The Problems of Communitarian Politics

The Problems of Communitarian Politics

Unity and Conflict

ELIZABETH FRAZER

OXFORD
UNIVERSITY PRESS

OXFORD

UNIVERSITY PRESS

Great Clarendon Street, Oxford OX2 6DP

Oxford University Press is a department of the University of Oxford
It furthers the University's objective of excellence in research, scholarship,
and education by publishing worldwide in

Oxford New York

Athens Auckland Bangkok Bogotá Buenos Aires Calcutta
Cape Town Chennai Dar es Salaam Delhi Florence Hong Kong Istanbul
Karachi Kuala Lumpur Madrid Melbourne Mexico City Mumbai
Nairobi Paris São Paulo Singapore Taipei Tokyo Toronto Warsaw

and associated companies in Berlin Ibadan

Oxford is a registered trade mark of Oxford University Press
in the UK and in certain other countries

Published in the United States
by Oxford University Press Inc., New York

British Library Cataloguing in Publication Data

Data available

Library of Congress Cataloging in Publication Data

Data available

ISBN 0-19-829563-4
ISBN 0-19-829564-2 (pbk.)

10 9 8 7 6 5 4 3 2 1

Typeset by Hope Services (Abingdon) Ltd.
Printed in Great Britain
on acid-free paper by
Biddles Ltd.,
Guildford & King's Lynn

For Robert, and Scott, Remi,
Tobias, and Heidi—
with thanks and with love.

Preface and Acknowledgements

This book brings together and substantially revises a number of articles, lectures, and seminar papers written since the publication of *The Politics of Community*, co-authored with Nicola Lacey.[1] In that book we critically examined both sides of the liberal versus communitarian disputes, finding that, when they are viewed from the perspective of feminism—a political project which seeks to establish a world characterized by sexual equality—both camps are revealed to be unable to provide models of person, society, social institutions, and political processes which are adequate to that task.

The papers reworked here continue to elaborate, refine, and in some cases amend our analysis and criticisms of the communitarian side of that divide. In this book I offer a much more detailed study of communitarianism, paying particular attention to what I call 'political communitarianism'. Political communitarianism is the political platform from which would-be political entrepreneurs, political commentators, and some established politicians, attempt to propel communitarian analyses, programmes, and projects into practical politics. In particular, I have had the opportunity to study in some detail the relationship between political communitarianism and recent debates about local government, about family policy, and about democracy in general. I have also taken the opportunity to elaborate the methodological arguments and themes—about the role and nature of conceptual analysis, and about interpretivism and social constructionism in political theory—that Nicola Lacey and I identified to be central in the liberal versus communitarian disputes.

I am indebted to countless individuals and groups, then, for keeping me focused on these subjects by inviting me to write papers, by listening attentively, challenging my analyses and arguments, making suggestions, reading and commenting on drafts, and writing me letters about the ever-engaging, so it seems, subject of community. I have had endless encouragement, stimulating questions, and some robust challenges from conference participants at: the ESRC conference 'Rethinking Local Democracy', St John's College Oxford in 1994; 'Citizenship and Cultural Frontiers', Staffordshire University, 1994; 'Difference and Political Community', University of Hull 1995; the 10th International Congress of

---

[1] Elizabeth Frazer and Nicola Lacey *The Politics of Community: A Feminist Critique of the Liberal-Communitarian Debate* (Hemel Hempstead: Harvester, 1993).

Logic, Methodology and Philosophy of Science, Florence, 1995; 'Ideas of Community' at the University of West of England, 1995; 'Morality and Ideology', University of Oxford, 1996; Political Thought Conference, University of Wales, Swansea, at Gregynog 1997; 'Community and Morality in a Democratic Society' New York University, 1997; 'Liberalism and Communitarianism', Australian National University, Research School of Social Sciences, 1997; and the 10th Annual International Conference on Socio-Economics, Vienna, 1998. In this period I have given seminar papers at the University of Edinburgh, Department of Politics; University of Kent, Departments of Politics and Philosophy; University of East Anglia, Department of Social Sciences; University of Cambridge, Seminar in Political Theory and Intellectual History; University of California at Los Angeles, Centre for the Study of Women, and Law School; University College, Dublin, Department of Politics; University of Oxford, Politics Research Seminar; University of Sussex, Social and Political Thought Seminar; ANU Research School of Social Sciences Philosophy seminar. I am particularly indebted to the Director and members of the Research School of Social Sciences, Australian National University, Canberra for their hospitality, civility, and intellectual stimulation when I was fortunate enough to have a visiting fellowship there from October to December 1997.

Some of the arguments and analysis from the chapters that follow have appeared in: Caroline Wright and Jill Jagger (eds.) *Changing Family Values* (Routledge, 1999); Adam Lent (ed.) *New Political Thought* (Lawrence & Wishart, 1998); Andrew Vincent (ed.) *Political Theory: Tradition, Diversity, Ideology* (Cambridge University Press, 1997); Desmond King and Gerry Stoker (eds.) *Rethinking Local Democracy* (Macmillan, 1996); *Imprints*, vol. 1 (1997); *Pouvoirs*, no. 82 (1997). I am grateful to all these people and publications for giving me the opportunity to write on these topics, and for very helpful comments on and reactions to drafts.

Finally many colleagues have read and commented on the original papers or drafts of chapters, have discussed the issues with me, and have provided all kinds of practical assistance. I am particularly indebted to: John Braithwaite, Valerie Braithwaite, Beatrix Campbell, John Campbell, Nick Emler, Amitai Etzioni, Max Farrar, Lawrence Goldman, Robert Goodin, Michael Hechter, Joanna Hodge, Richard Holton, Charles King, Chandran Kukathas, Nicola Lacey, Rae Langton, Susan MacRae, Chantal Mouffe, Vicki Nash, Glen Newey, Mike Noble, Noel O'Sullivan, Carole Pateman, Phillip Pettit, Anne Phillips, Mark Philp, Phillip Selznick, Quentin Skinner, Michael Smith, Teresa Smith, Adam Swift, Peter Wagner, Matthew Weait. I am particularly grateful to those colleagues and friends who read the complete first draft. This final version is very much longer and more detailed and contains attempts to respond to their criticisms and questions, no doubt prompting more in the process. I am grateful to Rebekah Lee and Zofia Stemplowska for help with the references and the bibliography. I would like to thank Dominic Byatt from Oxford University Press for his encouragement and assistance, and Amanda Watkins and Edwin Pritchard for dealing with what—despite my best endeavours, and thanks to my footnotes losing the battle with my word-processor—turned out to be a less than perfect typescript.

Finally, I owe a particular debt to the students who have worked with me in political theory during this period, from whom I learn so much year after year.

Contents

Introduction

This book takes as its starting point, and elaborates and develops, a number of problems with 'communitarianism' that Nicola Lacey and I specified and laid out as the culmination of our reading of the 'liberal versus communitarian debates'.[1]

There we criticized liberal models of individual, society, and state, and liberal analyses of the values of individual freedom, autonomy, formal equality, privacy, rationality, and the rule of law on a number of grounds. First, they fail to capture and *endogenize* a number of important social mechanisms of disadvantage and dominance. For instance, cultural and other social processes construct and position men and women at the outset as unequally endowed—unless these processes of initial endowment are understood by liberal theorists and brought within their theories, their models will fail to predict or identify the kinds of inequality that characterize modern societies. Similarly, liberal prescriptive distinctions between private, domestic life with its particularistic relationships and practices, and public political life with its abstract and universal laws and rules, prevent liberal theorists from accurately analysing the political nature of interpersonal relationships and social practices, or fully perceiving the roles of established quotidian social practices in the conduct of public life.

We find a structurally similar problem with communitarianism. Communitarian models feature a set of elements that contrast with liberal models: social individual, community, wider political society, and the values of tradition, settlement, socially constructed reason, intra-community trust, reciprocity, mutuality and interdependence, and the communal realization of values such as freedom, equality, and rights. But such models fail to endogenize the movement of individuals across social formations and the antagonism and conflict that this movement engenders. Communitarian theorists tend to emphasize the communal construction of social individuals and social formations, and of values and practices. A problem is that these constructive processes themselves need to be

[1] Elizabeth Frazer and Nicola Lacey, *The Politics of Community: A Feminist Critique of the Liberal-Communitarian Debate* (Hemel Hempstead, Harvester, 1993).

analysed in terms of power—power which can account for when individuals manage to reconstruct their circumstances, when they move from context to context, when they get trapped, when they rest content. Communitarians, that is, overlook precisely the *politics* of 'community'—to such an extent, we argued, that communitarianism barely looks like a political theory at all.[2]

We began, however, with a pronounced consciousness of the affinities between feminism and communitarianism. The feminist political project of changing social identities so fundamentally as to seek to transform *gender* (indeed, the very discontent with forms of femininity and masculinity that start feminist political projects off) relies on some version of social constructionism. It seems to be the social constructionist strand of the communitarian approach to political and social theory that attracts many feminist theorists in the first place.[3] Further, feminism shares with communitarianism an emphasis on the values connected with human relatedness—reciprocity, trust, solidarity. And feminist politics has tended to emphasize the significance of local and mundane contexts as the key centres of social, and therefore political, organization. On the basis of the theory that kinship and social structures are the site of women's oppression, feminist politics challenges and attempts to restructure family and social networks, and does so, furthermore, on the terrain of the family itself with the provision of refuges, helplines, advice centres, etc. as well as challenges to the conventions and norms of personal relationships, rhetorically and theoretically supported by the slogan 'the personal is political'. This strategic approach has been informed by feminist criticism of the principle that state power and conventional party political activity in pursuit of national legislation are the primary or only legitimate route to change.[4]

---

[2] See Elizabeth Frazer and Nicola Lacey, *The Politics of Community: A Feminist Critique of the Liberal-Communitarian Debate* (Hemel Hempstead, Harvester, 1993) 130, 137, 161; this apolitical nature of much 'political theory' is a theme that pervades a good deal of recent thought and critique within the subject—see for instance Bonnie Honig, *Political Theory and the Displacement of Politics* (Ithaca, NY: Cornell University Press, 1993); Richard Bellamy, *Liberalism and Modern Society* (Oxford: Polity Press, 1992); Chantal Mouffe, *The Return of the Political* (London: Verso, 1993).

[3] Note for instance the implicit and explicit references to social constructionism in Alison M. Jaggar, *Feminist Politics and Human Nature* (Brighton: Harvester, 1983) especially chs. 6 and 10; and in the essays in Sandra Harding (ed.) *Feminism and Methodology* (Bloomington: Indiana University Press, 1987), especially Nancy C. M. Hartsock, 'The Feminist Standpoint: Developing the Ground for a Specifically Feminist Historical Materialism'.

[4] See for example Anna Coote and Beatrix Campbell, *Sweet Freedom: The Struggle for Women's Liberation*, 2nd edn. (Oxford: Basil Blackwell, 1987); Suzanne Franzway, Dianne Court, and R. W. Connell, *Staking a Claim: Feminism, Bureaucracy and the State* (Cambridge: Polity Press, 1989); Gabriele Griffin (ed.), *Feminist Activism in the 1990s*

This analysis of the nature and limits of the affinity between feminism and communitarianism led us in the final section of *The Politics of Community* to propose a modified communitarianism—a model of social individual, social formations, and wider networks of these 'communities', in which values, practices, and meanings are shared, albeit contested. We proposed 'dialogic communitarianism'—dialogic, because it features a normative commitment to promoting the individual's engagement with others, and because value commitments are conceptualized as the upshot of dialogue (in contrast to the effective monologue of traditional communitarianisms and liberalisms alike). [5] This communitarianism would need to develop theoretical models of how individuals cross and recross the boundaries from 'community' to 'community' in the course of their daily lives and across their lifecourses. It also needs to develop models of how individuals with different community memberships and allegiances can relate to and engage with members of other communities. Such a model would potentially repoliticize political theory by emphasizing the contest for political power and authority. It is in the theoretical analysis of these processes that we can grasp both the possibilities for and constraints on political change.

Although I still believe that such a model is on the right lines, and should form the foundation of political theory and political endeavour alike, I have come to believe that the continued presence of the term 'community' in this formulation is regrettable. It seems to me now that conceptual and theoretical problems with 'community' are very far-reaching. They undermine the validity of models. They resonate in discourses, and

(London: Taylor and Francis, 1995); Nancy A. Naples (ed.), *Community Activism and Feminist Politics: Organising across Race, Class and Gender* (New York: Routledge, 1998).

[5] Our approach to 'dialogue' was influenced by Drucilla Cornell, especially 'Beyond Tragedy and Complacency', *Northwestern University Law Review*, 81 (1987), 693 ff.; Seyla Benhabib, 'Liberal Dialogue versus a Critical Theory of Discursive Legitimation', in N. Rosenblum (ed.), *Liberalism and the Moral Life* (Cambridge, Mass.: Harvard University Press, 1989); and 'Autonomy, Modernity and Community: Communitarianism and Critical Social Theory in Dialogue', in *Situating the Self* (Cambridge: Polity Press, 1992); but for dialogue and community see also Martin Buber, *A Believing Humanism: My Testament 1902–1965*, trans. and introd. Maurice Friedman (New York: Simon and Schuster, 1967); id., *I and Thou*, trans. and Prologue by Walter Kaufman (New York: Charles Scribner's Sons, 1970) (1st pub.German 1923) while dialogue has its place in Alasdair MacIntyre's communitarianism—*After Virtue* (London: Duckworth, 1985)—and in Michael Walzer's—see especially *Interpretation and Social Criticism* (Cambridge, Mass.: Harvard University Press, 1987); *Thick and Thin: Moral Argument at Home and Abroad* (Notre Dame, Ind: University of Notre Dame Press, 1994). Our argument in *The Politics of Community* was that MacIntyre's and Walzer's models of 'dialogue' are not robust enough to incorporate the kind of radical interventions and innovations in debate exemplified by feminist politics.

have particular (not progressive) rhetorical effects. They impact in policy and practice in perverse ways. In the chapters that follow I attempt to explain why and how this is so.

In *The Politics of Community* we also argued that 'political theory' needs an interdisciplinary focus and that both liberals and communitarians tend to misrepresent the nature of political relations, actions, and processes. In what follows I also explore these two themes in more detail. There is a bias in my discussion here towards the interrelationships between political theory and sociological and cultural theory (as opposed to psychology or economics). But my main point is not damaged by this bias. That point is, that having an eye on the interrelationships between politics and sociology (or anything else) does not entail that politics is reducible to sociology (or anything else).

These conceptual, theoretical, and methodological themes are explored in this volume in the context of *political* rather than philosophical communitarianism. By 'philosophical communitarianism' I mean the texts produced by philosophers such as Charles Taylor, Alasdair MacIntyre, Michael Walzer, and Michael Sandel that together constitute, for many readers, a coherent critique of late twentieth-century Anglophone 'liberal individualism'—a critique that focuses on questions of epistemology, metaphysics or ontology, and methodology.[6] As many have noted, the precise practical political implications of this philosophical critique of liberalism are by no means clear—it might be thought to rule some kinds of political order (radical anarchism, for instance) out, but it is potentially consistent with liberal, social democratic, socialist, welfare liberal, and certain sorts of conservative party programmes. The idea of 'community'—central to 'communitarianism'—is politically relevant for many kinds of political actor and political programme. It has been present in political discourse and in public policy (for example in the promotion of 'care in the community', 'community policing', 'community activism', and the like) for many years. For many activists and political actors, indeed, the idea and ideal of community is key in their understanding of political effort—political principles, goals, and strategies can come together in activists' lives and in political and social institutions so as to constitute a more or less clearly articulated and crystallized 'lay communitarianism' or

[6] Michael Walzer, *Spheres of Justice* (New York: Basic Books, 1983); Alasdair MacIntyre, *After Virtue* (London: Duckworth, 1988); *Whose Justice? Which Rationality?* (London: Duckworth, 1988); *Three Rival Versions of Moral Enquiry* (London: Duckworth, 1990); Michael Sandel, *Liberalism and the Limits of Justice* (Cambridge: Cambridge University Press, 1982); Charles Taylor, *Philosophy and the Human Sciences* and *Human Agency and Language* (Cambridge: Cambridge University Press, 1985).

'vernacular communitarianism'.[7] Participants in the economy, in local organizations, in civil society in general, deploy ideas and ideals of community, discuss theories of community—asking and debating why it has been lost in recent times, or how it might be regained. These discourses, and their interrelationships with action and organization, appear again and again in reports by sociologists and others, in journalism and elsewhere.

Recently some strands from these discourses have crystallized into a political platform, and been published in explicitly manifesto-like form, in a way that seems to me to be novel.[8] This platform has been occupied by would-be political entrepreneurs and established politicians, so the relationship of these ideas to established party programmes has now become a practical question, as has their relationship with the older, established traditions of community activism and vernacular communitarianism mentioned before. Political communitarianism brings to the forefront of practical politics some problems that critics of philosophical communitarianism had identified as problems in theory. One common theme in the 'liberal communitarian' debates is the nature of community—a vague concept and an elusive ideal.[9] This vagueness matters in a new way when, for instance, government policies enjoin bureaucracies and authorities to

[7] Jeremy Brent, 'Community without Unity', paper delivered to conference 'Ideas of community', University of the West of England, Sept. 1995, uses the term 'vernacular communitarianism'.

[8] See Amitai Etzioni, *The Spirit of Community: Rights, Responsibilities and the Communitarian Agenda* (New York: Crown Publishers Inc. 1993) which includes a copy of 'The Communitarian Platform' promulgated by the Communitarian Network in 1991. In the UK, see Henry Tam, *Citizen's Agenda for Building Democratic Communities* (Cambridge: Centre for Citizenship Development, 1995). On Tony Blair's communitarian beliefs and programme see Peter Mandelson and Roger Liddle, *The Blair Revolution: Can New Labour Deliver?* (London: Faber and Faber, 1996), and Tony Blair, *New Britain: My Vision for a Young Country* (London: Fourth Estate, 1996). This 'political communitarianism' has received considerable press coverage and journalistic comment on both sides of the Atlantic. It has also made its way into prominent political speeches: US President Clinton's State of the Union Address in January 1995 contained notable communitarian themes and was widely commented on as such; in British Prime Minister Blair's speech to the Labour Party Conference in September 1998 'communitarian' principles were also prominent.

[9] The elusive nature of the ideal is testified to by the number of books on the subject that contain the terms 'quest', 'search', and the like. For instance Paul Lichterman, *The Search for Political Community* (Cambridge: Cambridge University Press, 1996), Standish Meacham, *Toynbee Hall and Social Reform 1880–1914: The Search for Community* (New Haven: Yale University Press, 1987), Robert A. Nisbet, *The Quest for Community: A Study in the Ethics of Order and Freedom* (New York: Oxford University Press, 1953); Ken Young et al., *In Search of Community Identity* (York: Joseph Rowntree Foundation, 1996); Robert Wuthnow, *Sharing the Journey: Support Groups and America's New Quest for Community* (New York: Free Press, 1994).

'involve the community at every stage in the process'.[10] Similarly, some contributors to the liberal communitarian debates asked questions about the nature of local politics and governance, the difficulties and dilemmas of neighbourhood and social movement organization, controversies over sex-roles, parenting, and kinship and family relations. In the context of debates about philosophical communitarianism, such was their abstraction, detailed discussion of these issues seemed misplaced. Now that communitarianism is a political programme such discussion is of more obvious relevance and worth.

These then are the main issues treated in this book. Chapter 1 discusses and criticizes 'political communitarianism' and explores its relationship with philosophical communitarianism, with earlier community politics of the left, and with appeals to 'community' from the right. The discussion of the 'communitarian critique of liberalism' undertaken here is very quick and decidedly sketchy—it is not the purpose of this book to offer yet another detailed discussion of the debates, or make any further direct contribution to them. However, in the chapters that follow I do pick up themes from those debates where they have clearly relevant political implications. Chapter 2 takes up the concept 'community', examining its contested and indeterminate nature, and analysing a range of attempts at decontestation. Here I offer analysis and interpretation of the concept, and on the way I address the question of what we are doing when we analyse concepts.

Chapter 3 examines the relationship between communitarianism and interpretivism in political theory. The main focus of the chapter is on the role of 'the community' in communitarian accounts of how interpretations are grounded and validated. Critical political theories, which foreground the analysis of and role of social power, cast doubt on the view that invocation of the, or a, community can be a solution to the problem of adjudication of interpretations. In Chapter 4 I discuss 'social constructionism'—a prominent theme in communitarianism. It is a theme which is the key to the attractiveness of communitarianism to theorists in a number of disciplines. It is also a theme that, wherever it arises, causes extraordinary levels of hostility and apparent bafflement. It is also one, I would be the first to admit, which is often taken for granted in social and cultural theory and in related empirical research, but rarely rigorously analysed or tested. Disputes about it in epistemology and the philosophy of science and social science are more than usually unilluminating—it is frequently extremely difficult to discern exactly what is at issue.

---

[10] As does the British Home Office 'Guidance on Statutory Crime and Disorder Partnerships, 1998', foreword.

The following chapters attempt to assess the merits of three communitarian models—the models of locality as community, family as community, and polity as community. In Chapter 5 I discuss the relationship between 'community' and 'locality', and in Chapter 6 the political communitarian model of 'the communitarian family'. In both of these chapters the main burden of argument is that the category 'community' has perverse effects on theory and in practice. Conceptualizing locality and family *as* community works against the theoretical and practical appreciation of the structure and significance of households, kinship groups, families, neighbourhoods, and associations that the communitarians set out to establish. Finally, Chapter 7 examines the way the concepts 'community' and 'politics' are hooked together, not only by communitarians, but also by a range of liberal, social democratic, socialist, and feminist theorists. The main point the chapter makes is that the concept of community conduces to a model of political relations as based in shared culture and practices, and thereby bounded. A preferable conception of democratic politics emphasizes the unsettlement of boundaries.

It may be wise to offer some terminological clarifications at this point. In this book I wish to examine the concept 'community' and I shall be doing this in part by examining a number of discursive and practical political contexts. For instance, at a number of points I discuss the success and failures and dilemmas of 'community action' and 'community activism', or make reference to such policy initiatives as 'care in the community'. I take it that in such contexts 'community' means something, and that, although it may be impossible to give a definitive account of what that is, it is nevertheless open to critics and analysts to try to analyse what actors mean by 'community', how the term 'community' operates in these discourses and practices, in short to analyse the concept community. In the course of such analysis we will meet many different conceptions of community, different views of what community is and ought to be, and varying projects to try to realize or achieve 'community' as a kind of social group, formation, or system of institutions. Examples I discuss in what follows include 'local communities', 'national communities', 'political communities', 'religious communities', and so forth. As well as referring to a particular set of social groups 'community' also refers to the peculiar relations between persons that constitute those groups. My analysis of this element of the concept reveals less variation and vagueness than might be expected. There are theoretical disagreements, for instance over whether community implies equality or is consistent with hierarchy. But underlying all such theoretical disputes that I have read is a surprisingly definite set of concepts—the relation of community is centred on sharing; it inheres between human beings or persons as such (not individuals in social roles), and it involves an orientation on the part of each to the whole and to all.

One important set of discursive contexts in which the concept or term 'community' is very prominent is 'communitarianism'. 'Communitarianism' refers to a range of positions in social and political discourse, which, like other 'isms', consist typically of sets of concepts which are tied to beliefs, propositions and theories about the world, values, and prescriptions about acceptable and appropriate strategies for realizing these values. Just as there are a number of varieties of socialism and anarchism, so there are a number of varieties of communitarianism, and like others who try to write about 'isms' I face a number of methodological and analytical difficulties in judging what texts and thinkers should be included in the class of 'communitarianisms', how to characterize or analyse 'communitarianism as such' (which obviously can only be an abstraction or an ideal type), and within that class which texts and thinkers should be thought of as members of this or that subdivision. A number of subdivisions of the class of 'communitarianisms' are worth exploring—in particular it strikes many critics that it is important to distinguish between 'left' and 'right' communitarianism.[11] As we have seen, a number of theorists have set out to develop a dialogic, as opposed to what they understand to be the more monologic, communitarianism.[12] In this book, as I have already stated, I am interested in a distinction within the communitarian literature between a set of texts and theorists I think of as the 'philosophical communitarians' and a rather distinctive set of texts, thinkers, and discourses I label 'political communitarianism', paying more attention, here, to the latter than the former.

I want to make it clear that when I talk about political, as opposed to philosophical, communitarianism, I mean 'political' and 'philosophical' to modify communitarianism; I do not mean them to modify 'community'. What I mean by philosophical communitarianism is a set of propositions and values as analysed, with an eye primarily on their epistemological, metaphysical, logical and ethical implications, by writers who are addressing, for the most part, an academic audience and who are deploying, for the most part, familiar philosophical techniques. What I mean by political communitarianism is a set of propositions, values, and recommendations about strategies, as analysed and defended, with an eye

---

[11] Adam Crawford, 'Appeals to Community and Crime Prevention', *Crime, Law and Social Change*, 22 (1995), 97–126; Eugene Kamenka (ed.), *Community as a Social Ideal* (London: Edward Arnold, 1982).

[12] For example Benhabib, *Situating the Self*.

primarily on their political implications, by writers addressing a mixed audience of academics and political actors, with a view to making a persuasive case for a particular direction to political and social change.[13]

In both philosophical and political communitarianism the concept 'community' is, unsurprisingly, central. However, it is also important to note that the concept 'community' is likewise salient for non-communitarians—for liberals, socialists, feminists, conservatives, and others.[14] It is also salient in a number of discourses that, although they are relatively coherent, should not be thought of as 'isms'—for instance, in discussions of policy in the field of criminal law, such as 'community justice', or projects for non-custodial sentencing.[15] A central purpose I have in this book is to argue that in many although not all contexts the concept 'community' should be displaced by a more precise set of group or network concepts, the application and relevance of which needs to be established, theoretically and empirically, on a case-by-case basis. Association, society, network, group—perhaps in a limited number of cases, community itself—are some politically and socially salient formations, governed by differing rules or norms of membership and participation, given unity and identity by different kinds of boundaries with different conditions and constraints governing boundary crossings. Why there has been a tendency in political theory and philosophy to label all of these, indiscriminately, 'community' is one question I now set out to address.

[13] I am harping on my intended meaning here, because some readers have understood me to be talking about 'political community' as opposed to 'philosophical community' when I draw this distinction. The idea of a 'political community' is one I analyse and question in this book; but this is an idea which can be elaborated by both political and philosophical communitarians.

[14] See particularly Eugene Kamenka (ed.), *Community as a Social Ideal* (London: Edward Arnold, 1982).

[15] Adam Crawford *The Local Governance of Crime: Appeals to Community and Partnerships* (Oxford: Clarendon Press, 1997); *Crime Prevention and Community Safety: Politics, Policies and Practices* (London: Longman, 1998); on 'community care' see Martin Bulmer *The Social Basis of Community Care* (London: Unwin Hyman, 1987).

1

Communitarianism, Philosophical and Political

POLITICS AND COMMUNITY

Since the 1970s in western democracies the idea of community has been prominent in politics in two particular ways. First, there have been a number of programmes and ideas in the field of public policy—such as 'community policing', community justice, community health, and 'care in the community'. These have been discussed extensively by politicians and practitioners, commented on by journalists, studied and analysed by academics, and debated by interested parties in the mass media and other forums. So anyone who is ever involved in talking or thinking about politics or public policy, in almost any context, can hardly fail to be aware of 'community' as a key term. These projects are connected—although not in a very straightforward way—to a longer, older tradition of political practice, which includes 'community development projects' (often funded by central and local governments in the 1960s and 1970s), and a tradition of 'community organization' and 'community action' which has had its place in democracies throughout the modern, industrial period.[1] Thus for many political actors 'community' is an important term in their thinking and action in connection with democracy, freedom, equality, empowerment, government accountability, and so on. Second, these policy developments and projects have been accompanied by a moral and political debate about the relative responsibilities and rights of individuals, communities, society, and the state—debates to which politicians, activists, government ministers, academics, journalists, and other public figures such as church leaders and heads of companies have been party.

In these debates, some voices have urged the importance and role of community above all (above, in any case, the role of the individual, or the importance of wider society and state). Among community activists and

---

[1] See Robert Booth Fowler, *The Dance with Community: The Contemporary Debate in American Political Thought* (Lawrence, Kan.: University Press of Kansas, 1991), esp. pp. 32–6; Hugh Butcher *et al.*, *Community Groups in Action: Case Studies and Analysis* (London: Routledge and Kegan Paul, 1980); Eugene Kamenka (ed.), *Community as a Social Ideal* (London: Edward Arnold, 1982).

community workers we can discern a strand of analysis which emphasizes the value of community as such, we can hear voices of people who wish more than anything to participate in building and sustaining communities—for whom the major political and social problem is 'the state of streets and communities',[2] or who believe that the only solution to housing problems or toxic pollution is community building.[3] I call this strand of discourse 'vernacular communitarianism', and in later chapters I shall discuss the hopes and aspirations of these actors. Within political philosophy and political theory, written for a mainly academic audience, there is a well-articulated and refined position, which has emerged mainly in the form of a critique of 'liberal individualism'. In this book I refer to this as 'philosophical communitarianism'. There has also emerged a body of analysis, theory, and political claims which, for the purposes of this book, I call 'political communitarianism'. By this term I intend to refer to the elaboration of the ideal of community, and prescriptions about the political and social institutions that could realize this ideal, in public political discourse, and commentary on it. Themes of philosophical communitarianism, and relevant social scientific theory and research, are presented so as to emphasize their practical political implications.[4] Journalists have discussed and made reference to these communitarian ideas[5] and a number of academic philosophers and political theorists have explained their ideas

[2] Dick Atkinson, *The Common Sense of Community* (London: Demos, 1994), 1.

[3] Paul Lichterman, *The Search for Political Community* (Cambridge: Cambridge University Press, 1996); some of his respondents 'did not distinguish political (agenda challenging, power challenging) work from other community betterment work—informed by an ethic of service', p. 127; Roberta M. Feldman, Susan Stall, Patricia A. Wright, 'The Community Needs to be Built by Us', in Nancy Naples (ed.), *Community Activism and Feminist Politics: Organising across Gender, Race and Class* (New York: Routledge, 1998), 258 on women who are motivated by a sense of necessity and by strong community ties: one activist says: 'We all volunteer together, and without a working relationship like that you can't do anything. But if you get a good working relationship, baby, you can do wonders!'

[4] Atkinson, *The Common Sense of Community*; id. (ed.), *Cities of Pride: Rebuilding Community, Refocussing Government* (London: Cassell, 1995). Henry Tam, *Communitarianism: A New Agenda for Politics and Citizenship* (Basingstoke: Macmillan, 1998); *Citizen's Agenda for Building Democratic Communities* (Cambridge: Centre for Citizenship Development, 1995); Amitai Etzioni, *The New Golden Rule: Community and Morality in a Democratic Society* (New York: Basic Books, 1996); id. (ed.), *New Communitarian Thinking: Persons, Virtues, Institutions and Communities* (Charlottesville: University Press of Virginia, 1995)—the blurb on this volume declares that it 'connects the ivory tower to the world beyond'; id., *The Spirit of Community: Rights, Responsibilities and the Communitarian Agenda* (New York: Crown Publishers, 1993); Robin Harris, *The Conservative Community: The Roots of Thatcherism—and its Future* (London: Centre for Policy Studies, 1989); Ian Taylor, *Releasing the Community Spirit: A Framework for the Active Citizen* (Cambridge: Tory Reform Group, 1990).

[5] For a sample of press coverage of community politics and communitarianism, see Appendix II.

and opinions in print journalism, and have made efforts to discuss their ideas more directly with politicians and policy-makers.[6]

Most importantly, the theme of community and related ideas have been taken up in the speeches and platforms of prominent political figures. For example, Gordon Brown wrote in 1990 that the problem in Britain included *inter alia* 'too little community': 'What the community can achieve by acting together to further individual well-being and freedom can be greater than anything individuals working only a free market ideology can achieve on their own. . . . the new agenda sees Britain as a community of individuals enabled by a public interest that ensures for them opportunities at critical points along the way.'[7] The redrafted Clause 4 of the British Labour Party Constitution features 'community' as a central value. In an interview Tony Blair, then Leader of the Opposition, said

We believe in the values of community, that by the strength of our commitment to common endeavour we can achieve the conditions on which individuals can realise their full potential. The basic principle is solidarity, that people can achieve much more by acting together than acting alone. I think that all this is best represented by the idea of community, in which each person has the rights and duties that go with community and we act together to achieve power, wealth and opportunity for all, not for the few.[8]

In his speech to the Labour Party Conference in Blackpool in 1998, now Prime Minister Blair said:

It is that same spirit of determination, and the power of community, that should be the country's guide in this year of challenge. . . . The challenge we face has to be met by us together. One nation. One community. Social Justice; partnership; cooperation; the equal worth of all, the belief that the best route to individual advancement and happiness lies in a thriving society of others. Words and concepts derided in the 80s. These are the values of today. Not just here but round the world. 'It's up to me' is being replaced by 'it's up to us'. The crude individualism of the 80s is the mood no longer. The spirit of the times is community.

---

[6] For example, Amitai Etzioni has produced a good number of press column centimetres himself—see Appendix II; the US 'Communitarian Network' have held seminars at the White House—'The First Communitarian Teach-In', *Responsive Community*, 2 (1991–2). *Tikkun*, 8/1 (1993) contains a reproduction of an appreciative and supportive letter dated 13 Dec. 1988 from Bill Clinton (then Governor of Arkansas), together with a number of memos to Clinton (now US President) about various aspects of public policy.

[7] Gordon Brown, 'Beware the Mask of Tory Social Concern', *Observer* (2 Dec. 1990), 20.

[8] Martin Kettle, 'Blair Puts Faith in Community Spirit', *Guardian* (13 Mar. 1995), pt. 1, p. 2. The redrafted Clause 4 was interpreted by more than one commentator as inspired by Amitai Etzioni: for instance Joe Rogaly, 'Blair's Community Spirit', *Financial Times* (18 Mar. 1995), Weekend Section p. 1, an inference apparently encouraged by Etzioni himself: Sarah Baxter 'I am the Way and I am the Truth', *Sunday Times* (19 Mar. 1995), 7. There is no reason, given Tony Blair's intellectual history, to accept this claim.

US President Clinton's State of the Union speech in January 1995 included similarly notable passages: 'The common bonds of community, which have been the great strength of our country from its very beginning are badly frayed . . .'; '. . . the great strength of America as de Toqueville pointed out when he came here a long time ago has always been our ability to associate with people who were different from ourselve and to work together to find common ground'.[9] US Senator (later Vice-President) Al Gore spoke at the 'Communitarian Teach-In' at the White House in 1991—although his remarks as reported focused on the one hand on the importance of recognition of the global environmental crisis, and on the other one the narrowing of moral judgement to the recognition of transgressions against individual rights only. His remarks about his 'inner life' during the US presidential campaign of 1991 were interpreted as speaking to 'spiritual communities' in a way that 'amazed them'.[10]

The relationships between these three communitarianisms—vernacular, philosophical, and political—are explored in the chapters that follow. Of course, these distinctions are analytic. I do not wish to suggest that 'philosophy', 'politics', and practical daily life are three completely separate enterprises. On the contrary, individuals who have contributed to the philosophical dispute between liberal individualism and communitarianism also make interventions in debates about policy, and address arguments to general rather than specialized audiences. Those who are engaged in practical political interventions are aware of the relevance of philosophical arguments (although as I go on to describe below it is not the case that philosophical communitarianism is the most important source for political communitarianism). So there is no very clear distinction of personnel, or of the origin of ideas, let alone the structure of philosophical as opposed to political argument. However, a number of factors support my view that it is valid to distinguish between philosophical and political communitarianism. First, the policy direction of political communitarianism has given some contributors, on the communitarian side of the philosophical debate, pause for thought, and they have dissented from some of the policy lines that are suggested by avowed political communitarians, denying that these are implied by their philosophical

---

[9] The speech was interpreted by one commentator as 'unmistakeably inspired' by Robert Putnam's 'Bowling Alone' thesis: Robert Putnam, 'Bowling Alone: America's Declining Social Capital', *Journal of Democracy*, 6 (1995), 65–78—William F. Power, 'Can a Nation of Individuals give Community a Sporting Chance?', *Washington Post* (3 Feb. 1995), p. D01.

[10] Martha Sherrill, 'Hillary Clinton's Inner Politics', *Washington Post* (6 May 1993), p. D01.

positions.[11] Second, the core philosophical communitarian texts indisputably are abstract and technical, as has been remarked on by commentators. Many words are spent on disputes in meta-ethics, and philosophical abstractions such as 'the self'. By contrast, the texts that I group under the heading political communitarianism are much more concrete in their analysis and prescriptions, much more strategic in tone, and have, by their very nature, been much more readily expressible and discussable within the conventions of print journalism. Political communitarianism now has a recognizable presence within political disputes and discourses, where it attempts to rival socialism, conservatism, liberalism, nationalism, and other 'isms' that make their way into party platforms, pressure group or social movement programmes, and projects in civil society. In contrast again, vernacular communitarianism—produced by activists and workers when they are discussing their projects among themselves or have been urged to talk about them with a researcher—is, of course, much more variable in its precision and clarity. We would expect that some individuals in such settings will be oriented in one way or another to political or philosophical communitarianism—there is no very clear division of personnel when it comes to people, in mundane contexts, talking about politics and community.

Within all of these kinds of communitarian discourse it is possible to distinguish between more and less left and right programmes and thinkers, although such labels and their significance will always be contested as would the allocation of thinkers and ideas to one or other end of a left–right continuum. It is also possible to differentiate between more and less libertarian and authoritarian communitarians, those with contrasting approaches to the design of democratic institutions, and, indeed, those who seem to deploy contrasting conceptions of community. I shall try not to lump all the views I examine together into one undifferentiated category. However, I believe that these communitarianisms are coherent enough objects for analysis.

First, I briefly outline the 'communitarian critique of liberalism' paying attention here mainly to philosophical communitarianism in my terms. The texts sketchily examined here are those that criticized the liberal political philosophy of John Rawls, Ronald Dworkin, and Robert Nozick—three important United States liberal thinkers who were constructed by

[11] For example, Charles Taylor, 'Cross Purposes: The Liberal Communitarian Debate', in N. Rosenblum (ed.), *Liberalism and the Moral Life* (Cambridge, Mass.: Harvard University Press, 1989), 161 argues that 'Taking an ontological position' (as the philosophical communitarians do on the nature of the individual, society, values etc.) 'does not amount to advocating something'.

their communitarian critics as representative apotheoses of 'the liberal tradition'.[12] In many ways communitarianism was a very negative position, organized as a series of criticisms of liberalism's alleged analyses of rights and the rights-bearing individual, rationality, the nature of social institutions and relations, the phenomenology of values, and so on. But out of these criticisms, and out of the subseqent elaboration of them in the course of the 'liberal–communitarian debates' in which a large number of social and political theorists joined, it is possible to construct a positive philosophical position which, like the liberal individualism it opposes, is an ideal type. Following that, I discuss political communitarianism: communitarianism as elaborated and rendered by political actors as a 'platform' or 'manifesto' or at any rate a practical political project, communitarianism framed as a direct political intervention or claim about the organization of governance and the framing of public policy.

THE PHILOSOPHICAL COMMUNITARIAN CRITIQUE OF LIBERALISM

In the academic context, the debate between liberals and communitarians has focused on, and been generated overwhelmingly by, the liberal theory of John Rawls.[13] Rawls's *Theory of Justice* derives and elaborates the principles of justice that should govern political, social, and economic institutions—the principles that would be chosen by rational, free, and equal individuals were they to have the opportunity and the need to sort out such principles from scratch. The resulting conception of justice features individual freedom guaranteed by rights, together with a measure of egalitarianism in the distribution of resources.

Some of Rawls's critics, notably Robert Nozick and Ronald Dworkin, share a number of Rawls's philosophical commitments, particularly to a tradition of ethics in which rights are 'deontological', that is to say not reducible to or explicable in terms of anything else. This tradition can be

[12] Michael Freeden, *Ideologies and Political Theory* (Oxford: Clarendon Press, 1996), 226–8, argues that they are unrepresentative of 'the liberal tradition', representing rather a decidedly novel turn away from a number of liberal themes; see also Richard Bellamy, *Liberalism and Modern Society* (Oxford: Polity, 1992), 217–18. Others argue that the 'individualism' attributed to at least Rawls and Dworkin is based on a partial or misreading of their work—see Stephen Mulhall and Adam Swift, *Liberals and Communitarians*, 2nd edn. (Oxford: Basil Blackwell, 1996), 13–18.

[13] So this debate can be dealt with distinct from, say, the Marxist critique of liberal individualism (which of course also featured the idea or concept of community), or the larger debate between 'Aristotelianism' and 'modernism'—although Alasdair MacIntyre deploys this distinction in his own intervention against 'liberal individualism' in *After Virtue*.

identified as 'Kantian'. This is not because it conforms in every respect with Kant's ethics (indeed these philosophers neglect Kant's deontological concept of duty).[14] But they embrace 'Kantianism' in two important senses. First, they conceive of human individuals as 'ends in themselves'—hence their strong emphasis on individual rights.[15] This is in contrast, by their own account, to philosophical and ethical systems such as utilitarianism which are focused on a 'social good', such that some individuals' well-being, welfare, or indeed rights might be diminished or even sacrificed for the sake of the collective or whole.[16] Second, we can point to an emphasis on the role of 'pure reason' in deriving ethical and political principles and theses. This is particularly marked in Rawls's *Theory of Justice* and Nozick's *Anarchy, State, and Utopia*.[17] Here, 'intuitionism', which traces ethical principles back to our 'sense' of right and wrong, and any creative, synthetic or eclectic way of putting together a moral code, is rejected.[18] 'Intuition', however, is not completely displaced in Rawls's theory. It is an important aspect of his method that the ethical principles derived deductively must be tested against our considered judgements about right and wrong, good and bad, justice and injustice—and considered judgements of course be subject to the force of intuition.[19] If there is a large distance between derived principles and our considered judgements then we need to look again at our derivation procedures; and critically at our judgements—in the end we will achieve what Rawls calls 'reflective equilibrium'.[20]

These explicit methodological and substantive commitments have led many critics to read Rawls's work as informed by and contributing to a long tradition that we might call 'liberal individualism'.[21] Not all liberals

[14] Ronald Dworkin, *Taking Rights Seriously* (London: Duckworth, 1978), esp. p. 175; John Rawls, *Theory of Justice* (Oxford: Oxford University Press, 1971), 342.

[15] Dworkin, *Taking Rights Seriously*, 198; Robert Nozick, *Anarchy, State, and Utopia* (Oxford: Basil Blackwell, 1974), 31, 32.

[16] Rawls, *Theory of Justice*, 180–1; Dworkin, *Taking Rights Seriously*, 275; Nozick, *Anarchy, State, and Utopia*, 28.

[17] In these works 'pure reason' discerns or generates the two principles of justice, and the legitimacy of the minimal state respectively.

[18] Rawls, *Theory of Justice*, 40; see also Dworkin, *Taking Rights Seriously*, 279—here Dworkin argues that there is a right answer to complex questions in law and political morality, against those who would argue, as might the intuitionist, that in many situations a plurality of possible answers are equally good and attractive.

[19] Rawls, *Theory of Justice*, 48.   [20] Ibid. 48–53.

[21] Charles Taylor, 'Atomism', in *Philosophy and the Human Sciences* (Cambridge: Cambridge University Press, 1985); Michael Sandel, *Liberalism and the Limits of Justice* (Cambridge: Cambridge University Press, 1982), 11, 59–64; Alison Jaggar, *Feminist Politics and Human Nature* (Brighton: Harvester, 1983), 31, 33–5; Anthony Arblaster, *The Rise and Decline of Western Liberalism* (Oxford: Basil Blackwell, 1984), 15–49; James

are or intend to be 'individualists'; but critics of 'liberal individualism' point to the way that the themes of individuality, autonomy, and disengaged rationality, which indisputably are central to liberal thought, tend to be resolved and crystallized in a coherent theory like the following:

- the self is understood as ideally rational, with capacities for self-awareness, assertiveness, and choice;
- in order that these capacities can be exercised, the self should be maximally untrammelled by emotional or traditional attachments, neurosis, or superstition;
- likewise the self must be protected from state power, social power, and the power of other rational, assertive selves;
- hence the importance of protective rights, which are guaranteed by the construction of a sharply delimited political and legal sphere, dominated by a sovereign but constitutional power;
- certain aspects of this individual's freedom are realized in a civil society which is dominated by market, contractual, relations guaranteed by the rule of law; while other aspects are realized in, again a sharply delimited, private sphere;
- this private sphere, in a reversal of some older understandings of human life, is no longer conceived of as a sphere of privation, but instead as a sphere of fulfilment and safety.

The status of this 'liberal individualist model' is, of course, controversial. Some theorists and scholars believe it to be very much at the heart of 'the liberal tradition', there explicitly or implicitly at least in the texts of Hobbes, Locke, Rousseau, Smith, and others.[22] Other scholars deny the validity of some elements of this interpretation, and put forward alternative readings of these texts—emphasizing, for instance, themes of rhetoric and unreason in Hobbes, or trust and mutuality in Adam Smith, or the pull of socialism for J. S. Mill, or the emphases on reciprocity and membership in Rawls.[23] Be that as it may, nobody can deny (and indeed these rereadings confirm) that individualism has been attributed to, and is in some measure attributable to, the liberal authors. This individualist interpretation of liberalism, it can also be argued, has then been an effective

Meadowcroft (ed.), *The Liberal Tradition: Contemporary Reappraisals* (Cheltenham: Edward Elgar, 1996), 129–30, 139–42.

[22] Arblaster takes this line in *The Rise and Decline of Western Liberalism*.

[23] Istvan Hont and Michael Ignatieff, 'Needs and Justice in the Wealth of Nations', in I. Hont and M. Ignatieff (eds.), *Wealth and Virtue: The Shaping of Political Economy in the Scottish Enlightenment* (Cambridge: Cambridge University Press 1983); Quentin Skinner, *Reason and Rhetoric in the Philosophy of Hobbes* (Cambridge: Cambridge University Press, 1996); Freeden, *Ideologies and Political Theory* 456–64.

factor in the design and workings of certain social and political institutions in modern democratic societies—for instance, in the procedures of representative institutions, the regulation (or absence of regulation) of labour markets, in systems of punishment and legal responsibility, and so on.[24] Critics of liberalism also are quick to point out how these 'liberal institutions' have effects that are the opposite of liberal (if liberal means sustaining the flourishing of the individual). Marx's strictures about the alienating and immiserating effects of liberal labour markets; Sandel's observations about the rise of bureaucracy in societies characterized by liberal equality; feminists' complaints about the consistency of liberal freedom with sexual exploitation; Foucault's analysis of the reinforced disciplining of the supposedly autonomous modern individual, are all examples of this line of critique.

Although critics of liberal individualism see it as lamentably dominant in modern and contemporary academic political theory, then, and enshrined and realized in certain social institutions and practices in modern societies, its dominance is not and never has been uncontested. There always have been social democrats, Marxists, anarchists, feminists, welfare liberals, socialists, republicans, conservatives, and those to the right of modern conservatism who challenge this liberal view of politics and society. Many (of course not all) of these theorists begin with an alternative analysis:

* phenomena such as roles, social relations, discourses and institutions, are conceptualized as 'socially constructed';
* the contexts within which individuals develop and live are conceptualized as 'non-natural';
* the individual, her choices, reasons, and actions are conceptualized as contingent but sociologically explicable;[25]
* these social conceptions of the individual are associated with the phenomenological, hermeneutic, and structuralist social scientific traditions, in contrast with the rational choice and empiricist social scientific approaches which are consistent with, and indeed intimately bound up with, liberal individualism;[26]

[24] On labour and capital markets see Karl Marx, *Capital* (London: Lawrence and Wishart, 1954), i. 165 (that is, Part II, ch. 6, 'The Buying and Selling of Labour Power'); N. Abercrombie, S. Hill, and B. Turner, *Sovereign Individuals of Capitalism* (London: Allen and Unwin, 1986); Nicola Lacey, *State Punishment: Political Principles and Community Values* (London: Routledge, 1988), esp. ch. 7; Anne Phillips, *Democracy and Difference* (Oxford: Polity Press, 1993).

[25] With reference to the first three points see Jaggar, *Feminist Politics and Human Nature*, 98 ff. ,125–32.

[26] Jürgen Habermas, *On the Logic of the Social Sciences* (Oxford: Polity Press, 1988); Michel Foucault, *The Archaeology of Knowledge* (London: Tavistock, 1972); Sandra Harding, *The Science Question in Feminism* (Milton Keynes: Open University Press, 1986).

• these social conceptions of the individual are associated with a normative emphasis on values that sustain social order and that are premissed on individuals' social nature (trust, reciprocity, mutuality, substantive equality, community).

Three works in particular—Michael Sandel's *Liberalism and the Limits of Justice,* Michael Walzer's *Spheres of Justice,* and Alasdair MacIntyre's *After Virtue* can be identified as responses to the kind of liberalism exemplified by Rawls, from perspectives that can be situated in these traditions of ethical and social scientific theory. The political theory that is constructed by these writers collectively (although not intentionally on any of their parts) has come to be identified as communitarianism. They take issue with Rawls's conception of the relationship between individual and society, emphasizing how an individual's identity, values, and understandings are socially constituted and expressed. They also argue against the Rawlsian project of deriving principles of justice which are universal in their applicability. These two strands of argument—social constructionism and particularism—are central to philosophical communitarianism.

These and related themes have then been developed, criticized, and elaborated in numerous books and articles in a wide-ranging debate which is not always explicitly focused on the work of John Rawls.[27] As the debates proceeded they came widely to be understood as between 'liberals' or 'individualists' on the one hand, and 'communitarians' on the other.[28] Later, perhaps inevitably, a number of contributions pointed out how the opposition between the two 'sides' was exaggerated, how each side tended to misread and misrepresent the other, how important 'communitarian' themes are in liberal philosophy, how clear a distinction must be drawn between liberalism and individualism, and how important liberal values are to those who are identified as communitarians.[29] In particular, Rawls himself denies that *A Theory of Justice* has any bias to individualism, and emphasizes the values and themes of reciprocity and associational life, stressing the importance of these to a specifically liberal politics.[30] In

---

[27] Although he tends to get a mention at least in practically all of them.

[28] A collection of articles which includes a good range of relevant contributions is Shlomo Avineri and Avner de-Shalit (eds.) *Communitarianism and Individualism* (Oxford: Oxford University Press, 1992); see also Michael Sandel, *Liberalism and its Critics* (Oxford: Blackwell, 1984), which includes older critiques of liberal individualism; also Mulhall and Swift, *Liberals and Communitarians.*

[29] Taylor, 'Cross Purposes: The Liberal Communitarian Debate'; Michael Walzer, 'The Communitarian Critique of Liberalism', *Political Theory,* 18 (1990); Ronald Dworkin, 'Liberal Community', *California Law Review* 77 (1989).

[30] John Rawls, *Political Liberalism* (New York: Columbia University Press, 1993), 190, 221 n.

Rawls's later work we find an emphasis on liberalism as a tradition, and the particularistic implication that this theory of justice applies only in the democratic and pluralist context in which it is built.[31] Dworkin's work features a prominent emphasis on interpretation and tradition, implying a sort of 'social constructivism'.[32] Nozick, in a later work, argues, against the line he took in *Anarchy, State, and Utopia* that the individual person is connected with others in ways that are not accountable by pure egoistically rational choice, and has concerns about the integrity and the unity of their lives in relation to others which cannot be accounted for in purely individualistic terms.[33]

The 'communitarian critique of liberalism' developed in the context of academic political philosophy and the conventions of that genre predominate. Although many contributors to the debates are eminently concerned about the practical upshots of their philosophical analyses, and are engaged in political disputes about the future of social welfare, the conduct of interstate and intergroup conflict, social justice and democracy, communitarians aim their fire at liberal philosophy, and engage with it on its own terrain; liberals reply in like terms. In addition, in this body of literature the role of philosophy in the world is itself one topic of analysis. Many communitarian critics emphasize the dominance of liberal individualism in the academy and outside, and the role of liberal individualism in the construction of social institutions. Communitarians argue that as liberal philosophy is so full of error, then a society built around liberal individualist institutions will unsurprisingly be a mess.

PHILOSOPHICAL COMMUNITARIANISM

If we trace communitarianism's philosophical origins we see that it is a coalescence of a number of strands of western philosophy, including hermeneutics (or interpretivism), phenomenology, and pragmatism. These contrast with the rationalism and empiricism that are associated with liberal political philosophy. They also contrast with the structuralism that has been associated with some varieties of Marxist politics and social

---

[31] John Rawls, *Political Liberalism* (New York: Columbia University Press, 1993), 14, 156.

[32] See Ronald Dworkin, *Law's Empire* (London: Fontana, 1986). I take up the questions of interpretation and social constructivism in Chapters 3 and 4.

[33] Robert Nozick, *The Examined Life* (New York: Simon and Schuster, 1989), 17 ff., 141 ff.

theory.[34] As I have said, the theorists whose work has been gathered under the heading 'communitarian' did not set out to be communitarians (and in later works have expressed their unease about the implications of the concept, and in a number of cases have reaffirmed their commitment to liberal values and institutions). So 'philosophical communitarianism' is a construct, and the process by which it is constructed is an interpretive reading of a range of texts which can be argued to have a number of substantive and methodological themes in common, and the distillation, summary, and re-expression of those themes.

If we can discern a single theme in communitarianism it is anti-individualism; and this can be analysed into three distinct theses:

- First, an ontological or metaphysical thesis: that it is not the case that all there is in the world is individuals. Communitarians, like many other social philosophers, are likely to argue for the non-reducibility and significance of collectives, institutions, relations, meanings, and so on.

- Second, an ethical thesis, which itself falls into two parts: (1) communitarians will argue that the locus of value is not only the individual as such, but also (or perhaps rather) the social individual, or even the community or society of which the individual is a member; (2) they will also argue for the importance of a range of values that have tended to be neglected in individualist philosophies: reciprocity, trust, solidarity, tradition, etc.

- Third, a methodological thesis: communitarians argue that the way to do ethics and to derive political principles is not to try to deduce and apply universally valid fundamental principles, but to interpret and refine values that are immanent in the ways of life of really living groups—societies, communities. This way, ethical principles can be accepted and owned by social actors.

These three theses generate a number of inferences.

- Communitarians take issue with the idea (which is a powerful idea in modern societies, and one that has been to some extent promoted in the development of modern legal systems and welfare states) that the individual stands and should stand in a direct unmediated relationship with the state and with society.

For example, in the liberal tradition there has been a tendency to think of the individual as threatened by society and by centres of traditional

---

[34] Ted Benton, *Philosophical Foundations of the Three Sociologies* (London: Routledge and Kegan Paul, 1977); id., *The Rise and Fall of Structuralist Marxism* (Basingstoke: Macmillan, 1984).

authority such as the village, family, church, etc., and as needing legal protection from these in the shape of rights that protect his individual freedom. Some accounts of the transition to 'modern society' stress the dismantling of diffuse centres of power and authority, or status strata and local groups and networks, all of which 'embedded' individuals and stood between them and sovereign power.[35] These have been replaced by the formal equality of all individuals before a central state authority; and the power of this central state authority is, in modern societies, felt directly by individuals in their dealings with state bureaucracies and the institutions of law. Communitarians argue that this picture underestimates the continuing significance of status and local networks, and the potential significance of other kinds of intermediate institutions. The individual may be idealized in certain theories and social practices as independent and subject to state and social power, but 'individuals' are only what they are thanks to social institutions and processes. Thus, the liberal project of freeing individuals from state and social power makes the mistake of equating power with oppression and underestimates individuals' interdependence.

• Communitarians dispute the place of a free unregulated market as the key social institution, and the idea that free market exchanges are a particularly right and even natural pattern of human relationships.

In place of the individual who has defensive rights against society, the individual who engages in instrumentally self-interested transactions with others, communitarian philosophers focus on a variety of mediate institutions and traditional norm-governed ways of doing things. The communitarian literature is full of references to corporations, voluntary organizations, occupational groups, families, religious institutions. In these institutions individuals enter into relationships with one another that are governed by a variety of shared norms and practices. When we consider this range of social institutions in total it seems clear that instrumental self-interest cannot be said to be the dominant motivating factor in human life (although, of course, it has its place). Even markets, it is observed, are founded on trust, shared understandings, and conformity to norms.

• Communitarians promote a distinctive set of values.

---

[35] Alexis de Toqueville, *Democracy in America*, vols i and ii (New York: Vintage Books, 1945); Emile Durkheim, *The Division of Labour in Society* (New York: Free Press, 1933); Ferdinand de Tonnies, *Community and Society* (Lansing, Mich.: Michigan State University Press, 1957). On the perennial nature of the tussle between the ideals of individual freedom and of community see Robert A. Nisbet, *The Quest for Community: A Study in the Ethics of Order and Freedom* (New York: Oxford University Press 1953).

A good way of thinking about political traditions is to analyse their lists of cherished values (such as liberty, fraternity, authority, equality) and their order (for instance, liberals tend to put liberty prior to equality, and socialists vice versa).[36] Communitarians value community itself, and tradition. Apart from that, they will argue that we cannot in advance of study of and reasoning about some particular society say what the cherished values should be and how they should be ordered—it all depends on the traditions and ways of life of the society in question. Furthermore, we cannot in advance of reasoning about some particular society, say what liberty, for instance, means—what the criteria are by which we judge whether an individual is free or not. The meaning of liberty, in respect of what properties or characteristics people ought to be equal with one another, how authority and power ought to be distributed—all such questions can only be answered from within the established framework of a society and its way of life.

THE SOURCES OF POLITICAL COMMUNITARIANISM

There are a number of sources for the ideas and analyses of political communitarianism. One, but only one, of these is the philosophical critique of liberal political philosophy that stems, as we have seen, from the hermeneutic, phenomenological, and pragmatist philosophical traditions, and which brings together consideration of the metaphysics of the self and the person, the ontology and epistemology of values, meta-ethical questions such as the nature of right and obligation, as well as first-order ethics or consideration of the good life for human beings. The significance of philosophical communitarianism is attested to by numerous mentions in political communitarian works, and in journalistic reportage and comment.[37]

But other equally important sources, taking political communitarianism all in all, are strands of religious thought, for example, elements of the monastic traditions of the major religions, or the collective and settlement traditions of Judaism and Christianity; Christian and Jewish socialism

[36] The order of value concepts, the pattern of relationships between them, of course alters their content and scope—so that 'freedom' for instance can both mean something rather different as between different theoretical contexts, and can refer differently.

[37] Etzioni's edited collection of communitarian thought *New Communitarian Thinking* includes papers by Michael Sandel, Charles Taylor, Michael Walzer, and other prominent North American contributors to the liberal communitarian debates; one journalist credits Gordon Brown with 'bringing the MacIntyre position into the Labour Party'—Melanie Phillips, 'The Race to Wake Sleeping Duty', *Observer* (2 Apr. 1995), 25.

and the ethical socialist tradition more generally; the thought and practice of such political and social groupings as populists and progressives (in the United States), the cooperative movement in Britain, republicanism, and elements of conservative thought such as those that value common membership, established institutions and settlement. Recent political communitarian writing features references to all these diverse traditions—in all of them the theme of 'community' recurs in suggestive and inspirational ways. Of course, 'community' is not univocal, and across these various traditions and strands of tradition there is a huge variety of conceptions of the nature of community and the conditions under which it might be realized, and its relation to other concepts such as freedom, love, work, equality, history, and more.[38]

Religious Thought and Practice

It is striking that themes from religious thought and practice are prominent in contemporary political communitarianism. In the major religions the ideal of community recurs—the Christian ideals of the communion of saints, and the congregation and the Eucharist as forms of community; the centrality of *umma* or community in Islamic tradition and contemporary practice and theology; community is a prominent theme in Judaism, and in Buddhism. (Confucianism is not, of course, a religion, but neo-Confucianism is closely intertwined with Buddhism and with traditional religious cults of the family and ancestors, and Confucian norms of family and community life are politically significant in many contemporary contexts.)[39]

In particular, a number of twentieth-century philosophers whose writing is mentioned as relevant to recent political communitarianism (but who predate the 'liberal communitarian debates') were preoccupied with the interrelationship between religious and political or social thought.[40] One of these is Martin Buber, who was concerned with 'endowing the

[38] I discuss concepts of community, with all their variation, and various theories of community, in more detail in the next chapter. In this I am merely concerned to show the significance if not the centrality of conceptions of community in a variety of traditions of thought and practice that seem to be relevant for recent communitarian discourse.

[39] See, for instance, Lisa Sun-Hee Park, 'Navigating the Anti-immigration Wave: The Korean Women's Hotline and the Politics of Community', in Naples (ed.), *Community Activism and Feminist Politics*, 176.

[40] In addition to Buber and MacMurray, discussed here, we can note that Michael Sandel makes reference to Josiah Royce, *The Problem of Christianity*, ii (New York: Macmillan, 1913), 85–6 (Michael Sandel, *Democracy's Discontents: America in Search of a Public Philosophy* (Cambridge, Mass.: Harvard University Press, 1996), 207).

social sphere with a religious dimension';[41] he was concerned also with Zionism, and this was prompted by his philosophical concern for the creation of a new way of life and 'a new type of community'.[42] In an essay on the subject Buber discusses the need for 'religious community' also to be a community of work[43]—he was intrigued by the elusive ideal of 'a genuine, hence thoroughly communally disposed community of the human race'[44] and espoused, as a political and a spiritual project, 'the rebirth of the commune. Rebirth, not restoration.'[45]

Tony Blair's communitarianism was influenced by the philosophy of John MacMurray.[46] MacMurray took issue with the 'individualist' analysis typical of liberal and empiricist political and social philosophy in the twentieth century which understands society to be for the sake of the protection of the individual from others, as presupposing fear; in contrast MacMurray analyses society as for the sake of friendship and presupposing love.[47] The celebration of communion is a crucial sign and affirmation of this conception of society.[48] Communion, and a shared orientation to a transcendent Other also overcomes the logical and practical problem that time and space do not allow us to realize the active relationship of friendship with all others. This friendship is symbolically realized in communion and in our personal relations with God.[49] In MacMurray's work 'the family' has a central place: 'Family is the original human community and the basis as well as the origin of all subsequent communities. It is therefore the norm of all communities, so that any community is a brotherhood . . . The more society approximates to the family pattern, the more it realises itself as a community, or, as Marx called it, a truly human society.'[50]

Prominent strands of the major religions feature monasticism or traditions of settlement or both. In both monasticism and settlement relatively small groups share material goods and burdens, participate in collective religious practices, and are tied together in dense networks of multiplex

---

[41] Martin Buber, *I and Thou* (1st pub. 1923; New York: Charles Scribners Sons, 1970) (trans. and introd. by Walter Kaufman), 30. Martin Buber has been mentioned as an influence on Amitai Etzioni: see Martin Walker, 'Community Spirit', *Guardian* (13 Mar. 1995), pt. 2, p. 10.

[42] Buber, *I and Thou*, 37.

[43] Martin Buber, 'Comments on the Idea of Community' (1st pub. 1951), in *A Believing Humanism: My Testament 1902–1965* (New York: Simon and Schuster, 1967), 89.

[44] Ibid. 87.   [45] Ibid. 91.

[46] Peter Mandelson and Roger Liddle, *The Blair Revolution: Can New Labour Deliver?* (London: Faber and Faber, 1996), 32–3; Tony Blair, *New Britain: My Vision for a Young Country* (London: Fourth Estate, 1996), 59–60.

[47] John MacMurray *Persons in Relation* (London: Faber and Faber, 1961), 151.

[48] Ibid. 157.   [49] Ibid. 158–64.   [50] Ibid. 155.

relationships. In visionary and perfectionist Christian social thought the monastery, conceived of as orderly, simple and harmonious has often stood as an institutional ideal.[51] In the high Anglican and Catholic Christian socialist tradition there is an emphasis on the special role and contribution to the wider world of individuals living in sacramental communities—a sacramental point can also be the base for effective social action.[52] Communion, realized in community, gives individuals in turn a generalizable ideal for all social relations—which ideal according to Christian socialists like F. D. Maurice and Thomas Mirfield, could only be realized through socialism.[53] This ideal of community goes hand in hand with 'kingdom theology'—the project of realizing the kingdom of God on earth.[54] And this fits, in turn, with the ambition to overcome division (especially class division) that was the avowed aim of the nineteenth-century settlements. A number of nineteenth-century settlements (houses inhabited by volunteers who carried out charitable work among poor people in the cities of the United States and Britain) embodied this combination of religious community with social action in the local community, and the wider world.[55] This pattern is evident wherever there are monasteries: not only is the religious house a focal point for the religious life of lay people living around it, but it is frequently conceived of as a point for social action.[56]

[51] Krishan Kumar, *Utopia and Anti-Utopia in Modern Times* (Oxford: Basil Blackwell, 1987), 17. Of course, studies of monasticism and monastic life emphasize the paradox and tensions within it—as between solitude and community, contemplation and active involvement in the world, the ascetic 'natural' life and the law-governed cultural life, withdrawal and continuing dependence on supporters. See Austin B. Creel and Vasudha Narayan (eds.), *Monastic Life in the Christian and Hindu Traditions: A Comparative Study* (Lewiston, NY: Edwin Mellen Press, 1990), esp. essays by M. Meister, R. B. Michael and J. W. Elder; Patrick G. Henry and Donald K. Swearing, *For the Sake of the World: the Spirit of Buddhist and Christian Monasticism* (Minneapolis: Fortress Press, 1989), 16, 19; Jane Bunnag, 'The Way of the Monk and the Way of the World', in H. Bechert and R. Gombrich (eds.), *The World of Buddhism* (London: Thames and Hudson, 1991), 167.

[52] On the Christian Socialist tradition see Peter d'A Jones, *The Christian Socialist Revival 1877–1914: Religion, Class and Social Consciousness in late Victorian England* (Princeton, NJ: Princeton University Press, 1986), 230; also Kenneth Leech, *The Social God* (London: Sheldon Press, 1981), 45, 84.

[53] Jones, *Christian Socialist Revival*, 230.

[54] See for instance the discussion of Tawney in Standish Meacham, *Toynbee Hall and Social Reform 1880–1914: The Search for Community* (New Haven: Yale University Press, 1987), 157.

[55] Fowler, *The Dance with Community*, 33; Meacham, *Toynbee Hall and Social Reform*; Asa Briggs and Anne Macartney, *Toynbee Hall: The First Hundred Years* (London: Routledge and Kegan Paul, 1984); Lawrence Goldman, *Trinity in Camberwell: A History of the Trinity College Mission in Camberwell 1885–1985* (Cambridge: Trinity College, 1985).

[56] Henry and Swearing, *For the Sake of the World*, 186; Jane Bunnag, 'The Way of the Monk and the Way of the World', 170.

Settlement Traditions

The idea of community as voluntary settlement is especially prominent in the Christian Socialist and Jewish traditions. It is possible to point to a huge number of examples from the religious kibbutz movement,[57] to the Garden City and City Beautiful movements whose founders were connected with Christian socialism,[58] some of the Settlement projects which were focused on a specific confessional or liturgical tradition,[59] to the ideals of the puritan settlers in North America.[60] One hope of such projects is that people might remake the manner of their living and relating, in new settlements of collective life, where their environment would be under the collective control of the members. It is also important to remember that for Jewish people in Europe from the Middle Ages to the nineteenth century and beyond community was important not as voluntary settlement but as a more defensive strategy—involuntary settlement and separation from the wider city—albeit one that could be idealized in religious terms. Jewish people in Christian cities were conscious of the difference between their own ' "natural" unit—a cell of an ancient body, dispersed but not broken up' and the 'artificial, voluntary association' of the Christian commune. The ideal 'to create a community of the Pious' recurs, although it was not an ideal easily realized.[61]

On the one hand, religious communities can see themselves as 'apart from the world', opposed to the dominant society and dissenting from the laws and customs of the state and the established church, as did such groups as the Ranters.[62] On the other hand, as we have seen, religious community can be seen as a source of resources for political engagement,

[57] Aryei Fishman, *Judaism and Modernisation on the Religous Kibbutz* (Cambridge: Cambridge University Press, 1992), 102 argues that many features of the Religious Kibbutz Federation's (founded 1935) religious ideology bear the imprint of the teachings of Maimonides, notably 'a religious political ethic based on self-rationalisation and aimed at creating a perfected community through which individuals can realise their own improvement'.

[58] Jones, *Christian Socialist Revival*, 337–8; Kumar, *Utopia and Anti-Utopia*, 7.

[59] Goldman, *Trinity in Camberwell*.

[60] Kumar, *Utopia and Anti-Utopia*, 85–7 on the view that the Shakers were 'the foundation stone of American communitarianism' (p. 87); Fowler, *Dance with Community*, 31.

[61] H. H. Ben-Sasson, 'The Northern European Jewish Community and its Ideals', in H. H. Ben-Sasson and S. Ettinger (eds.), *Jewish Society through the Ages* (London: Vallentine Mitchell, 1968), 211–15.

[62] Kumar, *Utopia and Anti-Utopia*, 15; Leon H. Mayhew, *The New Public* (Cambridge: Cambridge University Press, 1997), 161; on puritanism and disjunction from the state, see J. G. A. Pocock, *The Machiavellian Moment: Florentine Political Thought and the Atlantic Republican Tradition* (Princeton, NJ: Princeton University Press, 1975); on the Franciscans, Victor Turner, *The Ritual Process: Structure and Anti-structure* (London: Routledge and Kegan Paul, 1969), 140 ff.

as an inspiration to those who live outside but in contact with it, and as a base from which its members can participate in the relations of society and state. (Certainly to the present-day churches, temples, and so on among all social institutions command available resources for 'community building'.[63]) And, as with the Puritan settlers in North America, religious community can be conceived of as the foundation, the template, for a new society and state,[64] or, as in the case of Jewish people, as elements of a society awaiting redemption.[65] Victor Turner discusses a tension within the ideal of community in Hinduism and in Franciscan Christianity. The Franciscan tradition is marked by the contrast between Francis's own vision of permanent marginality for the members of the existential community (or communion), and the developing settlement and structure symbolized and realized in the basilica at Assissi and the hierarchical relationships between Franciscan houses and the authority of the order. In Hinduism too an ideal of a 'community of withdrawal'—which transgresses social conventions—competes with the ideal of society (with settled relationships and orderly institutions) as itself a community.[66]

The idea of settlement is not always religious in any strong theological sense.[67] Toynbee Hall, which served as a model for community settlements in general, was criticized for its lack of a robust theology and mission.[68] Toynbee Hall was founded on the theory of the cultural bridging of class division—the community of shared experience, shared milieu, and shared values.[69] In Jewish history involuntary settlement in mainly hostile

[63] See Wuthnow, *Sharing the Journey*; on the Quakers Kamenka, *Community as a Social Ideal*, 24.

[64] Fowler, *Dance with Community*, 31.

[65] Jacob Katz, 'The Jewish National Movement', in Ben-Sasson and Ettinger, *Jewish Society*, 269.

[66] Turner, *The Ritual Process*, 140–61.

[67] The distinction between 'religious' and 'secular' is not always clear cut. On the interpenetration of religious and secular utopian communitarianism in North America see Krishan Kumar's discussion of John Humphrey Noyes (the founder of the Oneida community) in Kumar, *Utopia and Anti-Utopia*, 82, 87. More recently, Robert Wuthnow argues that small groups (to which, he estimates, 4 in 10 Americans belong) both make 'the sacred' more personal and more manageable, and suffuse everyday life with the equivalent of prayerfulness—Wuthnow, *Sharing the Journey*, 3–4, 7, 19. Below I mention recent Jewish secular moves to incorporate (partially) secularized versions of Jewish religious festivals and rituals into kibbutz community. The theme of making the secular quasi-sacred, and secularizing the sacred, seems to me to be a prominent one in recent communitarian thought and it is one to which I shall return.

[68] See Goldman, *Trinity in Camberwell*, 6–9 on the centrality of the gospel in the Trinity project.

[69] See Meacham, *Toynbee Hall and Social Reform*, 4. There was tension between this ideal and the professionalism and participation in governmental policy-making that was a later preoccupation of Toynbee Hall; see Briggs and Macartney, *Toynbee Hall: The First Hundred Years*, 147 ff.

societies has its redemptive mirror image in voluntary settlement in Palestine.[70] Secular practical Zionism has supported a variety of forms of collective life: cooperative production, communal domestic living, nomadic labour gangs.[71] For many participants in early experiments the socialist values and projects of the international labour movement were their guide: 'the collective provides the proletariat with its means of struggle', wrote one woman.[72] The practical commitment to collectivism was connected perforce with the material forces of a hostile landscape and climate, the need for defence, and the pioneers' meagre material resources. However, it was also connected with socialist values: the principled and determined opposition to capitalist exploitation, the value of equality, an idealized conception of the relation between the people and the land, an ideal of relations between people—in communal life 'Soul encountered soul. There was a yearning to become a sort of sea of souls, whose tributaries would flow together and together create a fresh and mighty current of fraternity and comradeship.'[73]

Models of the kibbutz have evolved, and the guiding values have been adjusted by participants and commentators.[74] In many kibbutzim there has been a movement away from the radical rejection of market relations, to the acceptance of choice and autonomy in consumption and the holding of a certain amount of private, saleable, property. This acceptance and institutional support of choice and autonomy in consumption entails a move away from the 'old-style' view of the kibbutz as a 'community . . . in which all social and economic relations meet. . . . The best way to achieve unity, which every person needs, is by belonging to the organic human entity . . . The members' frame of reference always speaks of "us" '.[75] This loosening of collective life is nevertheless thought to be consistent

[70] It is reported that Amitai Etzioni's communitarianism is shaped by his liberal Jewish upbringing in Israel, where he lived on a kibbutz. Sarah Baxter, 'I am the way and I am the truth' (*sic*) *Sunday Times* (19 Mar. 1995).

[71] Henry Near, *The Kibbutz Movement: A History*, vol. i (Oxford: Oxford University Press, 1992), 11, 18, 26, 31. Erik Cohen, 'Persistence and Change in the Israeli Kibbutz', in Kamenka, *Community as a Social Ideal* argues that notwithstanding the protestations of secularism and materialism by many members the early kibbutz had many traits in common with religious sects (p. 124).

[72] Marya Wilbushevitz, a member of the Socialist Revolutionary Party in Russia, one of the founders of the Sejera Collective, quoted in Near, *Kibbutz Movement*, i. 18.

[73] Recollection of the period 1922–3, by a member of the Kibbutz Genegar, quoted in ibid. 81.

[74] Henry Near, *The Kibbutz Movement: A History*, vol. ii (Oxford: Oxford University Press, 1997); Avner de-Shalit, 'David Miller's Theory of Market Socialism and the Recent Reforms in Kibbutzim', *Political Studies*, 40 (1992), 116–23; Cohen, 'Persistence and Change in the Israeli Kibbutz'.

[75] De-Shalit, 'Recent Reforms', 119.

still with common cultural lives and values, and with collective production.[76]

Socialism

Another source for political communitarianism is the ethical socialist tradition and socialism more generally. Michael Freeden notes that 'All socialisms subscribe to some notion of group membership, to a view which regards individuals as constituting fraternities or communities, even—in some cases—as defined by their membership of such groups. The emphasis on human inter-relationships, and their consequent community structure, as a salient feature of human life appears in different but unmistakeable forms.'[77] The history of socialism notably contains numerous experiments in collective living and community construction, including John Humphrey Noyes' Oneida, Robert Owen's New Harmony, Etienne Cabet's Icaria, Charles Fourier's phalanstery, and even more designs for such experiments.[78] Nineteenth-century United States communitarian socialists could seriously consider that they held 'the key to America's future', believing 'in the small experimental community as the germ-cell of the future society'.[79] But the central values of solidarity, cooperation and reciprocity also underpin arguments about patterns of social relations at the level of society in the large (not the small, town or village sized, collective and cooperative community). For instance a British Commission on Social Justice[80] argued in 1994: 'A good society depends not just on the economic success of I, the individual, but the social commitment of we, the community', 'not just the idea that we owe something to each other, but the belief that we gain from giving to each other'.[81]

Socialist political theorists argue that the egalitarianism that is prescribed in socialist, social democratic, and left liberal thought must presuppose a particular quality of relationships between persons—a sense of common membership of some collective, a sense that our relations with other members are relations of reciprocity, fraternity, and concern about

---

[76] De-Shalit, 'Recent Reforms', 122–3. Near, *Kibbutz Movement*, ii. 281–6.

[77] Freeden, *Ideologies and Political Theory*, 426; Eugene Kamenka, 'Community and the Socialist Ideal', in *Community as a Social Ideal*.

[78] See Kumar, *Utopia and Anti-Utopia*; George Lichtheim, *A Short History of Socialism* (London: Fontana, 1975); Kamenka, 'Community and the Socialist Ideal'.

[79] Kumar, *Utopia and Anti-Utopia*, 95.

[80] Which was set up by the then Labour Party leader John Smith.

[81] The Commission on Social Justice/Institute for Public Policy Research, *Social Justice: Strategies for National Renewal* (London: Vintage Books, 1994).

the needs of others. Frequently, the term 'community' is used to characterize such relationships or clusters of relationships.[82] Others simply argue that 'community' itself is a core socialist value. Sometimes, this is on the grounds that sociability and altruism 'are human characteristics which were unnaturally made to give way to self-assertion and competitiveness'—so community is valued because it is essential or natural to human life.[83]

Republicanism

The communitarian tradition in the United States is often connected with the republican tradition, although scholars tend to argue that the discontinuities and differences between republic and community are as striking as the seeming continuities. Continuities, discontinuities, and differences have been found and analysed, between the seventeenth-century English republicanism of the Commonwealth, the Puritan 'community of the elect', the 'Elect Nation', and the political community as it was constructed in American republican thought and practice.[84] The communal nature of social and political organization in the medieval and Renaissance city republics has been noted.[85] United States 'New Republicans' have explicitly drawn attention to the convergence between republicanism and communitarianism.[86] Certainly, the Republican tradition has been much cited in recent communitarian thought, both political and philosophical, and the answer to the question what are the political implications of philosophical communitarianism has widely been taken to consist in some revised and revitalized form of republicanism.[87]

---

[82] G. A. Cohen, 'Back to Socialist Basics', *New Left Review*, 207 (1994), 9–11; David Miller, 'In what sense must socialism be communitarian?', *Social Philosophy and Policy*, 6 (1989), 57–60, p. 51.

[83] Alan Carling, 'Analytical and Essential Marxism', *Political Studies*, 45 (1997), 768–83; Freeden, *Ideologies and Political Theory*, 426; Kamenka, 'Community and the Socialist Ideal', 26.

[84] Pocock, *The Machiavellian Moment*, 345, 348; Leon H. Mayhew, *The New Public* (Cambridge: Cambridge University Press, 1997), 157–64.

[85] Anthony Black, 'Communal Democracy and its History', *Political Studies*, 45 (1997), 8.

[86] For example, Stephen A. Gardbaum, 'Law Politics and the Claims of Community', *Michigan Law Review*, 90 (1992), 685; Mark Tushnet, 'The Possibilities of Interpretive Liberalism', *Alberta Law Review*, 29 (1991), 276.

[87] Fowler, *Dance with Community*, 27, 31; Adrian Oldfield, *Citizenship and Community: Civic Republicanism and the Modern World* (London: Routledge, 1990); Walzer, 'Communitarian Critique', 20; Charles Taylor, 'Cross Purposes', 166–71.

Conservatism

There are also distinctly conservative sources of communitarianism. The conservative criticisms of liberal society, economy, and polity that were generated at liberalism's inception frequently invoked the value of settled relationships and ways of life, in the face of liberalism's emphasis on individual freedom and voluntarism.[88] Cultural conservatives like Coleridge emphasized the role of established institutions in binding individuals together in relations of mutual obligation.[89] Disraeli emphasized the common membership of the nation, which should be shared by rich and poor alike, in contrast to and settlement of the antagonism that is engendered by so-called liberal rights and liberties.[90] Such themes recur throughout conservative thought, although of course they jostle with the more libertarian themes of laissez-faire in conservative arguments about free trade in the nineteenth century especially, and the economic and social liberty of the individual in New Right discourses of the late twentieth century.[91] In response to these libertarian themes the communitarian strand of conservatism has become, if anything, more loudly insistent in the 1980s and 90s.[92] This is one factor in the success that communitarianism, as an idea, has had in politics.

POLITICAL COMMUNITARIANISM: AN ANALYSIS

In this section I set out an analysis of political communitarianism. This account is the product of reading a range of materials, including documents such as the 'Communitarian platform' published by the Washington DC based Communitarian Network, reports and political pamphlets in which the ideal of community is prominent, books by and about politicians, and journalistic comment and reportage both of community projects and politics and of 'communitarianism' as a set of political goals from the decade 1987–98.[93]

[88] Roger Scruton, (ed.), *Conservative Texts: An Anthology* (Basingstoke: MacMillan, 1991), 8–11; George L. Mosse, 'Nationalism, Fascism and the Radical Right', in Kamenka, *Community as a Social Ideal*, 27–8.
[89] Scruton, *Conservative Texts*, 71–7.   [90] Ibid. 40–58.
[91] Freeden, *Ideologies and Political Theory*, 364, 371, 373, 388—Freeden emphasizes the transformation of the meaning and theory of 'laissez-faire' between liberal and conservative discourses and platforms.
[92] See for example Taylor, *Releasing the Community Spirit*; Robin Harris, *The Conservative Community*.
[93] A complete list of my 'political communitarianism' sources, together with an account of the method I used for analysing them, is supplied in Appendix II.

Varieties of Political Communitarianism

On the basis of the material in this database a number of varieties of political communitarianism can be identified. First, there is the communitarian strand of the British left, which in the period in question came
practically to dominate Labour Party and 'centre-left' politics. As I have
mentioned a number of origins of this tradition are cited: 'Scots ethical
socialism', Christian socialism of various kinds, the cooperative movement, working-class practices of mutuality and solidarity, and so on.
Second (and most prominent in the press coverage), the recently formed
US-based self-styled 'Communitarian Movement' which prides itself on
going 'beyond right and left'—or, rather, in managing to get the support
of representatives of both the major US parties. The origins of this are
very diverse; they certainly include the philosophical communitarian critique of US liberalism, aspects of conservative social and political
thought, especially a distinctive analysis of 'the family'[94] and an emphasis
on duty and obligation, but also an appeal to religiosity, and to various
aspects of US political tradition including some of its republican elements.
Third, there is British conservative communitarianism—the examples I
have are from within the Conservative Party, but are marked by a distinctive set of themes deployed in order to appeal to a coalition which contrast
markedly with the 'New Right' elements of recent Conservative Party history. Fourth, there is a rival (and actually older established) US communitarianism centred around the journal *Tikkun*—'a bi-monthly Jewish
critique of politics, culture and society'. I call this a 'rival' of Etzioni's
communitarian movement as this is an unavoidable interpretation given
the criticism in *Tikkun's* pages of some of the projects and analyses of the
communitarian movement, and because as we shall see there are clear
intellectual distinctions. However, there is also some overlap of contributors. And as we shall also go on to see the themes that are shared between
these varieties of communitarianism are more striking and more numerous than are the contrasts.

This categorization of four 'varieties' of political communitarianism is
neither exclusive nor exhaustive. It is not exclusive, because some individuals have a foot in more than one camp, and there are no clear barriers to
hybridization. It is not exhaustive. For one thing, the classification is contingent on my sample of communitarian discourse: of course I am conscious that had I sampled different journals I might have found other

---

[94] I deal with 'the family' in detail in Chapter 6.

variants.[95] Further, there seem to be no barriers, on the face of it, to proliferation of variants—the ubiquity of ideals of community in a wide range
of religious and cultural traditions testifies to this. Finally, many individual authors of articles and books can't be classified (on the evidence I have
to hand) into any of these categories, although their work makes a clear
contribution to communitarian politics.[96]

Analysis of the database yielded an index divided under a number of
heads.[97] In addition to the *varieties of communitarianism* just enumerated
I found that writers and commentators referred to a range of *examples of
communities* and *kinds of community*.[98] More important for the purposes
of my present discussion are the *hypotheses* about social processes and
mechanisms, the *normative principles* and the *values* that communitarians
elaborate. Together these constitute the communitarians' account of what
makes and what sustains communities. In addition, communitarians are
more or less clear about what undermines and destroys community; these
items constitute a separate heading in my index.

There are some clear differences between the four varieties of communitarianism. Predictably enough whereas contributors to *Tikkun* mention
capitalism as an enemy of community—

individual rights are . . . certainly not the greater threat to community. The expan-
sion and abuse of property rights—now exercised by multinational corporations
on a global scale—has produced abandoned plants and ghost communities all
over America[99]

—conservative communitarians and the communitarian movement do
not. British Left communitarianism and commentary on it emphasizes
themes of mutual aid, reciprocity, and solidarity; for instance:

people can achieve much more by acting together than acting alone . . . we act
together to achieve power, wealth and opportunity for all, not for the few[100]

[95] For example, I am conscious that had I sampled the *Los Angeles Times* it is likely that
I would have found accounts of—and commentary on—a wider range of community
activism centred on more recent migrants to the United States, and this might have made a
difference to my interpretation. And of course, the lack of a wider European reference begs
a number of important questions that I am simply not able to answer from the confines of
this project.

[96] I haven't included journalists who write sympathetically about community activism
(for example, Melanie Phillips) in any of these categories; nor the British communitarian
Henry Tam, or communitarian activist and entrepreneur Dick Atkinson.

[97] A complete list of the index headings is supplied in Appendix I.

[98] I discuss these in some detail in Chapter 2.

[99] Charles Derber quoted by Jonathan Steele, 'Clinton Policies are Caught in
Communitarian Crossfire', *Guardian* (12 Apr. 1995).

[100] Tony Blair quoted by Martin Kettle, 'Blair Puts Faith in Community Spirit',
Guardian (13 Mar. 1995), 2.

and

not just the idea that we owe something to each other, but the belief that we gain from giving to each other.[101]

As Michael Young writes,

British socialism owed more to Methodism than Marxism. But also in its beginning it owed much less to doctrines of public ownership than to mutual aid and self help as represented in the Victorian friendly society . . . but above all in the everyday exchanges of mutual aid in every working class community in the land.[102]

There is a discourse of class here, which is also very evident in the pages of *Tikkun* whose draft Social Responsibility Amendment to the US Constitution requires that corporations 'serve the common good, give [their] workers substantial power to shape their own conditions of work and [have] a history of social responsibility to the communities in which they operate, sell goods and/or advertise'[103] but which is absent from presentations and discussions of the Communitarian Movement, and from British conservative communitarianism.

However, what is shared—albeit inflected rather differently due to what is not shared—is the more striking. Civic spirit, responsibility for self and for the community, mutuality, are central in all varieties of political communitarianism. Responsibility, as commentators noted, was ubiquitous in Tony Blair's speeches as leader of the opposition;[104] a conservative communitarian laments the 'attitude that assisting those around us who are less fortunate than ourselves is the responsibility of someone else';[105] while the editor of Tikkun discusses the decline in such values as loyalty and responsibility to others.[106]

Values, Principles and Hypotheses

The normative principles that communities should have authority, that the individual should participate in the community in which she or he is rooted and which has shaped her or him, that communities can produce and distribute goods that neither the commodity market nor governments

---

[101] Commission on Social Justice, *Social Justice*, 307.
[102] Michael Young and Gerald Lemos, 'Roots of Revival', *Guardian* (19 Mar. 1997), Society p. 2.
[103] *Tikkun*, 12/4 (1997).
[104] 'Communitarianism: Down with Rights', *The Economist* (18 Mar. 1995), 31; Joe Rogaly, 'Blair's Community Spirit', *Financial Times* (18 Mar. 1995), Weekend p. 1.
[105] Taylor, *Releasing the Community Spirit*, 4.
[106] Michael Lerner, 'Pain at Work and Pain in Families', *Tikkun* 6/1 (1991), 18.

can, are common. Etzioni argues, for example, 'the community must be provided with the constitutional tools that will prevent [drug] dealers from destroying whole neighbourhoods'.[107] And from a conservative communitarian:

the formulation of a hierarchy of communities, each with importance in its own right, began as a matter of law—the legal theory of corporations. . . . the Conservative government has strengthened the autonomy of those real units of social life which are the natural focus of people's loyalties.[108]

While another conservative asks that as

a strong and happy society can best be achieved as a partnership between the government and active individuals and families which comprise the communities in which they live—what are we doing to encourage community activity and responsibility?[109]

Amitai Etzioni insists that 'the community has a moral standing coequal to that of the individual'.[110]

In answer to the old theoretical question, and the current practical problem, about the relationship between individual and community we find a number of answers. I coded four distinct views: first, that the individual and the community both exist and both are important (more strongly, in Etzioni's words, they have moral equivalence); second that the individual is rooted in and shaped by the community; third, that the individual should, for various good reasons, participate in his or her community or communities; fourth, that the individual has responsibility for others severally and for the community collectively. Tony Blair articulates the first view very clearly:

[Labour believes] that individual liberty is best secured through a strong and just community, where people recognise their interdependence as well as independence and where action by society as a whole is used to help fulfil the aspirations of the individuals within it. . . . The need for cooperation, for action by government, for a resurgence of community values is clear; but it will be supported only if the balance between individual and collective is right for the age in which we live.[111]

[107] Charles Trueheart, 'The Case for the Group Ethic', *Washington Post* (5 Feb. 1991), p. C07.

[108] Robin Harris, *The Conservative Community*, 37.

[109] Taylor, *Releasing the Community Spirit*, 4.

[110] Etzioni, *The Spirit of Community*, 31; Charles Trueheart, 'The Case for the Group Ethic', p. C07; Martin Walker, 'Community Spirit', *Guardian* (13 Mar. 1995), pt. 2, p. 10.

[111] Tony Blair, 'The Right Way to Find a Left Alternative', *Observer* (9 May 1993), 20; also Blair, *New Britain*, 215–22.

That individuals are 'rooted' in community is expressed most clearly in *Tikkun*, many of whose contributors emphasize the existential alienation in societies organized along individualist lines. According to Michael Lerner the message from both right and left has been:

'You are fundamentally alone, you can't really trust other people and all relationships start with the individual'. By our account, human beings are most fundamentally in relationship. they are part of a family and part of a people and it is this rootedness in community that is ontologically prior and ethically funda-mental.[112]

A key theme in communitarianism is participation. For instance, the UK Institute for Citizenship Studies has as one of its basic principles 'Encouraging people to value and recognise the obligations and respons-ibilities of being fully involved as members of their community'; and as one of its strategies 'Promoting activities which assist individuals to par-ticipate in communities, however defined.'[113] More strongly, and most associated with the US communitarian movement, is the view that mod-ern societies are overly 'rights centred' and that this tendency should give way in part to 'duty centredness': that the duties and responsibilities of citizens to each other and to the community should balance individual rights.[114]

Shared by all the communitarians too is the hypothesis that the strength of families and the strength of communities are mutually reinforcing: 'Strong families make strong communities' says Tony Blair;[115] 'Individual families get their strength and meaning through participation in a larger community, and the community at any given moment gets its strength and meaning by its relationship to the historical chain of generations that have

---

[112] Michael Lerner, 'Founding Editorial Statement', *Tikkun*, 1/1 (1986).

[113] Institute for Citizenship Studies, *Encouraging Citizenship http://www.citizen.org.uk/*; see also Atkinson, *Common Sense of Community*, 42 ff., 56.

[114] See Paul Taylor, 'An Agenda Focussed Less on Rights and More on Responsibilities', *Washington Post* (19 Nov. 1991), p. A19. An important book on this sub-ject, by a signatory to the US Communitarian Agenda, is Mary Ann Glendon, *Rights Talk: The Impoverishment of Political Discourse* (New York: Free Press, 1991). See also Blair, *New Britain*, 236–43.

[115] Mandelson and Liddle, *The Blair Revolution: Can New Labour Deliver?* (London: Faber and Faber, 1996), 20; Blair repeated this in his speech to the 1998 Labour Party Conference: 'I challenge us to accept that a strong family life is the basic unit of a strong community'; and in the Ministerial Group on the Family's discussion document (*Supporting Families*) the Home Secretary begins the Foreword with 'Family life is the foundation on which our communities, our society and our country are built'. See also Atkinson, *Common Sense of Community*, 11.

preceded us and will follow us,' writes Michael Lerner;[116] while Ian Taylor argues that 'the family is a basic component in the resurgence of community spirit [so] it is important that policy makers begin here'.[117] There is a similar level of consensus about the threats to community: selfishness on the part of individuals, ineptitude and betrayal on the part of bureaucratic government, crime—from low level but nevertheless damaging littering and vandalism to assault, burglary, and theft. Poverty is mentioned by the US, British conservative, and British left communitarians only to be disavowed as a key factor in 'community breakdown'.[118]

Within each of these varieties of political communitarianism, too, we find pairs of values which communitarians strive to 'balance', notably liberty and authority, and religiosity and secularism or humanism. The pull between libertarianism and authoritarianism is central to the thought of all communitarians who are determined to steer a middle way or, alternatively, go beyond the dichotomy. Henry Tam's book is organized throughout as a rebuttal of objections to communitarian policies from libertarians on the one hand and authoritarians on the other.[119] Etzioni insists on the compatibility of communitarian and consensual social organization with the fostering of democracy and autonomy.[120] Conservative Robin Harris expresses concern about 'the social disintegration which flows from libertarianism' and argues that the conservative state must 'combine a high degree of consensus about [values which are essential to the 'good life'] with emphasis on the importance of private life and personal freedom'[121]

The balancing of secularism and religiosity is also a common feature, although here we find more contrasts in detail than in the problem of liberty and authority. On the one hand political communitarians are quite sensibly reluctant to suggest that their programme is tied to any confessional tradition or faith, and it is fair to say that much of the press coverage of the relevance of religious tradition is the product of commentators' questions and imputations. But the editors of *Tikkun* are quite clear about the importance (and the disadvantages) of stressing the place of Jewish heritage and spirituality in their politics:

---

[116] Michael Lerner, 'Founding Editorial Statement'. I discuss communitarians on the family in much more detail in Chapter 5 is worth noting here that the approach to family life evident in *Tikkun* is in many respects different from that shared by the other varieties of communitarianism—more informed by psychoanalysis and conflict theories.

[117] Taylor, *Releasing the Community Spirit*, 12.

[118] Ibid. 8; Etzioni, *The Spirit of Community*, 69.

[119] Henry Tam, *Communitarianism: A New Agenda for Politics and Citizenship* (Basingstoke: Macmillan, 1998).

[120] Etzioni, *Spirit of Community*, 37–8.

[121] Harris, *The Conservative Community*, 6.

The healthy human being is not the one who has learned to stand alone but the one who can acknowledge his/her need to be in deep relationship with other human beings and with the community. . . . it is in these relationships with others and in community that we gain access to God. . . . we are ethically and religiously bound to the healing, repair and transformation of this social order.[122]

A British conservative communitarian argues that 'religion, even be it a secular religion, will be the single most important continuing influence on society', while also holding that

the religion of the Conservative—insofar as he is a Conservative—is not just any religion, but rather Christianity. This is not to say that all Conservatives are Christians—which would be absurd. It is most emphatically in no way to ignore the wisdom and virtue of many non Christians—particularly Jews—who share fully in liberal, democratic, Western values. It is to do no more than to state that the tradition and values from which Conservatism has sprung—and which continue to inspire it—are Christian.[123]

The importance of various strands of Christian socialism to figures such as Tony Blair, Gordon Brown, and Frank Field from the British Labour Party, and Methodism to Hillary Clinton, are commonly remarked on by journalists and other commentators.[124]

The tension between religious impulse and secular society is resolved by emphasizing non-material goods and values—'meaning' and 'spirit'. There is an emphasis on the things money can't buy. The battle between profit, on the one hand, and state-sponsored redistribution, on the other, has generated a vacuum which can't be filled by right- or left-wing policies:

a society unable to fulfil the basic psychological, spiritual and ethical needs of its members. It is this failure to deliver the goods on these fundamental levels that creates a deep hunger for love, meaning and purpose . . . This is the most central problem facing many Americans . . . The crisis in the meaning of life has to be the center of a Democratic agenda in the nineties.[125]

What is lacking in this country is a communitarian spirit . . . The economic success of the Reagan years has left Americans uneasy with their own selfishness, concerned about whether they are doing enough for their fellow citizens . . .[126]

The sense of community not only has a long tradition in Conservative thought, but is entirely compatible with modern day Conservatism. A stable society is

[122] Lerner, 'Founding Editorial Statement', 7.
[123] Harris, *Conservative Community*, 49.
[124] Blair, *New Britain*, 57–61 (this piece, entitled 'Why I am a Christian' links Christianity and community. It was first published in the *Sunday Telegraph* (7 Apr. 1996)).
[125] Michael Lerner, 'Surviving a Bush Presidency', *Tikkun*, 4/1 (1989), 17.
[126] Michael Barone, 'After Reagan, How About a Great Communitarian?', *Washington Post* (29 Nov. 1987), p. L01.

possible only with the active sense of involvement of its citizens. As Douglas Hurd MP commented when he was Home Secretary: 'Freedom can only flourish within a community where shared values, common loyalties and mutual obligations provide a framework of order and self-discipline. . . .' The government has already initiated a number of important measures that constitute an important step in releasing community spirit . . .[127]

This metaphor of 'spirit' pervades communitarian discourse and in the chapters that follow I have a good deal to say about it. For now I just want to note the way it implies a transcendence of concrete and material relations although political communitarians are always ready to gloss their references to community spirit with sketches of what material transactions it entails: volunteering, taking responsibility, acting cooperatively.

The Communitarian Consensus

In US communitarianism we also find a pervasive theme of 'beyond left and right'.

'I prefer my own view . . . a community based participatory politics that's neither left nor right wing but the whole bird'[128]

This is not the kind of stern catalogue of shoulds and shouldn'ts that either the Democrats or the Republicans are likely to serve up. That's because the [Communitarian] platform comes from a different realm.[129]

These ideas about the need to restore our sense of community supersede left-right political debate. When I'm attacked by both sides I know I'm in the right place.[130]

We are not uncritically committed to liberalism. When liberal values are used as a cover for materialism and individualism we say clearly that they are not our values. We are also very critical of the Left. The Left has almost always tried to force Jews into a false universalism—denying the particularity of our historical experience. . . . The irony is that although the Right is able to manipulate the language of community and family it actually supports a social and economic order that at root shatters solidarity and fragments community and places individual pursuit of private gain as the highest value.[131]

British socialist and Tory communitarians, of course, do not embrace this 'beyond left and right' thesis; rather they are preoccupied with the project of capturing the communitarian ground from the opposition: as Ian

---

[127] Taylor, *Releasing the Community Spirit*, 9.
[128] Sam Smith, 'Bringing Politics Back Home', *Washington Post* (01.11.1994), p. A23.
[129] Taylor, 'An Agenda Focussed Less on Rights . . .'
[130] Amitai Etzioni, quoted in Martin Walker 'Community Spirit', *Guardian* (13 Mar. 1995), pt. 2, p. 10.
[131] Lerner, 'Founding Editorial Statement'.

Taylor remarked, 'we must avoid the danger that the mood [the kinder, gentler mood that President Bush saw emerging in the USA at the 1991 Presidential election] is seen to be matched by the "new" socialism rather than, as in reality, best satisfied by traditional Conservatism'.[132] Labour Party members have been concerned equally to establish the socialist credentials of the ideal of community. Roy Hattersley, associated with 'traditional' socialist Labour, argued: 'During the eighties we were all encouraged to forget that we are dependent one on another. Labour must now reassert the idea of community.'[133] And Tony Blair asserts repeatedly: 'The founding principle, the guiding principle, of the Labour Party is the belief in community and society. It's the notion that for individuals to advance you need a strong and fair community behind you.'[134]

Although British socialist and conservative communitarianism is not committed, exactly, to a 'beyond left and right' position, it nevertheless is the case that political communitarianism is committed to consensus, rather than majority, building. There are three aspects of communitarian politics that I wish to draw attention to here.[135] First, communitarianism, according to both its promoters and its critics, focuses on 'what we all share'—values, beliefs, goals. What we all share forms a substructure which supports and enables the disagreement and conflict that are essential in democratic, liberal, and indeed communitarian societies.[136] Communitarians insist that on virtually every issue there are shared values, meanings, and goals that can be appealed to. A key strategy is to build on the 'communitarian traces' within the society: firms know, already, that communitarian management and external relations reap dividends, and in every economy some firms are consistently committed to such policies. The common understanding that this is so can be appealed to in disputes between citizens and corporations.[137] Residents and developers agree that something must be done to improve the mess that exists at present; this shared goal forms the basis for political agreement.[138] Second, communitarians emphasize the importance of participation. Community activism forges civic bonds, and promotes individuals' and groups' independence from state bureaucracies. It fosters political participation and the

---

[132] Taylor, *Releasing the Community Spirit*, 6.
[133] Roy Hattersley, 'Let's Proclaim Our Beliefs', *Observer* (29 Sept. 1991), 23.
[134] Blair, *New Britain*, 217.   [135] I take these issues up in more detail in Chapter 7.
[136] See Gerard Kelly, 'Off the Self Sociology', *Times Higher Education Supplement* (24 Mar. 1995), 21; also Robert N. Bellah, 'Community Properly Understood: a Defence of "Democratic Communitarianism" ', *Responsive Community*, 6/1 (1995–6), 49–50.
[137] Tam, *Communitarianism*, 172–3, 180–81.
[138] Daniel Kemmis, 'A Question of Locus: Sovereignty and Community', *Responsive Community*, 1/3 (1991), 14.

discharge of democratic obligations.[139] Third, and connected, is that community politics brings politics down to its proper human level—the level of the person, and the human encounter.

We must learn and teach and make a central part of our politics that while small is not always beautiful it has—for our human ecology, our liberties and our souls—become absolutely essential. . . . political power is what transforms our civic spirit from mere desire to real community life. The fact that most politics has become corrupt, abusive and far removed from such a generic purpose is no reason to shun it. It is rather all the more reason to demand its return to its proper place as a natural, integral and pleasurable part of our lives. It is all the more reason to bring politics back home.[140]

This passage admirably brings together a number of the key themes of political communitarianism: spirit and the soul, human life and relationships, individual liberty and community (and Mr Smith begins this piece by going 'beyond left and right'). So there, for the moment, we can leave the analysis of political communitarianism, and turn to some theoretical and practical problems with it.

PROBLEMS WITH POLITICAL COMMUNITARIANISM

If we look at political communitarianism with an abstracting eye, we can see that within it there are two distinct formal arguments. Some communitarians *begin* with the concept 'community': community is a valuable thing and the theoretical and practical problem these communitarians try to tackle is, crudely, how to get it, and how to secure it once it has been got. Obviously, this project begs the question what community, or 'a community', is. Usually communitarians are talking of social organizations and arrangements in which people are related to one another as whole persons, in contrast to the partial relations such as buyer–seller, employer–employee, that are typical of markets, or the multiple (and, taken separately, partial) roles we play in complex modern societies, such as teacher–pupil, constituent–representative, or neighbour. Sometimes, the idea of relations between whole persons has an explicitly spiritual dimension. Some communitarians really mean that in community people relate to each other 'soul to soul', or at some level that transcends the mundane

---

[139] Melanie Phillips, 'The Race to Wake Sleeping Duty', *Observer* (2 Apr. 1995), 25; 'Riddle behind Howard's Volunteers', *Observer* (10 Mar. 1994), 27; Martin Wainwright, 'People Power is Bringing Hope', *Guardian* (6 Dec. 1995), 4.

[140] Sam Smith, 'Bringing Politics Back Home', *Washington Post* (01.11.1994), p. A23.

and the bodily. For others, the point is that in 'whole person' relations we have relations with others that are more meaningful than are the partial relations of modern societies and markets. I analyse and discuss these ideas in more detail in Chapter 2. Meanwhile, let us turn to the second formal argument that is discernable in political communitarianism.

Other theorists begin with the premiss that 'persons are fundamentally related to each other'. This can be meant in several senses. First of all, of course, there is the trivial sense that we are spatially related to each other because we share the same territory or planet. Second, as persons making our way in the world we inevitably encounter one another—sometimes we are compelled or choose to interact with one another. So far, this account is acceptable to social theorists from individualist traditions of social theory, such as rational choice and rational expectations: they presume that persons encounter one another and interact, engaging in exchange, reciprocity, and even altruism. But these theoretical approaches take it that this is consistent with the premiss that the individuals who engage with each other are, in theory at least, disconnected from one another. Many communitarians think of connectedness in a stronger sense than this. First, they emphasize *sharing*—shared fate, shared social identities, shared practices (language, religion, culture), shared values. They emphasize that the world we enter is a world in which we must participate in these collective enterprises and partake of these collective states—this is not optional, as some individualist social theories seem to suggest. Second, we are *dependent* on others—when young we are dependent on our carers, and our socialization into adulthood involves the transformation (not the cessation) of that dependence into a range of material, psychological, and social attachments. These are *attachments*; not simple interactions.

This emphasis on interaction, sharing and attachment is taken by communitarians to generate a number of inferences. First, any political or social system that emphasizes above all the freedom and rights of the individual, and in particular assumes that market mechanisms, worked by the aggregation of individually self-interested decisions, is the best solution to social dilemmas of distribution, morality, and stability, is likely to fail. On the other hand, second, this also goes for the kind of social and political system in which it is assumed that the first allegiance of the individual is to the state, and that distribution, morality, and stability are the business of the state. The individual, on the one hand, and the state, or nation, or people, on the other, are less salient than a variety of social organizations and institutions such as kinship groups, neighbourhoods, voluntary associations for work, sociability or fellowship, communities, parties, religious organizations, corporations, and other economic enterprises. These are the focuses of human attachment, sharing and interaction, of human connectedness.

However, communitarians also infer that what this all adds up to is community. As we have seen, they infer both that these mediate institutions should be and can be communities (and to the extent that they are not, in contemporary societies, that itself is an explanation of what's going wrong in those societies) and that these mediate institutions are themselves the building blocks of community.[141] A prominent strand of the argument in this book is that community is a very specific form of association or organization. The communitarian theory that mediate institutions individually and in aggregation should and can be communities does not follow from their own premises about human and social life. There is a fallacious inference, that is, from an appeal to the proper recognition of the *relational basis* of social identity and social institutions (taking it that institutions are dense clusters of relationships), to the prescription of *community* as the ideal form of social organization.

Within communitarian writing we find a peculiar combination of acknowledgement and denial of this. A recurrent theme is that community has been lost. This is consistent with the familiar sociological thesis, associated with a number of the founders of modern sociology, which focuses on the conditions and consequences of the historical transition from traditional to modern societies, from community to society, from status to contract as the dominant normative basis of social relations, from particularism to universalism in knowledge claims and social relations, and so on. The details of this sociological thesis are, of course, argued about. And the thesis itself is disputed by some sociologists and historians who are inclined to emphasize continuities rather than discontinuities, or incremental change rather than dramatic restructuring. But undoubtedly the early sociologists were preoccupied with the ills of modernity—alienation and the brutality of capitalist relations, anomie, the iron cage of bureaucratic rationality. At least part of their project was to seek resolutions to these new conflicts and contradictions. But it is by no means a valid inference to associate these ills with the loss of community itself, nor, further, to presume that the solution to the ills of modernity is the reinstatement of community.

This argument that there is a fallacious inference in communitarianism itself begs the question I have already mentioned, namely the question of the concept 'community'. In the first place, philosophers and political communitarians both have produced very little in the way of systematic

---

[141] Atkinson, *Cities of Pride*, section 2.

analysis of this concept. If we compare the number of print words devoted to the analysis of community with the number devoted to liberty, or equality, or authority, or exploitation, the difference is very striking. In the second place, usage—not only in the political discourses that comprise my dataset of 'political communitarianism' but also in political science and political theory—is extremely ambiguous and vague. The term is used in shifting ways. Sometimes it seems to denote a particular kind of *social entity*, sometimes it denotes a particular kind of *relationship* between persons. Sometimes it is used as a general noun to encompass all kinds of groups and collectivities. We frequently find that writers offer us examples of communities, in the stead of analysis. Alasdair MacIntyre makes community a term which encompasses a range of subcategories: he mentions 'communities such as those of the family, the neighbourhood, the city and the tribe'.[142] By contrast, Michael Sandel thinks of communities as one kind of institution of which we might have membership (like families, or nations, or peoples).[143] Amitai Etzioni implies that all sorts of social groups should and can be communities: firms, schools, families, neighbourhoods, nations, and states.[144] However what exactly makes a community a community, or what makes a firm or school etc., a community, is vague.

One analytic tradition which might seem to promise clarity about the concept 'community' is community studies within sociology. Here we find that there has been disagreement about whether community entails any or all of:

- a bounded geographical area;
- a dense network of non-contractual relations including those of kinship, friendship and cultural membership
- a network, dense or otherwise, of multiplex relations
- a particular quality of identification on the part of members with place, or culture, or way of life, or tradition—usually involving emotional attachment, loyalty, solidarity or unity, and/or a sense that the community makes the person what they are
- shared symbols, meanings, values, language, norms; shared interests such as occupational interests (as in a 'fishing community') or political and cultural interests (as in 'the gay community').

It is not necessary for all these to be present together, evidently. Equally, no one of these characteristics alone seems to be sufficient for

[142] Alasdair MacIntyre, *After Virtue*, 221.
[143] Michael Sandel, *Liberalism and the Limits of Justice*, 172.
[144] Amitai Etzioni, *The Spirit of Community*, 32.

community.[145] However, in political philosophy and theory, communitarians often seem to propose or imply that one particular element is a necessary and sufficient condition for community—that is shared symbols, common meanings, a common language or at least a common understanding.[146] The trouble with this is that it can be interpreted to mean nothing more than that we live in the same society, or on the same planet—there's no more to community than that; or it can be interpreted as sociologically very demanding, a condition almost impossible to meet in late modern societies.

It is important to see that this very vagueness in the concept 'community' is one of its strengths—it acts as a mechanism for holding a coalition together, for community can mean different things to different parties. Insofar as communitarianism is politically significant, it is because it appeals to a potential diverse coalition. Unless individuals and groups are willing to go in for allegiance across difference, change cannot occur politically. But coalitions are frequently fragile and invariably susceptible to a variety of destabilizing forces. And, importantly, critics are quick to denounce coalitions as unholy alliances, putting coalition members on the ideological defensive. This has certainly been the case with communitarianism: liberals accuse them of authoritarianism; socialists accuse them of liberalism; feminists accuse them of patriarchalism—notwithstanding that all parties are attached to the idea of 'community'. It is the key term that members of the coalition are most going to contest—so as well as being a strength, it is also a weak link in the communitarian chain.

[145] Colin Bell and Howard Newby, *Community Studies: An Introduction to the Sociology of the Local Community* (London: George Allen and Unwin, 1971); Margaret Stacey, 'The Myth of Community Studies', *British Journal of Sociology*, 20 (1969), 134–47; Graham Day and Jonathan Murdoch, 'Locality and Community: Coming to Terms with Place', *Sociological Review*, 41 (1993) 82–111.

[146] e.g. Charles Taylor, *Philosophy and the Human Sciences*, 39, 96. This theme is prominent in political communitarianism, in the emphasis on consensus.

2

The Concept 'Community'

CONCEPTUAL ANALYSIS

Any reader who is curious about the meaning of the term community, and
is interested in analysis of the concept, will be struck by the absence of
such analysis in the communitarian texts and in political theory more generally. If the amount of print devoted to the analysis of such terms as
equality, liberty, exploitation, or authority is compared with that devoted
to community, the difference is very striking. Yet, the concept itself is ubiquitous—the importance of community is declared, we are given examples
of it, the relationship between more or better community with more or
better social order or welfare is elaborated, politicians appeal to communities, and so on. Although philosophers and others are reluctant to
analyse the concept of community, they cannot proceed without, as one
might say, helping themselves to it.

Now, many readers will be suspicious about this demand for 'analysis'.
They might read it as based on such a naive assumption as that concepts—
including abstract concepts like community—have a definite content
which the analyst can simply set out, as though concepts can be analysed
as chemical compounds can. Moreover it might seem to have the authoritarian implication that once a philosopher has kindly conducted this conceptual analysis the results will authoritatively guide subsequent language
users. Conceptual analysis is associated by a range of critics who don't
have much else in common with a form of philosophical analysis (widely
condemned as 'sterile' and the like) premised on the assumption that
many so-called metaphysical, epistemological, and ethical problems could
be cleared up if only ambiguity and vagueness were eliminated from language use.[1]

---

[1] This philosophical programme is strongly associated with 'Oxford'—I've had to con-
tend with a few raised eyebrows when I have presented the material for this chapter at seminars. I recently came across the story (*possibly* apocryphal!) of an 'Oxford philosopher'
who offered a series of lectures on 'The Meaning of Life' and who devoted all his time to
the semantics of the word 'life'. Anyway . . . let me plough on regardless with analysis of the
concept 'community'.

Some critics of this approach emphasize that language *is* ambiguous and vague, and our philosophical explorations are explorations in language, so are likely to have far less briskly authoritative results than the analytic philosophers hope for. In this case the analysis of concepts in order to yield a definitive result is an impossibly vain project.[2] Philosophical realists find irksome and unconvincing the suggestion, sometimes imputed to analytic philosophers, that philosophy is properly confined to the domain of language, and see in language no insuperable barrier to the analysis of things and states of affairs themselves.[3] And it was as a riposte to the analytic programme as applied to political philosophy that John Rawls's *Theory of Justice*—with its construction of a formal model constrained by deontological values—caused a stir, and is now widely cited as the key text in the renaissance of political philosophy after its near demise at the hands of 'Oxford'. Rawls insists that political philosophy must be done in the domain of 'theory'. An accurate *theoretical* account of our moral conceptions indeed may have the effect of showing that questions of meaning (and justification) are either easier to answer or turn out no longer to be real questions at all.[4] Conceptual analysis does not help us build robust models of how the world ought to be, but building robust models may well bring about a profound transformation in our analysis of concepts: 'It is possible that convincing answers to questions of the meaning and justification of moral judgements can be found in no other way.'[5]

In this chapter I agree that concepts are closely connected to theories, but propose that the repudiation of conceptual analysis has been overdone by some social theorists. Indeed, one of the notable characteristics of the wide-ranging 'debates with Rawls' is the frequency with which critics take issue with his theory precisely on conceptual grounds—the theoretical developments associated with his work have not settled the conceptual questions. Whereas it clearly is the case that theoretical (and practical) physics have settled that the concept 'atom' should no longer be understood to include the idea of 'unsplittability', social theory is still marked by genuine disagreement about concepts such as 'community' and 'politics'. One ground for taking a sceptical view of Rawls's 'political liberalism' is the way it construes the concept 'politics'.[6] Similarly, com-

---

[2] This view is associated with a range of philosophers from the pragmatist, hermeneutic, phenomenological, and deconstructionist traditions.

[3] See for instance Roy Bhaskar, *Reclaiming Reality* (London: Verso, 1989).

[4] John Rawls, *A Theory of Justice* (Oxford: Oxford University Press, 1971), 51.

[5] Ibid. 52.

[6] Elizabeth Frazer and Nicola Lacey, 'Politics and the Public in Rawls' Political Liberalism', *Political Studies*, 43 (1995), 233–47.

munitarian critics can take issue with Rawls because he denies that a liberal society can be a community, on the grounds that the maintenance of community requires authoritarian institutions inconsistent with liberalism.[7] A communitarian might argue that Rawls has misconstrued the concept of community.[8]

I shall return to this question of the relationship between theory and concepts, but first it will be as well to consider the concept of concept. Whichever way you look at it, a 'concept' is a highly abstract thing. One plausible way of analysing 'concept' is 'that which you have to have grasped before you can correctly use a term'.[9] Observers watch children learning language move from *saying* 'blue' or 'dog' to correctly and reliably identifying blue things, or dogs—one way of expressing what has occurred at this point is that the child has grasped the concept 'blue' or 'dog'. But to say this is to beg many questions. Is it implied that the child has had direct contact of some sort—'seeing', 'knowing', or 'understanding'—with the concept itself? Or is saying 'she has grasped the concept' to say no more than that she now uses the word 'blue' acceptably? With complicated concepts like 'community' we might expect certain language users to be able to explain that they call a particular group a community because it is small, it is cohesive, it is not simply an aggregation of persons, etc. Should we reserve the judgement that 'she's grasped the concept . . .' just for those people who can do that?—in which case people who can use a word like 'blue' appropriately but would be stumped if asked to explain why would not count as having grasped the concept. Peacocke suggests that the exact form of 'possession conditions' for a concept will vary from concept to concept. For 'blue' perhaps simply picking out blue things is enough; for community we may demand a grasp of the relevant theory of groups and relationships before we accept that a user has a grasp of the concept.

In some philosophical traditions concepts are thought of in the first of those three ways—as the kind of things we (as rational and educated persons) can come in some way directly to discern, understand, and of course analyse. According to such views, concepts are independent of all language

---

[7] Rawls, *Political Liberalism* (New York: Columbia University Press, 1993), 42.

[8] In fact, they have tended to do this in a rather oblique way, as if conceding that Rawls is entitled to define community as authoritarian, and to reject it for that reason.

[9] Christopher Peacocke in *A Study of Concepts* (Cambridge, Mass.: MIT Press, 1992), begins with the idea of 'mastery of a concept' going on to argue that if we embark on analysis of this idea then we must be committed to the existence of concepts. Conventionally, in current analytic philosophy concepts are related to the content of thought, while meaning attaches to terms and words. Concepts and meaning are connected because a concept is what you have to have grasped before you can use a term correctly.

users' use of a term. Plato's theory of the forms is sometimes interpreted like this: the form 'beauty itself' or 'good itself' gathers all instances of beauty (although in the sensible world beauty is often combined with ugliness) and it governs the philosophically correct use of the term 'beautiful'. Philosophical knowledge is knowledge of the forms themselves, not just the unsystematic jumble of judgements about beauty and ugliness.[10] Although Hegel's philosophy is different, it can be read similarly as regards the independent existence of concepts. According to Hegel, philosophers are concerned with Ideas, which are a complex of 'the concept together with the actualisation of that concept'. Concepts are not 'the mere abstract category of the understanding which we often hear called by the name'; concepts alone are 'actual' and further 'it gives this actuality to itself'. That is concepts are dynamic.[11] Philosophical systems like Plato's and Hegel's suggest that 'concepts' are (will turn out to be) perfect: clear, clearly distinct from other concepts, unitary, non-contradictory.

An alternative understanding of concepts is that they are mental entities. Some philosophers think of them as mental representations—representations that have the form and function of kinds of prototypes for the relevant categories and qualities. This view is challenged by, for example, Peacocke, according to whose analysis 'a thinker who has mastered a concept has propositional attitudes to thoughts and sentences that contain it'.[12] These attitudes of course have a mental component, but this analysis is also consistent with an emphasis on linguistic usage and human practice rather than mental content as such.

Rival philosophical approaches focus just on linguistic usage and human practice. Human practices of hunting, husbandry, companionship, and the like have produced a class of animals, dogs, which are now quite distinct from the wolves from which they are descended. The coining of a term to classify them, and the various expert and lay discourses governing our use of terms, have generated the abstraction, the concept 'dog'.[13] Children have to learn that the wolf at the zoo is not, despite appearances, a dog. This emphasis on coming to understand a concept by reference to

[10] Plato, *The Republic*, trans. and introd. Desmond Lee, 2nd edn. (Harmondsworth: Penguin, 1974), 264–6 (translator's note), ss.476a, 479a–e (pp. 269–76).

[11] G. W. F. Hegel, *The Philosophy of Right*, trans. T. M. Knox (Oxford: Clarendon Press, 1952), 'Introduction', s. 1 (p. 14).

[12] Peacocke, *Study of Concepts*, 5.

[13] Willard van Orman Quine, *Word and Object* (Cambridge, Mass.: MIT Press, 1960), develops this sort of account of what he calls 'conceptualisation', emphasizing the dynamic nature of 'concepts', although concepts arrest dynamism. He says (p. 10): 'actual memories are mostly traces not of past sensation but of past conceptualisation. We cannot rest with a running conceptualisation of the unsullied stream of experience; what we need is a sullying of the stream.'

what it is not, what it contrasts with, is featured in structuralist and systemic approaches to language. The structuralist linguist Saussure emphasized the 'arbitrary' nature of the conceptual classes languages construct. In Saussure's terminology 'dog' is a sign which amalgamates an aural and a visual symbol—the word 'dog'—with the concept dog. The concept 'dog' as explained above picks out a class of 'things' and differentiates members of that class from members of other classes. According to one interpretation of Saussure's linguistics an important aspect of this theory of language is that it all could have been otherwise: we can easily imagine alternative worlds in which the concept 'dog' incorporates wolves and foxes too.[14]

Despite all this, 'dog' is a pretty simple and straightforward concept. Some are much more complex, encompassing a wider and fuzzier set of 'things'. Wittgenstein famously explores the concept 'game' in the course of observation that many philosophically interesting and socially salient concepts encompass a range of 'things' that resemble each other in the way that family members resemble and are connected with each other—or, rather, a 'word must have a family of meanings'.[15] Chess and football have something in common with each other; and something in common with the 'power games' people play in some places of work, and these have something in common with 'dressing up'. But 'dressing up' doesn't have that much, or perhaps anything, in common with chess. Yet they belong to the same 'family' of things—are encompassed by the concept 'game'. Using a different metaphor, Wittgenstein elsewhere says they are connected in the way all the fibres that constitute a thread are connected—no one fibre runs for the entire length of the thread, or across its entire width, but the thread itself is a robustly unified thing.[16]

This analysis has some unsettling implications that Wittgenstein remarks on in the course of his investigations. It means that the boundary of a concept is blurred. It means that the extension of the concept—the extent of the group of things in the world properly encompassed by it—is not fixed with clarity. It means that the boundary that you might draw around a concept won't be the same as the one I would draw (were I to want to draw one at all).[17] Wittgenstein entertains the view that by now we are not talking of concepts at all: 'is a blurred concept a concept at all?'

[14] Ferdinand de Saussure, *Course in General Linguistics*, trans. R. Harris (London: Duckworth, 1983), 65–9; see Deborah Cameron, *Feminism and Linguistic Theory* (Basingstoke: Macmillan, 1985), 9–21; Michael Freeden, *Ideologies and Political Theory* (Oxford: Clarendon Press, 1996), 49–51.
[15] Ludwig Wittgenstein, *Philosophical Investigations*, trans. G. E. M. Anscombe (Oxford: Basil Blackwell, 1958), I, ss. 67, 77.
[16] Ibid. I, s. 67.   [17] Ibid. I, ss. 68–71, 75–7.

But he rejects this thought: 'Is an indistinct photograph a picture of a person at all? . . . Isn't the indistinct one often exactly what we need?'[18]

Whichever way we look at the matter 'concepts' are related to language
use—they are thought to govern correct language use, or to be abstractions from language, or both.[19] It is rather different to say, as many
philosophers and theorists do, that they are related to theory. The analysis of the 'theory ladenness of concepts' has had some disruptive effects in
epistemology and the philosophy of science, where it seems to turn the
relationship between 'the world' and our knowledge of or theories about
it the 'wrong way round', and thus has given rise to considerable philosophical controversy. By contrast, in political philosophy the view that
concepts follow from theory has become something of an orthodoxy. But
it is important to sort out different senses of theory, and different accounts
of the relationship between theory and concept, here.

First, we meet the idea that language use itself embodies 'theory'—
nouns and pronouns, verbs, and adjectives all classify and individuate
'things' and embody, implicitly at least, someone's or some group's view of
how the world works or how it ought to be. An implicitly different theory
about how the world works is embodied in the locution 'it yellows' from
that in the locution 'it is yellow'. Different pronoun systems embody contrasting theories of the relations between persons.[20] These theories are
part and parcel of the concepts 'yellow' or 'I'. Second, we meet the view
that some theories are particularly authoritative and acceptance of them
can radically alter the meaning of terms. For instance, 'atom' used to
describe some thing that was indivisible and fundamental; thanks to modern physics 'splittability' must now be part of the meaning of the term
'atom' (or an element of the concept atom).[21] The concepts that interest

[18] Ludwig Wittgenstein, *Philosophical Investigations*, trans. G. E. M. Anscombe
(Oxford: Basil Blackwell, 1958), I, s. 71.

[19] This does not imply that concepts are necessarily tied to language—some or all concepts might not require language mastery for their possession; see Peacocke, *Study of
Concepts*, 31.

[20] For instance, see Peter Mulhausler and Rom Harre, *Pronouns and People: The
Linguistic Construction of Social and Personal Identity* (Oxford: Basil Blackwell, 1990), 5
and *passim*.

[21] This view is associated with Thomas Kuhn's analysis of theory change in the natural
sciences: *The Structure of Scientific Revolutions*, 2nd edn. (Chicago: Chicago University
Press, 1970); *The Essential Tension: Selected Studies in Scientific Tradition and Change*
(Chicago: Chicago University Press, 1977). See also Hilary Putnam, 'The Meaning of
Meaning', in *Mind Language and Reality*, Philosophical Papers 2 (Cambridge: Cambridge
University Press, 1975), 225–8. It is interesting, though, that elements of the old meaning
of 'atom' do linger on in certain discursive contexts. In the field of political theory 'atom-
ism' is still intelligibly used to convey a theory of society and individual human beings that
trades on the old sense of 'atom' as a separate and internally uniform element. See Charles

political theorists and philosophers—state, community, democracy, liberty—are not so clearly subject to theoretical authority; rather they are contested by rival theorists who stand in rival traditions of moral thought such as liberalism, socialism, and conservatism. Notably, philosophers and theorists who have attempted to present analyses of 'community' emphasize these theoretical divergences—the rival ways Marxist, British Hegelians, Burkean conservatives, liberal and social democrats, anarchists, and others understand the concept.[22]

Third, even absent such unifying -isms, social positions involve perspectives and understandings of the world which make a difference to understandings of meanings and concepts. The social perspective of an activist in a particular neighbourhood will condition her understanding of 'community'. Similarly, turning to more specialized academic settings, preoccupation with theoretical and practical problems such as the possibility of 'dialogic democracy', or 'racial purity' or individual liberty, will make a difference to one's understanding of, and analyses of, other concepts. As we have seen, John Rawls argues that we need to get our theories of and arguments regarding such values and their realization right—then the concepts will come right.

If we ask what 'conceptual analysis' consists of then, many theorists will be inclined to answer that it must be this—the study and analysis of the way concepts are differently construed in rival theoretical schemes. Theorists will pay attention both to what we can provisionally call the concept's content, and to its relationship with other salient concepts. Thus, Plant shows that for Marxists 'community' means an unalienated social formation—a group of individuals equally situated vis-à-vis one another, integrated by relations of solidarity, reciprocity, and cooperation, united by shared goals, beliefs, and a common material situation. By contrast, conservatives think of 'community' as a hierarchically organized human group, integrated by obligations, united by an orientation to a common tradition, common set of institutions, and so on.[23] Michael Freeden, in his thorough analysis of liberalism, socialism, and conservatism, emphasizes

Taylor, 'Atomism', in *Philosophy and the Human Sciences* (Cambridge: Cambridge University Press, 1985). In my dictionary, come to that, the 'old' sense is part of the 'new' meaning: 'a body or particle of matter originally thought to be incapable of further division'. *Cassell Giant Paperback Dictionary* (London: Cassell, 1993).

[22] See Robert Booth Fowler, 'Community: Reflections on Definition', in Amitai Etzioni (ed.), *New Communitarian Thinking: Persons, Virtues, Institutions and Communities* (Charlottesville: University Press of Virginia, 1995); Raymond Plant, 'Community: Concept, Conception and Ideology', *Politics and Society*, 8, (1978), 79–107; Robert A. Nisbet, *The Quest for Community: A Study in the Ethics of Order and Freedom* (New York: Oxford University Press, 1953).

[23] Plant, 'Community', 90–9.

how 'community' is affected by the concepts with which it coexists within an ideology and with which it theoretically interacts. In socialism, the concept 'community' is affected by socialist theory of the role of the state, and of class, both of which in some variants 'stand in' for community. Community is also equated with 'fraternity'.[24] In anarchism the ideal of community affects and is affected by the primary value of liberty.[25]

There are two independent sources of complexity then. First, some concepts are complex structures of simpler concepts: for instance the concept 'colour' is an element of the concept 'red'. The concepts 'human group', 'reciprocity', and so forth are elements of the complex concept 'community'. A second complicating factor in social theory is the role of evaluation or prescription, and the role of normative theory as well as theory in its descriptive sense. In his discussion of 'essential contestability' William Connolly suggests that in addition to the fact that contests about, for instance, democracy involve the deployment of other terms that are themselves contested (politics, power), the fact that adherents to rival theoretical perspectives will value different aspects of democracy differently accounts for the 'endlessness' of conceptual disputes.[26]

This analysis of the relationship between theories and concepts takes us far, then, from any straightforward exercise of conceptual analysis as 'definition'. Indeed, a good deal of doubt has been cast over the whole idea of 'definition of terms'. Yet the idea of definition continues to grip social theorists and scientists in an odd way. A number of papers on the subject of community, for instance, take something like the following form. They ask whether it is possible to come up with or arrive at a 'definition' of 'community'; they survey the extant literature both theoretical and empirical, descriptive and normative; they list fifty-six[27] ways 'community' is defined in this literature; they argue that these various definitions don't 'boil down' or 'add up' to a definitive solution. They conclude either with a 'core concept' or working definition which, as Raymond Plant says tends to be so formal and abstract as to be empirically vacuous; or they conclude that the concept community is hopelessly vague or non-existent.[28]

[24] Freeden, *Ideologies and Political Theory*, 446–9.   [25] Ibid. 312.
[26] William Connolly, *The Terms of Political Discourse* (Oxford: Basil Blackwell, 1983), 10–11, 32.
[27] Or thereabouts.
[28] Plant is commenting on David B. Clark, 'The Concept of Community', *Sociological Review*, 21 (1973), 403; Plant, 'Community', 87–8. Margaret Stacey, on definitional and other substantive grounds, concludes that 'community' is hopelessly vague: 'The Myth of Community Studies', *British Journal of Sociology*, 20 (1969), 134–471; those who come up with a minimal definition and then carry on include Graham Crow and Graham Allan, *Community Life: An Introduction to Local Social Relations* (Hemel Hempstead: Harvester Wheatsheaf, 1994); Colin Bell and Howard Newby, *Community Studies: An Introduction to*

One philosophical reason why the project of 'definition' grips analysts is undoubtedly that philosophers have often taken a view of 'concepts' that approaches the idealism that earlier I associated with Plato and Hegel. Wittgenstein and others have vigorously opposed this, but it is still tempting to think that concepts must exist, are definitely analysable, and will have a perspicuous and consistent content. Another reason for emphasizing definition might be a continuing conviction that the analysis of relatively simple cases is a guide to the method for analysis of complex ones. G. E. Moore, for example, reasoned that the adjective 'good' must apply to the substantive 'that which is good' or 'the good'. 'The good' is the concept which governs our proper use of a range of words and expressions such as good, best, better, well, and so on.[29] According to Moore, to define a word or term is not the same thing as to give an analysis of that word (to give an analysis of a word would involve setting out its various meanings (these may be effectively independent of each other, as in the case of the English word 'crane' which means both a wading bird and a machine for hoisting loads), setting out the etymologies for these various senses, analysing its syllable structure, and so on. However, to analyse a concept is the same thing as to define it. Moore gives the example of the concept 'brother' which can be analysed as a combination of the concepts 'male' and 'sibling'. 'Male sibling' is both analysis and definition of the concept 'brother'.[30] But it does not, contra Moore, seem plausible that analysis of 'good' or 'community' can be as neat, as definite, as analysis of 'brother'.

A third reason why the procedure of 'defining terms' seems to retain its grip on theorists is because of its connection with two 'scientific' motifs— formality and operationalizability. If a theorist can define a term, the idea is that the definition can be treated as stable and fixed, and can thereafter

the Sociology of the Local Community (London: George Allen and Unwin, 1971); A. P. Cohen, The Symbolic Construction of Community (London: Routledge, 1985). Peacocke makes a resonant point in his discussion of concepts as such: 'We should be sceptical of arguments that take the following form: First they explore various candidate identifications of concepts with entities of some kind or another; then they find each such candidate defective in some respect or other, and finally they conclude that there is no such thing as concepts.' (A Study of Concepts, 122.)

[29] G. E. Moore, Principia Ethica (Cambridge: Cambridge University Press, 1903), 9. It is interesting, by the way, that 'community' is one of those terms that is often joined with a definite article—'the community' (like 'the academy', 'the right and the good'). I'm not sure what to make of this. Sometimes it seems to have a unitary empirical referent—as in 'the people', i.e. those individuals who constitute the political citizens or subjects. (I discuss this usage further in Chapter 7). Other times it seems that it is a unitary abstract object that is being invoked.

[30] Moore, 'Reply to my Critics', in P. A. Schilpp (ed.), The Philosophy of G E Moore (Evanston: Northwestern University Press, 1942), 666.

be substituted in arguments and hypotheses by formal symbols like x and y. If a term can be analysed into a series of variables (for instance, community might be operationalized as network density, relationship complexity, smallness of membership, confinement to locality, and perhaps one or two more) then social scientists can treat 'community' as measurable—can make it operational—and can explore the relationships between these variables and others, for instance, human welfare or incidence of crime. The fact that network density, relationship complexity, smallness of membership, and confinement to locality is not, really, what ordinary speakers *mean* by 'community' is deemed irrelevant for these scientific purposes, as is the point made by Connolly and others that the concept 'community' takes on very different contents in different theoretical contexts.[31]

So, according to these views, to analyse a concept is to do three things. It is, first, to set out a definite list of the concept's elements—its content, or to borrow a term from the philosophy of meaning, its intension. As we have seen, these elements will themselves be conceptual. It is, second, to have specified the set of things in the world the concept gathers up—its scope, or its extension. By virtue of these two, it is to have specified a list of rules governing the proper use of terms that refer to the concept, to have specified a list of 'criteria for belonging to that extension'.[32] It is also implied, fourth, that to use a term correctly is to have a grasp of these rules and the relevant concept's elements. That is, we can't make sense of what language users are doing, according to this model, unless we presume that concepts are mental properties of competent speakers. Even if we think that concepts are abstract rather than mental entities, grasping them has usually been thought of as 'an individual psychological act'.[33] Critics have taken issue with all four points of this model, and with a number of its further implications.

To begin with, we have already met the view that a concept's elements, and the relationships between them, can vary from one theoretical or discursive or practical context to another.[34] Other theorists emphasize the

---

[31] Connolly criticizes political scientists' view that the operationalization of concepts can be theoretically and normatively neutral—it follows from his model of contestability that the decision to measure some and not other elements inevitably makes scientific concepts 'theory-laden'; so they cannot then be used as independent sources of data, the measurement of which rigorously tests the theory in question—rather, the 'theory in question' has itself contributed to the operationalization of the concept. *Terms of Political Discourse*, 11 f.

[32] Putnam, 'Meaning of Meaning', 219.   [33] Ibid. 218.

[34] Freeden puts it that concepts are 'decontested' differently in different ideological contexts, *Ideologies and Political Theory*, 76.

extent to which concepts shift not with theory as such, but with the changes in human practice—concepts like 'state' and 'politics' change as human institutions and standards change.[35] According to these views there is no simple concept, there, to be analysed, independent of our theories about the world or our ways of engaging with it and with each other. Secondly, the implication that concepts are clearly demarcated one from another is not borne out in practice. Our linguistic lives are characterized by the fuzziness of the boundaries between one concept and the next, with language users making different judgements as to whether something is a book or a pamphlet, a house or a palace.[36] Wittgenstein also observed that the model of concepts as giving us sets of rules or criteria is spoiled by the consideration that 'rule-following' is not determinate, or in any case, rules are not transparent. 'How can a rule shew me what I have to do at this point? Whatever I do is, on some interpretation, in accord with the rule.'[37] The paradox is resolved when we realize that following a rule is not a mechanical, algorithmic procedure; it 'is analogous to obeying an order. We are trained to do so; we react to an order in a particular way. But what if one person reacts in one way and another in another to the order and the training? Which one is right?'[38]

Hilary Putnam also takes issue with the implication that the meaning of a term consists in the criteria for its use, and that competent speakers know the meanings of terms, and apply the criteria (follow the rules) in this sense. On the contrary, competent speakers may well not know the meaning of a term that they perfectly well use. Meaning for Putnam as for others is a theoretical matter, and furthermore societies are characterized by theoretical divisions of labour. The important point that Putnam makes is that for many terms we have a 'division of linguistic labour': everyone to whom gold is important has to acquire the word gold, but he

---

[35] This is a view that is strongly associated with the philosophical communitarians especially in connection with the concept 'justice' and critique of Rawls's particular conceptualization of it: see Michael Walzer, *Spheres of Justice: A Defence of Pluralism and Equality* (Oxford: Basil Blackwell, 1983); Alasdair MacIntyre, *After Virtue: A Study in Moral Theory*, 2nd edn. (London: Duckworth, 1985); Charles Taylor, 'The Nature and Scope of Distributive Justice', in *Philosophy and the Human Sciences*, 289–317. See also Ronald Dworkin, *Law's Empire* (London: Fontana, 1986), 69.

[36] These two examples are taken from Dworkin, *Law's Empire*, 40—he also makes the important point that these disputes don't make linguistic life and communication impossible between intelligent people; as competent communicators we can note that one of us thinks of a certain building as a house while the other considers it to be a palace. Wittgenstein also emphasizes that the blurred edges of 'concepts' don't stop us: 'Someone says to me 'Shew the children a game.' I teach them gaming with dice, and the other says: 'I didn't mean that sort of game.' Must the exclusion of the game with dice have come before his mind when he gave me the order?' *Philosophical Investigations*, I, p. 33e footnote.

[37] Wittgenstein, *Philosophical Investigations*, I, s. 198.   [38] Ibid. I, s. 206.

does not have to acquire the method of recognizing that something is or is not gold. The 'way of recognizing' possessed by *expert* speakers is also through them possessed by the collective linguistic body even though it is not possessed by each individual member of the body, and in this way the most *recherché* fact about gold may become part of the social meaning of the word while being unknown to almost all speakers who acquire the word.[39]

Thus, the fixity and clarity of the content of concepts, and the clarity and followability of the criteria of applicability that concepts allegedly include, are cast into doubt. This doubt is reinforced by consideration of some other aspects of meaning and how we analyse it. We have already met the points that, in the first place, it is difficult to specify the content of a 'concept', and second that it is difficult precisely to demarcate one concept from the next. Critical conceptual analysis with a historical cast reveals how often philosophically relevant concepts are given 'content' by reference to their negation, to what they are not.[40] So reason is analysed by reference to the emotion which is its opposite; 'masculine' is conceptualized by reference to the rejection of 'feminine', community is analysed by contrast with society, and so on.[41] The difficulty here, as 'deconstructive' critics have pointed out, is that this inevitable and indispensable reference to what is rejected or repudiated paradoxically brings what is rejected into the heart of the concept at issue. Thus, masculinity cannot be conceptualized or analysed except by reference to femininity; so masculinity's negation is an element of the concept masculinity itself. That is, the dualistic project of separation and repudiation is defeated. The analysis of a pure uncontaminated concept of masculinity is found to be impossible. To be poles apart, after all, is to be connected by a pole.

This theme of the openness of concepts, implies the openness of meaning of terms, and of utterances (speech, writing, signals, signs). If our terms and utterances are not 'governed' by and fixed by our concepts then their meaning is relatively open. There are several aspects to this. First, the intentions of utterers, not fully governed by conceptual criteria, are vague, as Wittgenstein points out with his example of teaching children to gamble with dice (see footnote 36 above). 'I didn't mean *that* kind of game' someone might say. True enough. But neither what was nor what was not

[39] Hilary Putnam, 'The Meaning of Meaning', 265; also Peacocke, *Study of Concepts*, 30.
[40] This follows from Saussure's view of language: *Course in General Linguistics*, 115; Freeden, *Ideologies and Political Theory*, 49.
[41] See Genevieve Lloyd, *The Man of Reason: 'Male' and 'Female' in Western Philosophy* (London: Methuen, 1984).

meant was not clearly delineated. Second, meaning attaches to utterances and terms which can connote more than either the utterer intends or than the hearer understands. We have already met the idea that the attempt to use terms, or analyse concepts, with clarity in such a way as to fix their meaning, always produces an 'outside', a rejected, that which is repudiated, which then is present, so to speak, in the use of the term. There are many explorations of this theme, using theories of language and theories of subjectivity such as psychoanalysis, focused on the great political dualisms of gender and 'race'.[42] More prosaically utterances convey impressions, and echoes—of sadness, of violence.[43] Texts and discourses address particular audiences. Individuals who are physically in the audience can 'know' that they are not being addressed, perhaps notwithstanding the good intentions of the speaker. Or readers can engage in a kind of negotiation with written texts, positioning themselves, partially, in the subject position of the 'implied reader' (or alternatively, putting themselves in the position of overhearing a discourse addressed to someone else).[44] All of this means that communicators improvise, infer meaning using their knowledge of the world and of social context, exploit the openness of meaning strategically, engage in repair when things do go wrong, note the excess of meaning in utterances, remark on the connotations of utterances.

A further important aspect of the openness of meaning is that much language use is performative. It is commonplace enough that uttering 'I promise' in speech or writing can constitute making a promise, and thereby entering into a new relationship with the relevant promisee.[45] It is also notable that the interpretation of what this means, exactly, in the way of obligation, the justification of sanctions, and so on is itself a matter for inference, and individuals' inferences will vary depending on their, so to speak, theory of promising. Both promiser and promisee have to use social and institutional knowledge to proceed with the upshots of a promise, and there is room for disagreement—for example, what constitute good grounds for breaking a promise?[46] Some performatives are constitutive: another commonplace example is the registrar or clergy person who, by

[42] For example, Judith Butler, *Bodies that Matter* (New York: Routledge, 1993); Renata Salecl, *The Spoils of Freedom: Psychoanalysis and Feminism after the Fall of Socialism* (London: Routledge, 1994); Gayatri Chakravorty Spivak, *In Other Worlds: Essays in Cultural Politics* (New York: Routledge, 1988).

[43] Diane Blakemore, *Understanding Utterances* (Oxford: Blackwell, 1992), 50.

[44] See Ros Ballaster, Margaret Beetham, Elizabeth Frazer, and Sandra Hebron, *Women's Worlds: Ideology, Femininity and the Woman's Magazine* (Basingstoke: Macmillan, 1991).

[45] J. L. Austin, *How to Do Things with Words* (Oxford: Clarendon Press, 1962), *passim*.

[46] Blakemore, *Understanding Utterances*, 49; cf. Putnam on theory and meaning in 'The Meaning of Meaning'.

uttering the words 'I now pronounce you husband and wife' in the appropriate institutional setting thereby marries two people. But others are not—rather what is happening is that an utterer is engaging in a performance—an acting out—of some part, in part by linguistic means. So 'This room is a pigsty' enables the speaker to act out the role of critical and exasperated parent, or whatever, providing her interlocutor is intelligent enough to know that the utterance does not mean, literally, that the room is a pigsty (or, perhaps, that it means: 'Don't take me literally. This room is a pigsty).[47]

All this—the indeterminacy of concepts, the centrality of theory, the contestation of authority, the openness of meaning, the importance of connotation, the need for contextual interpretation, the importance of performatives—could seem to have a devastating effect on any aspiration to the analysis of concepts. Certainly, it all implies that the analysis of concepts cannot be an exercise like chemical analysis: a straightforward laying out of the concept's elements. It certainly also implies that a philosopher or theorist who has analysed a concept is not thereafter in a position to present it as normative and authoritative—'this is the concept of freedom; any usage which does not conform to this is invalid'. However, that something is vague and open does not imply that we can't have a quite precise account of its vagueness and openness. A conceptual analysis can, first of all, be based on a reading of the relevant terms in use. It can show something of the layers of meaning—the relevant connotations. It can reveal the points at which instability, disagreement, and shifts occur, and locate sources of inconsistency in use. It can describe some of the overlaps and resemblances that hold a 'family' of things together. Most importantly, it can seek to justify some, but not other, conceptual interpretations and uses of terms and words.

'Community' is a concept with open frontiers and vague contours, which seems to extend across a very heterogeneous class of things, which conveys a wealth of meaning—it appeals to people's emotions, it is shot through with value judgements, it conjures up associations and images from a wide, wide range of discourses and contexts. It excludes a good deal, and what is excluded comes back to haunt those who deploy the concept. It encompasses more than one contradiction. This complexity of the concept has been dealt with in a number of partial ways in the literatures of philosophical communitarianism, and political sociology and political communitarianism. I survey these in the next section. After that, in the

---

[47] Blakemore, *Understanding Utterances*, 95–108 on complexities in the analysis of 'performatives'.

final section of this chapter, I attempt to set out an extensive analysis of the concept, which reveals its complexity.

COMMUNITY IN POLITICAL AND SOCIAL THEORY

The work of the 'communitarian critics of liberalism'[48] is remarkable for the absence of any extended analysis of the concept 'community'. It was a common complaint, or remark, in the course of the 'liberal v communitarian debates' and commentary on them that 'communitarians characteristically avoid or evade the definition of "community".'[49] This might be testimony to the degree to which the label 'communitarian' was not their choice—their works are philosophical considerations of the nature of the subject, the nature of virtue, the nature of language, and of society, and the concept of community simply was not uppermost or even particularly prominent in their thinking at the time of writing. However, the term does turn up in the work, and it is difficult to read the relevant passages as insignificant. For the most part, the philosophical communitarians were intent on theorizing about the *relation* of community. But their discussions of the value of the relation of community frequently feature lists or mentions of the kinds of communities they have in mind. Theories of community as a relation trade on or presuppose the conception of community as an *entity*—specifically a social formation. However these two are not, in this literature, rigorously distinguished or brought together.

MacIntyre for example, in the course of his discussion of virtues and traditions, and his criticism of aspects of individualism, says:

the story of my life is always embedded in the story of those communities from which I derive my identity. . . . Notice also that the fact that the self has to find its moral identity in and through its membership in communities such as those of the family, the neighbourhood, the city and the tribe does not entail that the self has to accept the moral limitations of the particularity of those forms of community.[50]

---

[48] By which I mean the core texts that started the whole recent debate off—Michael Walzer, *Spheres of Justice*, Charles Taylor, *Philosophy and the Human Sciences,* Alasdair MacIntyre, *After Virtue*, Michael Sandel, *Liberalism and the Limits of Justice.* I do not mean to imply that the work of these four is 'communitarian' from first to last; neither does this list exhaust philosophical communitarianism. (But incidentally, Shlomo Avineri and Avner de-Shalit (eds.) identify these four as the key communitarian critics of Rawls in the relevant respect too: *Communitarianism and Individualism* (Oxford: Oxford University Press, 1992)).

[49] Jeremy Waldron, 'Particular Values and Critical Morality', *California Law Review*, 77 (1989), 512.

[50] MacIntyre, *After Virtue*, 221.

Walzer refers to 'communities' throughout *Spheres of Justice*: 'the political community is probably the closest we can come to a world of common meanings'; 'the sharing of sensibilities and intuitions among the members of a historical community is a fact of life';[51] 'in any community, where resources are taken away from the poor and given to the rich, the rights of the poor are being violated';[52] 'The interest in this case [i.e. the case of professional standards] doesn't have to do with God or the community as a whole . . .';[53] 'if the community underwrites the general education of some of its citizens as we do today for college students . . .';[54] '. . . to uproot a community, to require large-scale migration, to deprive people of homes they have lived in for many years; these are political acts . . .';[55] and so on and so forth. Analysis of the relation of community depends upon reference to particular kinds of community qua entity. In a later paper Walzer is more explicit about community as a relation: 'community is the home of coherence, connection and narrative capacity', in contrast to liberal society which is 'fragmentation in practice'.[56] In this paper too Walzer mentions communities. Although 'community itself is largely an ideological presence in modern society, intermittently fashionable because it no longer exists in anything like full strength' nevertheless communities do exist, are fragile, and warrant sustenance.[57]

'Community' turns up far less in Taylor's essays, although 'common', 'communal', and 'society' are very frequent. However, it does have a significant place in Taylor's theory of language:

Common meanings are the basis of community. Inter-subjective meaning gives people a common language to talk about social reality and a common understanding of certain norms, but only with common meanings does this common reference world contain significant common actions, celebrations and feelings. These are objects in the world that everybody shares. This is what makes community.[58]

. . . each one has an interest in the same flood prevention, and this is so irrespective of whether they have some common understanding of it, or indeed, whether they form a community at all. By contrast, shared goods are essentially of a community; their common appreciation is constitutive of them.[59]

. . . for this common good of living in a family, or a community, or whatever, we are all in each other's debt.[60]

---

[51] Walzer, *Spheres of Justice*, 28.   [52] Ibid. 83.   [53] Ibid. 131.
[54] Ibid. 208.   [55] Ibid. 301.
[56] Michael Walzer, 'The Communitarian Critique of Liberalism', *Political Theory,* 18 (1990), 6.
[57] Walzer, 'Communitarian Critique of Liberalism', 16, 20.
[58] Taylor, *Philosophy and the Human Sciences*, 39.   [59] Ibid. 96.   [60] Ibid. 298.

Taylor's writing contains fewer examples of communities; but community is individuated as an entity—a community—in places, although it most often lacks either definite or indefinite article and seems then to refer to a relation.

These passages offer us three modes of analysis. First, exemplification, as in MacIntyre's enumeration of 'communities such as those of the family, the neighbourhood, the city and the tribe'.[61] Second, classification— as in Walzer's mentions of 'historical communities', 'political communities', and others.[62] Third, we find here suggestions of criteria for the use of the term: as in Taylor's discussion of shared goods, shared meanings, and Walzer's mention of shared sensibilities and intuitions.

Michael Sandel offers an extended critique of Rawls's theory of community, which rests in part on conceptual critique. Sandel finds in *A Theory of Justice* two distinct theories. First, there is an individualistically instrumental account whereby 'by living in a community men acquire needs and interests that prompt them to work together for mutual advantage in certain specific ways allowed for and encouraged by their institutions'.[63] But second and further

We are led to the notion of the community of humankind the members of which enjoy one another's excellences and individuality elicited by free institutions, and they recognise the good of each as an element in the complete activity the whole scheme of which is consented to and gives pleasure to all. This community may be imagined to extend over time, and therefore in the history of a society the joint contributions of successive generations can be similarly conceived.[64]

Sandel calls this a 'sentimental' as opposed to an 'instrumental' account of community: 'Where community on the first account is wholly external to the aims and interests of the individuals who comprise it, community on Rawls' view is partly internal to the subjects, in that it reaches the feelings and sentiments of those engaged in a cooperative scheme.'[65] Sandel argues that Rawls's account of 'common assets' actually entails a conception of community stronger than this second sentimental one. In order for the redistribution of goods that Rawls's model of justice requires to be motivated, Sandel argues, we need a conception of community as

not just a feeling but a mode of self-understanding partly constitutive of the agent's identity . . . On this strong view to say that the members of a society are

---

[61] MacIntyre, *After Virtue*, 221.
[62] 'Sovereign communities', 'autonomous communities', 'typical medieval European Jewish communities', all on p. 71 of Walzer, *Spheres of Justice*.
[63] Rawls, *Theory of Justice*, s. 79, p. 522.   [64] Ibid. s. 79, p. 523.
[65] Sandel, *Liberalism and the Limits of Justice*, 149.

bound by a sense of community is not simply to say that many of them profess communitarian sentiments and pursue communitarian aims but rather that they conceive their identity—the subject and not just the object of their feelings and aspirations—as defined to some extent by the community of which they are a part. For them, community describes not just what they have as fellow citizens but also what they are, not a relationship they choose (as in a voluntary association) but an attachment they discover, not merely an attribute but a constituent of their identity.[66]

Martin Buber in one place mentions communities as one of the constitutive elements of 'society': society is not composed of individuals or families alone but 'societies, groups, circles, unions, cooperative bodies and communities, varying widely in type, form, scope and dynamics'.[67] Elsewhere, in a beautiful essay, he does dwell on the concept: 'community . . . proclaims itself above all in the common active handling of the common, and cannot endure without it'.[68] We find counterfeit, fictitious community where there is 'a unity not established out of real communal living of smaller and larger groups that dwell and work together, and out of their reciprocal relationships'.[69] Genuine community is

the inner constitution of a common life; in commonness of need, and only from this commonness of spirit; commonness of trouble, and only from this commonness of salvation.[70]

The real essence of community is undoubtedly to be found in the—manifest or hidden—fact that it has a centre. The real origin of community is undoubtedly only to be understood by the fact that its members have a common relationship to the centre superior to all other relations: the circle is drawn from the radii, not from the points of its periphery.[71]

The concept 'community' also plays a prominent part in the work of Ronald Dworkin. In his theory of legal interpretation and adjudication, Dworkin from the outset refers to the unit to which laws apply as a 'com-

---

[66] Sandel, *Liberalism and the Limits of Justice*, 150. In a relevant contribution Robert Goodin asks what kind of community might emerge in a society of rational individuals. Even 'sovereign artificers' would form communities of interest, of meaning, of generations, of regard. Rational individuals have the capacity to express 'we-oriented' sentiments, but they do this from their own as well as a collective standpoint: they cannot be as 'encumbered' as Sandel's conception of community seems to entail. Robert Goodin 'Review Article: "Communities of Enlightenment" ', *British Journal of Political Science*, 28 (1998), 531–58.

[67] Martin Buber, 'Society and the State' (1st pub. 1951) in *Pointing the Way*, ed. and trans. Maurice S. Friedman (Freeport, NY: Books for Libraries Press, 1957).

[68] Martin Buber, 'Comments on the Idea of Community' (1951), in *A Believing Humanism: My Testament 1902–1965* (New York: Simon and Schuster, 1967), 87.

[69] Ibid. 88.   [70] Ibid. 89.   [71] Ibid. 89.

munity'.[72] At the centre of Dworkin's theory is the 'principle of integrity [which requires that] lawmakers try to make the total set of laws morally coherent, and . . . which instructs that the law be seen as coherent in that way as far as possible [by judges]'.[73] In the course of explicating and defending this principle Dworkin decides that the most promising line of defence will use the concept 'fraternity, or to use its more fashionable name, community'.[74] The argument then goes through several stages of conceptual and theoretical development together. Dworkin argues that practice already defines states such as Great Britain, and the several states of the USA, as 'bare political communities'—meaning among other things that 'the officials of these communities have special responsibilities within and toward their distinct communities'.[75] We can also imagine or think of examples of 'political communities' in which members treated their association with each other as a 'de facto accident of history and geography'. They share territory, and cooperate with each other if it is advantageous, but this barely counts as a community at all. In another model 'the members of a political community accept a general commitment to obey rules established in a certain way that is special to that community'.[76] The third model of community is the 'community of principle', which 'insists that people are members of a genuine political community only when they accept that their fates are linked in the following strong way: they accept that they are governed by common principles, not just by rules hammered out in political compromise'.[77] The community of principle accepts integrity. It can therefore claim the authority of a genuine associative community and can therefore claim moral legitimacy in the name of fraternity.[78]

What, at this point, can we say about 'the concept of community'? On the one hand, we could take the disarming Wittgensteinian view and answer: 'not much'. Here we have a variety of uses of the term 'community'; they make a certain amount of sense. The philosophers themselves haven't done anything so prosaic as try to set out systematically any analysis of the meaning of community—rather, they seem to count on their

---

[72] Dworkin, *Law's Empire*. 'The community as a whole' is used in Dworkin's explanation of *McLoughlin* v. *O'Brian* [1983] 1 AC 410, on p. 27; his discussion of 'interpretation' begins with the problem of the case where 'members of particular communities who share practices and traditions make and dispute claims about the best interpretation of these' (p. 46) and goes on to discuss the nature of practices and interpretation in a hypothetical, invented community (pp. 47 ff.). See also Ronald Dworkin, 'Liberal Community', *California Law Review*, 77 (1989), 479–504.

[73] Dworkin, *Law's Empire*, 176. I discuss Dworkin among other theorists on 'interpretation' in Chapter 3.

[74] Dworkin, *Law's Empire*, 188.   [75] Ibid. 208.   [76] Ibid. 210.
[77] Ibid. 211.   [78] Ibid. 214.

readers knowing already what they mean. It seems obvious that we can't specify a set of criteria, or a set of necessary and sufficient conditions, for the use of the term. On the other hand, we could take the Rawlsian, theoretical, view: the important thing is the validity of these social theories—theories of legal adjudication, theories of justice, theories of social institutions including language. There's not much to say about 'community' as such apart from the role 'it' plays in the theory; if you want to ask questions about the concept 'community' attend to the validity of the theoretical framework first, then look and see what 'community' means. However, it strikes me that there is more to be said than this, and that saying it is not an entirely trivial waste of time.

First, 'a community' is an entity: a group of people or an institution or series of institutions. Diagram 2.1 shows some of the examples of commuity that are mentioned in the philosophical and the political literature on comunitarianism. Second, community means a particular kind of relation between persons. Up to this point we have met many references to sharing—shared principles, laws, meanings, goods, goals; a shared 'centre'; shared life. To the left of Diagram 2.1 are examples of 'groups that dwell and work together'; all across it are groups that are (if they are to count as communities) integrated by shared goals, practices, structures.

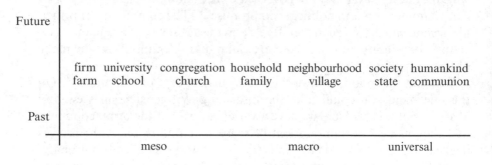

Diagram 2.1 Political and philosophical communitarianism: examples of
community

The relation of community has both subjective and objective or intersubjective elements. We have met references to 'the sense of community', the 'acceptance' by members that they are related in this particular way, the sentiments felt about others and about the group. It involves certain practices and actions—the common handling of the commons, governance by particular rules and principles. Finally communitarians tend to emphasize the temporal continuity of these 'communities'—one important thing that is shared is a past and a future, past generations and future descendants. I have represented this temporal dimension on the vertical axis of Diagram 2.1.

In sociology and related social science we find a somewhat different set of approaches and preoccupations. One preoccupation is whether the concept can be operationalized for research purposes—so that communities can be identified and studied, so that the degree to which some group is a community can be measured. Another strand takes the view that this preoccupation is misguided. It falls foul of 'the fallacy of misplaced concreteness'[79] and the task of social science can only be to trace the idea of community in discourses and practices. I shall deal with these two tendencies in turn, as well as some literature that attempts to take a middle way.

Sociologists have thought of community as a locality with settled denizens, a stable social structure consisting of dense networks of multiplex relations, and a relatively high boundary to the outside.[80] Within this variable framework there is a good deal of dispute over which elements should be emphasized.[81] One contested issue is spatiality. In one strand of sociological analysis a community is a locality within which there is a particularly dense and spatially restricted network of relations. 'Community studies' frequently focus on a relatively small local area. Other sociologists are more expansive and emphasize simply the density of social interactions regardless of their spatial extension.[82] The importance of spatial restrictedness is one of the major topics of dispute in sociological theory, and one that many critics identify as accounting for fatal (from the social scientific point of view) ambiguity in the concept, and for its sociological invalidity.[83]

A complicating factor is that in sociology 'community' has been conceptualized in contrast with 'society', and hence as 'the other' of sociology.

[79] Robert Booth Fowler, *The Dance with Community* (Lawrence, Kan.:, University Press of Kansas, 1991), 2.

[80] 'Density' refers to the extent to which each member is connected to each member; 'multiplexity' refers to the extent to which social relations in a dyad consist of more than one kind of tie. Examples of simple ties are kinship, economic exchange, cultural co-membership, religious co-membership, the co-worker relation, etc..

[81] Colin Bell and Howard Newby, *Community Studies*, ch. 1.

[82] See Graham Crow and Graham Allan, *Community Life*, pp. xv, 1.

[83] Margaret Stacey, 'The Myth of Community Studies', 134–47 argues both that the concept is ambiguous as regards whether spatial restrictedness is a criterion, and that, in any case, empirical research shows that most people even those living in what look like 'communities' such as rural settings, working-class housing estates, etc.—inhabit social networks, which are economically, affectively, and socially significant and fateful and which are not confined by geographical boundaries.

The work of sociology's founders can be interpreted, at any rate, as founded on a dualistic distinction between modern and pre-modern or traditional social relations. Sociology came into being as a distinct discipline in order to tackle the novel problems of modernity: increased social and geographical mobility; the problems of urbanization, industrialization, and forms of democratization; the decline of religion. The normative basis of modern societies is voluntarism and contract, and acquired power and resources; the normative basis of community was ascribed social status and authority. And so on.[84]

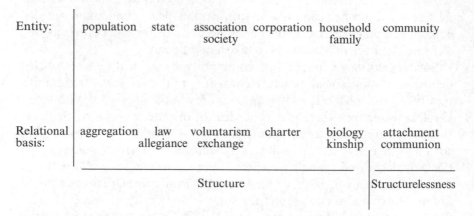

Diagram 2.2 'Community': contrast terms

Diagram 2.2 sets out some of the prominent contrast concepts, the categories that 'community' is not, according to social theorists. Most importantly, in communitarianism, 'community' is seen as a third way between bureaucratic state structures and processes, and voluntaristic, egoistic market exchanges. A community is certainly not a simple aggregation, as a population is. For some, the contrast between association and community is clear: associations are voluntaristic, are premissed on the individual's rational calculation of his interests, and feature exchanges of goods; whereas a community is a source of attachment, in Sandel's words

---

[84] These dualistic ideas are visible particularly in Emile Durkheim, *The Division of Labour in Society* (1st pub. French, 1893), trans. George Simpson (New York: Free Press, 1933); Karl Marx and Friedrich Engels, 'The German Ideology' (1845), 'The Communist Manifesto' (1848), in Karl Marx, *Selected Writings*, ed. David McLellan (Oxford: Oxford University Press, 1977); Max Weber, *Economy and Society* (1st pub. German, 1921; New York: Bedminster Press, 1968); and Ferdinand de Tonnies, *Community and Society* (Lansing, Mich.: Michigan State University Press, 1957). See Robert Nisbet, *The Quest for Community*.

an attachment that is discovered, not chosen. However, this distinction is controversial—some theorists work on the premiss that in modern societies, morally defensible 'communities' will be associations, based on voluntary relations of exchange. Similarly, there is controversy about the relationship between community and family. For many theorists, community refers to a series of relationships and institutions beyond the household and family. Whereas kinship, and biological ties, are a notable feature of family and household life, they are not a feature of community: that is based on shared ties such as culture, language, and so on. However, for other theorists family *is* a kind of community, if not 'the original community'.[85] Similarly, 'corporation'—including older social institutions such as guilds—with their legal basis, charters, and the like, stand in contrast to 'community' which refers to an informal formation.

One common if not ubiquitous theme is the nature of the boundary around the community. It is a commonplace that although communities might not have formal or ritualized modes of membership[86] nevertheless membership can be difficult to obtain, resting as it does on acceptance by the existing members. It is an important characteristic of communities that their members will draw very clear distinctions between insiders and outsiders.[87] Like Margaret Stacey, sociologists J. A. Barnes, and Elizabeth Bott, employers of network analysis, emphasize that 'community' denotes 'incorporation', 'encompassingness', boundedness; whereas what network analysis reveals is the absence of an external boundary.[88]

Sociology has been caught between seeing 'community' as a residual trace of an older social order enduring in modern societies, and seeing it more structurally as an element of contemporary social orders. As to the latter, 'community' is thought of as the social grouping, or the range of social institutions, that inhabit the space between the individual and the family, on the one hand, and the state and the society, on the other.[89] Crow

[85] I discuss this in some detail in Chapter 6.

[86] Some might of course. For example, joining a religious group such as a convent involves formal and ritualistic processes of education, avowal, and admission. But arguably, joining the order, or the institution (house etc.) is not the same as joining 'the community'. Just as becoming a member of a department or college—which requires credentials, contracts etc.—is not the same as becoming a member of 'the community' of the college or department (if there is such a thing).

[87] Crow and Allan, *Community Life*, 7–10, 68; A. P. Cohen, *The Symbolic Construction of Community*, 13, 28.

[88] J. A. Barnes, 'Class and Committees in a Norwegian Island Parish', *Human Relations*, 7 (1954), 39–58, p. 43; Elizabeth Bott, *Family and Social Network* (1st pub. 1957; 2nd edn. London: Tavistock, 1971), 99.

[89] Although, as we shall see in Chapter 6 many communitarians think of 'family' *as* community.

and Allan take this view. Community is 'the interlocking social networks of neighbourhood, kinship and friendship, networks which together make up community life as it is conventionally understood. Community stands as a convenient shorthand term for the broad realm of local social arrangements beyond the private sphere of home and family but more familiar to us than the impersonal institutions of the wider society.[90] This seems a clear enough structural analysis; but the theme of residuality lingers on. For 'community' is neither state (with its legal and bureaucratic structures and procedures), nor market (with its rational material transactions). As such, there is the continuing sense that here we have something older, more authentic, more originally human.[91]

Victor Turner emphasizes the 'structurelessness' of community and its contrast therefore with the structures of association, state, market, corporation, religious institutions, and the like. In community individuals relate to each other in an inchoate polymorphous fashion. Hence, according to this reading, community as a relation can only be marginal and liminal in human societies with their order and structure, but it is a mode of relating which in many human societies is yearned for. So it does have its (marginal) place; and members of a community are different from 'ordinary' people in ordinary social roles.[92]

So far we have examined sociological analyses which take actual material objects—particular lots of people, in particular patterns of social relations and distributions of resources, particular physical spaces—as their objects. But a significant strand of analysis dwells on the imagined, symbolic, and otherwise immaterial nature of communities. For example, A. P. Cohen focuses on individuals' and groups' own deployment of the term community in their understanding of their own lives—their attachment to their own community, the ways they distinguish insiders from outsiders, their evident attachment to the idea of community, their conception of it as a valuable thing. By surveying a wide range of ethnographic evidence, Cohen focuses on variation in the nature of community boundaries—in some cases they are grounded in language practices, in others in ritual, in others in politically constructed demarcations of one group from another.[93] He also focuses on variation in exactly what is shared by the members of communities: beliefs, norms, symbols, etc.[94] But more importantly he can focus on other variation and instability between mem-

[90]   Crow and Allan, *Community Life*, 1.
[91]   Martin Buber somewhere called it 'the between': quoted in Peter Gabel, 'The Desire for Community and the Defeat of Health Care', *Tikkun*, 10/1 (1995), 36.
[92]   Turner, *The Ritual Process*, e.g. 128.
[93]   Cohen, *Symbolic Construction of Community*, 44–5, 50 ff.   [94]   Ibid. 70 ff.

bers of 'a community' as regards their conceptions of their community and its outside. A community collectively may behave in very different ways to different 'others' and even differently to the same 'other' on different occasions.

Cohen insists that the project of trying to specify the social structural characteristics of communities as opposed to other social formations is vain. None of the criteria adduced by social scientists, such as complexity, ascribed status of members, pre-modernity, structurelessness, can be empirically validated. He cites Wittgenstein in support of his view that the only valid procedure is to explore how the concept is used; and he proceeds to examine its use in a number of contexts, as reported and analysed by social anthropologists, by 'members of a group of people who a) have something in common with each other, which b) distinguishes them, in a significant way, from the members of other putative groups'.[95] However, it is notable that the research data analysed does not come from any old groups of people, but from groups who share either a locale such as a village, or who share an 'ethnic' identity, such as members of ethnically distinct tribes.

There is an ambivalence in practice here then. On the one hand, 'operationalization' of the concept is disavowed, on the other hand certain sorts of groups—shopping crowds, theatre audiences (members of which have something in common which distinguishes them from other groups)—are not included in the category whereas villagers, tribespeople, religious, and linguistic groups are. If the answer is that shopping crowds and theatre audiences are definitely not 'communities' I want to ask how that judgement is made. After all, that a concept's boundaries are fuzzy does not mean we cannot say anything about it at all. Community is clearly one of a 'family' of social group concepts, and it is not the case that the terms for social groups are simply substitutable one for another.

We find a similar equivocation among those communitarians whose background discipline is social science. For example, Phillip Selznick recommends a 'principle of vagueness' when it comes to social science concepts: 'definitions for social science should be weak, inclusive and relatively uncontroversial'.[96] He defines community as consisting of two variables: 'a group is a community to the extent that it encompasses a broad range of activities and interests, and to the extent that participation implicates the whole person rather than segmental interests or activities'.[97]

[95] Ibid. 12.
[96] Phillip Selznick, *The Moral Commonwealth: Social Theory and the Promise of Community* (Berkeley and Los Angeles: University of California Press, 1992), 358.
[97] Ibid. 359.

In an earlier paper Selznick also mentions another variable: commitment. 'A community cannot be formed when the conditions of commitment are too weak, but it may turn into a parody of itself if commitment to a distant symbol or to leadership undermines the continuities and dissolves the bonds of person-centred life.[98] This analysis (or definition as Selznick calls it) strikes me as not very vague, after all. And it is clearly consistent with his theoretical endeavour, which is to explore the conditions under which societies can endure both stably and fully morally. The answer, for Selznick as for other communitarians, is when moral persons live in socially integrating structures to which they are committed (in the right way) as well as being committed to each other. Such a society, Selznick theorizes, will be characterized by mutuality, plurality, autonomy, participation, historicity, an emphasis on identity, as well as the integration already mentioned.[99]

A question that arises here, and elsewhere in the work of the political communitarians, is the extent or scope of community. Sociologists mainly have thought of communities as limited in extent—confined to a locality, or an ethnic group or its equivalent. It is also suggested that such organizations as firms, churches etc. can be 'communities'. We have also met the idea that whole states—society, Great Britain, etc.—can be a community. Another way of putting the question is: 'is community a macro, a meso, or a micro phenomenon?' Amitai Etzioni is quite clear about the answer to this. He is very reluctant to get bogged down in conceptual questions, offering only that in community 'we care about each other's wellbeing', and that 'the community can lay moral claims on its members'.[100] What he is clear about is the long list of organizations, groups, and other social entities that can be communities: families, neighbourhoods, local village, towns, nations, cross-national groupings e.g. the European Union, professional groups, occupational groups, etc. The state-society formation altogether should become a community; power and authority that has been accrued by individuals on the one hand, and the state and its bureaucratic agencies on the other, should be given back to 'the community', meaning intermediate and interlocking social formations; and the meso and micro level organizations that have in modern times themselves been weakened by individual sovereignty and state power, must be reforged as 'commun-

---

[98]   Phillip Selznick, 'The Idea of a Communitarian Morality', *California Law Review*, 77 (1987), 449.

[99]   Selznick, *Moral Commonwealth*, 360–5.

[100]   Amitai Etzioni, *The Spirit of Community: Rights, Responsibilities and the Communitarian Agenda* (New York: Crown Publishers, 1993), 31.

ities'. All these various communities and potential communities are 'nested' inside one another.[101]

Phillip Selznick is more equivocal on this point. He tends to characterize community as a macro phenomenon—the framework within which autonomous groups and institutions can operate.[102] 'Participation in communities is mediated by participation in families, localities, personal networks and institutions.'[103] However, meso and even micro organizations might become communities, to the extent that they encompass a broad range of interests, and to the extent that participation in them implicates the whole person rather than segmented interests or authorities.[104] For example, a firm might become a community if employees and employers began to interact with each other in multiplex relations—adding to the economic exchange of work for wage, cultural exchanges of sociability, shared leisure, participation in the locality, the organization of voluntary work, education, etc.

However, this requirement of multiplexity, which Phillip Selznick in particular has taken from sociology into communitarianism, strikes many theorists these days as too constraining. What many communitarians want, it seems, is community without multiplexity—hence the common emphasis on 'partial communities' such as 'the gay community', or 'a linguistic community'. The partial communities mentioned in the literature can be grouped in various ways. Looking at the list it struck me that many of them refer to place—from the world community at one end, to the community of a street or cluster of houses at the other. Others—ethical community, political community, traditional community, etc.—pick out a group which is tied by its foundation. Perhaps the most familiar cluster of 'partial communities' in recent discourse is the one that refers to groups tied by practice or belief—such as religious communities, linguistic communities, 'the business community', and the like. Finally, we find many references to communities of interest, communities of sentiment, communities of fate, etc. Such familiar formations as 'the gay community', the feminist community, and the like might be located as communities of fate or interest, or as practice based—sharing as they do cultural etc. norms.

What is most significant about all these 'communities' though is that for each one of them there is a perfectly serviceable descriptive name which does not use the concept 'community'. Why call a neighbourhood or a locality 'the local community'? Why call speakers of English or any other natural language a 'linguistic community'? Why call a polity, or a state, a

---

[101] Ibid. 32.　　[102] Selznick, 'Idea of a Communitarian Morality', 449.
[103] Selznick, *Moral Commonwealth*, 367.　　　　　　[104] Ibid. 358.

(The) Community . . . (A)				
Place	*Foundation*	*Scope*	*Practice*	*Resource/ constraint*
the local c urban c rural c	ethical c political c traditional c	total c universal c partial c	linguistic c religious c cultural c	c of fate c of interest economic c business c policy c
Alternative terms				
neighbourhood locality area denizens etc.	polity society nation democracy etc.	humankind group etc.	anglophone world Inuit speakers Jewish people etc.	producers capitalists policy makers workers etc.

Diagram 2.3   Varieties of partial community: community without multiplexity

'political community'? What, if it is not too crude a question, is the pay-off of the predicate community in these usages?

By contrast to this political project of making social organizations and institutions into communities, and them in turn into a 'community of communities' (or at the very least, calling groups and collectives commun-ities) Robert Booth Fowler takes as the object of his analysis ideas or images of community as constructed in various recent discourses within US politics. Movements for democracy, the 'New Republicans', and oth-ers propose the 'creation of political community', 'public spiritedness and public community', and the like.[105] By contrast, political projects based on the perception of crisis, such as environmentalism, invoke ideas such as 'the community of the human race', world government, and so on—thought to be the only answer to the planetary crises facing us.[106] Meanwhile thinkers who are concerned with the loss of tradition, the loss of stability, emphasize building up local and traditional institutional life, building up networks of mutuality and reciprocity, and so on.[107]

This last group of thinkers tends to emphasize the role of religious revival in building community. 'While there is rarely any assumption that

[105]   Robert Booth Fowler, 'Community: Reflections on Definition', 89.
[106]   Fowler, 'Community', 89.   [107]   Ibid. 91.

enhanced religious community will be a path to perfection, the feeling that its strengthening will help revise national public community rests on the assumption that religion celebrates community and challenges in principle the individualistic, not to say disintegrative, sides of American life.[108] We saw in the previous chapter the apparent connection between varieties of religious identity—socialist Christianity, non-Conformism, Judaism—and communitarian commitment.[109]

Another strand of analysis looks at the history of the concept community, using etymology to trace elements of its current meaning. One connection that has been pointed out is between community and Communitas—the transcendent or symbolic universe that embraces all souls.[110] For many theorists, and for many social actors as we have seen, community is the site for the realization of communion, and communion—connectedness, the meeting with another soul to soul—is the ideal for social relations that can be more nearly realized in community than anywhere else.[111] Another pertinent etymological strand links community with 'communitas' (with a small c)—the 'internally self-governing group which ordered its affairs through consensus of all its members', which stood in contrast with societas (association) and civitas (city). The communes were sometimes territorial associations, sometimes based on function, such as religious communities.[112] Historically, the term 'commune' has been used to refer to units of sentiment and jurisdiction—to units to which members have a feeling of belonging, and in which they can rule themselves. This sense carries over from the original communitas, to voluntary, unofficial communes of our own time (groups of families, single individuals, and children who attempt to share goods, resources, and burden, and who sometimes attempt to live self-sufficiently) to the legally recognized units of local government still common in Europe.

---

[108] Ibid. 92; Robert Wuthnow, *Sharing the Journey: Support Groups and America's New Quest for Community* (New York: Free Press, 1994), 105–9.

[109] The sociological, political, and philosophical literatures are full of pertinent references. Here is another: the British Home Office Official who was a driving force behind the Callaghan government's Community Development Programme, Derek Morrell, was concerned by the growth of bureaucracy and the disintegration of our sense of community; this was reinforced by his own Catholic commitment to community. Martin Loney, *Community against Government: The British Community Development Project 1968–78—A Study of Government Incompetence* (London: Heinemann, 1983), 44.

[110] John Fraser, 'Community, the Private and the Individual', *Sociological Review* 35 (1987), 796.

[111] Kenneth Leech, *The Social God* (London: Sheldon Press, 1981), 45, 84; John MacMurray, *Persons in Relation* (London: Faber and Faber, 1961), 157.

[112] Antony Black, 'Communal Democracy and its History', *Political Studies*, 45 (1997), 6.

Political philosophers who emphasize the importance of historical change in concepts are conscious of a particular hazard of language. Their worry is that if the history of the concept is lost from consciousness and use, we lose an invaluable element of our history, and hence our sense of who we are.[113] The construction of a conceptual history opens up conceptual argument, and forecloses on the dogmatic 'definition' of terms. (In fact, it seems to me that in the case of community, the openness of the concept is very evident—no danger here of dogmatism in definition as we have seen.) The historical associations with self-governance and autonomy on the one hand, and communion—the meeting of soul with soul, the human encounter which transcends the mundane and the material—on the other are still very much present as connotations of the term, whatever the context for its use.

THE CONCEPT 'COMMUNITY'

In this section I present an extensive analysis of the concept 'community'. I hope that this analysis will not be read as a definition of the concept, nor as an attempt to specify a set of necessary and sufficient criteria for use of the term. It is not meant as a legislation for the concept. Rather, it lays out the range of elements of the concept, in such a way as to enable analysts to say something about the kinds of connotations and echoes the term generates in use, the ways that elements that the concept excludes nevertheless are salient, and the points at which theories about how the world works are relevant. By 'elements of the concept' I mean elements of the meaning of the term in use: this analysis is based on reading uses of the term 'community', in academic discourses, and in the discourses presented in other chapters. I take it though that there are no barriers in principle to there being additions to and even subtractions from this set of elements. Diagram 2.4 presents this analysis. There are a number of points to note.

First, 'community' is a *value*, or an ideal, and it appears as such in ethics, in moral or normative discourse in other contexts, as in political and vernacular communitarianism, and in social science which attends to respondents' beliefs and values. Second, as we have seen it is a descriptive *category*, or set of variables. Of course, these two trade on each other; in particular community as an ideal begs the question of community as a descriptive category. So although we can make an analytic distinction between a descriptive and a prescriptive deployment of the concept, in

[113] Terence Ball, James Farr, and Russell L. Hanson, 'Editors' Introduction' to *Political Innovation and Conceptual Change* (Cambridge: Cambridge University Press, 1989), 1.

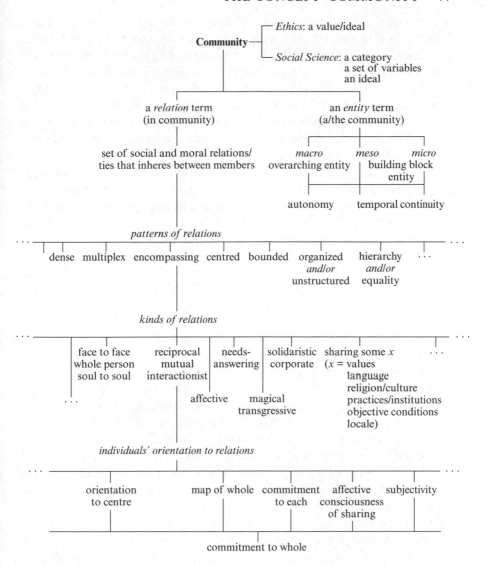

Diagram 2.4 The concept 'community'

practice it is difficult to hold the two apart. Second, as I have discussed before, 'community' is used sometimes with an '*entity*' sense dominant— it refers to a group of people and institutions, whether this is on the macro or global scale where it is an overarching entity which encompasses other groups and other communities, or on the micro scale so that communities are thought of as among the building blocks of the wider society. Sometimes it is used (usually without a definite or indefinite article) with a '*relation*' sense dominant. It refers to a set of social and moral relations and ties that inhere between members, and between members and non-members. Of course, these two trade on each other, too—the entity community consists of persons in the relation of the community; and persons in the relation community make 'a community'. But nevertheless there is an analytic distinction here; and that analytic distinction is tracked in different discursive contexts.

I have already discussed a number of issues that arise in connection with the range of elements of the *pattern of relations* that is taken to be typical of or normative for community—for example, the questions of density and multiplexity, the theoretical controversies over the nature of the boundary around a community, and Martin Buber's contention that a community must have a centre. I have included also in this analysis the idea that community relations are 'encompassing'. This has something to do with multiplexity—some characterizations emphasize that in a community, as opposed to other kinds of aggregate and collective, a person can live a good deal of their total life—economic, sociable, spiritual, cultural, etc. This is what I mean by encompassing. But it has another connotation, which flows into some common theories of community—that the community makes and holds the individual as what they are (rather than the individual, fully formed, entering the community as she or he pleases). This of course, is a key theme in philosophical communitarianism and it flows into the emphasis that the community can be a kind of agent, or a kind of subject. For example, Sandel argues that community can denote 'the subject, and not just the object, of shared aspirations'.[114] and Etzioni develops a normative theory of the 'moral voice of the community'.[115] Clearly, we need social theory here to account for how a collective becomes a subject. One way of reading it is that 'the community's voice' etc. is 'in the head of' the individual—it is the internalized 'other' or the equivalent of the Freudian superego which controls and socializes the individual's egoistic and impulsive behaviour. According to such psychological or psychoanalytic theory 'the community that speaks' is a psychological construct. However, another way of reading it is more sociological and literal: under the right conditions individuals can enter into solidary community relations with one another and can speak with a collective voice.

[114] Sandel, *Liberalism and the Limits of Justice*, 151.
[115] Amitai Etzioni, *The New Golden Rule: Community and Morality in a Democratic Society* (New York: Basic Books, 1996), 123 ff.

What is most notable about this analysis of the patterns of relations that constitute community are two points at which the concept contains a tension. Community often implies an *unstructured* set of relations—as we shall see this is connected with certain aspects of the nature of community relations. But 'a community' is also conventionally thought of as an *organized* set of relations—this is entailed in the nature of the community boundary which as we have seen has a definite form (whether symbolic or material). Relations cannot be both organized and unstructured. Yet in uses of the term we find sometimes one and sometimes the other emphasis. And sometimes (for instance in the work of Martin Buber) we find both. The tension can be resolved by an emphasis on the distinction between (structured) social relations and (unstructured) spiritual, soul to soul, relations. In the ideal of 'human to human' relations the two ideas can coexist. There is also a common theoretical dispute whether relations within community must be *equal*, or whether inequality and *hierarchy* of status, material resources, power and authority are consistent with community. Although equality is often associated with the socialist traditions, while hierarchy is associated with conservatism, it is more remarkable that in many practical and theoretical contexts both the ideals of equality and hierarchy coexist and their coexistence is expressed in and by the concept community. This is notable, for instance, in the liberal and socialist settlement projects discussed in the previous chapter.

Two elements in the list of *kinds of relations* that are characteristic of community reliably appear to be part of the concept of community for all users of the term. First, that in a community members *share some thing*. It is not obvious to me whether there are any *x*'s the sharing of which do not, potentially, constitute the sharers as a community, according to some version of communitarian theory. Certainly, as we saw above when I discussed 'partial communities', economic competitors can be referred to (without irony, seemingly) as 'the business community'; warring parties can be discursively incorporated into 'the political community'; individuals who happen to have an interest in, say, a particular level of state taxation are referred to, sometimes, as 'a community of interest'. Sharing itself is a complex concept. In the first place it denotes just the division of some quantity between two or more parties. If one of the parties is sacrificing her capacity or right to enjoy the whole this might be a morally laudable relationship. Second, it denotes 'having in common', where the good (or bad) in question is a collective good (collectively produced, or collectively consumed, or both). This is a meaning of 'shared' that, we saw, is very prominent in Charles Taylor's theory. Third, though, is another sense of sharing that is often implied in discussions of community: where sharing augments the quantity of a good, or diminishes the quantity of a bad. Certain goods which are collectively produced and consumed—like trust,[116] and according to Hannah Arendt, political power[117] can have the quality of augmenting, not diminishing, with use. (Of course this quality depends on the absence of or the overcoming of too many free riders). Shared practices, shared understandings, gain with use rather than being depleted—these are the goods that communitarians have often been impressed by.[118] We can note too that even scarce, conventional goods can be stretched by sharing. This is the phenomenon captured in the adage 'two can live as cheaply as one', and is part of the experience of people who remember a lost community life, in which all were poor and individuals shared what they had. In this kind of circumstance we have both the enhanced good of mutual help, but also a sense that although there was very little, collective effort and mutuality helped stretch what there was.

Second, all users of 'community' imply that the relations in question are human or *personal relations*. When we are in community we do not relate simply in our partial social roles, nor can we be indifferent to the others' humanity, and personal and particular existence. It is this aspect of the concept that accounts for the frequent theoretical inference that community is transcendent, rising above mundane and material relations, that in community we relate to others soul to soul. And it is this aspect of community relations that more than any other accounts for the elusive, fleeting, nature of community, and the way it engages (some) individuals at the affective level and at the level of fantasy.

Let us now turn to the issue of the *individual's orientation* to the relations of community. The philosopher Martin Buber emphasized that in community individuals must have 'a living reciprocal relationship to a single living centre, and they have to stand in a living reciprocal relationship to one another'.[119] Other philosophers do not make reference to this *'centre'*, but do emphasize the *reciprocal* relations between individuals—the concern, respect, of each for each.[120] It is an implication of this kind of relationship that the individuals will also have an idea of, or a kind of *mental map* of, the whole thus constituted. Many theorists emphasize the need for individuals to have such a map if the concept 'community' is to apply. For instance,

[116] Diego Gambetta, 'Can we Trust Trust?', in Gambetta (ed.), *Trust: Making and Breaking Cooperative Relations* (Cambridge: Cambridge University Press, 1988), 225.

[117] Hannah Arendt, *The Human Condition* (Chicago: University of Chicago Press, 1958), 200–1.

[118] This theme is captured, of course, in the term 'social capital', which can grow with use. See James Coleman, 'Social Capital in the Creation of Human Capital', *American Journal of Sociology*, 94 suppl. (1988), 95–119.

[119] Buber, *I and Thou*, 94.   [120] Dworkin, *Law's Empire*, 199 ff.

Benedict Anderson discusses the display of geographical maps in constructing the politically forged 'communities' of modern nation states.[121] Sociologists use the existence or retrievability of respondents' mental and discursive maps of their 'community' as a crucial variable in measuring the presence or absence, strength or weakness, of community among some population.[122] We have already met A. P. Cohen's argument that communities exist by virtue of symbolic work—symbols stand in for and construct boundaries around the community. The articulation of the existence of a community, in interaction and practice, is itself a symbol whose purpose is to invoke the boundary.[123] Participation in ritual and other integrative practices heightens consciousness of the difference between insider and outsider, by rehearsing and institutionalizing the attachment of insiders and outsiders respectively to such qualities as trustworthiness, purity, religiosity, etc.[124] The boundaries are mental, imaginative, symbolic constructs.

I discussed earlier the recent communitarian desire to have community without multiplexity. Arguably, what we have here are theories of community without density. For instance, Dworkin acknowledges that in modern conditions societies cannot meet the criteria of true community (each caring reciprocally for each). However, he argues that these personal and special relations are implicit or immanent in practices such as law, and democratic or republican politics. Community is therefore not a psychological matter—although an emotional bond to '*the whole*' is necessary. Rather it is 'an intepretive property of the group's practices of asserting and acknowledging responsibilities.'[125] Jeffrey Weeks argues that in the face of political and social disadvantage, and crises like the HIV epidemic, gay people have felt that community should exist—a diasporic consciousness results and constructs it. Webs of narrative then give meaning to the idea of sexual community.[126] With the construction of symbolic boundaries, the display of unifying symbols and representations like flags and maps, narratives of unity and history, or individuals' imagination of all the people in a locality as 'in community',[127] the material density of social relations that has traditionally been thought to be a necessary element of the concept community is eclipsed.

[121] Benedict Anderson, *Imagined Communities*, 2nd edn. (London: Verso, 1991), 170–8.
[122] John E Puddifoot, 'Some Initial Considerations in the Measurement of Community Identity', *Journal of Community Psychology*, 24 (1996) 327–36.
[123] Cohen, *Symbolic Construction of Community*, 15.
[124] Ibid. 50.   [125] Dworkin, *Law's Empire*, 201.
[126] Jeffrey Weeks, 'The Idea of a Sexual Community', paper delivered to conference 'Ideas of Community', University of West of England, Sept. 1995.
[127] Paul Lichterman, *The Search for Political Community* (Cambridge: Cambridge University Press, 1996), 129.

Earlier I posed the question: what is the pay-off to calling Francophone people, or cockneys, or those who share gossip, a linguistic community or a speech community? What is the point of calling a university department, or an interest group, or a congregation, a community? The question can be partly answered by reference to a feature of the concept that is much remarked upon: its positive evaluative connotations. Despite the best endeavours of critics of communitarianism in recent years to point out that dense and multiplex relations, reciprocity and mutuality, sharing, affective consciousness, and all the rest can encompass vicious xenophobia and hostility, cultures of criminality, indifference to the suffering of outsiders, the prevention of exit by disadvantaged insiders, and so on and so forth,[128] the concept 'community' has the warm and positive connotations now that it had when Raymond Williams wrote *Keywords*.[129] In turn this means that (almost) invariably the description of some formation or relation as a community is a commendation. At the same time, there is an irony to many such speech acts, for competent users of the term themselves know that it is empirically pretty demanding—with its connotations of at least some of commitment, reciprocity, solidarity, wholeness, personalism, and so on. Thus, announcements of meetings of the community, appeals to the community to organize to prevent crime or fight injustice, are exhortations to individuals to form the very 'community' whose existence is (in some sense) presupposed. That is, they are exhortations to all relevant individuals to come together in a formation that realizes some number of these connotations of community.

But the question remains: exactly what is the call to form? We have seen that density and multiplexity are not thought by most to be practicable political or social aims. But one particular quality that is, still, desirable, is boundedness. A community is a corporate, rather than a merely interactive, entity. I have not come across any usage which does not imply, at least, that some subset of the five kinds of orientation to the relevant social relations is necessary in addition to the relations themselves. These kinds of orientation, in turn, imply *orientation to the whole and to its boundary*, which as we have seen involves the use of the imagination, symbols, ritual, and so on. For the

---

[128] Marilyn Friedman, 'Feminism and Modern Friendship: Dislocating the Community', *Ethics*, 99 (1989), 257–90; Adam Crawford, 'Appeals to Community and Crime Prevention', *Crime, Law and Social Change*, 22 (1995) 97–126.

[129] Raymond Williams, *Keywords* (London: Fontana, 1976), 75–6. Phillip Selznick pointed out to me that it does not follow from the fact that a concept has positive connotations that every instance of the phenomenon is good. I agree that it does not in logic. But one point I wish to make in the course of this analytic exercise is that meaning can defy logic, so that a case of a 'bad community' while not illogical seems odd. Given the current use of the concept it would have to be glossed, or explained.

communitarian, no matter that this whole will have uncertain, fuzzy, or constantly shifting boundaries, elusive to analyst and participant alike because the use of imagination, interpretation, and symbol to establish boundaries is necessary if any group, aggregation, or collective is to experience itself as a community.

Given these conditions, I argue that the experience of community will be both euphoric and fleeting. On occasion or at such times members experience a centred and bounded entity that includes the self as such; they engage in exchanges and sharing that are personalized; the orientation to each and to the whole engages the person and, as some are tempted to put it, his or her soul. It is from such occasions that 'the spirit of community' or 'the sense of community' is achieved. Here I think we have the answer to my question about the 'pay-off' of community—although I realize that here I am mixing a profane and calculative metaphor with a transcendent and sacred one. In the relation of community concrete patterns of material social relations are felt to be transcended. The etymology of 'communion' is relevant, the engagement of the whole person in the relationship of community is an element of the concept for all theoretical perspectives religious and secular. I have discussed the role of imagination, symbol, and affect at some length. What this all adds up to, I think, is that the aspiration to community is an aspiration to a kind of connectedness that transcends the mundane and concrete tangle of social relations.

The centrality of this aspect of the phenomenology of community implies, I think, strictly that the term is not applicable to a group which is oppressed such that its members share only misery. This is consistent with common contemporary usage. If members of misery-sharing groups or formations ever experience themselves as a community, or if an outsider is tempted to describe them as a community, it is because they are engaging in the kind of productive, augmentative sharing that such groups can sometimes achieve—where the little there is stretches further, or where the miserable food is a feast because of the social setting in which it is consumed. What is for sure is that individuals do not acquire the 'sense of community' or 'spirit of community' from experiences such as not being able to find anyone to deliver the neighbourhood newsletter, or getting a disappointing turnout at a meeting, or as a committee member being left to make decisions which the wider population then disown because they were made by the committee. They don't acquire it from immiserated persons failing to share and thereby rise above their misery.

It is also important to underline the fleeting and elusive nature of community. When the euphoria subsides what people are left with is the stuff of social life—networks of concrete social relations of exchange, trust or its absence, obligations and duties, friendship, uncertainty. That is, we are left—in the terms of Diagram 2.3—with neighbourhoods and local people, interest groups and parties, activists and voters, people who share religious or cultural institutions, and so on. Some groups are better integrated and organized than others, some have more potent holdings of material and symbolic resources than others—that is, some are better able to achieve cohesion and some measure of agency.

From this analysis, and these observations, I derive a number of hypotheses. First, community as a sustained and enduring social formation is likely to be even rarer than inspection of the elements of the concept suggest. The theory is that community can only be realized and lived in episodic and fleeting moments. Second, though, numerous social formations, muddles, or networks of social relations, of course do exist and endure, and form the basis for the aspiration to community. Third, it is precisely the theoretical connotations of transcendence, the wholly human encounter, and so on which makes many critics hostile to community—I mean both philosophical or theoretical critics, and also those who practically resist calls for community formation, resist the idea that gay people form a community, and so on. Some individuals do undoubtedly value encounters at the human-to-human level—there are individuals who want to socialize with their colleagues, share cultural pursuits with their political allies, do business with their neighbours. But others value the partiality of modern human relations—the absence of the need to socialize with colleagues, or to be friends with business partners. There is a clash of values, and a significant political dispute, here. And many individuals feel ambivalent about these options, and pulled both ways.

Fourth, I am sceptical about the power of a specifically communitarian analysis and communitarian politics to actually forge the kind of relationships that will deliver the social power, at the meso level of intermediate groups, that communitarians aspire to in the first place. The problem is that the 'spirit of community' or fostering a 'sense of community' is inadequate for the subsequent action and organization, absent the right kind of concrete social relations. Yet organizers' and theorists' focus on the absence and longed for presence of a 'spirit of community' precisely diverts attention from the material conditions that might generate this agency. Rather it focuses attention on the big occasions. Certainly, from the point of view of activists there is a difficulty here. Rhetorically, exhortations for action by 'networks with loose ties'[130] lack a certain something

---

[130] Mark Granovetter, 'The Strength of Weak Ties', *American Journal of Sociology*, 78 (1973) 1360–80; 'The Strength of Weak Ties: A Network Theory Revisited', in Peter V.

that appeals to community do not lack. But calling for 'community action' and even achieving a transcendent moment in some event, does not institute the networks of loose ties, the interest groups, the alliances and allegiances, that are the basis for effective social action.

I anticipate that this argument will invite from communitarian and other users of the concept the objection that their use does not involve anything like the transcendence or euphoria I have identified. All it means, they will say, is some subset of elements from Diagram 2.4. Theory adds that, for instance, community can only be realized in conditions of high interpersonal trust; or low levels of family breakdown, or the devolution of governmental power to neighbourhoods. All very concrete and material. Communitarians will object that their attention really is on the networks of relations that will be the basis for effective social action and a just society.

But the question I then want to ask is: why insist on that term when a more precise range of terms, that more specifically describe the shapes of networks of social relations, is available? What is the difference between co-membership of an interest group, or association, corporation or network, and co-membership of a community? I think the answer must be along the lines that the relation of community is not straightforwardly anchored in concrete social relations. To analyse how members of a department, in rather muddled and perhaps contradictory ways, have a variety of interests in the continued existence of the department, and a variety of strategies for ensuring its continuance, is exactly to draw attention to the way such a collective—with its variety of social relations and alliances—is not a community. For communities 'rise above' or 'transcend' this muddle of relations. And it is this that communitarians want and are striving—by exhortation, or by theory, or by action—to achieve.

Marsden and Nan Lin (eds.), *Social Structure and Network Analysis* (Beverly Hills, Calif.: Sage Publications, 1982).

3

Communitarianism, Interpretation and Politics

COMMUNITARIANISM AND INTERPRETIVISM

'Interpretivism' is a prominent theme in political and philosophical communitarianism. First, communitarians tend to argue that the best, most coherent and effective way to do ethics and political philosophy is not to try to deduce and apply universally valid, fundamental principles, but to interpret and refine values that are immanent—that is, lived and enacted although not necessarily explicitly articulated or codified—in the ways of life of actual groups, societies, or communities. For example, this is an important aspect of Michael Walzer's theory of complex equality. He says in his preface: 'A society of equals lies within our own reach. It is a practical possibility here and now, latent already, as I shall try to show, in our shared understanding of social goods. *Our* shared understandings: the vision is relevant to the social world in which it is developed . . .'. By contrast to deductive philosophical methods premised on a priori principles Walzer sets out another way of doing philosophy:

to interpret to one's fellow citizens the world of meanings that we share. Justice and equality can conceivably be worked out as philosophical artefacts, but a just or an egalitarian society cannot be. If such a society is not already here—hidden as it were in our concepts and categories—we will never know it concretely or realise it in fact.[1]

Alasdair MacIntyre argues that values—what is valued—are posterior to practices and traditions.[2] So, ethical arguments about how life ought to be lived, our obligations to others and ourselves, have to be based on the reflexive consideration of an already existing way of life, on the interpre-

---

[1] Michael Walzer, *Spheres of Justice* (New York: Basic Books, 1983), p. xiv; also *Interpretation and Social Criticism* (Cambridge, Mass.: Harvard University Press, 1987), 19.
[2] Alasdair MacIntyre, *After Virtue* (London: Duckworth, 1985), 219; *Three Rival Versions of Moral Enquiry* (London: Duckworth, 1990), 7 ff., 349 ff. See also Charles Taylor, 'The Diversity of Goods', in *Philosophy and the Human Sciences* (Cambridge: Cambridge University Press, 1985), 234 ff.

tation of tradition, and the understanding thereby of values, their meaning, and their practical possibility.[3]

The political communitarians, notably Amitai Etzioni, make a good deal of the idea that ethical principles or values are only powerful if they are in some sense already part and parcel of ordinary people's ideas in and about their daily lives. Communitarians appeal to people's tacit understandings that community really does matter, that our unchosen obligations to others are as important as our voluntaristic choices and freely entered into contracts. Ethical argument is then a combination of interpretation of the values and understandings that are explicit or implicit in ways of life, the refinement and development of certain aspects of these, and a prescriptive analysis of what life could be like under ideally moral conditions in which these values were properly and thoroughly realized.[4] Political communitarians, that is, rely on the existence of what I call 'vernacular communitarianism' in the societies in which they campaign. They wish to elevate this aspect of social life to the level of articulation and institutionalization.

Second, communitarians argue that social scientific models and theories must have an interpretive basis. This means that social scientific practices such as measurement and model building can't proceed without an interpretive understanding of the practices of the society in question.[5] It means that scientific understandings of how people live and the outcomes of their actions, will reflect the understandings and decision-making processes of the actors themselves, and will, therefore, be recognizable to the actors themselves. Most importantly, it incorporates a theory about the mechanisms that explain regularities, changes, and effects in the social world—these are actors' interpretations of their situation, and their actions which are undertaken in the light of the understanding thus formed.[6]

For the philosophical communitarians, notably Taylor and Walzer, there is a deeper connection with interpretivism—they emphasize that interpretation itself is a community practice. There are two aspects to this. First, in an extension of the argument set out before, Walzer argues that political philosophers must engage in philosophy as interpretation. This interpretation will on the one hand be recognized by the community

[3] MacIntyre, *After Virtue*, 221–2; *Three Rival Versions*, 350–3.

[4] Amitai Etzioni, *The Spirit of Community: Rights, Responsibilities and the Communitarian Agenda* (New York: Crown Publishers, Inc., 1993), 101, 258–9.

[5] MacIntyre, *After Virtue*, 104, 81; Charles Taylor, 'Neutrality in Political Science', in *Philosophy and the Human Sciences*.

[6] Charles Taylor, 'Social Theory as Practice' and 'Interpretation and the Sciences of Man', in *Philosophy and the Human Sciences*, 40 ff., 93; MacIntyre, *After Virtue*, 85–6.

addressed, and on the other hand will have a critical element. After all, there may be contradiction between the principles immanent in a culture and the practices, or some of the practices, actually to be observed there.[7] It may be that members of a community have imperfectly understood the implications that follow from their principles—the long deprivation of working-class, female, and black people in liberal societies of the franchise and other civil rights might be an example of this.[8] Walzer discusses, for instance, Marx's critique of capitalist society, in the course of which he observes that the capitalist class is impelled to present itself as a universal class embracing standards of rationality and freedom that it cannot (in existing social conditions) live up to. The Marxist critique of capitalism 'condemns capitalist practice by elaboration of the key concepts with which capitalism was originally defended'.[9] A second aspect of interpretation as a community practice is that in the living of a tradition, or way of life, in the reproduction of social institutions and norms, participants themselves must engage in a continuous interpretive process. Rules, norms, standards, traditions are not just mechanically followed—participants interpret the rules before they attempt to follow them.[10] Neither can participants straightforwardly coordinate or cooperate with each other—cooperation and coordination (and by that same fact, competition) are premissed on interpretation of what others are doing and what their signals mean.[11] Furthermore, the adjudicators regarding the goodness of our interpretations, those who inform us when we have gone wrong and from whom we get indications that our understanding and actions are right, are members of our community.[12]

For the communitarians, then, community is significant in connection with interpretivism, in two important ways. First, values and practices are the property of communities and their ways of life, so interpretation of and argument about values and practices has to begin in a community and its way of life. Second, as 'interpreting animals' we refer to other members of our community, interpreting their actions and meanings, before we decide how to interpret a rule or a custom or a norm, and thereby decide how to act. Predictably enough, with the argument and analysis of

[7] Walzer, *Interpretation and Social Criticism*, 29.

[8] Ibid. 43; MacIntyre, *After Virtue*, 222 on the reflexive development of tradition.

[9] Walzer, *Interpretation and Social Criticism*, 43.

[10] Taylor, 'Interpretation and the Sciences of Man', 27–30, 33–5; see also Michael Walzer, *Thick and Thin: Moral Argument at Home and Abroad* (Notre Dame, Ind.: University of Notre Dame Press, 1994), 7.

[11] Taylor, 'Interpretation and the Sciences of Man', 31.

[12] Walzer, *Interpretation and Social Criticism*, 48; MacIntyre, *Whose Justice? Which Rationality?*, 355; Taylor, 'Interpretation and the Sciences of Man', 17.

Chapter 2 in mind, I want to ask what 'community' means in this context. In addition, of course, this model of community and interpretation begs the question of the nature of interpretation.

INTERPRETIVISM

The term 'interpretivism' turns up in a wide variety of contexts. In sociology and cultural studies it is often contrasted with 'empiricism' or 'naturalism'.[13] In ethics, as we have seen, it is contrasted with 'deontology' and with teleology.[14] In metaphysics and epistemology, interpretivism contrasts with empiricism, rationalism, and idealism.[15] In literary studies interpretation is distinguished from other analytic techniques.[16] In jurisprudence it is often contrasted with 'black letter law' or the idea that 'the law' is just what the relevant statutes and cases say it is, and with 'realism' or the theory that the law is just what judges say it is.'[17] In these various settings theorists and analysts focus on a variety of objects of interpretation. These include texts proper (legal cases, statutes, poems, books, films, the life's work of an author or group of authors), and text analogues (including utterances, gestures, symbols, social events, performances, practices, actions and behaviours, and states of affairs).

There are two focuses for contention here. First, what are proper objects of 'interpretation'. It can be disputed, for instance, whether any classes of 'facts' are not subject to interpretation; or whether an action like 'making an offer' really is to be interpreted in the same way a poem is. Second, how radical are the implications of a commitment to 'interpretivism', especially in the fields of social science and theory? At one extreme we find the strong view that interpretivism fundamentally undermines the pretensions of a number of other social scientific programmes—in particular their aspiration to the objectivity of analysed data, and to predictive causal models that converge on determinism.[18] The argument that the world is a text (or,

[13] See, for example, Alexander Rosenberg, *Philosophy of Social Science* (Oxford: Clarendon Press, 1988), 20, 83 ff.

[14] Walzer, *Interpretation and Social Criticism*, 21.

[15] Jürgen Habermas, *On the Logic of the Social Sciences*, (1st pub. German, 1967), trans. T. McCarthy, (Oxford: Polity Press, 1988), ch. 8; James Bohman, *New Philosophy of Social Science: Problems of Indeterminacy* (Oxford: Polity Press, 1991), 113.

[16] I. A. Richards, *Practical Criticism* (London: Routledge and Kegan Paul, 1929), 13–14; Stanley Fish, *Is There a Text in this Class?* (Cambridge, Mass.: Harvard University Press, 1980), e.g. p. 9.

[17] Ronald Dworkin, *Law's Empire* (London: Fontana, 1986), ch. 1; Georgia Warnke, *Justice and Interpretation* (Oxford: Polity Press, 1992), 2.

[18] Habermas, *On the Logic of the Social Sciences*, ch. 8; Bohman, *New Philosophy of Social Science*, ch. 3.

more weakly, that the world is like a text) contrasts with a number of other familiar representations of 'the world' from the history and philosophy of the social sciences. It contrasts with the world as like a billiards table, with elements (atoms, organisms) colliding with each other and affecting each others' paths in a way that can be explained in terms of mechanistic causal connections. It contrasts also with behaviourists' views of persons and other animals, responding to stimuli, learning about the pleasurable or painful effects of these stimuli, and developing avoidance or attraction behaviours.[19] It contrasts too with the rational choice theorist's view of the individual as calculating the best means to the satisfaction of (given) preferences or goals. For the 'world as text' view means that individuals are readers, meaning makers and meaning finders. They interpret and reinterpret their preferences, desires, constraints and opportunities, and the actions, behaviours and demeanours of other individuals.

According to this approach models of human action and its aggregate effects could not be once and for all valid, as for instance we may hope that models of the interaction and behaviour of protein molecules at a certain temperature are, because meanings are protean, and the connections that an actor makes, which explain his actions—his preferences, his actions in pursuit of preference satisfactions, his conduct towards other agents, and so on—are similarly changeable. This is not to say that an actor's actions are inexplicable to others, or completely idiosyncratic or random. For meaning is intersubjective. But what the analyst needs in order to render a subjects' actions explicable is an understanding of the meanings of his world for the actor himself. Getting hold of these data is not a neutral matter of observation and measurement; it requires 'sensibility', 'understanding', and 'insight'—which are unformalizable and unstandardizable.[20]

It can be objected to this approach in social science that there are many circumstances in which it is perfectly proper to measure and correlate variables without regard to what anyone thinks of them, or what meaning is attached to them. For instance, given that income and holdings of material goods are powerful predictors of life chances (levels of material welfare, life expectancy, etc.) it is sufficient simply to measure income, savings, investments etc., for predictive purposes, without asking subjects anything about meaning, or engaging in any interpretation at all. In other words, in many contexts, the billiard table model of cause and effect (more material holdings causes longer life expectancy) or the rational choice model of preference satisfaction (individuals with more resources satisfy more of their material needs) best model the processes in the world.

[19] Rosenberg, *Philosophy of Social Science*, ch. 3.
[20] Taylor, 'Interpretation and the Sciences of Man', 53.

But in reply to this, the interpretivist can make two points. First, the specification of scientific variables, even very simple ones like 'income' are the upshot of scientists' interpretation of the reality they seek to understand, their arguments about these interpretations, and their settling on more or less standard ways of measuring 'income'. Second, if we are to understand properly why increased material resources increase life expectancy, or whatever, then we need to know why people expend their resources in the way they do—we need, in other words, to understand the meaning of various goods and bads for people. For example, we might reasonably hypothesize that the more material resources a person has, the more she will spend on life-damaging commodities such as harmful drugs, fatty food, and so on. In order to understand how spending power transforms into health and welfare we have to understand what various commodities mean to the relevant individuals—we have to understand their understanding In the social sciences, then, the issue of interpretation is closely connected with the issue of understanding, or *verstehen*. The problem is accurately to grasp the interpretations and understandings of those subjects whose actions are being modelled and explained (and by extension to accurately model the outcomes when interpretation-based actions are aggregated and interact with one another). One question is how we know when our (the analyst's or scientist's) interpretation is a valid or otherwise correct grasp of the subject's understanding or interpretation. In social science, arguably, predictive capability is one such measure, although in the case of interpretations we cannot assume as readily as we do with some other kinds of events and processes—despite the strictures of Humean sceptics—that the past is a reliable guide to the future.

A second controversial problem that exercises political theorists, philosophers, and literary scholars, is how to interpret texts like books, especially those written in cultural and historical contexts some distance from our own; and how to validate particular interpretations. There are various kinds of challenges and disputes in this connection. First, there is a controversy about the extent of the context that lends meaning to a text. Is it acceptable to read a book like Thomas Hobbes's *Leviathan* on its own and produce an interpretation of the meaning of Hobbes's terms, the structure and validity of his inferences, and the implications of his model of politics? Or do we have to know the context out of which and into which Hobbes was writing, the audience he was addressing, what he was saying as opposed to the meaning of his words?[21] The question then arises how

---

[21] The saying *v.* meaning distinction is ambiguous in ordinary English. On the one hand we draw the distinction as follows (using an example from Diane Blakemore *Understanding Utterances* (Oxford: Blackwell, 1992), 5): on a television holiday programme the presenter

extensive this contemporary context is: it incorporates Hobbes's other works, his correspondence, the pamphlets and books that he himself read, the debates he was engaged in. Does it also extend to the popular culture of his time, which plausibly affects the assumptions and understandings of Hobbes and his colleagues? To the wider social context? The problem, clearly, is how to differentiate this 'context' and establish what is significant and what not in the production of Hobbes's meaning.[22]

This controversy is complicated by consideration of the readers' context too—some strains in literary theory emphasize that texts mean what readers take them to mean. Thus, if contemporary liberal thinkers, who are preoccupied by the relationship between natural and legal rights of the individual the constitutional limits on state and social power, and the maximization of individual freedom and autonomy, read Hobbes for what he has to say about these matters, the fact that Hobbes himself had quite other issues on his mind (and would have been read as saying very different things by his contemporaries) constitutes no criticism of the current readers' interpretations. 'What the text says now matters more than what the author meant to say.'[23] But the extent of the context which affects the recent readers' readings matters, and is a bone of contention, too. Some critics of recent liberalism, for instance, consider that liberals ought to widen their frame of reference to take into account a range of social processes by which social, political, cultural, economic, and interpersonal power is distributed. Some argue that liberals ought to take account of more realistic and plausible models of the human subject and the structure of personality. One way of putting the issue is that there is no *one* thing that 'the text says now'; different readers' different contexts and preoccupations produce different readings.

I continue discussion of that issue in the final section of this chapter. Meanwhile, though, I want to note that another controversy is introduced

utters the following: 'Obviously, in the outer islands nobody speaks English. So brush up your English.' That's what she *said*; what she *meant* was '. . . So brush up your Greek.' On the other hand we also draw the distinction this way (using an example from John B. Thompson, *Studies in the Theory of Ideology* (Oxford: Polity Press, 1984), 268): one person in some domestic partnership says to the other: 'Don't you think the rubbish is beginning to smell?', in which case his or her interlocutor might well ask (as if she or he didn't know!) 'What are you *saying*?' Philosophers disambiguate the saying *v.* meaning distinction the former way. (In the latter example the second speech should perhaps be glossed as 'What are you not saying?')

[22] Jonathan M. Wiener, 'Quentin Skinner's Hobbes', *Political Theory*, 2 (1974), 251–60.

[23] Quentin Skinner, 'From Hume's Intentions to Deconstruction and Back', *Journal of Political Philosophy*, 2 (1996), 142–54, p. 145 (in the section from which this quotation comes Skinner is presenting the strong 'reader response approach' associated with Stanley Fish.)

here—rather than the question of context as such we meet the question of 'surface' versus 'deep' readings. An obvious example is recent feminist readings of Hobbes and other canonical political theorists. Usually, conventional political philosophers and historians of political thought have either failed to find any interest in the conceptualizations and theories of gender, marriage, and kinship in the work of political thinkers, or they have acknowledged their characteristic views of marriage, femininity, household, and so on but argued (with unusual brevity) that these are irrelevant to the important questions about governance, state, society and individual sovereignty, liberty, equality, and so on.[24] By contrast, feminist interpretation of Hobbes's and others' work brings the treatment of gender, sex, marriage, and household to the centre, revealing the relations between these concepts and others, and their place in theories of political relations, freedom, state, equality, and so on.[25] Thus far, this interpretive process is focused on the surface of the texts: the words are there plain to see, passages that have traditionally been thought to be relatively uninteresting are brought to the reader's attention, and put in the context of gender theory. In the process concepts like politics, state, and equality are re-presented—shown to have a gender component.

But feminists have been motivated to go further, and to read texts in order to elucidate what is not said—the unspoken and tacit assumptions, the conceptualizations of key terms which must underpin the argument if the text is to make sense. A most notable example of this is Carole Pateman's reading of the social contract tradition. The absence of women from the social contract, their irrelevance in the described processes of construction of state, civil society, and laws, can only be accounted for if we presume that the question of women has been dealt with before the story begins, so to speak. Pateman traces in the social contract texts hints of a story of exactly this process.[26] Here we have a reading of the text that not only notices what is generally ignored, but also takes what is said to license inferences about what is not said. Authors do not explicitly address the questions that are on the agenda of their readers and critics, but we can

[24] For example, neither of the Introductions to the two editions of Hobbes's *Leviathan* I have on my shelf mention the themes of family, marriage, gender, or sex: introd. Kenneth Minogue (London: Dent, 1973); introd. J. C. A. Gaskin (Oxford: Oxford University Press, 1996).

[25] Carole Pateman, *The Sexual Contract* (Oxford: Polity Press, 1988); 'The Fraternal Social Contract', in *The Disorder of Women* (Oxford: Polity Press, 1989), 38–57; ' "God Hath Ordained to Man a Helper": Hobbes, Patriarchy and Conjugal Right', in Mary Lyndon Shanley and Carole Pateman (eds.), *Feminist Interpretations and Political Theory* (Oxford: Polity Press, 1991).

[26] Pateman, *Sexual Contract*, throughout.

nevertheless validly enquire what the author would have said, must have said, had he addressed the issue explicitly or in the form the critic poses it.

A third set of controversies arises in connection with the relationship between interpretation and conceptual analysis. We met in the last chapter four ways of conceptualizing concepts. First, they might be thought of as bounded entities with a clear and determinate relationship with their referents. According to this view, the analyst's job is to delineate for the benefit of others the exact boundary of the concept's extension, the relationships between the concept and relevant others (neighbouring ones, contrast terms and so on), and the exact content of the concept. This view implies that philosophy provides us with special tools for the identification and characterization of concepts.[27] However, we also met the view, associated with Wittgenstein, that concepts should be thought of as having boundaries that are only drawn by specific language users for specific purposes, and are not stable or determinate.[28] Hence, the analyst's job perhaps is to interpret for the benefit of others where the boundaries have been drawn, by whom, under what circumstances, with what success. A third approach to concepts emphasizes that they are intimately bound up with 'theories'. Our theories of how the world works structure our concepts (hence, disputes about the meaning of 'freedom' or 'community' and changes in the meaning of 'atom').[29] And concepts, concomitantly, are 'theory laden'—our understanding and use of them, whether we know it or not, predispose us to particular theoretical commitments. A fourth and recently influential way of thinking about concepts almost denies the validity of the concept 'concept' altogether. It sets out to show that concepts (certainly many of those of interest and importance to political theorists, such as 'woman', 'community', liberty'), are unstable and perhaps unsustainable. This instability can be shown by examining the terms in use, in texts. Here conceptual analysis is intimately bound up with textual analysis and reading.[30]

Arguably, whichever of these four ways of conceptualizing concept we favour, the process of analysing begins, at least, with interpretation. For

[27] Hegel thought that philosophy, eventually, could discern the outline and content of 'concepts', G. W. F. Hegel's *Philosophy of Right* (1st pub. 1821), trans. T. M. Knox (Oxford: Clarendon Press, 1952), Preface, pp. 12–13; in Chapter 2 I associated this model of conceptual analysis also with G. E. Moore.

[28] Wittgenstein, *Philosophical Investigations*, I, ss. 71, 76.

[29] William Connolly, *The Terms of Political Discourse*, 2nd edn. (Oxford: Basil Blackwell, 1983); Raymond Plant, 'Community: Concept, Conception and Ideology', *Politics and Society*, 8 (1978), 79–107.

[30] Judith Butler, *Gender Trouble: Feminism and the Subversion of Identity* (New York: Routledge, 1990), p. ix; Jacques Derrida, 'Différance', in *Margins of Philosophy* (Hemel Hempstead: Harvester Wheatsheaf, 1982).

nobody has ever argued that the object of analysis—a concept—is obvious. Concepts don't parade before us, with all their elements labelled, their referents indicated by arrows, and their connotations attached. Rather, terms are used in texts, and their relationship to concepts is inferred by reading. The 'content' of concepts can only be analysed by way of reading and interpreting use—by interpreting what writers and speakers include, exclude, imply, and refer to when they use a term (deploy a concept).

But all of this begs the question 'What is interpretation?'

A MODEL OF INTERPRETATION

There is a vast literature on interpretation and hermeneutics, and there is no space in this work for an exhaustive analysis of its philosophical history, the varying approaches to interpretation in social science, philosophy, and elsewhere, and the disputes between them. Instead I propose to approach the question of the relationship between community and interpretation by constructing a model of interpretation. First, I shall set out the elements and relations of a skeleton model of interpretation, and then use this to indicate which aspects of interpretation are subject to controversy, and where different theories of interpretation compete with each other.

I	II	III	IV	V	VI
Thing	Author of thing interpreted	Meaning of thing interpreted	Interpreter	Interpretation (Product of process of interpretation)	Audience

Diagram 3.1 The elements of a model of interpretation

This is a very minimal 'model of interpretation'. But it is not minimal enough to be quite uncontentious. For instance, discussions of interpretation that commence by setting out some basic elements often omit the audience at the outset. For example Charles Taylor's analysis of interpretation begins with 'object' or 'field of objects', its/their meaning, and the subject 'for whom these meanings are'.[31] Taylor remarks that the identification of this 'subject' is likely to be problematic; I would argue that the

---

[31] Charles Taylor, 'Interpretation and the Sciences of Man', 15–16. Dworkin in *Law's Empire* begins his analysis of interpretation in a 'community' setting—in which the 'interpreter' has as an attentive audience his community co-members—p. 46.

subject is invariably complex, consisting of the Author, the Interpreter, and the Audience, (although, of course, these may conceivably coincide in one physical person). Often, but not invariably, the Author may be a person: a writer, a speaker, the author of a gesture, or otherwise producer of a text or text analogue. I say not invariably, because for some theorists a contested abstraction like God, or 'nature' might be positioned as the Author of the kind of Thing that is susceptible to interpretation. There is also the question whether non-human animals, like dogs, or even amoebas, can be thought of as authors in this sense. George Herbert Mead contrasts the reflexive abilities of human beings as compared to other mammals. Two dogs encountering one another have a 'conversation of gestures' which can be wholly modelled in stimulus-response terms. In contrast, symbolized and mutually recognized meanings emerge out of human interaction: 'the organism is able to point out meanings to others and to himself'.[32] The Author and the Interpreter may be the same individual—it is quite common for us to engage in interpretation of our own texts (utterances, writing, gestures, etc.). The Interpreter and the Audience may be the same individual. I may, as it were, say to myself, 'Whatever does that mean?' and then, having engaged in interpretation, respond to myself 'Oh it means . . .'. And, of course, live Authors will often be members of the Audience for Interpretations of their own work.[33]

A good deal of confusion stems from the fact that theorists and philosophers focus on different kinds of 'Thing'. Philosophy has often focused on sentences, propositions, or utterances. Aesthetic and cultural critics focus on poems, films, symphonies, novels, and paintings. Social theorists focus on the one hand on gestures, actions, signs, and symbols, and on the other on practices, discourses, and states of affairs. It is controversial whether Interpretation bears the same analysis in the cases of these various objects. Ronald Dworkin, for instance, draws a distinction between 'conversational interpretation' and the 'creative interpretation' of an entity which has been made by people but which is then independent of the Author—texts, pictures, films, social practices, and social institutions. Dworkin argues that conversational interpretation 'assigns meaning in the

[32] George Herbert Mead, *On Social Psychology*, (ed). Anselm Strauss (Chicago: University of Chicago Press, 1956). Mead's account of interpretation does incorporate 'audience', in the shape of the I *v.* Me distinction—I am my own interlocutor and audience.

[33] For rueful accounts of the experiencing of hearing and reading interpretations of one's own work see Judith Butler, *Bodies that Matter* (New York: Routledge, 1993), pp. ix–xi; Fish, *Is There a Text in this Class?*, 303–4. According to Margaret Canovan, Hannah Arendt was 'unmoved' by misreadings of her books: Margaret Canovan, *Hannah Arendt: A Reinterpretation of her Political Thought* (Cambridge: Cambridge University Press, 1992), 2–3.

light of the motives and purposes and concerns it supposes the speaker to have, and it reports its conclusions as statements about his "intention" in saying what he did'.[34] By contrast in creative interpretation intentions cannot have this privileged position. Dworkin considers and rejects the argument that Author's intentions, on the contrary, do and should have a central place in the interpretation of pictures, music, novels, and social practices. He does this on the grounds that in the interpretation of such entities the interests and purposes of the Interpreter come into play.[35]

Some of the most animated debates in connection with interpretation concern the issue of the relevance of the Author's intentions.[36] In the case of conversation many philosophers, like Dworkin, incline to take it for granted that here speaker's intention exhausts meaning. However, this theory is unconvincing. Rather, speakers' intentions do make some difference, but they do not settle the matter. Choices of words, gestures, expressions, and demeanours are often bones of contention, and it is not simply up to speakers to say what they meant. There can be a gap between what a speaker wants to say or do and what she or he actually says or does, and the gap is bridged by the meaning of the words, gestures, etc. which is not simply a matter of the speaker's intentions.[37] Further than this, discourse and conversation analyses reveal many examples of dialogue and utterances where speakers' intentions are opaque (including to themselves), or exceedingly complex, and themselves susceptible to endless interpretation.[38]

In the case of texts, it is also a common view that meaning coincides with just what the Author intends the text to mean. The Interpreter, on this theory of meaning, has recourse to the intentions of the Author, to what she or he was trying to say, when determining what the thing means. For their part, Audiences will make reference to the Thing, and to the Author's intentions, when they assess the goodness of the Interpretation.

---

[34] Dworkin, *Law's Empire*, 50.   [35] Ibid. 52.

[36] Quentin Skinner, 'Some Problems in the Analysis of Political Thought and Action', *Political Theory*, 2 (1974), 277–303; 'From Hume's Intentions to Deconstruction and Back'; Dworkin, *Law's Empire*, 55 ff.

[37] Morally, of course, not intending to be offensive—being offensive accidentally, as it were—may mean that a speaker is less blameworthy than she or he would otherwise have been, just as accidentally hitting someone with your umbrella is less blameworthy than deliberately doing so. From the point of view of the recipient of the offence or the blow, though, it must be acknowledged that the pain is considerable either way.

[38] Examples include such familiar conversations as 'I've failed, I know I've failed . . .' repeated, where the speaker's intentions are complex to say the least of it (from Blakemore, *Understanding Utterances*, 32–4), or the kinds of conversational interjections where it is not obvious that the speaker has any intentions at all—the absence of intentions does not make utterances meaningless.

Clearly there is a complication where the nature of 'Authorship' is contested—for instance in the case of holy writings; or where the existence of an Author at all is a question, for instance, with such Things as thunderbolts and plagues. But more significantly, many theorists emphasize, in the first place, that Authors are not in control of the Meaning of Things they produce: there can be a significant gap between what they intended or were trying to mean, and what they mean. It is now a familiar (although not uncontested) view in some literary theory and associated critical methods that the intentions of the Author are discounted in the process of critically setting out, responding to, and otherwise rendering the meaning of a novel or a poem. The important relationships here are between readers of various sorts, and the text they read.

We should consider, although it will not detain us long, that the Meaning of the Thing interpreted is a simple property of, or somehow intrinsic to, the Thing, as, for example, its size is. If this were so there would never be any dispute about meaning. In terms of Diagram 3.1 this state of affairs would be depicted by superimposing (III) on (I). More often than this, theorists and philosophers consider the Meaning of the Thing to inhere somewhere and somehow in the space of relations between the Thing, the Author's intentions, the Interpreter's process and production of Interpretation, and the Audience. That is Meaning depends on the relation between Things and social subjects (Authors, Interpreters, observers, and interested parties)

Diagram 3.2 introduces a number of sets of relations between the various subjects, things, and meanings. First, and most commonsensically we

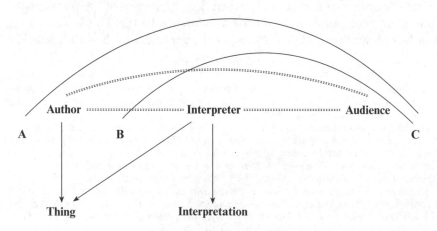

Diagram 3.2 The relations of interpretation

can think of the Author, where there is one, as producing the Thing, while the Interpreter produces the Interpretation. (The relations 'produce' is represented on the diagram by arrows.) However, some theorists emphasize that there is a significant sense in which the Interpreter produces the Thing too—that the act, the practice of interpretation is constitutive of the Thing, it is not independent of interpretation. For example, in the case of literary studies Stanley Fish argues that 'the text' including its formal properties (such as 'sections', 'passages' etc.) is 'always a function of the interpretive model one brings to bear, (they are not "in the text"). Indeed, the text as an entity independent of interpretation and (ideally) responsible for its career drops out and is replaced by the texts that emerge as the consequence of our interpretive activities.'[39]

Secondly, I have been talking about Author, Interpreter, and Audience quite conventionally as social beings: they may be one and the same person, or they may be many persons variously distributed among these functions. As such they are connected by complex strands of social relations: as critic and audience, conversationalists, communicators, and receivers; and there may be temporal gaps or complicated chronological links (such as the link that connects 'us' to the Athenian democrats). (These social relations are represented on the diagram by dotted lines.) But theorists of interpretation often emphasize a particular set of links between these parties—that is, that they share Background Meanings, or 'live within a horizon', or 'participate in a language game', or 'inhabit a conceptual scheme'.[40] Charles Taylor puts it that 'Things only have meaning in a field, that is in relation to the meanings of other things', and that our interpretation of some Thing as, for example, a symptom of 'shame' depends on our inhabiting a shared world of actions, practices, and meanings: 'In the end we are in on this because we grow up in the ambit of certain common meanings.'[41] The rightness, correctness, defensibility of the Interpretation of some gesture as, for example, symptomatic of shame, equally, depends upon our Audience sharing those practices and meanings (that is, on there

---

[39] Fish, *Is There a Text in this Class?*, 13.

[40] 'Live within a horizon' is an image from phenomenological philosophy—see H. G. Gadamer, *Truth and Method* (London: Sheed and Ward, 1975), 245 ff., 302 ff.; see also Habermas, *Logic of the Social Sciences*, 151–3; 'participate in a language game': Wittgenstein, *Philosophical Investigations*, I, ss. 7, 23; 'inhabit a conceptual scheme': W. V. O. Quine, *Word and Object* (Cambridge, Mass.: MIT Press, 1960), 123; Thomas Kuhn, 'Second Thoughts on Paradigms', in id., *The Essential Tension: Selected Studies in Scientific Tradition and Change* (Chicago: University of Chicago Press, 1977), 293–7; for criticism Donald Davidson, 'On the Very Idea of a Conceptual Scheme', *Inquiries into Truth and Interpretation* (Oxford: Oxford University Press, 1984), 183–98.

[41] Taylor, 'Interpretation and the Sciences of Man', 24; also Habermas, *Logic of the Social Sciences*, 151–3.

being an incorporating arc of 'background meanings' represented in Diagram 3.2 by B–C) or indeed, on the Author of the action or gesture in question also being an individual who inhabits a culture or way of life in which 'shame' and its cognates feature (that is, there is an arc of background meanings represented in Diagram 3.2 by A–C).

Things typically do not come with their meaning written plain upon their faces. As we have seen, a complex set of relations—linguistic, social, and cultural—contributes to the production, (and the acceptance, or currency), of an Interpretation. Different Interpreters might produce different, rival, Interpretations. This, of course, raises the problem of adjudication between competing Interpretations. Most philosophers and theorists agree that some Interpretations can certainly be said to be false. It follows from this that the severe anxiety (or anger) expressed by many critics who protest that interpretivism slides inevitably into a radical relativism in which, according to its apologists, anything can mean anything, is misplaced—this is not an implication of interpretivism, and it is difficult to find a real theorist (as opposed to a straw person) who seriously proposes this.[42] For Wittgenstein that interpretations can be wrong seems to be a conceptual matter: 'Now it is easy to recognise cases in which we are *interpreting*. When we interpret we form hypotheses, which may prove false.'[43] Others are less epistemologically confident than Wittgenstein seems to be at this point. Stanley Fish, for instance, argues that interpretation is constrained—there are limits to what it is possible to interpret any utterance, symbol, or more discursive text as meaning in any given context. However, there seem to be few limits on what, in possible worlds not very different from our own, texts could mean.[44]

We might take issue also with Wittgenstein's drawing of a clear-ish distinction here between 'seeing' and 'seeing as' ('seeing is a state') and interpreting ('To interpret is to think to do something').[45] He also draws a clear-ish distinction between 'just obeying a rule' and interpreting the rule: 'there is an inclination to say: every action according to the rule is an interpretation. But we ought to restrict the term "interpretation" to the substitution of one expression of the rule for another'.[46] Against this, Habermas argues that, indeed, Wittgenstein overlooks that

He who has learned to apply . . . rules has learned not only to express himself in a language but also to interpret expressions in this language. Translation with respect to what is outside and translation with respect to what is inside must both,

---

[42] Fish, *Is There a Text in this Class?*, chs. 15, 16.
[43] Wittgenstein, *Philosophical Investigations*, pt. II xi (212e).
[44] Fish, *Is There a Text in this Class?*, 346–9.
[45] Wittgenstein, *Philosophical Investigations*, II xi (212e).   [46] Ibid. s. 201.

in principle, be possible. Along with their possible application, grammatical rules also imply the necessity of an interpretation.[47]

Joseph Raz, like Wittgenstein, takes it that interpretation must be intentional and conscious 'One has to offer it as an interpretation to be interpreting'. Interpretation 'has to be meant as such'.[48] Yet, when we consider the complexity of social relations between Interpreter and Audience, we can see how an Interpretation can shift modality from the status of Interpretation proper to that of 'fact' or 'accepted as true' or 'commonsensical' or 'authoritative'. In this process audiences can lose sight of the interpretive status of interpretations. They can become sedimented as, to all intents and purposes, as brute a set of facts as one could wish to meet. But, contrary to Raz's and Wittgenstein's view, they are no less Interpretations. The problem seems to be in the 'process-product' ambiguity: 'interpretation' as I have taken some pains to signal throughout this analysis refers both to a human action or practice, and to the product of that action or practice. Raz and Wittgenstein in insisting on the role of conscious intentionality are focusing only on the 'process' side; but what exercises many interpretivist theorists is the role and place of 'interpretations' (the product) in the social world.

It seems clear enough that social power must be a relevant factor in the acceptance or sedimentation of interpretations (or to put it a different way, in the convergence on a conventional interpretation). On the one hand we have clear cases—administrative state power has a role in establishing that red lights mean 'stop', to be interpreted as having a similar meaning to a police officer's hand raised with palm towards you, the words 'stop' uttered by parent to small child, and so on. On the other hand we have contested cases. It is unlikely (although not inconceivable) that anyone would wish to challenge the meaning of red lights; but very familiar that individuals and groups wish to challenge the meaning of gestures, ways of speaking, signs, and symbols. Social life is marked by explosions of conflict about what words, gestures, classes of actions mean—what they signify, what connotations they have, what they do in the contested space of social relations. (A recent problem in British life is the public kiss of greeting, especially but not only between men. The authoritative answer from a problem page journalist to a worried correspondent is that this is not a sign of erotic attraction, effeminacy, nor other moral degeneracy.[49]) There

---

[47] Habermas, *Logic of the Social Sciences*, 149.

[48] Joseph Raz, 'Morality as Interpretation: On Walzer's *Interpretation and Social Criticism*', *Ethics*, 101 (1991), 403.

[49] I regret that I can't give the reference for this—I read it in a magazine in my doctor's waiting room.

are many familiar examples associated with civil and political life, which is frequently marked by the political display of symbols and symbolic actions intended by their promoters to change their moral value, from 'deviant' to 'normal', or from 'shameful' to 'proper'. Rival interpretations of the meaning of these are typically offered by participants who have the chance publicly to articulate their interpretations and intentions through the available media, by journalists and editors, by onlookers.

Or consider the major political innovation that is the subject of this book—the promotion of the value of community, the interpretation of social goals as the building of community, the identification of groups and networks as communities. Political communitarianism is studded with interrogations of meaning, with clashes of interpretation. A report of a poor woman's 'work in the community' gives pause for interpretation—it seems to mean 'work in the neighbourhood'.[50] The hope that 'localities come to life as communities' begs the question 'as what?'[51] Gordon Brown argues that the 1980s were characterized by 'too little community and too little fairness'.[52] 'What do these warm words of community and duty actually mean?' asks a sympathetic journalist,[53] and answers theoretically— that is, she gives an account of the conditions under which community might be realized: a new equilibrium between rights and responsibilities, local community activism, the development of 'extensive social networks', and 'the traditional family'.[54] The connotation of 'warmth' is taken as read; other connotations, such as 'timelessness' and 'immediacy' are not spelled out. Such connotations impress themselves on critics who are then sceptical about the value of community, and sceptical about the possibility of the conditions for its realization.[55] And in response to this, communitarians recast the concept of community, suppressing some of its elements (immediacy, collectivism) and emphasizing others (reciprocity), and retheorizing it into 'a community of individuals'.[56] But the theoretical work that sets out to show that we can coherently conceptualize com-

[50] Marcia Davis, 'Open Arms', *Washington Post* (20 Feb. 1996), p. B01.

[51] Michael Young and Gerard Lemos, 'Root of Revival', *Guardian* (19 Mar. 1997), pt. 2, p. 2.

[52] Gordon Brown, 'Beware the Mask of Tory Social Concern', *Observer* (2 Dec. 1990).

[53] Melanie Phillips, 'The Race to Wake Sleeping Duty', *Observer* (2 Apr. 1995), 25.

[54] Phillips, 'The Race to Wake Sleeping Duty', and 'Getting Lone Parents off Benefits . . .' *Observer Review* (14 Dec. 1997), 2.

[55] For example William F. Power, 'The Lane Less Travelled', *Washington Post* (3 Feb. 1995), p. D01, says: 'There is one really sublime moment in bowling . . . you stand, all by yourself . . . They say we are bowling alone. And so we are.'

[56] Brown, 'Beware the Mask'.

munity as consistent with individualism[57] does not settle the interpretive issue, which is that readers vary in their understanding of the meaning of the term, and engage in disputes about what is a defensible or valid interpretation.

Doubt is cast, when we consider this kind of example, on the principle that interpretations should be adjudicated, as Taylor puts it, by reference to 'our understanding', 'an ultimate appeal to a common understanding of the expressions, of the "language" involved'.[58] Of course, 'our understanding' might yield to us an appreciation of the range of possible ways that these gestures in that social context might be interpreted by a variety of kinds of social actor. As the foregoing discussion suggests, we can see that welfare liberals will wish to construct an analysis of community such that it is consistent with rational individualism: libertarians will tend to emphasize those aspects of community that are antithetical to individuality; sympathetic writers' deployment of the connotations of 'warmth' will be taken by radical critics to connote 'suffocation'. But 'our understanding' does not get us very far in adjudicating between these competing interpretations. However, taking the view that all of these competing understandings are justified, as it were, raises the spectre of the idiosyncratic and subjective multiplication of interpretations between which adjudication is well nigh impossible.[59] In the communitarian literature we can find two main kinds of response to the dilemma in which Charles Taylor's approach to interpretation seems to leave us. First, there are liberal responses from Michael Walzer and Ronald Dworkin. Stanley Fish proposes a much more uncomfortable (for both liberals and philosophical and political communitarians) view of the nature of institutional power.

Michael Walzer attempts to steer a middle course between subjectivism and objectivism. He characterizes the interpretive task in ethics and political theory as the retrieval of the understandings a community has of itself, its values, and the world: 'to interpret to one's fellow citizens the world of meanings that we share'.[60] But he also emphasizes the critical social role of the Interpreter—shared meanings and everyday practices might be incoherent, there might be contradiction between principles and practices; the best reading might be a new reading.[61] Critics can exploit the larger meanings of key terms to reveal weaknesses in conventional usage.[62]

---

[57] For instance Robert Goodin, 'Review Article: Communities of Enlightenment', *British Journal of Political Science*, 28 (1998), 531–58.
[58] Taylor, 'Interpretation and the Sciences of Man', 17.
[59] Warnke, *Justice and Interpretation*, 10.
[60] Walzer, *Spheres of Justice*, p. xiv.
[61] Walzer, *Interpretation and Social Criticism*, 29–30.   [62] Ibid. 43.

Ronald Dworkin in his analysis of the interpretive process also emphasizes the key social roles of the political philosopher, the judge, the Interpreter. According to Dworkin the Interpreter studies the history of an institution, or practice, or a concept, and responds to the normative question how that institution, practice, or concept ought to be in light of this history, and in light of the requirements of coherence, consistency, intelligibility. This Interpretation is 'creative'.[63] There can be nothing 'value-free' or 'neutral' or strongly objective about his judgement. On the other hand, it is the practices, of interpretation itself in open societies, and of law, morality, art, conversation, communication, etc. which validate these interpretations.

Stanley Fish considers, for the most part, competing Interpretations of texts such as poems and novels. He is concerned to establish that two competing and inconsistent Interpretations of the meaning of a poem can't be adjudicated by appeal to the text itself (because it is precisely textual elements that are presented as evidence for both the interpretations), nor to the intentions of the Author which are, given existing data, obscure on the point in question (and, indeed, rival Interpreters can each point to biographical and related details in support of their interpretations).[64] Fish's 'solution' to the problem is that 'interpretive communities' are prior to Interpreters. (In the terms of my Diagram 3.2 that is, all those individuals who are incorporated in a relevant arc of background meanings, or who are within the same horizon, or who share a field of background meanings). At one point Fish refers to 'those who share interpretive strategies', then corrects himself:

Even this formulation is not quite correct. The phrase 'those who share interpretive strategies' suggests that individuals stand apart from the communities to which they now and then belong. In later essays I will make the point that since the thoughts an individual can think and the mental operations he can perform have their source in some or other interpretive community, he is as much a product of that community (acting as an extension of it) as the meanings it enables him to produce.[65]

How then are rival interpretations to be adjudicated? Fish sees them as clashes between rival communities, or sub-communities. There is a 'literary community', there are sub-communities such as New Historicists and Deconstructionists, which map (although not perfectly) onto departments in this or that university. Within any community 'the boundaries of the acceptable are continually being redrawn', individuals move from one community to another, and within communities there are influential or

[63] Dworkin, *Law's Empire*, 50.   [64] Fish, *Is There a Text in this Class?*, 339–42.
[65] Ibid. 14.

authority figures who may have significant influence on innovation or its absence.[66] This plurality of interpretive communities makes agreement about an Interpretation (and interpretive methods) plausible and likely. It also means that disagreement (between communities) is equally inevitable. And it means that the promotion of Interpretations is a matter of persuasion, or authority.[67]

This conclusion about the importance of the authority of the Interpreter is implicit, I would argue, in Walzer's and Dworkin's emphases on the social roles of critic, philosopher, and judge. Dworkin represents a scene in which people from a society or 'community' ask a philosopher to elucidate their institutions for them, and make a judgement in the case of disagreements; he also, in trying to lay out the complex structure of legal interpretation, uses 'an imaginary judge of superhuman intellectual power and patience who accepts law as integrity. Call him Hercules.'[68] Thus Dworkin's heuristic for the acceptance of interpretation involves the use of expertise, wisdom, charisma—and power. Walzer emphasizes, by contrast, that 'Marginality has often been a condition that motivates criticism'. Marginal people are ambiguously connected to 'the community', but they are not 'detached' or 'dispassionate' or 'estranged'.[69] Also important are 'local judges', the 'connected critic',[70] and the 'mundane critic' whose discourse comes close to common complaint, and is very ordinary and familiar.[71]

COMMUNITY AND INTERPRETATION

What does 'community' mean here? First, it seems clear that in these contexts these theorists mean: a group of persons who share meanings. As we saw in Chapter 2, according to some communitarian philosophers this is more or less it. Charles Taylor says shared meanings are the basis of community

Common meanings are the basis of community. Inter-subjective meaning gives a people a common language to talk about social reality and a common understanding of certain norms, but only with common meanings does this common reference world contain significant common actions, celebrations, and feelings. These are objects in the world that everybody shares. This is what makes community.[72]

---

[66] Ibid. 343.   [67] Ibid. 15–16.
[68] Dworkin, *Law's Empire*, 68–73, 239; *Taking Rights Seriously*, 106 ff.
[69] Walzer, *Interpretation and Social Criticism*, 37–8.   [70] Ibid. 38.
[71] Walzer, *Thick and Thin*, 51.
[72] Taylor, 'Interpretation and the Sciences of Man', 39.

Shared meanings aren't all there is to community, for Taylor then, but they are a necessary basis for the other shared objects, practice, etc. that constitute community. And common meanings ground interpretations. This means that it is not acceptable to interpret 'all other societies in the categories of our own';[73] and it means as we saw earlier that 'we can only convince an interlocutor [of the validity of our interpretation] if at some point he shares our understanding of the language concerned'.[74] Likewise, for Sandel, common meanings—a common vocabulary and a background of implicit practices and understandings—constitute community. A spirit of benevolence, shared aims, and particular values are not sufficient.[75] For Sandel, common meanings are necessary, although by themselves insufficient, for community. For Dworkin, community presupposes shared meanings, institutions, practices—it is not clear to me whether Dworkin thinks that any one of these is likely as a practical matter to involve the others; but as we saw in Chapter 2, in a 'true community' members will not only share meanings, institutions, and practices but each member will feel commitment to the meanings, practices, and institutions, and to the whole constituted by these. This will be a community of principle which will have moral legitimacy.[76] For Fish what is shared is understandings, specifically of literary meaning. His use of the term 'interpretive community' suggests that this is a partial community, as I called them in Chapter 2. Presumably, for Fish community can also be constituted by shared habitat, shared cultural identity, and so on. He does not here spend time exploring the relationship between 'interpretive community' and other forms.

To summarize, communitarians use the term 'community' very ambiguously. To begin with they propose that shared meanings are necessary for community. Only where there are shared meanings can there be the shared principles, values, ways of life, and institutions that constitute community. However, second, they sometimes seem to suggest that shared meanings might be a sufficient condition for community—sufficient to generate the other characteristics of community such as personalized relations and so forth. On the other hand, there is some warrant for thinking that the better way of interpreting the relevant passages is as discussions of a particular kind of 'partial community'. A linguistic community, an interpretive community, a community of meaning, are to be thought of as the same sort of partial communities as 'the business community', a 'local community', etc.—that is to say, as a group of people who are tied by the relation of sharing some good or some bad. But there is a lack of conviction here:

---

[73] Taylor, 'Interpretation and the Sciences of Man', 42.   [74] Ibid. 18.
[75] Sandel, *Liberalism and the Limits of Justice*, 172.
[76] Dworkin, *Law's Empire*, 214.

would not communitarians rather wish to say that a 'business community' can't really count as a community unless there are the shared meanings in addition to the other things that are shared? My reading of communitarianism is that this would be the case (i.e. shared meanings are necessary for community, any kind of community). And vice versa, it is often strongly suggested that where there are shared meanings there will be shared values—so that the category 'community of meaning' is misleading, because a community of meaning will be a community of much more than that. But the difficulty of reading communitarian and other texts about community so as to elucidate the meaning of that term is severe.

How should we conceptualize the background meanings by reference to which new things are interpreted and understood, which constrain new interpretations of old things? Clearly, we cannot think of these as anything like a straightforward corpus of definitions, a dictionary of meanings to which all speakers in principle have access, as though the background or horizon just is the *Oxford English Dictionary*. Some terms do have widely agreed 'core meanings' but none that is entirely resistant to change or contestation. Most interesting concepts either lack such core meaning or consist just in partially overlapping imperfectly convergent usage. As we saw in Chapter 2, too, the connotations, echoes, traces of suppressed or almost abandoned reference, traces of old or superseded or potential performances, form a shadowy and elusive aura around any instance of use of a word. The partially disclosed and the half-remembered, the shifting and coming into articulation of new meanings in new contexts, mean that meaning cannot be thought of as determinate—even within 'the community' (if we consent to call it that) of meaning.

This implies that between people who 'share meanings' or share language, interpretation is unavoidable. We cannot reserve the term 'interpretation' as Wittgenstein recommends for cases of conscious confrontation with some thing not understood. According to this view, to 'understand' is to have interpreted, and there need be no conscious moment of not understanding. However, this brings to the centre of the picture lack of coincidence between conversationalists, disagreement between language users, and conflict over meaning.

My discussion so far hints that what might generate new interpretations is new or newly understood social and political positions. The theorists discussed here emphasize the role of community in on the one hand validating interpretations and on the other explaining lack of agreement. We saw that implicit or explicit in these communitarian theories is the function of social roles, social positions, or social standpoints (the professor, the philosopher, the critic, the judge, the marginal) from which both to interpret and to promote or have accepted these interpretations. But more than this, the examples of conflict over gestures, words, and practices problematize differences in social position at the same time that they presuppose shared linguistic position. Subjects inevitably occupy a social standpoint, and this social standpoint is every bit as important as linguistic standpoint. The disputes about the meaning of community are political disputes; the disputes about kissing in public are generated by social and political disagreements about the nature of gender and sexuality and politeness.

This insight has generated a large corpus of interpretation—of texts, of social practices, of theories, of concepts—which makes social standpoint explicit. A considerable amount of this is premissed on the specificity of the position 'woman' or 'feminine'—women face particular ethical dilemmas, are unable to evade certain knowledges and responsibilities.[77] Other theorists emphasize the epistemological and ethical significance of the standpoint of 'the oppressed', or the 'subaltern'.[78] Debates about the relative merits and demerits of these projects focus on a variety of issues. An obvious objection is that, although a good many philosophers patently fail to abstract themselves away from their social standpoint (this is evident from the pervasiveness of particular varieties of masculinity in philosophical works) it should nevertheless be an enduring aim of philosophy to do this. But this philosophical project will not be furthered by substituting the standpoint of woman for that of 'detached man'. Philosophy, unlike social life, should not consist of competition and conflict between social positions. This challenge takes us right back to claims of 'neutrality' which interpretivism reveals to be unsustainable. Specific social standpoints will be present in philosophical analysis and interpretation. Importantly, we do not lack the tools to analyse just this.

However, communitarian theorists do not follow through completely the significance of the presence of standpoints in interpretation. Stanley Fish is quite clear about the significance of being a professor as opposed to a student, and in one university department rather than another, when

[77] For example Nancy Hartsock, 'The Feminist Standpoint: Developing the Ground for a Specifically Feminist Historical Materialism', in Sandra Harding and Merrill Hintikka (eds.), *Discovering Reality: Feminist Perspectives on Epistemology, Metaphysics and the Philosophy of Science* (Dordrecht: Reidel, 1983); Annette Baier, *Moral Prejudices: Essays on Ethics* (Cambridge, Mass.: Harvard University Press, 1994), 7; Virginia Held, 'Mothering versus Contract', in Jane Mansbridge, *Beyond Self Interest* (Chicago: Chicago University Press, 1990).

[78] Gayatri Chakravorti Spivak, 'Subaltern Studies: Deconstructing Historiography', in *In Other Worlds: Essays in Cultural Politics* (New York: Routledge, 1988); Dorothy Smith, 'A Sociology for Women', in Sandra Harding (ed.), *Feminism and Methodology* (Milton Keynes: Open University Press, 1987).

it comes to the promotion of interpretations. But this theme has implications for the conduct of politics and the conduct of interpretation which are not adequately dealt with by the concept 'interpretive community'. The communitarian philosophers emphasize membership of this rather than that 'community', and the difficulties of interpretation across community boundaries. As we have seen they emphasize special roles in the interpretive process. However, they tend not to follow up the implications of role differentiation and stratification within a 'community', nor the political implications of these, and, more important, the way the politics of interpretation are disruptive of 'community' relations.

Disputes about meanings are important political disputes. Theorists and activists face the problem of how to validate and secure acceptance of their interpretations. Undoubtedly, at moments when material relations are changing it is easier to secure rather widespread acceptance of meaning change. But this is not to say that meaning change follows passively on material change—rather the particular interpretations of material change that become widespread themselves depend upon prior efforts to redefine material relations. Acceptance of reinterpretations requires shared understandings—shared, that is, across alliances or coalitions; or by those who stand on a threshold of agreement about values and understandings. But it is important that at the self-same time as this is an appeal to or deployment of shared meanings, it is also a rejection of, or dissent from, some accepted meanings.

Now of course, in itself, this point does not invalidate the model of 'shared meanings' altogether. For it is consistent with that model that the meanings in question are unstable and contested. All that is needed is that members have the resources and the ability to communicate about meaning, and to attempt to explain to one another why they interpret as they do. But if the model of 'shared meanings' is held to make agreement about interpretations highly probable (as in Fish's 'interpretive community') then I think these considerations do give us grounds for rejecting the model. Dissenters from shared meanings in certain circumstances might make progress with individuals who maintain a conventional understanding. First, where they are moments, thresholds, over which communication occurs. It seems to me that with rival interpretations of terms like community this is likely to be so—it is a concept with some (albeit only liminal) core about which rivals can debate. However, as is common in political dialogue, the communication is likely to be a slow and possibly painful process, and the threshold is likely to be elusive—looking sometimes more like a barrier. Meaning transformation relies on difficult dialogue within shifting coalitions of interlocutors. Second, meaning change relies on the exertion of power within a range of institutions such as those of popular culture, in public spaces (such as the mass media), and in places of governance. If kissing among men ever becomes commonplace and conventional in Britain it will be because of the exertion of this kind of power in representation and in public conduct. Within these alliances and institutions it is important for individuals to be aware of who their fellows are, if they are to make reliable judgements about assent to or dissent from interpretations. That is, subtle and detailed knowledge about social identities and social standpoints is indispensable in the promotion of new interpretations and meanings.

Indeed, decisions to accept or reject existing interpretations involves, in part, considering the social identities of the producer of the interpretation, and the audience he was addressing—the conventional and shared meanings he was banking on in his efforts to have his interpretations accepted. Production of reinterpretations involves considering the social identities of the relevant audiences and partaking of (or exploiting) shared elements of meaning. In attending to the social standpoint of an interpreter, or members of the audience for our own interpretations, we have to attend not only to people's material position, but also to their sense of who they are and with whom they feel allegiance and alliance. That is to say, there is a reflexively political aspect to interpretation itself.

4

Social Constructionism

Social constructionism is a key strand in communitarianism. For instance, wherever philosophical communitarians protest against liberal individualism that what we *are* depends upon our social context, tradition, culture, or relations with others, they are making a social constructionist claim. When they argue that what counts as 'justice' or 'freedom' cannot be determined from some ahistorical non-particular vantage point, then they are arguing that values and ethical judgements are in some sense socially constructed. But in what sense? What, exactly, does this mean? In my view it means something quite precise, and I intend in this chapter to spell that out.

It is notable that this is an aspect of communitarianism that its critics tend to take violent exception to. 'Social constructionism', to its adherents seemingly the most commonsensical analysis of social reality, ethics, human action, and so on, strikes its detractors as contemptible if not beneath contempt.[1] It seems to have this polarizing effect also in the social sciences and humanities more generally. The concept 'social reality' is peculiarly controversial in the philosophy of social sciences, and even more so among social scientists and researchers. When it is teamed with the concept 'construction' all kinds of theorists, researchers, and philosophers are inclined to sneer. And the term 'social construction' can make them positively apoplectic.

Partly, this is a simple matter of the hostility to 'metaphysics' common among social scientists. There is particular impatience on the part of some with debates about reality and realism—these seem to irritate social scientists much more than the equally thorny concepts 'truth' and 'validity'. Among others there is the principled view that questions of ontology (the nature of existence and what exists) are irrelevant,[2] or the view that

---

[1] If conversations I have been involved in and had reported to me are anything to go by.

[2] For example, the anthropologist and social theorist Clifford Geertz argues, 'The thing to ask about a burlesqued wink or a mock sheep raid is not what their ontological status is. It is the same as rocks on the one hand, and dreams on the other—they are things of this world. The thing to ask is what their import is: what it is, ridicule or challenge, irony or anger, snobbery or pride, that, in their occurrence and through their agency, is getting

too much focus on ontology inclines analysts to make mistakes—to reify processes, procedures, and algorithms into entities.[3] Equally significant for my present purposes is that among philosophers there is an unaccountable aversion to serious analysis of the predicate 'social', even where they feel the need to deploy the concept in critiques of explanation, the analysis of concepts, or whatever.[4]

Unfortunately, debates on the topic of social constructionism tend to be unedifyingly bad tempered, with social constructionists and their critics frequently at cross purposes.[5] It is often difficult to discern what is at issue—whether, for instance, it is the argument that *anything* might be socially constructed, or whether it is a specific claim that *some particular thing or class of things* is socially constructed, that causes offence.[6] In

said.' 'Thick Description: Toward an Interpretive Theory of Culture', in *The Interpretation of Cultures* (1st pub. 1973) (London: Fontana, 1993), 10. It is notable that Geertz is inclined to find questions of ontology uninteresting by virtue of his view that 'things of this world' all have the same ontological status.

[3] For example, Henrietta L. Moore, *A Passion for Difference* (Oxford: Polity Press, 1994), 47: 'much social science theory . . . consists of ontologising local norms'.

[4] For instance, Bernard Williams in *Making Sense of Humanity* (Cambridge: Cambridge University Press, 1995) discusses why biological approaches and analyses of human life are insufficient. First, we need at the outset an ethological understanding of the phenomena that the biological explanation purports to explain (p. 81); second, some intentions must be explained in 'irreducibly social terms' (p. 86). But Williams offers no analysis of what that means—he offers us examples of 'what count as social factors: matters of class etc'. There are some relevant analytic papers: Maurice Mandelbaum, 'Societal Facts', *British Journal of Sociology*, 6 (1955) repr. in Alan Ryan (ed.), *The Philosophy of Social Explanation* (Oxford: Oxford University Press, 1973), 105–18; Stuart Hampshire, 'Social Objects', *Proceedings of the Aristotelian Society*, 76 (1975–6), 1–27.

[5] The first version of the argument in this paper was written in 1995. Reading the theoretical and philosophical material on social construction was a dispiriting experience as the debate seemed ill-focused. Responses to my paper, which I delivered at two conferences and a couple of seminars, also ranged from the lukewarm to the frankly impatient. Whilst freely admitting that that could have been because of the quality of my presentation I also harbour the view that it was something to do with the unsatisfactory nature of the whole debate. After finishing the third draft of this chapter in the summer of 1998 I read a new collection of papers: Irving Velody and Robin Williams (eds.), *The Politics of Constructionism* (London: Sage, 1998), which treats the topic with the seriousness I think it deserves, sorts out many confusions, and is unmarred by the petulance and vitriol (Velody and Williams more mildly call it 'irritable suspicion' (p. 3)) of some of the existing literature. It also contains a paper by Ian Hacking ('On Being More Literal about Construction') that, sadly for me, makes a number of the points I want to make in this chapter, only better. My argument for more specificity in social constructionism appears in outline in 'Construction and Social Construction' (review of John Searle *The Social Construction of Reality*), *Imprints*, 1 (1997), 71–9. I have incorporated references to some of the material from Velody and Williams into the final version of this chapter.

[6] For example, see Mario Bunge, 'New Sociology of Science, Part I', *Philosophy of the Social Sciences*, 21 (1991), 524–60. Bunge distinguishes between the view that knowledge is socially constructed, which he concedes is acceptable, up to a point, and the view that reality is socially constructed, which 'flies in the face of evidence'. He takes exception to the

response, I argue that it is certainly not preposterous to presume that some things might be socially constructed. Presuming that some things might be socially constructed does not, of course, entail that we presume that *all* things are socially constructed. Of course, theorists and researchers must specify

- what is constructed (or not); and, if it is constructed,
- what it is constructed out of; and
- how.

And it is true that in many arguments and disputes it is difficult to get this quite clear. This is a pity.

It is worth noting at this point that the term 'social construction' is ambiguous. Construction (like interpretation) encompasses the process-product ambiguity, to begin with. This is significant, because some objections to constructionism dwell on the emphasis on process, while others dwell on the emphasis on product, adding to the general sense of confusion if the ambiguity is not spelled out. For example, some critics seem to say that 'social constructionism' reifies into a 'thing' or, rather, a pseudo-thing, sets of phenomena and processes which should be properly analysed out—are not actually thing-like at all. A range of critics are very irritated with social constructionism on these grounds, including some who would normally be surprised to find themselves in the same camp on any matter. For instance, rational choice theorists are frequently very suspicious of 'thing talk', preferring to focus on the individual's subjective perceptions of constraints and opportunities, his preferences and his rational calculations. Better strategies spread as routines; norms become constraints.[7] But to think of these things as 'entities' is inappropriate (mainly, I think, because rational choice theorists fear it will shift theoretical focus from endogenous (to the actor) action to exogenous determination). Phenomenologists and ethnomethodologists are equally averse to any emphasis on 'things' as they too focus on the individual actor's intentional and active attitude to the world he inhabits.[8]

Other critics, by contrast, are suspicious of social constructionism's emphasis on process. For philosophers and researchers in the positivist and empiricist traditions, constantly harping on how 'things' came to be, and the implication that they may have been and yet might be otherwise,

view that scientific theories, 'facts', etc. can be socially constructed, but his way of approaching the problem seems to be, first, to lump all 'social constructionists' together, and, second, to imply that *nothing* could be socially constructed, really.

[7] Jon Elster, *Nuts and Bolts for the Social Sciences* (Cambridge: Cambridge University Press, 1989), 79.

[8] I discuss these 'actor centred' objections to social constructionism further below.

is scientifically unsound or politically objectionable or both. Scientifically unsound because scientific endeavour should concentrate rather on elucidating the causal and other relations between observables and measurables, and seeking the universal laws which in turn explain our observations. Politically objectionable because positivists in principle believe that science must stick to a 'value-free' approach which accepts just what there is. Going 'behind' the 'facts' to reveal how they came to be constructed misses the important scientific point. To compound the fault, theorists who are inclined to treat 'things' or 'facts' as social constructs, are inclined to go on to approach 'theories' and even 'knowledge' as socially constructed too; and, worse, to think of social constructionism itself as socially constructed.

Yet other critics are quite happy with the social constructionist's approach to the constructive process, but consider social constructionism to be wrong-headed because of its relativistic implications. These are thought to be discredited by developments in evolutionary and biological theory and research, which is behind a good deal of recent resurgence of universalism. Arguments for the 'social construction' of, for instance, standards of human beauty or conventions of human parenting, have come under sustained attack from evolutionary biologists and geneticists who set out to show, first, that alleged cross-cultural or cross-historical differences don't exist, and second that the uniformities in human behaviour are explicable in evolutionary terms.[9] Rational choice theorists who conceive of a particular structure of rationality, and particular standards of rational behaviour as universal take this kind of line too.[10]

Yet other critics might take the line that the emphasis on process is fair enough for many kinds of things, but that the process in question is not 'construction'. Rather, for a large class of things, we should talk about 'emergence' or 'evolution'. The process of construction entails an agent— a builder or builders, a maker or makers. A better, more parsimonious account of the ontology of a range of phenomena can dispense with any 'constructor'—processes of emergent properties and evolving entities are quite sufficient.[11] Alternatively, we can conceptualize many things as the upshot of a process of 'accretion'—the gradual laying down and harden-

[9] Devendra Singh, 'Adaptive Significance of Female Physical Attractiveness: Role of Waist to Hip Ratio', *Journal of Personality and Social Psychology*, 65 (1993), 293–307; Paul Ekman, 'Facial Expressions and Emotion', *American Psychologist*, 48 (1993), 384–92, are two examples.

[10] Michael Hechter, 'The Role of Values in Rational Choice Theory', *Rationality and Society*, 6 (1994), 318–33.

[11] In a rational choice, rational expectations mode, Martin Hollis argues this way in *The Cunning of Reason* (Cambridge: Cambridge University Press, 1987).

ing of layers of material. This metaphor just begs the question of the meaning of construction—we do talk of 'geological construction' after all—to which I return below.

CONSTRUCTIONISM

This term is deployed and explored in many philosophical, theoretical, and scientific contexts. In many branches of philosophy—logic, language, mind, science, epistemology, metaphysics, ethics, and no doubt others— arguments proceed between constructivists, realists, positivists, empiricists, phenomenologists, and other -ists.[12] What does construction mean? So what does constructionism focus on? In this discussion I do not survey what philosophers have taken it to mean and imply, nor exactly in what respects it differs from realism, empiricism and so on. Instead, I just try to focus on the concept 'construction', and consider some of the controversies in the communitarian and the relevant social science literatures in the light of that conceptual analysis. Construction means both the process of making things, and the thing that is made. More specifically, to construct something is to shape materials, to assemble and to join together more basic elements, to make a complex entity. Users of the term construction vary, predictably enough, in what they seem to mean by it. An obvious (to me) meaning is the product of fixing different elements or parts, made of different kinds of materials, together. Analysts vary as to whether they think of materials—many of which are made of a complex of ingredients—also as constructions (rather than just as mixtures). I mentioned above the question whether a process of accretion is a process of construction. Also, is the cutting, shaping, moulding etc. of the material construction? It is safe enough to say, then, that 'construction' is a concept with fuzzy boundaries. The resulting equivocation in use contributes to the sense that constructionist theories are vague.

However, they are also prominent and important. For example, John Rawls takes a constructivist approach to moral and political theory. In Rawls's work, an ideal deliberator who is ignorant of many of his personal characteristics and of his social position, constructs a procedural model of justice. The model is built up, based on axioms and fundamental principles, but also shaped to fit its context—the context of culturally and socially rooted values, beliefs, and moral practices. As we saw in Chapter 1 the method of 'reflective equilibrium' governs the final content and

[12] Hacking, 'On Being More Literal about Construction', 52–5 covers some of the varieties of constructionism in philosophy.

structure of a moral theory.[13] Ronald Dworkin takes, as we saw in Chapter 3, a 'constructivist' approach to philosophical interpretation. The philosopher begins with an interpretive problem, say the need to say what justice for a particular society should entail. He looks at what different people and groups of people seem to mean by justice, he tries to work out what is the 'trunk' of this 'conceptual tree' and what are the various branches that have grown out of the trunk; he considers the various branches in relation to the trunk, and also considers the trunk itself, bringing to bear the philosophical canons of consistency, coherence, right, etc. He builds, and presents to members of the society, a coherent model of justice which is true to their concept and conception, but which has eliminated incoherence and inconsistency, and perhaps has developed its strongest features.[14] These are two cases of 'construction' which are not, according to their authors, *social* construction (although some critics may argue with this). Rawls and Dworkin are both talking about philosophical construction, i.e. construction, of a philosophical theory, or of a concept, by a philosopher.

In social science, too, a constructivist approach to theory is commonplace, and by no means controversial in itself (although some of the resulting constructs are). All kinds of theoretical concepts—such as social class, the oedipal process, the authoritarian personality, gender—are constructs. That is to say, social theorists and scientists conceptualize them as a complex aggregation and interaction of a number of phenomena, processes, and variables. An important aspect of social science research is the establishment of 'construct validity'—social scientists try to establish that the unified entity they have made out of a range of elements really does behave like a unified entity.[15] Here, the constructor is the scientist or theorist (or, perhaps, scientists and theorists collectively, in departments, research programmes, and schools of thought). What is constructed is a 'scientific concept' or a 'theory' or a 'hypothesis'.

In these and other contexts then, to say some thing is a construction has a number of implications:

1. it is made up of a complex sticking together of a number of other, simpler, components;

---

[13] John Rawls, *A Theory of Justice* (Oxford: Oxford University Press, 1971); 'Kantian Constructivism in Moral Theory', *Journal of Philosophy*, 77 (1980), 515; *Political Liberalism* (New York: Columbia University Press, 1993), 8.

[14] Ronald Dworkin, *Law's Empire* (London: Fontana, 1986), 68–76.

[15] For example, John Bynner and Keith M. Stribley, *Social Research: Principles and Procedures* (Harlow: Longman, 1978), 246.

2. we might, in principle, see how it was made—that is, discover the mechanisms, or processes, or agency that put the bits together;
3. we might, in principle, see how the bits stick together;
4. we might, in principle, undo it;
5. we might, in principle, re-make it some other way.

Note that (2) docs not entail or even imply (3)—these are independent of each other, and are separate research projects. In turn, (4) is a separate project from (2) and (3)—splitting atoms is not the same as understanding the structure of atoms, although in the case of a theory or a constructed concept like class the two steps of seeing the structure and separating all the elements out are more closely linked. But (5) is something else altogether. Chemists succeed in making in laboratories ('artificially') compounds that heretofore were made in nature. Scientific and philosophical theories and concepts are certainly scrutinized and change over time.

Implication (2) highlights the process or mechanism by which the thing, whatever it is, is made. In philosophical and theoretical literature we come across a huge variety of 'constructionisms': conceptual construction, cognitive construction, mental construction, social, legal, psychological, linguistic, cultural, philosophical, etc. etc. construction. Here is another source of ambiguity and resultant confusion—for these adjectives can apply to either the mechanism of construction or the nature of the thing constructed or both. Thus, 'social construction' can mean three things:

1. a social thing which is constructed; or
2. a thing which is constructed socially; or
3. a social thing which is constructed socially.

If we take into account the other horn of the ambiguity it can mean three further things:

4. the process of making social things;
5. the social process of making things;
6. the social process of making social things.

For completeness we can add that this does not exhaust the possibilities as far as social constructionism, a methodological position or research programme in science, theory, and philosophy, is concerned. A social constructionist may

- take social constructs as her topic;
- for any thing, hypothesize that it is socially constructed, and test this hypothesis;
- for any thing, treat it as if it is a social construct, and see how far this gets her in understanding, prediction, etc.

- for any thing, presume (or treat it as axiomatic) that it is socially constructed.

That is, like rational choice theorists, symbolic interactionists and others, social constructionists will vary as to the dogmatism with which they hold that social constructionism is universally or globally true, and the extent to which they see it as an instrumentally successful theory (as measured by predictive or explanatory power).

There is no real reason why these ambiguities should result in confusion about what, exactly, theorists and analysts are talking about. However, it would be wrong to deny that in many cases this is quite unclear to audiences.

The huge literature which comes under the headings 'construction of social reality' and 'social construction of reality' is replete with discussions of the construction of a wide range of things—social identities and kinds of relation between persons, crime and deviance, illnesses, 'social problems', trust and its absence, economic and other social institutions.[16] Some of the most contentious analyses are of 'knowledge', scientific knowledge, 'facts', scientific theories, and the like.[17]

SOCIAL

The next term that needs to be analysed is 'social'. There is a good deal of controversy and scepticism about 'social mechanisms' and 'social processes' both from outside and within the social sciences and social theory.

First, we meet a kind of pervasive scepticism about the reference or sense of 'social' at all. Some analysts, including many professional sociol-

[16] For example, Celia Kitzinger, *The Social Construction of Lesbianism* (London: Sage, 1987); Ian Hacking, *Rewriting the Soul: Multiple Personality and the Sciences of Memory* (Princeton: Princeton University Press, 1995); Mark Granovetter, 'Economic Institutions as Social Constructions: A Framework for Analysis', *Acta Sociologica*, 35 (1992), 3–11, Edward H. Lorenz, 'Flexible Production Systems and the Social Construction of Trust', *Politics and Society*, 21 (1993), 307–24.

[17] Peter Berger and Thomas Luckmann, *The Social Construction of Reality* (Harmondsworth: Penguin, 1967); Thomas Kuhn, *The Structure of Scientific Revolutions*, 2nd edn. (Chicago: Chicago University Press, 1970); Michel Foucault, 'Questions of Method', in G. Burchell, C. Gordon, and P. Miller (eds.), *The Foucault Effect: Studies in Governmentality* (Hemel Hempstead: Harvester Wheatsheaf, 1991), and 'Power/Knowledge', in *Power/Knowledge: Selected Interviews and Writings* ed. and trans. Colin Gordon (Brighton: Harvester, 1980) are cited inspirations and antecedents for these analyses. For criticism of much of the 'social construction of knowledge/reality' literature see Wil Coleman and Wes Sharrock, 'Unconstructive', in Velody and Williams, *The Politics of Constructionism*, 100–8.

ogists, take the view that talk of 'social reality', or social anything else is only a way of talking, a folkway, that will be eliminated in scientific or other rigorous discourses. Some analysts seem to accept a way of talking that features 'social reality' or 'social things', but are distinctly unhappy with the view that mechanisms or causes might be genuinely social, or that social things might have genuine causal powers. The theme underlying all this scepticism seems to be that if a thing is 'social' it is epiphenomenal— apparent, to be sure, and part of people's experienced world, but caused by something else, some process or mechanism which is more basic. Second, as I mentioned before, there is a distinct absence of serious analysis of 'social' in the philosophical and theoretical literature (although writers often enough feel compelled to help themselves to the concept). For the most part, any elucidation of the meaning of 'social' is done by way of exemplification—'We have some rough idea of what will count as social factors: matters, presumably, of class, social roles, political power, economic organisation and so forth'[18]—or by contrast. Often the contrasts are presented as though they are dualistic. And frequently, 'social' is a kind of residual term that will mop up anything left over when biology, or rationality, or whatever is exhausted.[19]

A prominent contrast with 'social' is 'individual'. There are two possible implications—one that 'social' is simply an aggregative term; the other that it is a holistic or systematic term. According to individualists such apparent (and indeed experienced and understood) 'social phenomena' such as marriage, or society, are decomposable (without remainder) just into the individuals that make them up.[20] That is, 'social' can only refer to an aggregation, not to a whole, a system, or a unit which might itself have causal powers or effects.[21] Some varieties of rational choice theory make

[18] Bernard Williams, *Making Sense of Humanity* (Cambridge: Cambridge University Press, 1995).

[19] The philosopher Larry Laudan argued that all rational scientific practice was to be explained by cognitive factors, while anything left over could be explained by sociologists or psychologists. Stephen M. Downes, 'Socialising Naturalised Philosophy of Science', *Philosophy of Science*, 60 (1993), 452–68.

[20] Stephen Lukes, 'Methodological Individualism Reconsidered', *British Journal of Sociology*, 19 (1968), 119–29; Stuart Hampshire, 'Social Objects', *Proceedings of the Aristotelian Society*, 76 (1975–6), 1–27.

[21] We ought to distinguish between: 'methodological individualists' whose position is that for the purposes of social scientific analysis we should treat any alleged 'wholes' or 'systems' as aggregations, and that we should treat individual consciousness, intention, and action as the level that bears, as it were, all the explanatory weight in a model; 'metaphysical individualists' who believe that it really is the case that all there is are individuals and that 'wholes', 'structures', 'systems', etc. have only an abstract ontological status; and 'ethical individualists' who are committed to treating only individuals as the bearers of value. None of these individualisms entails any of the others. The individualism-wholism debate

the strong claim that the apparent form, shape, and nature of so-called 'social institutions', norms and the like, is the aggregate outcome of individuals' rationality (that is, self-interested utility, or satisfaction maximizing decisions and actions). As this kind of rationality is an aspect of humans which is independent of the society they are in (or in some versions, is to be thought of as philosophically prior to society) then it cannot be said to be social. Therefore, so-called social reality has a non-social or pre-social cause or ontological foundation. For these thinkers *social* and *rational* are disjunctive.

Another common disjunction is *social* versus *biological*. Biological analyses of 'social' phenomena have focused on various explanatory levels. 'Socio-biology' concentrated on the organism or beast with innate drives (the reproductive drive above all) and instinctive behaviour (hunting, killing, fleeing from danger, eating, mating, parenting).[22] More recent developments focus on the replication mechanism at the level of the gene, linking this to the requirements of selection. Thus, for biologists and geneticists, the organism's consciousness—what it thinks it is up to—is irrelevant to the scientific explanation of its behaviour and of course might be quite false. This is especially true of human organisms who conceive of their motivations and actions in terms of God's law, or morality, or reason, or freedom and choice. Human accounts of human life have tended to overlook and even deny the relevance of biological mechanisms, and where these have been taken into account they have been imperfectly understood. Daniel Dennett goes even further than the biochemical mechanism of gene replication to the algorithm that mathematically describes it: the algorithmic level is the level that best accounts for diversity, mechanisms, and so on—a blind algorithmic process that, potentially, will also account for intentionality, creativity, and all of the aspects of human mental and social life that have, up to now, been taken as those that distinguish 'us' from other organisms.[23] This last point alerts us to the fact that the disjunction between social and biological can be, and has been, made from both sides of the disciplinary divide. Biologists have repudiated 'the social' and located causal and explanatory power in the biological; philosophers and social theorists and scientists have, one way or another, repudiated

is a debate about human or social reality; however, it can get confounded with the debate about the relations between systems and elements, or whole and elements, in physical reality or in nature.

[22] E. O. Wilson, *Sociobiology: The New Synthesis* (Cambridge, Mass.: Belknap Press, 1975).

[23] Daniel Dennett, 'Darwin's Dangerous Idea', *The Sciences* (May 1995), 34–40.

and denigrated the biological and set 'man' apart from his biological nature emphasizing his ability to transcend and overcome it.[24]

This dualism turns our attention to another very common one: that between *social* and *natural*. In this disjunction, 'social' comes to be equated with, or mapped on to, 'artificial'. This dualism is very common in the 'state of nature' literature than underpins modern social contract theories, although it is not unique to that tradition. It is very prominent, notably, in the work of Jean Jacques Rousseau, and of Mary Wollstonecraft, both of whom were preoccupied, among other things, with the distorting effects that society has on human nature. The argument that some phenomenon or process is 'natural'—as for example Rousseau argues that the patriarchal family is—constitutes a powerful defence of that thing. For both Rousseau and Wollstonecraft 'reason' is a natural human capacity which can, nevertheless, be corrupted by social power. The social versus natural dualism has generated a vast literature. Scholars have recorded and analysed episodes in the history of the contrast.[25] They have pointed out that various specifications of the contrast are inconsistent one with another.

Others have, in a number of ways, attempted to go beyond the dichotomy. If social things are constructed by biological or natural processes, then social things are natural. That does not imply that 'the social' can be eliminated. Conversely, many theorists emphasize that since 'our' knowledge of, experiences of, and theories about 'nature', 'biology', and so forth themselves have a history, and depend on 'social' factors such as an economic surplus that can support an intellectual class, then the categories nature, biology, and rationality are themselves assimilable into the realm of sociality. Further, these very contrasts, by way of which the concept 'social' is given content by virtue of contrast with what it is not, are themselves, of course, heuristics—they are ways human beings contrive of understanding the world and structuring their knowledge and understanding. The fact that in different social contexts, and at different times, various contrasts to 'social' are deployed to illuminate it conduces to the argument that the very distinctions between social and everything else are socially made.

[24] See Val Plumwood, *Feminism and the Mastery of Nature* (London: Routledge, 1993), esp. ch. 2; Moira Gatens, ' "The Oppressed State of My Sex": Wollstonecraft on Reason, Feeling and Equality'; Lydia Lange, 'Rousseau and Modern Feminism', both in Mary Lyndon Shanley and Carole Pateman (eds.), *Feminist Interpretations and Political Theory* (Oxford: Polity Press, 1991).
[25] Evelyn Fox Keller, *Reflections on Gender and Science* (New Haven: Yale University Press, 1985), Part I; Plumwood, *Feminism and the Mastery of Nature*.

In this connection, modern physical and social science has constructed a new and distinctive set of contrasts to 'social': physical, biological and chemical, and psychological. In turn, social science offers us a set of sub-categories, or components of 'social'. For instance, we can distinguish between economic, psychological, cultural, political, legal, linguistic, discursive, sexual, etc. processes, phenomena, institutions, and relations. Whether a particular set of mechanisms and processes, and body of knowledge, is considered to be a *contrast class* to 'social' or a *subcategory* of it, is of course itself a matter of dispute and controversy. For example, some sociologists and, indeed, many psychologists, would argue that a good many of the processes that psychologists study are actually aspects of or subsets of social processes. Many biologists would object strongly to my classification of 'sexual' as a subset of social here; and the same goes for linguistic.

The history of the term 'social' reveals several elements that are still salient.[26] First, is association and sociability: to be social is to associate with others, to be in company, in personal relations. Second, social implies 'civil'; that is to say, the aggregation is ordered in a particular way. (We can note that this connotation of civility can be metaphorically extended to the social formations and patterns of sociability of non-human animals, many of whom certainly live in orderly social groups). Third, we can note a distinction (and, by the same token, an overlap) between 'social' and 'societal'—societal pertains to 'society' and 'society' is itself a complex concept which includes elements which lead to equivocation. On the one hand, it is a general term for the whole formation of interrelated groups and institutions in which people live. On the other, it is an abstract term which stands for the preconditions necessary for such life to be possible. This distinction (between social and societal) is in practice often glossed over, and 'social' does for both—adding yet more equivocation into the concept. Theoretically, it is commonplace to differentiate what we might call levels of sociality: distinguishing between the 'lower' levels of encounter and inter-action between individuals, 'higher' levels of organization and the institutionalization of norms, identities, and roles, and the even 'higher' level at which all these organizations and institutions are themselves interrelated.

So far, in discussing the meaning of 'social construction' I have pointed out two disambiguations of the term: first, some thing which is made by a social process or mechanism; second, some social thing that is made by some process or mechanism, social or otherwise. What could count as a social thing, and what can count as a social process? To take the first—

[26] See for detail Raymond Williams, *Keywords*, revised edn. (London: Fontana Press, 1976).

according to what has gone before social things will clearly include human groups such as families, schools, parliaments, markets and states. These are organized groups of human individuals together with organizations of organizations. By the same inference, the class of social things will include prides of lions, packs of dogs, nests of ants, and those groups of animals that include individuals from more than one species living together, permanently or temporarily. Second, the class of social things will include practices and discourses: traditions of living particular kinds of moral lives, narratives that give coherence to a culture or tradition and lend meaning, for good or ill, to individual lives, 'the rule of law', theories of justice, the scientific pursuit of knowledge. These practices and discourses, of course, are intimately interrelated with particular kinds of groups and institutions. Similarly, at least some of the species-specific, group-specific, and idiosyncratic patterns of socialization, parenting, discipline, play and aggression that are observable among groups of non-human animals come into this class of social things. What can count as a social process or mechanism? There are some clear cases. If one group of individuals organize themselves so as to either prevent some other group from, say, entering an institution or engaging in some activity, or organize themselves so as to coerce the other group into a particular activity, that is a social mechanism. The organized or concerted exercise of power, or an individual exercise of power that exploits the individual's membership of a social group (using that as a resource), is a clear case of social power. Second, some processes and mechanisms do not involve goal intentionality: interaction among individuals generates particular social outcomes which themselves are unintended. Rational choice, and its variants such as preference adaptation, can fall into this category.[27] Third, whether you are inclined to think of norms as independent of rationality (as does Jon Elster, for some norms) or as emergent for good reasons out of interaction between rational persons (as does James Coleman), norms operate to constrain action and to motivate it.[28]

Commonly however, we meet a much weaker conception of 'social construction'. All that it seems to mean, often, is some thing that is of social origin,[29] and the import of 'construction', let alone the project of specifying the mechanisms that built it, is ignored. Sometimes, scholars imply that the thing *could only* be made in a social context, or in the particular social context—but again without specifying mechanisms or processes. In

---

[27] Elster, *Nuts and Bolts*.

[28] Ibid. 113–24; James Coleman, *The Foundations of Social Theory* (Cambridge, Mass.: Harvard University Press, 1990), 241–300.

[29] Sergio Sismondo, 'Some Social Constructions', *Social Studies of Science*, 23 (1993), 521.

this weaker kind of formulation theorists and researchers enumerate the resources, roles, and relations that are the condition for some thing existing, without sticking their necks out so far as to hypothesize or specify any causal mechanism. Even more weakly, socially constructed can seem to mean no more than socially situated. This comes perilously close to being trivially true—even the planet Venus is, in part, socially situated, occupying as it does a place in the same universe that 'we' inhabit, in cosmological theory, and in human practices like contemplation of the skies, navigation, etc.

It is important to note that there are two defensible reasons why theorists may give only one of these weaker accounts of a social construct. First, because it is just too difficult, and perhaps not worthwhile for the purposes at hand, to specifically hypothesize, let alone test, the putative causal connections. Second, because for principled reasons one is sceptical about this causal project. Some social research programmes which are intellectually and philosophically rooted in phenomenology, sociological research programmes like symbolic interactionism, and other interpretive sociologies might take something like this latter line.

Phenomenologists in social science are sceptical about the sustainability of causal models in social studies, and emphasize instead actors' ongoing achievement of a precarious 'social order'. According to them individuals negotiate meanings (their own, and those they impute to others) and act or behave accordingly. This process is resolutely *local*. Even where social scientists, for instance, construct accounts of macro phenomena like GNP or class struggle, or the transition from feudalism to capitalism, they do so deploying resources which are local and immediate to them—SPSS spreadsheets, or books of Marxist theory, or historical documents—which they assimilate and interpret. In such a process, statements about distant phenomena or events, or abstractions, are incorporated as local and immediate—precisely within the phenomenology of the individual. This means that analysts must be very careful about ontological and epistemological assertions: assertions that something exists independently of the subject are illicit, as are postulations of causal mechanisms. The kind of thing objected to is: 'the dominant construction of gender in society S positions women in a subordinate relation to men in society S'. The phenomenologist insists, reasonably enough, that 'it is people acting together, not social contexts, that use, make and change meanings in social life.'[30]

---

[30] Joseph W. Schneider, 'Defining the Definitional Perspective on Social Problems', *Social Problems*, 32 (1985), 233. Note the convergence with rational choice theory which similarly resists the idea that contexts 'make' things, including human actions, happen.

Phenomenological empirical research describes the process (as apprehended by the individual social researcher) whereby agreement is reached about interpretations and descriptions, and about the social stages, the interactive processes, whereby a transaction is achieved, 'normal life' is maintained, an event completed.

Interpretivist sociologists, too, think in terms of how context gives meaning to text, text analogues, and signs. Human interactants engage in the interpretation of these meanings. Meanings take on an objective 'thing-like' and causal quality: that is the correct way to behave, or that is a gesture of politeness while another gesture is rude, or red means stop. These meanings have a certain causal power. That is, they are causally connected with what agents will do next—carry on interacting, or turn away in disgust, or come to a halt. But that doesn't, really, make them objects. They are meanings. It is true that as participants and as observers, if we come to understand the meanings as the agent understands them we will have good predictive power with regard to the agent's actions. But this predictive power has a quite different basis from the mechanical calculations that enable a physicist or a weapons expert to know where to search for a bullet given a specification of the gun that shot it, the position from which the shot was fired, the direction and angle to the ground, etc.

Interpretivists and phenomenologists object to the reification of meanings and actions into things that they detect in social constructionism. Their argument is that the shifting and protean nature of meaning, the indeterminacy of 'rule-following', is quite different from the operation of physical laws (all things being equal) such as the laws of mechanics and thermo-dynamics. Constructionists actually doubt this—certainly for the purposes of social science model building. Buildings are constructions, and the position of the doors and windows in walls constrains one's physical movements in and out of the building. Institutions with rules and norms are constructions, and the rules and norms can constrain one's movements, behaviour, and actions. The building is a physical construction; the institution is a social construction. They are equally concrete and material; equally causal and constraining.

From a contrasting critical viewpoint though 'social construction' implies 'mere social construction', and to social constructionism is imputed the view that 'reality itself is but a social construct, alterable at will, and subject to future changes as "we" see fit'.[31] This sort of view is extremely common, and very peculiar—undoubtedly prompted by the historical association of phenomenological philosophy with studies of the

---

[31] John Searle, *The Construction of Social Reality* (Harmondsworth: Penguin, 1995).

social construction of 'knowledge'. To many critics, 'social constructionism' is equated with phenomenology and rejected accordingly. But 'social
constructionism' is quite consistent with realism, rationalism, and empiricism, among other 'isms'. For this reason, confusingly, some phenomenologists and interpretivists attack social constructionists, when what
they actually dislike is the realism or empiricism associated with the attribution of causal powers to constructed entities.

That something is a construction does not mean that it is particularly
fragile or easy to dismantle—take atoms. The point of a man-made construction (as opposed to just a heap or aggregation) is its stability and its
viability in its environment. Many man-made constructions are no easier
to dismantle than are natural constructions such as hills and valleys (or,
about equally easy). Of course, a house of cards might fall down when a
door opens, but most constructions are more robust than this. The same
goes for social constructions. If we think for a minute about how social
mechanisms operate we will see that the converse to fragility is likely to be
the case—social constructions will be exceedingly difficult to dismantle. In
fact, in the case of a building, it is often surprisingly easy to alter the position of the doors, windows, walls, and so on—to bring the building into
line with our desired movements. It is, as the historical record testifies, far
less easy for groups to get access to institutions that have hitherto excluded
them: this requires changing hearts and minds, changing constitutions, it
sometimes needs state legislation, it requires altering formal and informal
rules, norms, conventions, and mores, and, worse, it means altering practices and discourses. By comparison alterations to a physical building are
the work of a moment (and if it is difficult to get them done it will be for
human and social reasons). Further, many social mechanisms operate
behind actors' backs, so to speak, so that conscious agents are not aware
of aggregate and unintended processes that are in train. Many mechanisms operate at the aggregate level—the many individual decisions and
actions of individuals add up to regular and powerful but unintended
forces and consequences. The project of trying to get everyone, or some
critical mass of the relevant people, to change reality is a daunting project
indeed.

SOCIAL CONSTRUCTIONISM AND COMMUNITARIANISM

Where does social constructionism figure in communitarianism? It is
present in a number of ways. First, contrary to Rawls's and Dworkin's
philosophical or rational construction of moral and political theory, the

philosophical communitarians insist on the social construction of moral and political theory. Second, communitarians emphasize the social construction of values (what is valued in a particular society or 'community'), social roles, and social institutions. Third, communitarians develop theories of the social construction of the subject or as it is often put, the self. I shall go on to discuss these aspects of communitarian philosophy.[32] It is also notable that 'community' figures in a good deal of social constructionism; I shall return to this point. So, what is socially constructed in communitarianism? I have mentioned: moral and political theory or philosophy, values, roles, institutions, and individuals.

Michael Sandel emphasizes the social or community construction of 'the self'. The 'self' or subject who is able reflexively to think about its own characteristics preferences, values, identity, social relations with others, knowledge of the world—and which is the *subject* of which the preferences, values, etc. are *predicates* does not have an existence independent from those preferences, values, etc.[33] Sandel's model, and his attack on Rawls, have been much criticized. Rawls argues that the human capacity for reflexivity involves that we can scrutinize, criticize and 'form, revise and pursue' our own conception of 'the good', our values, our understanding of virtue, etc.[34] It is nowhere required that we be able to do this all at once, wholesale—rather we can isolate elements of our social identity, system of beliefs and values, and evaluate them individually and in light of the whole. This is what is meant by 'form and revise'. Neither does the Rawlsian model entail (contrary to many readings of it) that we can literally step outside all of our values, commitments, and all the social aspects of our identity, and still operate as fully-fledged reasoners. All it entails is that we can imagine just for these limited constructive purposes being ignorant of these aspects of our selves.[35] So Sandel's critique is misplaced.

It is notable, though, that this view of the reflexive self (the one found in the rebuttal of Sandel) is quite consistent with Sandel's existential point. It is also consistent with the social constructionist position that the

[32] But not in great detail: there is a huge literature on this aspect of communitarianism, and I don't have anything to add at this stage. What I do want to do in this chapter is to make clear the constructive mechanisms that the communitarian philosophers (in my interpretation) hypothesize and argue for, and to argue that this use of social constructionism is not preposterous.

[33] Michael Sandel, *Liberalism and the Limits of Justice* (Cambridge: Cambridge University Press, 1982), e.g. 182–3.

[34] Rawls, *Political Liberalism*, 72.

[35] Stephen Mulhall and Adam Swift, *Liberals and Communitarians*, 2nd edn. (Oxford: Blackwell, 1996), 196.

conditions of possibility of the kind of reflexive scrutiny and revision of values that Rawlsians value are social conditions. Rawls does not deny that in some societies the kind of liberal autonomy he is concerned to promote is either impossible or difficult to live—as the necessary modes of education and socialization are absent, or sanctions against 'independence' are severe.[36] Indeed, the modern western conception of the independent self can only be explained by reference to the particular pattern of social relations and values that are bound up with the material and psychological conditions of modern society.

MacIntyre acknowledges the power of the idea of what he calls the 'detachable self'—the moral idea, that can be especially associated with existentialism, that the subject can be detached from its context, society, history, roles, and statuses. This idea is prominent in twentieth-century western societies and is exploited when individuals deny any responsibility for their family's or their society's actions: the white US citizen who believes that the continuing effects of slavery's legacy are nothing to do with him, the Englishman who has no interest in the problems of Ireland, the young non-Jewish German who thinks that Nazi policies do not effect his moral relationship with Jewish people.[37] The point of MacIntyre's argument is that these individuals, and the philosophers who purport to uphold this view of subjectivity, are making a philosophical mistake. Individuals are part of a history, inheritors of a specific past, members of a particular society. It is this that endows them with the roles they can play and the values they can negotiate. This is as true for the 'detached' self as for any other. This social constructionist theory of the self accounts for 'the facts' of dissociation and detachment; 'rebellion against my identity is always one possible mode of expressing it'.[38] The point is that detachment and the denial of responsibility for the legacy of the past is an aspect of 'liberalism as a tradition'.[39] This kind of approach to the question of individual identity and subjectivity is shared by other communitarian philosophers. Charles Taylor, for example, has traced the historical detail of the processes and mechanisms by which individuals have come to view themselves and each other as independent, rational, and reflexive individuals.[40]

[36] Stephen Mulhall and Adam Swift, *Liberals and Communitarians*, 2nd edn. (Oxford: Blackwell, 1996), 20, on Rawls's view of liberalism as a tradition.

[37] Alasdair MacIntyre, *After Virtue: A Study in Moral Theory*, 2nd edn. (London: Duckworth, 1985), 220.

[38] Ibid. 221.

[39] Alasdair MacIntyre, *Whose Justice? Which Rationality?* (London: Duckworth, 1988), ch. 17.

[40] Charles Taylor, *Sources of the Self: The Making of the Modern Identity* (Cambridge: Cambridge University Press, 1989).

The next set of 'things' that for communitarians are socially constructed are values, goods, and virtues (and their obverse: bads, vices). In MacIntyre's work there are several aspects to this. First, conceptions of 'the good life', and what 'the good life' is, vary with different social circumstances. 'What the good life is for a fifth century Athenian general will not be the same as what it was for a medieval nun or a seventeenth century farmer.'[41] MacIntyre doesn't give us much detail here, but clearly these contrasting social circumstances vary as to the dominant and alternative cosmologies (conceptions of the relationships between man, God, the universe, animals, etc.), and available technologies and the interaction of these with patterns of social relationships. The purposes and conceptions of satisfaction thus will vary greatly as between these three differently socially situated individuals. But second, within their broader social context these individuals are also specifically situated in networks of kinship, work, cultural and religious institutions, a political order. This closer context also endows the individual with 'a variety of debts, inheritences, rightful expectations and obligations. These constitute the given of my life, my moral starting point.'[42] This set of social contexts situates individuals, in turn, as participants in a series of social practices: the achievement of grace, the pursuit of scientific knowledge, excellence in competitive sport.[43] Whatever the detail of the practice in question, certain virtues such as courage (the courage to defend those things one cares about), truth, and justice must flourish if the practices, qua practices, are to be sustained.[44] The point, for MacIntyre and other communitarians, is not that values are entirely contingent but that their development is tied to our human purposes (and these may vary somewhat in detail). Another equally important point for MacIntyre is that the solitary asocial individual cannot pursue a practice. The lone runner, the solitary contemplative, even the nauseated existentialist, is only able to pursue his detached life *by virtue* of the collective enterprise that sets him on his way. The danger in a society that values independence, solitude, and autonomy above all is that the collective foundations that generate these goods will disintegrate.

Michael Walzer follows a similar train of thought. What is valued, what counts as a good, varies from social context to social context. Time away from labour—whether we term this rest, leisure, or whatever—is a good in all societies we know about. But exactly in what the good lies varies: between Aristotle's view of the good of non-instrumental activity, to Veblen's analysis of the role of leisure as a conspicuous consumption good; from the emphasis on rest and bodily reproduction, to an emphasis on

---

[41] MacIntyre, *After Virtue*, 220.   [42] Ibid.   [43] Ibid. 187 ff.
[44] Ibid. 191–3.

freedom and happiness.[45] And specific forms of free time also vary historically, in familiarly socially conditioned ways.[46] An important emphasis in Walzer's analysis is the question whether goods are thought of as collective goods or private goods. Holidays, including the Sabbath, have been thought of as collective goods, and the ways of filling them, the symbols and rituals associated with them, have all been significant modes of social, national (or as the communitarians prefer) community cohesion. The enjoyment of a traditional holiday depends in part on the intrinsic pleasure of feasting, partying, gifts, and so on, and in part on the fact that the others are also doing the same—otherwise the food, the decorations, the events wouldn't have the meaning they do. 'Holidays are for members.'[47] By contrast, vacations are individual consumption goods, the objects of individual choice provided one can pay. But of course, and only somewhat paradoxically, the provision of holidays as commodities is contingent upon a particular social organization of productive and distributive resources.

The final socially constructed thing I wish to discuss is political theory, moral philosophy, etc. itself. At various points in this book I have already indicated and discussed the distinction between a view of political theory as a philosophical construct (as Rawls and Dworkin conceive it), and as a social construct as the communitarians conceive it. Walzer's approach is that social, political and moral theory is not just given to us by a *deus ex machina*, nor is it constructed by a disengaged purely rational philosopher. Rather, political, social, and moral practices are constructed by social processes and mechanisms, by social actors, and these are interpreted, refined, and criticized by philosophers among other critics.[48] The disagreement between Rawls and the social constructionists is fairly clear. In *A Theory of Justice* Rawls's method was to begin with the philosophical construction, and then subject it to the tests and adjustments of 'reflective equilibrium'. In later work Rawls is more clearly explicit that his theory of justice is one designed for an already liberal polity and society—he does not intend that it could be a pattern to be either taken up by or imposed on societies with very different approaches to individual identity, religious observance, and operations of power. This latter formulation seems to have moved dramatically towards the social constructionist view, because Rawls is quite clear that 'the philosopher' is of the liberal society on whose

[45] Michael Walzer, *Spheres of Justice* (Oxford: Basil Blackwell, 1983), 184–7.
[46] Ibid. 190–6 on the contrast between 'holidays' and 'vacations'.
[47] Ibid. 194.
[48] Michael Walzer, *Interpretation and Social Criticism* (Cambridge, Mass.: Harvard University Press, 1987), 5.

institutions he comments.[49] Dworkin, as we have seen, takes it that the philosopher's job is to examine and subject to philosophical scrutiny morally relevant practices—of justice, of courtesy—that are already entrenched in 'a community'.[50] The philosopher may be an outsider; he needs interpretive skills in order to understand the 'logic' of the relevant practices from the community's point of view.

Why should either a Rawlsian or a Dworkinian be hostile to 'social constructionism' as regards moral and political practices and institutions? They can hardly deny that the history of the practices and institutions they are interested in—the framing, amendment, and interpretation of the Constitution of the United States of America, the institutionalization and defence of human rights, the achievement of a political and social state of affairs in which people are 'free and equal'—have been shaped by social factors: religious beliefs and their impact on human organization, technology, the regulation of markets, the regulation of disputes in the areas of kinship and culture, the structures of power. They cannot deny that the individuals who strove for freedom, equality, rights, and constitution were people with religious, cultural, economic, and domestic purposes—purposes which doubtless were shaped by the political institutions they bit by bit constructed, dismantled, lost in battle, regained, and restructured, but purposes also that shaped the institutions (and the theories about the institutions) they built. As we have seen, both Rawls and Dworkin are wary of the philosopher (or the sovereign) who attempts to impose a new (albeit internally consistent) system of institutions and judgements on a society. The relationship between society and institutions is more organic than this.

Scepticism about (although not hostility to) social constructionism is justified if social constructionists are vague about mechanisms and processes. It is undoubtedly true that readers have to do a certain amount of reading between the lines to garner a clear idea of the mechanisms and processes the communitarians hypothesize. But accounts certainly are there in their texts. First of all, we have seen that the communitarians put a good deal of emphasis on community membership. This is both a good, a valuable resource (and therefore a good the distribution of which is subject to reasoning as to its justice), and it is a social state, a social condition for an individual and for collectives. Community membership subjects individuals to constraints of various kinds: to the articulation and the enforcement of norms, and to the configuration of power (economic, cultural, kin-based, political) that applies. Concomitantly, the enforcement

[49] Rawls, *Political Liberalism*, 93–8.
[50] Ronald Dworkin, *Law's Empire* (London: Fontana, 1986), 68 ff.

and the revision of norms, the distribution and redistribution of power shapes and reshapes institutions. Community membership also is a resource for understanding and interpretation, according to the communitarians. Thus individuals' interpretation and understanding of rules, norms, the way to go on, desirable possible revisions to the context in which one is situated, depend on their membership of an 'interpretive community' which generates and also approves of particular interpretations.

John Searle argues that the stability of institutions relies on their members, 'and a sufficient number of members of the relevant community' continuing to recognize and accept their existence.[51] Searle acknowledges that there might be a plurality of understandings and interpretations of institutions. For instance, a complex social institution like 'marriage' or 'family' is susceptible to a predictable range of contrasting interpretations. Searle's point is that these particular and conflicting points of view are only possible given that some number of participants share a basic intentionality that constitutes the institutional fact that two persons who have been through this or that, but not another, ceremony and legal process count as married; or that this group of people, but not that one, are a clear case of 'a family'. But there is room, in Searle's analysis, for dissensus— some members of 'the relevant community' might cease to share in the collective intentional state, might come to recognize some alternative fact or institution. There is room, in short, for disagreement. And this means that social factors (agreement, disagreement, sufficient numbers) enter into the ontology, as Searle would put it, of institutional facts—without agreement the institution can vanish.[52]

I have introduced Searle's analysis at this point because of his own use of the term 'community'. This is unexplained. Intepreting it in context produces two possibilities. First, that it refers to some population of individuals who consequent upon being in such a spatial and temporal relationship that they share collective intentionality, and consequent upon being co-parties to the process (and products) of construction of institu-

[51] Searle, *Construction of Social Reality*, 117.

[52] It is important to note that Searle himself does not want to concede the *social* construction of social reality. According to him, social reality is constructed by collective intentionality, which is a biologically primitive phenomenon, and language. So social reality is constructed by a non-social (pre-social) mechanism. But it seems to me that by his own analysis he allows social factors into both the construction and the maintenance of social institutions. The answers to questions about what counts as what, actually, have to refer to power and authority, as well as intentionality and acceptance. The question 'Who must accept?' cannot be avoided. That is, the actual quality of the social relations that are constructive of institutions must be taken into account.

tional reality, *ipso facto* constitute a community. Alternatively, community might refer to just that group of individuals who share collective intentionality, whether or not they are parties to institutions. In this latter case, hyenas in a pack also count as a community. This seems to me to be stretching terms a bit far, although nobody would deny that hyenas in a pack are behaving socially. Equally, the first meaning is a very weak form of community.

In their very influential, phenomenologically informed, work on social construction Berger and Luckmann offer a particular and clear analysis of the process by which it comes to be that the reality of everyday life is taken for granted as real, as intersubjective and shared, as objective and external to us and to all. They emphasize how the structure of social reality is practically invisible to participants in their day-to-day contexts.[53] It is the same with physical reality: the structure of atoms, the atomic structure of everyday objects, the structure of buildings and bridges, and microchips and cars, is more or less invisible. Unless one knew better we might 'naturally' believe that a microchip just is what it appears, to our normal eyesight, to be. The extent to which this is so even for those individuals who have specialized technical knowledge probably varies. Some mechanically minded persons can and do routinely visualize everything that is happening under the bonnet and inside the engine of a car as it is driven, as they drive it. But this takes imagination—they don't see the workings of the car directly; and presumably even mechanical fanatics do sometimes have the experience of driving automatically, focusing only on the road, the passing scene, the events and places to come. Engineers and builders know with only a cursory glance the structure of bridges and buildings; physicists presumably have a dimension to their consciousness of physical materials that I lack, understanding as they do its molecular and atomic structure. But even if you have a D.Phil. in physics, you don't directly apprehend the molecular structure of the desk, you see or feel a desk. So it is with marriages, families, states, and refectories. Berger and Luckmann theorize that two mechanisms are key in this process. First is objectification—this is the social process of institutionalization and legitimation that brings it about that we take things for granted as just there, independent of us. Second is socialization—the internalization of norms and interpretations, the learning of definitions, routines, descriptions, and theories, the taking on, in short, of a social identity.[54]

Other models of social construction, and social constructionist studies, offer variations on this constellation of mechanisms of socialization,

[53] Berger and Luckmann, *The Social Construction of Reality*, 106 ff.
[54] Ibid. *passim*.

objectification, normative constraint, and resources for action. For example, Sue Wilkinson and Celia Kitzinger focus on individuals' negotiation with on the one hand meanings and on the other hand political imperatives, and the interaction between the two. This is the process whereby individuals arrive at a personal construction of various sexual roles.[55] (By 'personal construction' they mean the individual's own analysis of, images of, and account of sexual roles including their own). The mechanism by which identities and avowed identities are made, then, is: a subject negotiates with meanings that are independent of her; these meanings have been politically made and are elements of a discourse. What people can and cannot say in certain political and social circumstances is systematically connected with, constitutive of, those same individuals' subjective experience of their own identity. That is, this particular discourse and the conceptions that constitute it are a political construction, and the respondents' affirmed identities are a discursive, practical, political, and personal construction. That is, personal constructs have a multiple causality.

In this theoretical account discourse is identified as a key mechanism in the making of 'personal constructs' and social identities. Discourse is yet another term that needs careful analysis. For linguists it means, technically, 'language above the level of the sentence'—thus encompassing all kinds of passages of speech and writing. In social theory, it has taken on some additional connotations and implications. Social theorists tend to conceptualize discourse in three main ways. First, as the speech and writing of a particular kind of social subject or subjects. So, 'journalism', 'tabloid journalism', or 'literary criticism' or 'scientific discourse' or 'Labour Party speak' are discourses. Second, as all speech and writing produced, no matter by whom, on a particular topic—for instance, on sexuality, or crime. Third, in a way that combines the first two, so that, for instance, literary discourses of crime or sexuality are distinguished from scientific discourses of the same topics. Analytically, this is clear enough. Empirically, analysts face a problem with allocating particular texts to particular bodies or fields of discourse—'discourse' is very much an ideal-typical, or abstract, category. In social theory, the point of studying discourses is because they are agreed to be capable of influencing and shaping human action and social reality. Certain discourses are both powerful and influential—they are prescriptive, as they classify the world and, especially, define what is normal and what is deviant.[56]

[55] Sue Wilkinson and Celia Kitzinger, 'The Social Construction of Heterosexuality', *Journal of Gender Studies*, 3 (1994), 307–16.

[56] See especially aspects of the work of Michel Foucault: *Madness and Civilisation* (London: Tavistock, 1967); *The Birth of the Clinic* (London: Tavistock, 1973). Foucault's

A common theme in critical social theory is that the modern social sciences have endowed those structures that higher-order (that is theoretically interpreted and statistically measured) knowledge makes visible with an enormous degree of stability and solidity.[57] The division of 'spheres' for example—the common sense understanding in modern societies that there are public and private spheres, that economics, politics, and kinship are distinct systems with distinct norms and rules—exists empirically as a mode of justification for individuals.[58] Peter Wagner concentrates on how the academic and scientific disciplines have produced understandings and interpretations of society which are widely promulgated in the form of such representations as texts, statistical tables, charts, and maps; and are just as widely deployed by governments, policy-makers, and 'ordinary people' in a variety of diurnal settings.

Representations of stratified societies, which start out as the results of statistical surveys, become part of the common sense and mundane understanding of society that is deployed by ordinary members in their decision-making. For example, children who understand society to be stratified will deploy that knowledge in their rational calculations about education, employment, etc.[59] In the move from measurement and discovery (we can ignore for the purposes of this argument the prior role of theory, and the place of mundane meanings in scientific theory and hypothesis construction) to scientific representation of society, and from thence to common sense knowledge and know-how, the reality of social stratification is buttressed and reinforced and it becomes more difficult to dismantle. However, in some social scientific traditions measurable facts are treated as more 'objective' than they should be. The metaphors of biology and geology, when applied to social reality, can get in the way of an accurate understanding of the ontology of these facts and states of affairs. By contrast, a properly constructionist analysis of this ontology will keep us aware of the made, and mutable, nature of the social reality we inhabit.

In a useful contribution Mark Granovetter dicusses how and whether we may conceptualize economic institutions as socially constructed.[60] He

method and theoretical framework is influential in many social constructionist studies: see Irving Velody and Robin Williams 'Introduction' to *The Politics of Constructionism*.

[57] Peter Wagner, *A Sociology of Modernity: Liberty and Discipline* (London: Routledge, 1994), 186.

[58] Ibid. 187.

[59] See Diego Gambetta, *Were They Pushed or Did They Jump?* (Cambridge: Cambridge University Press, 1987) for an analysis of young people's formation of expectations of their chances, and the likely returns to 'investment in education' in a society they know to be unequal.

[60] Granovetter, 'Economic Institutions as Social Constructions', 3–11.

emphasizes individuals' intentional building of material institutions and networks of institutions (firms, business groups, banks) out of the materials to hand, so to speak. Here the process is a bit like the making of a desk or bridge. In certain contexts actors set out to solve problems; they have to work with materials which are independent and therefore are liable to be wayward and tractable. In this case the 'materials' are people, related to each other in particular ways, such as kinship, friendship, shared geographical locality, shared or clashing cultural norms, and so on. Out of this some novel artefact can be fashioned—a credit union, or a local bank, or a network of manufacturing firms engaged in relations of contracting and subcontracting.

Granovetter's empirical examples are of institutions of which the relevant actors are quite conscious. Furthermore, the relevant actors are perfectly capable of talking freely about the bases on which they judge others to be trustworthy, how existing social networks generated concentrated cooperation, and hence about the process of building the institutions. This kind of account is quite consistent with the tenets of rational choice theory. However, social constructionists tend to focus on the context of action, and on constraint. Some rational choice theorists focus on the actor's given preferences or goals, his calculation of the optimum course of action, in order to maximize his own preference satisfaction, and his free action following this choice. By contrast, social constructionists will focus on the norms and other prescriptions (including laws, and the coercive power of better-endowed individuals) that constrain actors; on their uncertainty, both about what other people are going to do and about the consequences of their own actions; on the need for actors to engage in reflection and interpretation of their own preferences, the goods on offer, the acceptability and possibility of the various means or courses of action available.

POLITICS AND SOCIAL CONSTRUCTIONISM

An important implication of social constructivism, if it is an accurate account of the ontology and nature of a thing, is that the thing might be dismantled. The thesis that some things are socially constructed, if true, holds out more hope of social change, regarding those things at least, than if it turns out they are biological constructs. However, it is important not to exaggerate this point. Human beings have not been wholly unsuccessful in manipulating and even eradicating biological entities, given the resources, institutions, and the will and desire to do it. Equally, as I remarked earlier, the view that a 'social construction' will be 'alterable at will' begs a number of questions. How is such a shared or collective will to be formed? How are the processes of reinterpretation and meaning change to be got in train and completed? How are the relevant coordination problems to be overcome? When we think about a reasonable answer to these queries we see that the adjective 'mere' as in 'mere social construction' is quite out of place. Nevertheless, although social constructions are not easy to dismantle, we might acknowledge that they are, in principle, dismantleable. This insight is a very important one for a number of political projects.[61]

To recap, I have been trying to argue that social constructions:

* are reasonably thought of as 'entity-like';
* are not very fragile nor easy to undo;
* are based on and constructed out of social processes and relations;
* so, will alter insofar as social processes and relations alter.

The second point, as I have insisted, is very important, and goes against the grain of a good deal of comment about social constructionism. The second, third, and fourth points are central to a number of recent political projects.

The kinds of political projects that are connected with or generated by social constructionist analysis are rather distinctive. Liberalism—as a political project—has been predicated on the idea that reason and rationality must prevail. It has been the hope of many individuals and groups that if the irrational, contradictory, false, nonsensical, meaningless, invalid, nature of many beliefs about the world, arguments, and so-called justifications can be exposed, and alternative rational, consistent, true, sensible, meaningful, and valid arguments and propositions put forward, then the latter must in the end prevail. The problem with this is that reason is not its own vehicle. Liberal reform has relied on two main vehicles—education, and laws, especially laws that construct and protect individual rights.

By contrast, socialisms have emphasized not only laws to construct and protect individual rights, but also the use of laws and state power to enforce redistribution of material resources, and to alter the power of groups who are relatively poor in material goods *vis-à-vis* those who are relatively rich—labour *vis-à-vis* capital, employees *vis-à-vis* employers,

---

[61] Again, Michel Foucault is very influential for the drawing of political implications from social constructionism: 'It is a matter of shaking this false self-evidence, of demonstrating its precariousness, of making visible not its arbitrariness, but its complex interconnection with a multiplicity of historical processes, many of them of recent date'. 'Questions of Method', quoted in Velody and Williams, 'Introduction' to *Politics of Constructionism*.

tenants *vis-à-vis* landlords, and so on. Socialists share with liberals the belief in reason, but their analysis of material power and interests makes them less inclined to think that reason has any chance of prevailing absent legal coercion or the state administered alteration of incentives. In the long term, though, socialism is predicated on the thesis that if economic relationships and distributions can be got right, then other forms of power (cultural, sexual, political), individual motivations, private and public morality, and so forth, will come right. Conservative political programmes have been premissed on the entrenchment of traditional social power, and sovereign political power, and the legal defence of property rights. Anarchists and libertarians by contrast presume that the key political aim is the maximum loosening of all kinds of bonds—cultural, legal, political, familial—from the individual.

This list of political projects could go on. My purpose is to highlight that social constructionist political and social theory turns political attention away from reasoned argument, the use of laws, and the use of authority (whether traditional, or the authority of the individual over himself), to the assault on meaning and practice in an effort to undermine and dismantle social constructions. This is a theme that has been expressed in a number of ways in recent politics. For example, those who speak for, and those who study social movements emphasize the importance of working outside and in the interstices of established, state-linked, political institutions such as parties, pressure groups, and bureaucracies.[62] Feminists have expressed scepticism about the use of laws in changing social reality. Laws, if they are useful, are useful for their symbolic standing for a certain range of values, rather than for the outcomes of the litigation they generate—indeed these can, notoriously, have perverse results. Feminists have also focused (their critics would say, to a fault) on meanings—vocabularies, metaphors, representations, on the content of popular culture and science, all in the framework of 'the discursive construction of reality'. They have concentrated on encouraging individuals to make 'small changes' in their interpersonal relations—with colleagues, friends, kin, sexual intimates, political allies—with the aim of making networks governed by new kinds of social norms, with a generative, constructive, effect.[63] Such strategies, and others from a variety of sources, have been picked up and developed by political communitarians.

[62] Alberto Melucci, 'Social Movements and the Democratisation of Everyday Life', in John Keane (ed.), *Civil Society and the State* (London: Verso, 1988); Claus Offe, 'New Social Movements: Challenging the Boundaries of Institutional Politics', *Social Research*, 52 (1985).

[63] Anne Phillips, *Democracy and Difference* (Oxford: Polity Press, 1993).

Within political communitarianism is a clear focus on the normative, rather than the legal, level. Amitai Etzioni's emphasis on norms rather than laws (and the limited value of laws without corresponding norms and morals) is undoubtedly accentuated by the widespread view that one of the most glaring symptoms of the malaise of United States society is the massive volume of litigation.[64] He also argues that values cannot be imposed legally, although there is wisdom in expressing strongly held values in law—but here, laws are expressive rather than primarily coercive. Henry Tam emphasizes the role of networks sustained by local organizations within which citizens make decisions about distribution and protection, rather than state legislation, in solving social dilemmas.[65] The emphasis is on the construction and reconstruction of norms through mediating organizations and associations, and the generation, thus, of rational expectations that the norms will continue to operate. This constructive project of building new norms is matched by projects of building new relationships. A good example of this is the (now government-sponsored) project of 'mentoring' where adults take on the role of counsellor and adviser to young people, in cooperation with parents and schools.[66]

An important aspect of this socially constructive politics is the exploitation of what Harry Boyte calls 'free spaces':

the vast middle ground between private identities and large scale organisations. They are places that ordinary people can often 'own' in important ways, spaces grounded in the fabric of daily communal life with a public dimension that allows mingling with others beyond one's immediate circle of family and friends. They are institutions which people can sometimes shape and re-shape, use as alternative sources of information about the world, employ as media for connecting with others in ways more substantive than transitory coalitions or other brief encounters.[67]

Another way of describing this spatial context of constructive politics is, in Martin Buber's words, 'the between',—it is an inter-space.[68]

---

[64] Amitai Etzioni, *The New Golden Rule: Community and Morality in a Democratic Society* (New York: Basic Books, 1996), 142–9.

[65] Henry Tam, *Communitarianism* (Basingstoke: Macmillan, 1998), 131 ff., 199 ff.

[66] Peter Mandelson and Roger Liddle, *The Blair Revolution: Can New Labour Deliver?* (London: Faber, 1996), 93, 136–7. The policy is set out in Department of Education and Employment, *Excellence in Schools*, Cm. 3681 (London: The Stationery Office, July 1997).

[67] Harry C. Boyte and Sara M. Evans, 'The Sources of Democratic Change', *Tikkun*, 1/1 (1986), 49.

[68] Peter Gabel, 'The Desire for Community and the Defeat of Healthcare', *Tikkun*, 10/1 (1995), 36.

These strategies, to construct new norms by practising new social relations, to construct novel social relations, to work from the spaces between
subjects and between institutions, can properly be described as socially
constructive strategies. They are not, as I have made clear, confined to
political communitarians, but are pursued also by activists in other political and social movements. Perhaps what is explicitly communitarian is the
more general aim of 'building community'. A truly constructive aspiration, reference to community building turns up again and again in political communitarianism. On the one hand, the work in 'the between'
referred to above is thought of as, ultimately, community building. On the
other hand, communitarians also are concerned to develop a series of
constructive mechanisms that are far less indirect and circuitous.

Political communitarians, in recent years, have been emphasizing the
role of 'community entrepreneurs' and 'community organizers'—individuals who play the role of builders in the constructive process. To be successful these people cannot be bureaucrats, cannot be politicians (in the
party political sense of that term).[69] A number of suggestions are made in
the literature. It is suggested that there is evidence that 'entrepreneurial
headteachers may provide a more cost-effective input in the long term generation of depressed areas than high levels of finance or artifically created
community entrepreneurs in the form of civil servant consultants'.[70] The
role of these persons is to focus and coalesce resources in such a way as to
construct new norms and relationships. Social construction, then, is a
political strategy. In the next chapters I discuss in more detail communitarian political strategies and aims.

[69] Tam, *Communitarianism*, 250; Charles Leadbeater, *The Rise of the Social
Entrepreneur* (London: Demos, 1997).
[70] Inger Boyett and Don Finlay, 'The Social Entrepreneur', in Dick Atkinson (ed.),
Cities of Pride: Rebuilding Community, Refocussing Government (London: Cassell, 1995).

5

Community, Locality, and Politics

INTRODUCTION

The relationship between community and locality is taken for granted in
many contexts. However, it has been disrupted in a number of ways
in recent theory. In this chapter I examine the place and role of 'locality'
in communitarian theory, and the place and role of 'community' in recent
theories of local government. These two topics raise the issue of the relationship between the concept 'community' and patterns of human relationships on the one hand, and the individuation of locales on the other.
They also raise the general question of the nature of 'community politics'.
There have been two main strands to this. First, 'community development'
is a public policy and strategy for addressing poverty and deprivation.
Second, 'community action' is a democratic strategy by claims-makers.
The literatures on community development and community action reveal
a number of dilemmas and tensions among which are problems regarding
the role of professionals, and the vulnerability of the ideals of community
organization and autonomous local social order to the workings of state,
bureaucratic, corporate, and other forms of social power exogenous to the
locality. Ambiguities in the concept and ideal of community itself are particularly highlighted when patterns of power endogenous to the locality
become the occasion of conflict. So finally, these problems raise the question of the true value of 'locality'.

COMMUNITY AND LOCALITY IN COMMUNITARIAN
THOUGHT

As we saw in Chapter 2, 'community' can be taken to denote, perhaps
above all, a particular quality of human relationships. It is not necessary
for individuals to live in proximity for this quality of relationship to inhere.
It may, perhaps, be necessary for them to meet physically. But perhaps not
even this. For instance, relatively recent formations with a self-conscious
'community' identity, like 'the gay community', the 'feminist community',

the 'business community', do not rely on shared locale or physical meetings for their existence. In the modern period, the press and other media
technologies have constructed a series of forums that transcend locale, and
current developments in communications have made a further quantita-
tive change in the relationship, from the point of view of social subjects,
between space and time.[1] Communitarian thinkers emphasize the desir-
ability of self-regulation of 'communities'.[2] As the examples of many self-
regulating associations—voluntary, commercial and professional—show,
this does not require locality. Many viable associations are comprised of
memberships linked by mail and other communications technologies. It is
also notable that for many individuals a powerful allegiance is with a community (in my stronger sense of the term, where community membership
is a source of transcendent association with others) in diaspora. That is to
say, community members can, seemingly, even be denied any straightforward means of communication, yet still enjoy community.

Communitarianism, both philosophical and political, is highly ambivalent about this. On the one hand, communitarians are anxious to head off
accusations of nostalgia, the accusation that they are proposing a return
to a social order in which individuals are relatively immobile members of
communities which are centred on a definite locale. On the other hand, the
emphasis on place creeps back into their analysis. Often this is in the
explicitly localist sense of a recommendation to strengthen local government, and the recommendation to build up local and neighbourhood
organizations. The most pressing image of community still seems to be the
dwindling number of occupational communities—mining, fishing, agri-
culture, steel, or whatever—where participants in the primary occupation
are tied to a geographical area, and where a more or less bounded economy of goods and services centred on the prime product ties in with social
networks, cultural traditions, and so on. Following close behind is the
neighbourhood with a strong and spatially limited economy of aid, support, and regard, and intergenerational respect and authority. In vernacular communitarianism, such an important strand of political culture for
the political communitarians, it is in any case clear that place—where
people live, or parades of shops, or business centres where they work, or
the school and its neighbourhood—is frequently both the source of con-

---

[1] Peter Dahlgren and Colin Sparks (eds.), *Communication and Citizenship: Journalism
and the Public Sphere in the New Media Age* (London: Routledge, 1991), Introduction.
[2] For instance, Michael Walzer, *Spheres of Justice* (Oxford: Basil Blackwell, 1983), 304;
see also Michael Sandel, *Democracy's Discontents: America in Search of a Public
Philosophy* (Cambridge, Mass.: Harvard University Press, 1996).

flict or anxiety that generates activity, and the object of that activity, whose aim is to turn a place into, or back into, a community.

Political communitarians certainly see strong localities, together with strong families, well-ordered institutions like schools, hospitals, and firms, all linked together by the relation of community, as the proper social infrastructure for modern states. This clear emphasis makes communitarianism exceptional in recent political theory. In libertarian varieties of liberalism, in existentialism, and in the kind of romanticism that emphasizes transcendence, one central theme (expressed in rather different ways in these different discursive contexts) is the individual's need to consider her or his inner self rather than social setting, to dwell on his or her ability to rise above the 'now' and the 'here', to be detached from ties. A number of theorists and commentators stress that demands for local power and the value of locality have tended to come from the left, in response to the oppression of the bureaucratic capitalist state. (By contrast, the response from the right was to demand the institution of more or less free markets to undertake distributions that before had been managed by bureaucrats.[3]) However, theorists and scholars of socialism are quick to point out that in practice socialists have taken at best a pragmatic view of local power (promoting it only when it works in favour of their policies), and in practice have believed central state power to be necessary for the implementation of redistributive and public investment policies.[4]

But, as I have remarked, even in communitarianism the case for 'locality' is by no means straightforward. For the philosophical communitarians in particular it is a repressed but returning theme. Alasdair MacIntyre's conception of community is unspecific about locality. The repeated examples of the 'communities' that bestow us with social identity and a legacy of roles and obligations include guild, profession, clan, tribe, nation, family, city, neighbourhood.[5] For many, but not for all, of these collectives space or territory have a potent symbolic value. For all of them place can (but need not necessarily) be an important symbol—the guildhall, the family home, etc. Indeed, the key theoretical point about MacIntyre's communities is that they are social formations which engage the individual at the level of his identity (not just his preferences) and this

[3] Nicholas Deakin and Anthony Wright (eds.), *Consuming Public Services* (London: Routledge, 1990); Ray Lees and Marjorie Mayo, *Community Action for Change* (London: Routledge and Kegan Paul, 1984), Introduction; David Blunkett and Keith Jackson, *Democracy in Crisis: The Town Halls Respond* (London: Hogarth Press, 1987), 5.

[4] Andrew Sanction, 'British Socialist Theories of the Division of Power by Area', *Political Studies*, 24 (1976), 158–70.

[5] Alasdair MacIntyre, *After Virtue*, 2nd edn. (London: Duckworth, 1985), all on pp. 220–1.

engagement might logically transcend place. For Charles Taylor the important basis, and unifying stuff, of community is meaning. He emphasizes the role of constitutive historical events, of cultural and subcultural movements, in institutionalizing meanings which are, then, constitutive of social identities and our relations with others.[6] Place, or locality, here has only a marginal place—'the modern West' is, indeed, a space or region term, but not one that bears much literally minded investigation.

In Michael Sandel's theory the shift of power from local regions to the centre in US federalism and the nationalization of politics is a key process in the loss of community.[7] The importance of locality for this theory of community is underlined by his discussion in his recent book on the Community Action Programme for the War on Poverty which sought to enlarge the civic capacity of the poor by encouraging their participation in anti-poverty programmes at the local level.[8] New communications technologies seem to offer new forms of community, so that locality, in modern conditions, becomes unimportant. Yet, in a geographically dispersed, and geographically mobile, society, Sandel argues, 'Americans found themselves implicated in a scheme of interdependence that did not guarantee that they would identify with that scheme, or come to share a common life with the unknown others who were similarly implicated.'[9] The philosopher most explicit about locality and local government is Michael Walzer, although his reference is tantalizingly brief. Walzer's prescriptive analysis of polity involves political equality uncontaminated by other social inequalities. The republican tradition, admittedly, has been based on the possibilities and needs of small homogeneous communities where civil society is relatively undifferentiated. He argues that perhaps 'the doctrine can be extended to account for a "republic of republics". . . .' a considerable strengthening of local government would then be required in the hope of encouraging the development and display of civic virtue.'[10] In *Spheres of Justice* Walzer discusses some of the dilemmas and problems of locality: local autonomy and choice under current social and political conditions will likely lead, for instance, to practical racial segregation of neighbourhoods and schools. But politics is 'always territorially based' and there are clear democratic advantages to people being close to home

[6] Especially in Charles Taylor, *Sources of the Self: The Making of the Modern Identity* (Cambridge: Cambridge University Press, 1989); also *Philosophy and the Human Sciences* (Cambridge: Cambridge University Press, 1985).

[7] Michael Sandel, 'The Procedural Republic and the Unencumbered Self', *Political Theory*, 12 (1984), 92–3.

[8] Sandel, *Democracy's Discontents*, 283.   [9] Ibid. 206.

[10] Michael Walzer, 'The Communitarian Critique of Liberalism', *Political Theory*, 18 (1990), 20.

where they 'are most likely to be knowledgeable and concerned, active and effective . . . The democratic school, then, should be an enclosure within a neighbourhood.'[11] Similar issues of the problems of locality arise elsewhere in Walzer's work; for the most part, like Charles Taylor, Walzer's conception of community is underpinned by shared meanings. To be sure, the metaphor of locality is prominent in Walzer's gloss of this kind of particularism: 'I don't claim to have achieved any great distance from the social world in which I live. . . . I mean to stand in the cave, in the city, on the ground.'[12]

By contrast, locality and neighbourhood are clear and literal central themes in political communitarianism. As I have emphasized before, they are not the only theme: political communitarians also wish the nation, and the international world, to be a community; and refer also to 'communities' that transcend locale. But, quantitatively speaking, the overwhelming amount of political communitarian discourse—theory, argument, reportage, analysis—focuses on locality. Discussions of corporate responsibility invariably include corporate responsibility for 'local community initiatives' as well as internal democracy and environmental responsibility.[13] The communitarian family, and the communitarian school, should be integrated with each other and with the locality.[14] And the major communitarian issues that are picked up by reporters and journalists are demands for the devolution of power and resources for local people to control and disburse in their locality,[15] questions about how to regenerate areas in which people suffer from multiple deprivations, and reports of community activism focused especially on poverty and crime.[16]

The political communitarian normative principles that emerge from analysis of the literature and coverage—principles such as that 'communities have the right to defend themselves', 'communities need the power to govern themselves'—are mainly focused on the rights, needs, and

[11] Walzer, *Spheres of Justice*, 225.   [12] Ibid. p. xiv.
[13] Henry Tam, *Communitarianism* (Basingstoke: Macmillan, 1998), 192; David Grayson, 'Business and the Community', in Dick Atkinson (ed.), *Cities of Pride: Rebuilding Community, Refocussing Government* (London: Cassell, 1995).
[14] Tam, *Communitarianism*, 76; Amitai Etzioni, *The New Golden Rule: Community and Morality in a Democratic Society* (New York: Basic Books, 1996), 154; Dick Atkinson, *The Common Sense of Community* (London: Demos, 1994), 19.
[15] Martin Wainwright, 'People Power is Bringing Hope', *Guardian* (6 Dec. 1995), 4; Bob Holman, 'Helping Self-Help', *Guardian* (11 June 1997), Society p. 9; Peter Hetherington, 'Well-Heeled Take on Kerb Crawlers', *Guardian*, (2 June 1997); Melanie Phillips, 'Riddle behind Howard's Volunteers', *Observer* (20 Mar. 1994); Sam Smith, 'Bringing Politics Back Home', *Washington Post* (1 Nov. 1994), p. A23— are some of the items from my database which have 'local power' as their main theme; many others mention it is a secondary theme.
[16] Melanie Phillips, 'When a Community Stands up for Itself', *Observer* (17 July 1994); Marcia Davis, 'Open Arms', *Washington Post* (20 Feb. 1996), p. B01.

obligations of local communities. For example, a senior police officer is reported as saying: 'It is not for beat officers to dictate standards of behaviour to the community. Communities must have their own informal rules which, in turn, are reinforced by legal ones.'[17] A Labour councillor is reported as saying: 'People with problems run to the council and say the gates are not working or the hedge needs trimming. I'm asking people to do things for themselves.'[18]

As well as such references which seem to me clearly to local community there are many to a much vaguer, unspecified, community made generic by the use of the definite article, as in:

What the community can achieve by acting together to further individual well being and freedom can be greater that anything individuals working only to a free market ideology can achieve on their own.[19]

In order to finance services to the community there has to be some form of common wealth . . .[20]

But the greater number of references to 'the community' and to 'community' are to locality.

I can here summarize the political communitarian theory of locality. First, neighbourhood, together with family and membership of other institutions, is a key source of meaning and identity for individuals. Their values, their conduct, their discharge of roles and duties, their well-being and welfare is crucially bound up with the nature of their area, among other social formations. Communitarians argue that if local resources and burdens are shared then solutions to seemingly intractable problems like vandalism, crime, squalor, and even poverty can be found. Local people know best, or at least as well as anyone, what the problems are, and local people can recognize a practical solution when they see one. There must be action against and to prevent abuse of the area—by vandals and criminals, but also by businesses who use a locale's amenities but either don't make any direct contribution to its social and material infrastructure, or worse, cause damage to these. A locality includes not just the people who live there, but those who work there, in businesses, in schools, and in voluntary projects. This action should be action by the local people themselves who need the rights, the authority, and their share of public resources, to carry their own projects through. This emphasis on the sharing of benefits and burdens by members, on the imperatives of mutuality

17 *Guardian* (2 June 1997), 10.
18 Melanie Phillips, 'The Race to Wake Sleeping Duty', *Observer* (2 Apr. 1994), 25.
19 Gordon Brown, 'Beware the Mask of Tory Social Concern', *Observer* (1 Dec. 1990), 20.
20 Gerald Holtham, 'It's not all over yet', *Observer* (24 Sept. 1995), 4.

and reciprocity, and on the importance of increasing the density and multiplexity of relationships in a locality all add up to the political project of building community in a locality, making a locality into a community.

We have seen, then, that locality and a measure of local autonomy, are central to political communitarianism. It is also notable that 'community' tends to be central in the thought of students and theorists of local government. A significant strand of this literature is concerned with the relationship between the spatial division of governmental and administrative powers, and the boundaries of 'communities'. The UK compares unfavourably with many European countries where the 'commune' (with its historic connotations of self-government and joint action) tends to be coextensive with meaningful social units such as villages or agricultural production areas. By contrast, in the UK over many decades there has been an overwheening emphasis on efficiency in service provision which has led now to centralization, now to a measure of decentralization, but has not acknowledged an intrinsic value in local self-administration and government.[21] On the other hand, among theorists of public administration the case for local government has been assumed, rather than argued for.[22]

In response to both these tendencies political theorists and scientists have developed a theory of 'community government'. For example, Desmond King argues, in defence of constitutional entrenchment for local government in the UK, that local governments are, at least in part, manifestations of local communities. The territorial division of power has a communal, as well a purely geographic, basis. There is a current crisis of local democracy, and that can be traced, in large part, to a decided and deliberate shift away from recognition of this idea in central government's policy on 'the local state'.[23] John Stewart argues that local government should take on a new role as community government. He is at pains to avoid the presumption that there just are genuine and strong communities

[21] John Stewart, 'A Future for Local Authorities as Community Government', in John Stewart and Gerry Stoker (eds.), *The Future of Local Government* (Basingstoke: Macmillan, 1989); Desmond King, 'Government beyond Whitehall: Local Government and Urban Politics', in P. Dunleavy et al. (eds.), *Developments in British Politics*, 4 (1993). However, it is important not to exaggerate the point—the Boundary Commission was expected to take 'community interest' into account when defining local government areas, and in the 1970s a Department of the Environment circular noted the importance of parish councils as 'communities of feeling'. (See Ken Young, Brian Gosschalk, and Warren Hatter, *In Search of Community Identity* (York: Joseph Rowntree Foundation, 1996), 4–5.) However, these rhetorical nods to 'community' did not make any clear impact on decisions.

[22] Gerry Stoker, *The Politics of Local Government*, 2nd edn. (Basingstoke: Macmillan, 1991), ch. 10.

[23] King, 'Government beyond Whitehall', 217.

already in existence, that will, given the opportunity, generate local autonomous governance and local democracy. But he argues that local authorities' primary role should be concern with the problems and issues faced by 'local communities'.[24] Gerry Stoker outlines a composite argument for 'localism' which chimes remarkably with political communitarianism: local democracy and autonomy would take diversity of conditions, needs, and practical solutions properly into account, it would maximize local participation, loyalty and legitimacy, it would institutionalize accountability.[25]

We have seen then a complex identification of community with locality: local communities are the most important (the most focused on) communities for political communitarians, and from some political scientists we have a demand that local government and administration should be responsive to 'communities'. In the next section I am going to consider a number of sets of problems with these theoretical relationships. First, a number of theorists question the relevance of the category 'community', in light of empirical findings about patterns of local life and the interrelationship of spatial and social relations. Second, nobody can deny that 'community' is a key concept for many political activists, political theorists, and policy-makers: community development, community action, community projects and programmes proliferate. These projects raise a number of questions: first, about their aims and objectives, second about the evaluation of their success or effectiveness. As ever, a central preoccupation in my discussion of these points is the relevance of the concept 'community'—its rhetorical effects, its empirical justification. Third, there is a good deal of evidence about the opportunities and barriers to 'community-building' projects; in discussing this evidence, once again, the significance of the concept is my main concern. In the final section of this chapter, I go on to discuss some ethical issues that have been problematized in relation to a political focus on locality and 'community'.

COMMUNITY, LOCAL POWER AND SOCIAL ORDER

The first set of problems we have met before. This is the objection to the sociological relevance of the concept community by theorists who are

24 Stewart, 'A Future for Local Authorities'.

25 Stoker, *Politics of Local Government*; also Gerry Stoker, 'Introduction: Normative Theories of Local Government and Democracy', in Desmond King and Gerry Stoker (eds.), *Rethinking Local Democracy* (Basingstoke: Macmillan, 1996), esp. pp. 11–14. See also Anne Phillips, *Local Democracy: The Terms of the Debate* (London: Commission on Local Democracy, 1994).

concerned to map people's actual networks of relationships. It may well be the case that in some societies individuals' significant relationships of exchange, solidarity, and identity are confined to a locality. However, it is not the case in modern industrial and post-industrial societies. Network analysis tends to reveal that for any individual most ties are not local— Margaret Stacey found this in Banbury, UK, in the 1950s and 1960s, Barry Wellman finds it in Toronto, Canada, in the 1980s.[26] Margaret Stacey also argues, based on locality studies, that it is not even the case that localities (towns, villages, estates, etc.) centre on particularly dense networks of relations. Stacey's argument against 'community' then is that the localities that community studies focus on are not communities in the sense of being bounded clusters of dense (and multiplex) ties which engage individuals in 'whole person' relations. It is notable that the UK studies that were conducted under the broad heading 'community studies' focused mainly on the significance of *kin* relations in a locality—rather than tracing the totality of social relations within and beyond the area.[27] A recent press article by Michael Young underlines the point. He emphasizes that the old interaction of kinship with the allocation of public housing (which kept kinship networks together in British cities) is (was) the infrastructure of community. Where kindred are local, informal aid and care will circulate easily. Where kindred are spatially scattered by housing allocation policies these networks crumble (this is illustrated even in Michael Young and Peter Willmott's original East London study, where they analysed the movement during the 1950s from Bethnal Green (London's traditional 'East End') to new housing developments in the Essex suburbs). The East London study also suggested that where kindred are local, ties of acquaintanceship and friendship beyond kin will also be more numerous and more dense, individuals will know, to greet or to talk to, individuals who are friends or neighbours of kin.[28] Phillip Abrams's work on neighbouring includes the observation that the traditional 'communities' in localities where the social networks were relatively dense and were efficient tracks for care and mutual aid tended to be rooted, if not in kinship, then in

[26] Margaret Stacey, *Tradition and Change: A Study of Banbury* (Oxford: Oxford University Press, 1960); *Power Persistence and Change: A Second Study of Banbury* (London: Routledge and Kegan Paul, 1975); Barry Wellman, 'Studying Personal Communities', in Peter V. Marsden, and Nan Lin (eds.), *Social Structure and Network Analysis* (Beverly Hills, Calif.: Sage, 1982).

[27] I am indebted to Teresa Smith for his point.

[28] Michael Young and Peter Willmott, *Family and Kinship in East London* (London: Routledge and Kegan Paul, 1957); Michael Young and Gerard Lemos, 'Roots of Revival', *Guardian* (19 Mar. 1997), Society p. 2.

occupation, religion, or race—that is, they were not local as such.[29] If 'community care' is to be a viable social policy it will be because it is based on kinship, religion, or ethnicity—not 'community' as such.[30]

This is an important point. A characteristic question in vernacular communitarianism is: 'is this a friendly or integrated area?', 'are people round here helpful/ friendly?' But studies suggest that the relevant variable is not the nature of people in a locality, but the spatial distribution of kin ties, or religious or ethnic identity, or occupation.[31] Where there are dense and multiplex networks based on these relationships, then two things can happen. First, all individuals in the area, including those who are not tied into the relevant networks, will be drawn into the generalized social practices of greetings and related exchanges. This affects individuals' subjective sense of attachment to the neighbourhood and to their co-residents.[32] Second, those individuals who are not tied into the relevant networks (but are nevertheless in the area) may be more easily overlooked—the sense on the part of the well-integrated that the area is inhabited by individuals who are not acquainted and do not interact will be less strong. So active and articulate people are likely to express the view that 'everyone round here knows each other' even though that is statistically far from the truth.

Wellman agrees with Stacey's point about community and locality. However he maintains the concept 'community', using it to refer to significant social relations, including kin (but not household)-based, and not market based. These are ties of intimacy, acquaintanceship, friendship, and co-membership, which can carry and channel support, aid, and care. Wellman's study has mapped 'personal communities'—that is, it has concentrated on individuals' personal networks of ties, rather than looking at the totality of ties within the area studied. The composition, structure, and content of these 'personal communities' varies with the individual's social structural location and status (in or out of the labour market, sex, marital status, etc.).[33]

---

[29] Martin Bulmer, *Neighbours: The Work of Phillip Abrams* (Cambridge: Cambridge University Press, 1986), 93–4.

[30] See Martin Bulmer, *The Social Basis of Community Care* (London: Unwin Hyman, 1987), 10.

[31] Graham Day and Jonathan Murdoch suggest that in the locality and community literature two distinct questions are frequently conflated: first, the question of the spatiality of social relations, second, the 'social construction of particular spaces as communities or localities'. 'Locality and Community: Coming to Terms with Place', *Sociological Review*, 41 (1993), 91.

[32] Cynthia Woolever, 'A Contextual Approach to Neighbourhood Attachment', *Urban Studies*, 29 (1992), 99–116.

[33] Wellman, 'Studying Personal Communities', 71.

The importance of networks does not, of course, mean that locality has no significance for individuals—it is significant in many ways, and in ways that vary from one individual to another. First, there is subjective sense of belonging. Notably, though, when individuals are asked about their sense of belonging to various spatial units (neighbourhood, town, district, county, etc.) multiple loyalties and identifications are expressed.[34] Furthermore, when individuals are themselves invited to describe the area they do or do not feel a sense of belonging in, and to describe the social relations within it, even more complexity and variation is revealed. Within a locale, different respondents will offer different 'maps 'of 'the area' and the social relations within it. They will also distinguish between their, subjective, map and what they perceive to be the public image of their area. There is also variation in the clarity of 'maps' between respondents from one locale to another (that is, some 'places' are more place-like than others). There is also variation, between individuals, and between respondents from different locales, in the strength of the antipathy expressed to other locales.[35] In light of these and other complexities, John Puddifoot proposes a fourteen-fold analysis of dimensions of community identity (to form the basis of interview and survey instruments)—and these do not include any more 'objective' measures such as the degree of network density and network multiplexity, or number of voluntary organizations in the locale.

Second are all the many ways that the areas in which individuals live, work, or socialize enhance or limit the quality of their lives. In social theory one important aspect of these questions about locality is the causal or explanatory one, and in particular debates about the significance of macro or large-scale structural processes such as 'class structure', 'industrialization', 'de-industrialization', and the like. Many theorists and scientists have argued that the impact of such processes is mediated by local factors, and individuals' actions and strategies in face of the dilemmas posed by these processes likewise. A number of studies set out to establish the extent to which this is so.[36] An important research question here is the effect of local authorities' actions in the face of economic change—whether declining employment levels can be halted, for instance, and who benefits

[34] Colin Rallings, Michael Temple, and Michael Thrasher, *Community Identity and Participation in Local Democracy* (London: Commission for Local Democracy, 1994); Geraint Parry, George Moyser, and Neil Day, *Political Participation and Democracy in Britain* (Cambridge: Cambridge University Press, 1992), 303 ff.; Young, Gosschalk, and Hatter, *In Search of Community Identity*, 11 ff.

[35] John E. Puddifoot, 'Some Initial Considerations in the Measurement of Community Identity', *Journal of Community Psychology*, 24 (1996), 327–36.

[36] Michael Harloe et al. *Place, Policy and Politics: Do Localities Matter?* (London: Unwin Hyman, 1990), Introd. and Conclusion.

from different local strategies.[37] More prosaically, the design and maintenance of the built environment, the provision of shops, green spaces, and buildings suitable for civic and social events, the layout of living, working, and leisure facilities and the routes between them, the routing of cars, heavy traffic, public transport, all make a difference to the quality of life. The exact interrelationship between such material structures, and social relations and processes (including crime, vandalism, civic and voluntary association, employment and work, education, and so on) is the subject of a wide range of theoretical and empirical literature.[38]

More importantly, these are also the issues that generate discontent, political consciousness, organization and political action. This political organization and action is often carried on in the name of 'the community'—that is, community is the key value that is promoted in this kind of local politics. By the same token, community building is frequently thought to be a necessary condition of success with the main goal—be that improved housing, the defeat of drug dealers, safer play areas, the removal of toxic or unsightly dumps, or saving shops or businesses from closure. For example, in a discussion of women residents' role in housing fights in Chicago the authors sum up the participants' view of politics: human connectedness in social networks is essential to politics[39]—Black Chicago women 'sustain the social fabric of community and help to foster a community identity, while at the same time they provide essential services'.[40] In this sense, community is instrumentally as well as intrinsically valuable. Organization of the community is carried out in the name of the community.[41]

[37] Phillip Cooke (ed.), *Localities: The Changing Face of Urban Britain* (London: Unwin Hyman, 1989), 10; Harloe et al., *Place Policy and Politics*; Peter Dickens, *One Nation? Social Change and the Politics of Locality* (London: Pluto Press, 1988); Paul Bagguley et al., *Restructuring: Place Class and Gender* (London: Sage, 1990); Richard Peet and Nigel Thrift, *New Models in Geography: The Political Economy Perspective*, vols. i and ii (London: Unwin Hyman, 1989).

[38] For example Adam Crawford, 'Appeals to Community and Crime Prevention', *Crime, Law and Social Change*, 22 (1995) 97–126; *The Local Governance of Crime: Appeals to Community and Partnerships* (Oxford: Clarendon Press, 1997); *Crime Prevention and Community Safety: Politics, Policies and Practices* (London: Longman, 1998); Kevin Robins, 'Prisoners of the City: Whatever Could a Postmodern City Be?', in Erica Carter et al. (eds.), *Space and Place: Theories of Identity and Location* (London: Lawrence and Wishart, 1993).

[39] Roberta M. Feldman, Susan Stall, and Patricia A. Wright, 'The Community Needs to be Built by Us: Women Organising in Chicago Public Housing', in Nancy A. Naples (ed.), *Community Activism and Feminist Politics: Organising Across Race, Class and Gender* (New York: Routledge, 1998), 261.

[40] Ibid. 260.

[41] See Ray Lees and George Smith, *Action Research in Community Development* (London: Routledge and Kegan Paul, 1975), 36–7 on different models of 'community development', 'community action', 'social planning', and so on, and 'community' as an instrumental value, or a deontological value, or both, in these.

This communitarian theory is also taken up by governments—central and local. In the United States President Johnson's 'War on Poverty' involved a government funded Community Action Programme.[42] The Callaghan Government funded the Community Development Programme, from 1972 to 1977.[43] The European Economic Community (now European Union) Anti-Poverty Programme financed an Area Resource Centre programme in the late 1970s.[44] The British government funded numerous local projects through the 'Urban Programme' throughout the 1980s.[45] British local authorities, increasingly through the 1980s, also decentralized the delivery of services (welfare payment, housing administration), and, in some cases, decentralized decision-making to the 'neighbourhood' level.[46] In the 1990s, a number of the many organizations and projects that had started in the 1970s and 1980s were themselves organised and structured by 'community development trusts' in the UK, and 'comprehensive community initiatives' in the USA.[47] As new drives to develop, empower or regenerate communities are announced by government after government it's *déjà vu* all over again.[48]

As numerous commentators point out, historically the theory behind these initiatives has tended to be vague, or muddled, or both.[49] Others

[42] Daniel P. Moynihan, *Maximum Feasible Misunderstanding: Community Action in the War on Poverty* (New York: Free Press, 1969).

[43] Martin Loney, *Community against Government: The British Community Development Project 1968–78—A Study of Government Incompetence* (London: Heinemann, 1983); Lees and Smith, *Action Research in Community Development*.

[44] Nick Bailey, Ray Lees, and Marjorie Mayo, *Resourcing Communities* (London: Polytechnic of Central London, 1980).

[45] Brian Robson, *Those Inner Cities: Reconciling the Economic and Social Aims of Urban Policy* (Oxford: Clarendon Press, 1988).

[46] See Colin Fudge, 'Decentralisation: Socialism Goes Local', in Martin Boddy and Colin Fudge (eds.), *Local Socialism? Labour Councils and the New Left Alternatives* (Basingstoke: Macmillan, 1984); Stoker, *Politics of Local Government*, ch. 5; Teresa Smith, 'Decentralisation and Community', *British Journal of Social Work*, 19 (1989), 137–49.

[47] James P. Connell and Anne C. Kubisch, 'Evaluating Comprehensive Community Initiatives', unpub. 1996; Stephen Thake, *Staying the Course: The Role and Structure of Community Regeneration Organisations* (York: Joseph Rowntree Foundation, 1995).

[48] The Cabinet Office Social Exclusion Unit began a consultation on 'deprived neighbourhoods' in 1998, publishing *Bringing Britain Together* Cm. 4045 (Sept. 1998).

[49] On paper, at least, the current UK government's policies are designed to head off the most obvious pitfalls and contradictions—there has been a concerted effort to work across governmental departments so that policy discussion and guidance from the Home Office (e.g. the *Guidance on Statutory Crime and Disorder Partnerships* (Crime and Disorder Act 1998), the Department of Education (*Excellence in Schools*, Cm. 3681), the Ministerial Group on the Family (*Supporting Families*, Nov. 1998), the Department of Environment, Transport and the Regions (*Guidance on Local Transport Plans*, Nov. 1998), and the Cabinet Office Social Exclusion Unit (*Bringing Britain Together*, Cm. 4045, Sept. 1998) are all singing the same community involvement and local participation tune. It remains to be seen whether policy implementation and development are successful in realizing this kind of local participation.

argue more cynically that in many cases they are a way of buying off local discontent by erecting a façade of democracy—for example, neighbourhood participation gave 'troublesome groups' representation within the local political system, but the key decisions about resources were always taken elsewhere.[50] In the case of the War on Poverty and the Community Development Programme it is undoubtedly true that certain sponsors of the programmes were influenced by normative theories of localism or communitarianism. For example, Derek Morrell, the Home Office official who was one of the main energies behind the Community Development Programme was

concerned with the growth of rigid bureaucracy and the disintegration of our sense of community. He said '. . . the profession of social work has a great deal to offer, not only to the more obviously dispossessed in our society, but also to the recovery or creation within Western social democracy of a genuine sense of community.'

Morrell was motivated by a religious, catholic, commitment to community.[51]

The Community Action Programmes (provided for in the Economic Opportunity Act 1964, itself part of President Lyndon Johnson's War on Poverty) similarly were ill thought out. Daniel Moynihan's account emphasizes several factors. First a theory of how social reform could be put in train—'by exerting smaller forces at points of maximum leverage to capture larger forces otherwise working against us'[52]—was articulated by political activists and became influential among academics and policymakers. Second, there was a new professional class of political, social, and community workers, centred on inner city community action agencies (the Henry Street Settlement in Lower East Side Manhattan was an important early focus for the programmes that were the precursors for the War on Poverty). Third, once the War on Poverty was under way hostility to 'research' from within Congress was extremely important—funds for projects were dependent upon 'action', something being done. Equally, Congress was hostile to the principle of 'maximum feasible participation

---

[50] Gerry Stoker and Stephen Young (eds.), *Cities in the 1990s* (London: Longman, 1993), 108. Chik Collins argues that the only way to understand the treatment of the umbrella organization for tenants' groups in Glasgow, both by the local authority, and in the context of an Urban Programme funded urban renewal initiative in the mid-1980s, is as 'co-optation', 'silencing', and eventually exclusion. Chik Collins, 'The Dialogics of Community: Struggle and Identity in a Scottish Working Class Housing Scheme', paper delivered to conference 'Ideas of Community', University of the West of England, Sept. 1995.

[51] Loney, *Community Against Government*, 44.

[52] Moynihan, *Maximum Feasible Misunderstanding*, 40.

by local people' that was articulated in early policy documents. Although professionals and activists held on to this as an ideal, in practice difficulties with questions of 'representation' meant that, for instance, neighbourhoods populated by black people were 'parachuted into' by white professionals. Add to this the antagonisms between the city authorities and the federally funded agencies, and the result was increased local conflict often focused on the projects themselves and little alleviation of poverty.

Seemingly, the theory or model underpinning the Community Development Project was the 'cycle of deprivation'.[53] The Home Secretary, announcing the project, said:

Although the social services cater reasonably well for the majority, they are much less effective for a minority who are caught up in a chain reaction of related social problems. An example of the kind of vicious circle in which this kind of family could be trapped is ill-health, financial difficulty, inability of the children to adjust to adult life, unstable marriages, emotional problems, ill-health—and the cycle begins again.[54]

The assumption was, must have been, that this kind of family was spatially concentrated—as funding was directed to restricted and bounded areas. That is, the implication was that families like this, and areas like this, needed a more tightly coordinated and targeted delivery of support services. And, governments hope, there will be cost and management savings if local people become more self-reliant.[55] Predictably, as the Inter-Project report submitted to the Home Office in November 1973, made clear, project leaders found little evidence either of the spatial concentration of the kind of 'problem family' the politicians had at the top of their minds, or of

[53] I say 'seemingly' because prominent individuals involved with the Community Development Programme apparently were in no wise committed to this theory: Loney reports that A. H. Halsey, who was the research director, was convinced that the problems of poor people in poor areas were a problem with the (national) structure of opportunities. Loney, *Community against Government*, 56.

[54] Quoted in John Benington, 'The Flaw in the Pluralist Heaven: Changing Strategies in the Coventry CDP', from Lees and Smith, *Action Research in Community Development*, (London: Routledge & Kegan Paul, 1975).

[55] John Benington quotes Richard Crossman announcing the Coventry Community Development Project: 'It is not just a matter of helping to get these people back on their feet by gearing up the social services for them in a fully coordinated way but of helping them to stand more on their own in the future by their own efforts without having to rely so much on external support.' (Benington, 'The Flaw in the Pluralist Heaven', 174.) Cynthia Cockburn quotes from a Department of the Environment consultation paper, July 1974, on the subject of 'neighbourhood councils' in support of the interpretation that the key impetus was the search for cost saving and the lessening of management burdens on local authorities. Cynthia Cockburn, *The Local State: Management of Cities and People* (London: Pluto Press, 1977), 108.

endogenous (and endogenously curable) problems of deprivation—the relevant problems were overwhelmingly external to the areas.[56] Poor public housing, development blight, badly designed roads and inadequate transport, disproportionate police surveillance and resulting stigma, and racism are all mentioned.

So the question has to be asked again, what is the point of 'community development' or 'community action'. Obviously, one response is that community action, involving organization, the marshalling of resources, the display of solidaristic political power, can help people frame, voice, and pursue their demands in public and political forums. And, indeed, this is the conclusion that many community workers quickly came to. The role of 'research' on the Community Development Programme was, in a number of projects, thought of not just as a means of evaluating practice, but as a resource for local people, giving them the chance to demonstrate the ill-effects of a ring road cutting an estate off from a town, or the problems of condensation in new housing. Account after account tells how local authorities fail to inform people of decisions that affect them (though they could); fail to consult people about the best way to go about some project or routine service delivery; fail to discover in advance of policy formation the needs of local people. It is reasonable enough that many local people and project workers concluded that improved channels of communication should be a relatively cheap way of overcoming a number of problems.

However, account after account also tells how the presentation of facts, diagnoses, ideas, options for change to local councillors, local government officers, and other decision-makers invariably failed to bring about even relatively simple and inexpensive or cost-free changes in policy and practice, no matter what dialogic strategy was tried.[57] These and similar examples are most significant for theorists of democracy, especially those committed to a dialogic or discursive model of democracy. The concept of 'dialogue' (as opposed to monologue, diatribe, and other politically relevant modes of discourse) connotes civilized, reason-governed, and reciprocal communication. These aspects of it in turn connote cooperation, or at any rate the lack of antagonism and friction. Yet, it is clear that for many individuals, and in many institutional contexts and practices, dialogue is agonistic in the extreme, and disruptive of established routine.

---

[56] It is possible that it was just that the 'wrong' areas were targeted—as Clive Payne and George Smith make clear there was very little detailed local data available, and no clear index of need was developed prior to the selection of the areas (in Lees and Smith, *Action Research in Community Development*, ch. 3).

[57] Ibid. 40; Loney, *Community against Government*, 98; Ann Curno, Anne Lamming, Lesley Leach, Jenny Stiles, Veronica Ward, and Trisha Ziff (eds.), *Women in Collective Action* (London: Association of Community Workers, 1982), 13 ff.

Many individuals have an extremely low tolerance of discussion, experiencing 'questioning' as violent and coercive, and find the obligation to explain or reason an intolerable burden. Dialogue *is* conflict.

As many commentators and analysts have noted, many bureaucrats and politicians seem to have a marked aversion to discussion with citizens, and furthermore are in an extremely powerful position to avoid this kind of conflict. How they do it is instructive.[58] Presenting tenants in damp housing as irrational and 'bad managers', arguing that they should send the television back to pay the heating bills and have the heating on full and the windows open,[59] not minuting requests for information, hearing requests for information from local people as 'rudeness',[60] arguing that suggestions from local people who have no formal organization are inadmissible,[61] viewing organized local people as unrepresentative and biased (and organization as a sign of illegitimacy).[62] That they do it is a challenge for democratic theory and practice. In particular, it points to the need for changes within political institutions rather than in 'the community' or at the level of locality.

These experiences with the 'normal political process' and the dialogic ideal of democracy turn attention to an alternative theory of politics and community. As John Benington reports, in Coventry local people didn't want any more communication: they were in dispute over their needs and aspirations.[63] A gap is revealed between the needs that are recognized and supported by politicians, governmental agencies, and, as we might put it, dominant social discourses, and the felt needs that are recognized and articulated by the participants. One aim of 'community development' is to enhance the capacity of poor people for social protest.[64] Among community workers in Britain this aim has often been connected with a 'conflict theory' of social relations (specifically class and state relations), and a commitment to 'conflict tactics' as the most promising way to social

[58] As well as the references in nn. 56–8 below see generally papers by Dennis, Jacobs, Thomas, and Benington in Peter Leonard (ed.), *The Sociology of Community Action* Sociological Review Monograph 21 (Keele: University of Keele, 1975).

[59] Curno et al., *Women in Collective Action*, 19.

[60] Collins, 'Dialogics of Community', 7.

[61] Maureen Mackintosh and Hilary Wainwright (eds.), *A Taste of Power* (London: Verso, 1987), 314.

[62] Leonard, *The Sociology of Community*, 182–3; on the contradictions of 'representativeness' also Moynihan, *Maximum Feasible Misunderstanding*, 124–5.

[63] Benington, 'Flaw in the Pluralist Heaven', 176.

[64] Loney, *Community against Government*, 63; Benington, 'Flaw in the Pluralist Heaven', 182; Harry Specht, *Community Development in the UK: An Assessment and Recommendation for Change* (London: Association of Community Workers, 1975), 9.

change.[65] And indeed, reports and accounts of community campaigns suggest that conflict tactics have brought results—disrupting a council meeting got a change where dialogue failed;[66] women chained themselves to the Town Hall railings to draw attention to the problems of heating and condensation and 'It was incredible. The press were coming, the television were coming. Suddenly, even our councillors greeted us.'[67] But the prominence of conflict tactics in local politics does beg the question why governments should fund these local projects.[68]

Cockburn argues that, like the devolution of a certain, limited, 'consultation' and administration to the neighbourhood level, conflict redeems the idea of democracy. It can be 'moderated into a style of governance'.[69] Cockburn clearly thinks of this as a cynical exercise, contrary to genuine political and economic justice. Norman Dennis argues that in their rhetoric politicians and officials will imply that they understand politics to be a process in which citizens' influence bears on the citizens' (via their representatives) authoritative decision-making, while they actually operate with a practical model in which politics is the process of bringing officials' and politicians' influence to bear on official decision-making.[70] But normative political theorists have not given up on the prospects for social conflict and democracy. One theme that emerges strongly from the community development and community activism literature focused on UK cases is that the partisan structure (the partisan conflict transformed into a mode of governance) presents a barrier to local organization, and to the solution to tractable local problems. One possibility is that disruption of this partisan conflict by the intervention of other groups and claims-makers—groups based on ethnicity, locality, generation, or other practical interests—might make governance more responsive to need.

However, Cockburn's argument chimes with another view that is prominent in the community development literature. Martin Loney, for instance, reports that some 'structuralist' community workers thought that these 'conflict' tactics used by their colleagues were an irrelevant waste of effort.[71] 'Structuralist theory' of course covers a range of hypotheses about the nature and workings of social reality—from the view that 'structures' are pre-social and even pre-cognitive and therefore unre-

---

[65] Loney, *Community against Government*, 100.   [66] Ibid. 98.

[67] Curno et al., *Women in Collective Action*, 14.

[68] Moynihan, *Maximum Feasible Misunderstanding*, 131.

[69] Cockburn, *The Local State*, 117–18.

[70] Norman Dennis, *Public Participation and Planners' Blight* (London: Faber and Faber, 1972), 269.

[71] Loney, *Community against Government*, 144 ff.

sponsive to human endeavours to transform them,[72] to the more moderate view that structures, because they are macro phenomena, the consequences of myriad actions, transactions, beliefs, and interpretations are unresponsive to local or isolated challenges, but not immutable.[73] Either way, being a 'structuralist community activist', or a 'structuralist community worker' is an interestingly paradoxical position—perhaps especially so if you are funded by the state. A structuralist social and political theory does not entail a view of the state as monolithic, but in practice, debates within community work and among activists have been organized around the problem of how to tackle the unified structure of state and class, as against a view of government and state as fractured and presenting opportunities for intervention and change.[74]

Loney remarks, though, that whichever view about the nature of state, class, race, and social change is dominant in a project, practical efforts are directed to a familiar repertoire of activities: the provision of advice, of play, leisure and associational facilities, attempts to provide employment and/or training to local people, on the one hand, and the organization of pressure about housing, environment, and transport, etc. on the other.[75]

[72] This is a view of 'structure' that proceeded into social and political theory from the structuralist approach to language associated with Saussure and the structuralist approach to cultural universals associated with Lévi-Strauss. An illuminating structuralist analysis along these lines is Pierre Bourdieu, 'The Kabyle House or the World Reversed', which is reprinted, in the context of an account of why Bourdieu now considers this kind of structuralism to be faulty, in *The Logic of Practice* (1st pub. French 1980), trans. Richard Nice (Oxford: Polity Press, 1990).

[73] This view is associated with Anthony Giddens's challenge to structuralism; see Anthony Giddens, *Central Problems in Social Theory: Action, Structure and Contradiction in Social Analysis* (Basingstoke: Macmillan, 1979). Similar approaches are taken in a wide range of 'post-structuralist' social theories.

[74] Loney, *Community Against Government*, 150–2; see Cockburn, *The Local State*, 42–7 for an analysis of the state as differentiated and layered; but she argues 'In spite of its multiplicity, however, the state preserves a basic unity. All its parts work as one' (p. 47). Specht, *Community Development in the UK*, 7 ff. also comments on the tension between the very idea of community work and theories of the state and government. See also Lees and Mayo, *Community Action for Change*, 39–44. Turner's opposition between community and structure is interestingly relevant here: Victor Turner, *The Ritual Process: Structure and Anti-structure* (London: Routledge and Kegan Paul, 1969).

[75] Loney, *Community against Government*, 149. Hugh Butcher, Patricia Collis, Andrew Glen, and Patrick Sills, *Community Groups in Action* (London: Routledge and Kegan Paul, 1980) identify two different attitudes to resource deployment: groups can use resources to directly provide goods to people who need them, or use these resources to modify the performance of larger resource allocation systems. They label these 'self-help' and 'influence' strategies. Of course, many groups will engage effectively in both. In a recent survey of 'community regeneration organisations' Stephen Thake finds the following activity headings: Childcare/youth work; education; training; business development; workspace; income enhancement; advice; security; housing; health; environmental improvement; culture/tourism/carnival. Thake, *Staying the Course*, 32.

These are all goods whose social provision is difficult to quarrel with. Obviously, there is the question whether the projects concerned are making a good job of the supply and distribution of these goods. And this raises the question of evaluation more generally. There are several reasons why this is a difficult issue to report on.

First, as has been pointed out time after time, it is difficult to escape the conclusion that although central governments and local authorities do (time after time) announce 'new' community initiatives and 'new' approaches to community regeneration, the programmes invariably have major design flaws (such as ambiguous, conflicting, or vague goals), lack crucial support in salient governmental quarters, and are funded for too short a time.[76] Second, a good deal of the literature to hand consists of researchers' and participants' accounts of what I can only call 'defeats and triumphs'.[77] These paint very vivid pictures of the difficulties of community organization, the resources that are necessary for sustained work (and the sacrifices individuals will make in order to marshall those resources), and the challenges to conventional practices of 'democracy' posed by local, participatory, politics which is focused on issues of justice in the distribution of goods and bads.[78] The difficulty with these accounts, riveting reading though they usually make, is that the tales of winning or losing battles with the local authority, or networking with groups engaged in similar conflicts elsewhere, rarely add up to a clear response to such questions as whether this kind of action does amount to 'community development' or 'community regeneration'; whether they make any lasting differences to distributions and patterns of relations; or about the significance for democracy of different modes of organization.

A third problem is that although the very ideal of 'community development' and 'community work' demands evaluation at the level of 'the community' (that is to say, the locality), most evaluation is carried out at the level of 'the organization'.[79] One important indicator is often taken to be

[76] Moynihan, *Maximum Feasible Misunderstanding*; Lees and Smith, *Action Research in Community Development*, ch. 2; Loney, *Community against Government*, 71, 85 ff., 108 ff.

[77] The 'triumph' genre is becoming dominant in UK government policy and consultation documents which are now packed with visually arresting vignettes which report 'impacts' like the following: 'There have been over 1,100 tenancies granted due to the Hotline since its establishment in 1997. . . . The Hotline has created stability in previously declining areas and given council housing a better image' (from Cabinet Office Social Exclusion Unit, *Bringing Britain Together*, 46).

[78] For example, Naples, *Community Activism and Feminist Politics*; Curno et al., *Women in Collective Action*; Leonard, *The Sociology of Community Action*; Paul Henderson et al. (eds.), *Successes and Struggles on Council Estates: Tenant Action and Community Work* (London: Association of Community Workers in the UK, 1982).

[79] I want to emphasize that the literature under review in this section of this chapter interprets 'community' just as 'locality' or 'area'.

relationships or networks between organizations in a locality.[80] The importance of informal networks between activists, professionals and funders, rather than formal and bureaucratic relations, is emphasized. This does not add up to evaluation of the locality itself—rather it is the success of organizations and individual workers in securing contracts and influencing policy that is at issue. Even so, evaluation of 'success' at the level of the single organization is anyway fraught with difficulty. To begin with, organizations are very often conflicted by funding matters: short-term funds—which have been dominant in the UK at least in the 1970s to 1990s—effectively rule out hope of any significant social change.[81] Further, with any new funding arrangements shifts in goals and strategies are also often required, and changing goals and strategies obviously make meaningful evaluation even more difficult.[82] In any case, evaluation is very difficult in the common circumstance where there is ambiguity, vagueness, and conflict about goals and strategies.[83] The 'community development' projects on both sides of the Atlantic show that governments and authorities wish for an easing of the burdens on state welfare agencies while community workers frequently move to increasing this 'burden' by way of the provision of advice to claimants about their rights. Participants and workers move to a conflict theory of social change and democratic politics, and frequently have resort to disruptive tactics, while governments and authorities wish for the optimum amount of participation in order to secure democratic legitimacy without any unpleasant disruption of established modes of decision-making (and all disruption is unpleasant). But there are also many disagreements about goals within community organizations. Bryant and Bryant, in a study of tenants' campaigns in the UK in the 1970s and 1980s, found that local people were far less inclined than professionals to focus on long-run (rather than short-run) goals. (When this is put together with funders' proclivity for short-term funding the result is a good deal of frustration for workers.) Secondly, while local people had very clear views about the kinds of material gains, for individuals and for the area collectively, that would count as 'success', they were

[80] See H. Clark, 'Taking up Space: Redefining Political Legitimacy in New York City', *Environment and Planning A*, 26 (1994), 940; Chris Skelcher, Angus McCabe, and Vivien Lowndes, *Community Networks in Urban Regeneration* (Bristol: Policy Press, 1996) also focuses on the conditions of 'organisational success'.

[81] Ian Cooke and Eddie Tunnah, 'Urban Communities and Economic Regeneration: A Liverpool Case Study', paper delivered to conference 'Ideas of Community', University of the West of England, Sept. 1995.

[82] Robert Kleidman, 'Volunteer Activism', *Social Problems*, 41 (1994), 271.

[83] James P. Connell and Anne C. Kubisch, 'Evaluation of Comprehensive Community Initiatives', unpub. 1996.

very divided in their views as to whether (in the absence of such material gains) they attributed any value at all to the 'community building process'.[84] According to those who value community in itself success and failure in the pursuit of material goals might be all the same—the community-building process, with all its benefits, will occur whether the group triumphs or is defeated in the matter at hand. Some individuals are persuaded by this argument (these are those who value community for its own sake); some are not.

Connell and Kubisch also point out that evaluation requires a measure of explicitness regarding the theory of change that guides a project. To return to a controversy already discussed it makes a difference whether organizers and workers are committed to a structuralist theory of change (in which case the amelioration of hardship might be seen as an undesirable goal) or a pluralist or conflict theory (in which case the provision of goods and resources to people engaged in conflict and claims-making will be a positive thing).[85] We can also add, following my remarks about different views of the value of community action as such, that different theories of democratic politics (as opposed to social change as such) will make a difference to commitments to different goals and strategies. Finally it is difficult (even in the best of circumstances) to attribute change to any intervention. Quite apart from the social scientific difficulties here, there is the problem that authorities are always reluctant to credit pressure with success. Politicians and bureaucrats both have a key interest in arguing that the authority would have done whatever it was anyway, and that pressure (let alone disruptive or conflictual tactics) were either irrelevant or actually a delaying factor.[86]

Some literature does focus on evaluation at the level of the community (that is, the level of the area or locality as a whole) rather than the individual organization.[87] Evaluation of the success of 'community building' is clearly not straightforward. Although it may be fairly clear when a locality is not 'healthy' there will be substantial disagreement about the degree of network density and multiplexity, and the patterns of interactions that are necessary for 'a healthy community'. Even if there were agreement on these matters, network analysis presents a number of technical difficulties, and requires extremely expensive and practically difficult data collec-

---

[84] Barbara Bryant and Richard Bryant, *Change and Conflict: A Study of Community Work in Glasgow* (Aberdeen: Aberdeen University Press, 1982).

[85] Connell and Kubisch, 'Evaluating Comprehensive Community Initiatives'.

[86] Richard Bryant, 'The New Slums—Community Action Response', in Paul Henderson et al. (eds.), *Successes and Struggles on Council Estates*.

[87] Marilyn Taylor, *Unleashing the Potential: Bringing Residents to the Centre of Regeneration* (York: Joseph Rowntree Foundation, 1995), 64.

tion.[88] Further, it is a theoretical question what is a reasonable expectation about 'community health' in a given framework of governance and distribution of social goods. What is it reasonable to expect, for instance, in the way of 'social capital' in a locality where people have a given level of household income?[89]

These problems with the evaluation of community building highlight the key problem that the concept 'community' is contested. The point is vividly illustrated by Paul Lichterman, in his study of several 'community campaigns' in the United States on the issue of toxic waste.[90] In this study he finds two kinds of commitment. There is the community commitment of 'Mrs Davies', who understands herself to be a concerned member of the community, who is enmeshed in locally shared traditions, local involvements and obligations, whose political campaigning against a toxic waste dump is an expression of this community membership, as well as having an obvious practical value—the achievement of a safer environment. There is the individual commitment of 'Carl', who sees the individual person as the locus of responsibility and political efficacy, who links changes in his personal life with changes in the social structure, and who believes that enlightened self-interest is sufficient reason to work hard in an anti-toxic waste campaigning group. Carl would have found Mrs Davis's certainty about 'the community' ('Everyone's community', she says) threatening to his individual identity in the first place and unconvincing in the second. Indeed, Mrs Davis's group had severe difficulties integrating people with differing interests into the bonds of communal obligation, and this caused them distress—they could not understand why people (people who shared their ethnic identity, at that)—disagreed with their aims. 'The language of community struggle in the name of a single communal black identity was a vernacular that limited [the organisation's] members' purchase on the conflicting issues in their locale.'[91] On the other hand, Carl's

[88] Computers now make the data analysis straightforward; but network analysis results are extremely sensitive to sample size, and sample boundary. See John Scott, *Social Network Analysis: A Handbook* (London: Sage, 1991).

[89] Taylor, *Unleashing the Potential*, 65.

[90] Paul Lichterman, *The Search for Political Community* (Cambridge: Cambridge University Press, 1996), 24. Lichterman sets his fieldwork data in the theoretical framework posed by Robert Bellah and his colleagues (Robert N. Bellah et al., *Habits of the Heart: Individualism and Commitment in American Life* (Berkeley and Los Angeles: University of California Press, 1985)) and other US communitarians: an individual, personalist basis for communal activity (like 'Carl's') is precarious and undependable; a true solid commitment to right, freedom, justice, etc. must be based on a more robust community identity which emphasizes 'we', not 'I' (pp. 4–14). Interestingly, Lichterman finds weaknesses, and a certain shrinking from politics, in both these styles.

[91] Lichterman, *Search for Political Community*, 129–34.

group, because of their emphasis on individual autonomy and conception of 'personal community' were rather unsuccessful in building an organization with any multicultural or multi-ethnic element. It was difficult to carry long-term processes through collectively, and the members' commitment to ambiguous boundaries, ambivalent and loose membership, meant that recruitment was difficult, as were stable alliances or coalitions with other groups.[92]

Community projects—from a play or event to get everyone working together, to setting up an advice centre, or an educational or social project—inevitably engender varying expectations, and these different expectations lead to conflict.[93] These are quite apart from the structured conflicts of interest that are a feature of any social setting: young and old people have very different views about the provision of play and leisure facilities,[94] men and women express different interests in employment; tenants and home-owners have different incentives and opportunities to settle with developers.[95] And the community development programme itself, especially where the distribution of material goods is involved, then engenders 'split interests'. In a refurbishment programme on a housing estate, those whose houses were soon to be modernized had an interest in securing adequate temporary accommodation from the housing authority before work started, while those whose houses were later in the schedule saw this group as delaying the programme. Later on, those whose houses were complete weren't so willing to keep up the pressure on the housing authority regarding standards, communications and so on, leaving those still in unmodernized houses unsupported and feeling abandoned.[96]

There certainly does seem to be a problem in many social settings with 'how to do conflict'. The 'parliamentary' method—of elaborate linguistic norms of politeness, speaking through the chair, using points of order and so on—which has been adopted in a variety of settings from local party meetings to committee work, has lost popularity, striking many as archaic, and is widely viewed as oppressive and exclusionary (as you have to know and be skilful with the rules to be successful). Skilful chairing of a heated discussion conducted more informally, on the other hand, can still strike some participants as overly manipulative, artificially smoothing over ruptures, and will strike others as impossibly aggressive. It is, indeed, difficult

[92] Lichterman, *Search for Political Community*, 138–45.
[93] Jeremy Brent,'Community without Unity', paper delivered to conference 'Ideas of Community', University of the West of England, Sept. 1995; Lees and Smith, *Action Research in Community Development*, 124.
[94] Leonard, *Sociology of Community Action*, 214.
[95] Feldman et al., 'The Community Needs to be Built by Us', 267.
[96] Lees and Smith, *Action Research in Community Development*, 75.

to attain the amount of 'closure' that allows people to go home feeling relatively comfortable, while still keeping the conflict and disagreements visible so that participants don't feel they've been swept under the carpet. Difficult, but not impossible.

Another set of problems is organization. Take for instance the difficulties stemming from the euphoria of a successful meeting in which it is resolved to take action about some problem or another, and the subsequent difficulty of keeping the work going.[97] This kind of problem has two aspects. On the one hand, activists who have energy, time, the inclination to work, and the ability to garner the necessary resources can nevertheless feel despondent if it seems (as it frequently does) that the public meeting once over they are left to do all the work. It is difficult to get people out to meetings after initial decisions have been taken, and certainly once the initial honeymoon period is over, and activists are likely to be much more aware of local complaints and feelings of dissatisfaction with their performance, than they are of congratulations, warm support, thankfulness, and so on. Second, well attended meetings which determine on action generally generate temporary coalitions which, as Farrar puts it, 'feel for a period like community'.[98] These cause a rush of feeling; but this rush does not solve the continuing problems of organization, and will not hold off indefinitely the incipient conflicts that are by definition a necessary aspect of any coalition. Nor, Farrar observes, are such rushes, and such temporary community-like coalitions usually equal to the challenges of such socially disruptive forces as the crack cocaine sellers that the people he writes about faced. These 'community-like' experiences, described in a variety of terms and from a variety of viewpoints, by students of community action and community development, are the empirical counterparts of the 'transcendence' element of the concept community, which I insisted upon in Chapter 2. Transcendence, conceptual analysis alone tells us, is inevitably fleeting; this aspect of 'community building' is borne out by the empirical analysis.

Of course, community projects endure, and individuals and groups continue to work hard and doggedly at delivering services to people in localities, or putting resources at their service, or attempting to represent them in the political forums of press and broadcast media, the council chamber and Parliament, and in the other spaces and relationships that constitute the political process. But it is difficult for the personnel of such organizations to avoid the perverse logic of democratic participation and

[97] Mackintosh and Wainwright, *A Taste of Power*, 343.
[98] Max Farrar, 'Agency Metaphor and Double Consciousness' paper presented to conference 'Ideas of Community', University of West of England, Sept. 1995, p. 7.

accountability.[99] Almost inevitably, workers and committee members have to use patronage or offer selective benefits to get the relevant local people along to the meetings that guarantee the project's democratic legitimacy.[100] Inevitably, the interests of the organization as such become a counter in the organization's work and decision-making.[101] The tendency is that structures which ideally should be transparent (and for the transparency of which the community project comes into being) are made opaque.

It might also be argued that problems of opacity are inescapable given the ideal of community. This is not to accuse community workers and community activists in general of obfuscation and the building of barriers around communities. But it is undeniable that there have been cases where the ideal of community has been invoked in defence of exclusionary social policies and projects, and furthermore in defence of the principle that decisions to pursue such policies are nobody's business but the relevant 'community's'.[102] In light of a broader theory of democracy and social justice, we may be pushed to thinking much harder about transparency in boundaries around communities and other kinds of social grouping.

THE VALUE OF LOCALITY

It is in the wake of such actual processes and developments that Adam Crawford has suggested that we be very suspicious of the implications that seem to be part and parcel of many community-building projects. He thinks particularly of 'neighbourhood watch', which yokes together 'community' and 'defensiveness' (the 'defended communities' that are becoming part and parcel of the housing scene on both sides of the Atlantic Ocean say it all explicitly). The localities that are constructed as 'communities' in these schemes are constructed according to criteria of socio-economic homogeneity—a typical neighbourhood watch area will be a set of streets with housing stock and occupancy of one type, inhabited by people who will potentially cooperate with one another—that is, people of a similar socio-economic status. Quite apart from the fact that rich neighbourhoods have the resources for organization that poor ones lack (absent dedicated and successful community work projects), Crawford questions

---

[99] Crawford, *The Local Governance of Crime*, 169–74.
[100] George Grosser, *New Directions in Community Organisation* (New York: Praeger, 1976), 184.
[101] Ibid. 264.   [102] Crawford, 'Appeals to Community and Crime Prevention', 107.

the ethical value of encouraging this development of intra-boundary lives.[103]

It is undoubtedly true that communitarian theory has explicitly valued the kind of living arrangements that Crawford criticizes. Remember Michael Walzer's view that 'the democratic school should be an enclosure within a neighbourhood'.[104] Contrary to this recommendation, critics might argue that important facilities like schools, leisure centres, medical centres, and so on should be sited on the edges of neighbourhoods—not at their heart—so that social mixing and the mingling of horizons is maximized.[105] For the question of social homogeneity cannot be avoided here. Undoubtedly there might be some advantages to relatively homogeneous localities. For instance, demand for shops selling very cheap goods will be more effective in inducing supply the more poor people there are in some locality. Where poor people are scattered—as they are in many rural and small-town areas in the UK—their deprivation in terms of purchasing power may be increased for the lack of ready availability of cheap shops.[106] They may also suffer greater cultural exclusion if the dominant local cultural norms rely on the possession of money and particular forms of cultural capital.[107] Yet boundaries marking prosperous from deprived locales are frequently barriers to information, effectively cutting people off from job markets, leisure, and educational opportunities and other valuable goods.[108] The ideal of community, with its emphasis on sharing, inevitably conduces to an emphasis on shared cultural identity and pronounced boundaries.

Another difficulty with the ideal of community as central to politics is that it raises the stakes too high. It is, as Farrar says, 'an expression of utopian desire', and invocations of community can generate the rush, the fleeting experience of transcendence. But it falls short of what is needed in the way of analysis of the nature of coalitions, conflicts, and social networks. What material, symbolic, and social resources are needed for action in concert, by people who have something in common, against the structures that oppress them? How can conflict be managed, without smoothing it over so that antagonists feel cheated? How, if antagonisms

---

[103] Ibid. 119.   [104] Walzer, *Spheres of Justice*, 225.

[105] Cabinet Office, *Bringing Britain Together*, 39.

[106] And vice versa of course—wealthy people might be deprived of opportunities to consume the kinds of goods, at the kinds of prices, they prefer, if they live in a very mixed area with lots of poor people.

[107] I am indebted to Mike Noble for a very helpful discussion of these issues.

[108] Cabinet Office/Social Exclusion Unit, *Bringing Britain Together*, 39. And the obverse of this, of course, is that those in the relatively prosperous areas have an unfair advantage as goods are shared among a restricted number of people.

really are unresolvable, can people in a group or a locality move on to decision and action?

At the beginning of this chapter I discussed the communitarian arguments for local government, and the argument that local government is uniquely suited to caring for the needs of communities (and therefore, uniquely, a necessary element of governance). I have also analysed some of the dilemmas and difficulties with conceiving of locality as community, and investing statutory, voluntary, and indigenous effort into 'community building'. Some of these difficulties are difficulties with *local* work, however it is conceived and whatever it is named. But others are specifically difficulties with *community* work, and these difficulties stem, at least in part, from the expectations that the invocation of community generates, the connotations that echo from its use.

But these difficulties by no means dispose of the argument that overly-centralized administration of local services is alienating, oppressive, and inefficient. The argument for the local administration of goods and resources, the need for people to be consulted about the likely upshots of decisions, about what is needed and how best needs might be met, still stands. The existence of local interests, and local people's identification with, and commitment to their area, can be seen as the focus for local government, a measure of local autonomy, and the basis for its legitimacy. However, we can no more rely on the givenness of localities and the existence of local interests than we can on the presence of local communities which generate their own values, social goods, and forms of governance. We need therefore to develop a distinctive argument for locality as a value, and for local democratic governance. That is, we need to develop arguments in favour of building and promoting local people's identification with their area, and for the significance of specifically local governance in this process.

We can begin with the empirical fact that in the course of the life cycle, as well as due to the exigencies of class and welfare, many individuals are immobile and many are, frankly, stuck.[109] Children in their educational years, young people prior to full adulthood, adults with caring responsibilities, and older people are situated in a particular place without the practical option of exit, and their well-being and welfare is crucially bound up with the health of their area. In particular, their immobility must not be in any way detrimental to their ability to live full and worthwhile lives. This means that relatively circumscribed geographical areas must have a full range of facilities and opportunities for work, leisure, and civic

---

[109] Bulmer, *Social Basis of Community Care*, 55–64.

participation. This immobility is an empirical fact, notwithstanding the high rates of geographic and social mobility which are undoubtedly a feature of modern societies. It is clear that many individuals' allegiances and relationships will transcend locality. We can be members of national and international organizations with headquarters and co-members distant from where we live and work. We may identify with an ethnic or cultural diaspora, and feel solidarities that are global. We may consume goods by post, bought via our TV sets; and we may conduct our friendships and work relationships by electronic mail. But even the most thoroughly postmodern individuals must also spend a great deal of time on the ground—the places where we live, work, and visit. And this ground must be civil—that is to say, safe, pleasant, and such as to promote citizenly relations between persons.

This then is the sociological context for consideration of a normative argument for locality as a value. At the heart of this argument is the principle that one key way in which individuals should enact their responsibilities for others is by way of care for the environment. In this connection individuals have particular relationships with particular areas by virtue of their habitual location there—for example, workplaces, residential neighbourhoods, leisure places, and the routes between these. People are not relieved from the obligation to care for other locations too—places they may visit or pass through, but living or working in a particular place generates a special relationship between an individual and that place.

Youth workers, social workers, local government officers and elected representatives have, of course, long had the value of care for place at the centre of their practical efforts. From the youth work point of view, this is a response to the relative immobility of young people, and the need to encourage and foster a sense of efficacy and empowerment of the individual *vis-à-vis* those institutions and sources of power which determine her environment.[110] However, 'changing society at a local level . . . by lobbying a local council or meeting a social need in their area' can only be one of several focuses for young people's attention. Working against racism, building international bridges, that is, allegiances and solidarities that transcend the local context are also important, as is working with and for disadvantaged groups in a locality—this, note, will often not be affirming of local communities. So also is political participation at the national level, for instance, taking issues to parliament.

Working on local projects with fellow citizens and in association with other social groups also ties people into reciprocal, responsible,

[110] British Youth Council, *The Voices of Young People* (London: British Youth Council, 1986), 4.

relationships.[111] This not only encourages an appreciation of civil relations, but aso contributes to the construction of cared-for social and public spaces. Of course, lasting and effective improvements to public spaces are not possible without governmental administration and resources; and the local youth club cannot work miracles in areas where social relations and institutions are damaged, or where flawed architecture and damaged infrastructure deplete the quality of life.

The facts of social immobility and the value of commitment to place, together conduce to a number of institutional recommendations. First, an emphasis on the use of local knowledge in the design of special projects—in education, training, community and youth work, social services, leisure provision, planning, employment policy, and so on. As others have pointed out, although the wider national and global contexts mean that many decisions cannot be made meaningfully at the local level, and although considerations of social justice and fairness in the relationships between groups of people and localities may make pressure against local decision-making, consultation, or autonomy, there are still many issues that are genuinely local.[112] A second institutional prerequisite for the commitment of local people to their locality is a mechanism for collective choice (as opposed to individual market choice or choices made by professionals, managers, or bureaucrats) in respect of public and some worthy goods—for example, the layout of public and associational spaces.

Third, the value of civil relations between strangers and the fostering of healthy public space means that the local administration of public and quasi-public spaces would have to be much more vigorous than is currently the case. Further, inequalities in provision (relatively clean town centres and tourist sites, and litter strewn residential estates and streets) would have to be corrected. This would not only be a matter of having high standards of cleansing and maintenance, but also a constant process of checking on the match between space and use, the competing demands of different kinds of users, the adjudication of conflicts, and so on. The maintenance specifically of civil relations means that the provision of police and security guards would have to be bolstered and supplemented, if not replaced, by civic positions such as caretakers, wardens and the equivalent of park-keepers.

I am aware that a number of objections might be levelled at this argument and the institutional recommendations I have sketched. They can invoke an unattractive picture of wardens dispensing summary justice to

---

[111] John Paley, et al., *Rethinking Youth Social Work* (Leicester: National Youth Bureau, 1986).

[112] Anne Phillips, *Local Democracy*.

children; the exclusion or harassment of homeless people or ethnic minorities or young men. There is a danger that proprietariness about spaces can militate against civic values—for example, housing developments can become inward looking and physically cut off. Small enclaves with hostile or distrustful attitudes to the outside will not enhance the quality of civic life; the value of locality can threaten to usher in the same problems of exclusion and coercion that we met in connection with the value of community.

But we are better off, theoretically speaking, with locality than with community—for there is in this concept no suggestion that a single or any particular set of values, norms, preferred social identities, patterns of relations, or tastes is privileged. Within the framework of social justice, the needs of existing users (residents, workers, visitors) in a place would all have to be considered if the value of democracy were to be realized. This means that questions of what counts as, say, social disorder, would always have to be on the agenda for critical debate and discussion. There could be no question of keeping particular kinds of people out of a public space. It is precisely the reclamation of public spaces (including quasi-public ones such as shopping centres) for the public that is important if civic life is to be possible.

Second, it might be objected that individual well-being would be better served by investment in the means of geographical mobility. However, given that even the most mobile people have an interest in the physical and especially the built environment offering the possibility of civil relations, the question is begged of how it is to be cared for. Local services—cleaning, maintenance—might be delivered by non-local, even international, firms. However, both the direction of services and the regulation of public spaces rely on local knowledge and demands, and crucially therefore on local organization.

Lastly, it might be objected that the subjective and indeterminate nature of 'localities' makes them an unlikely basis for the peculiar ethical relationship I have been sketching. But it is precisely the overlapping and indeterminate nature of localities, the importance of routes and communication between them—their contingency—that is a crucial ingredient of a normative theory of local democracy and civic life, and more particularly a theory of the political and social processes by which we might construct localities that will support civic values. It is quite clear that just as the existence of a 'community' or many social collectivities such as 'nation' is partly a matter of the imagination of its members, so a locality is not a naturally existing entity.[113] This means that the argument for the value of

---

[113] Benedict Anderson, *Imagined Communities*, 2nd edn. (London: Verso, 1991); A. P. Cohen, *The Symbolic Construction of Community* (London: Routledge, 1985).

locality is not an argument for rooting procedures and institutions in a given set of social relations. Rather if local government and local organizations address themselves to the maintenance of localities, a process of the making and unmaking of identities and relationships will occur.

Localities are contingent on a number of factors. First and most obviously, geographical and topological features are worked on by political and economic decisions: to draw boundaries in a particular way, and to site a city at a particular point, to build suburbs in particular patterns and directions, for example. That is, the exact shape of a locality will be contingent. Second, individuals will differ one from another as to their understanding of the shape and boundaries of the locality. These differences will be due to people's peculiar material circumstances—for example, their shopping habits, their routes to and from work, their habits of visiting friends or attending leisure facilities in one direction rather than another. That is, locality will be subjective.

A third factor is also significant—especially for social science. Localities are likely to be constructed (as objects of research) by researchers. When they find there is disagreement and difference in their subjects' understandings of the shape of a locality researchers will nevertheless make their own decisions about what and whom to include in and exclude from a locality study. Locality is also contingent in another important way. How people are related to each other depends on what resources are available, and where those resources are coming from. For example, people living on a particular estate will set up a tenants' association not only when they identify themselves as co-residents with interests and capacities in common, but when they perceive opportunities to obtain the necessary resources. The patterns of social relationships that proceed from, for example, the projects and activities of, say, a housing association are a supremely political matter.

6

Political Communitarianism and Family Life

In this chapter I wish to explore the ways 'family' and 'community' are connected in communitarian politics. The two are brought together in a number of discursive contexts, in debates about policy in academic journals, in journalism, and in political speech. A close connection between 'community' and 'family' is, of course, not an invention of communitarians—it is imputed in speech from the right, the left and the centre, conservative, liberal, and social democratic. The development of policies such as 'care in the community' (which usually means care in the family, with input and support from state employees like 'community nurses') command widespread assent among electorates and practitioners alike, although inevitably there are sceptical worries from sections of the public and professionals that there will not be adequate resources to carry out these policies.

The juxtaposition of 'family' and 'community' has an evident *rhetorical effect*—it invokes pictures of stable happy families and well-ordered communities on the one hand, and chaotic dysfunctional families and run-down neighbourhoods on the other. In the context of *ideological competition* the connection challenges new right social analysis whose elements are individuals, families, and states. It chimes with the more traditional conservative picture of an organic, but authoritative, social order. It also coheres with the traditional socialist view of organic, unalienated life, and on the way can take in a more radical socialist view which focuses on social movements and local, community, protest, and action. The connection between family and community is a challenge to the bureaucratic nexus between family and state which underlies welfare state institutions and ideology.

But in self-consciously 'communitarian' discourse, we also find a deeper, *conceptual connection* between the two. Families *are*, ideally at least, communities, and conversely the idea of community is analysed *as* 'family writ large'.[1] In some communitarian analyses, wider communities

[1] See for instance John MacMurray, *Persons in Relation* (London: Faber and Faber, 1961), 155.

are conceptualized as 'communities of communities'—communities of families and other institutions like firms and schools and neighbour-hoods.[2] The editor of *Tikkun* argues: 'Individual families get their strength and meaning through participation in a larger community, and the community at any given moment gets its strength and meaning by its rela-tionship to the historical chain of generations that have preceded and will follow us.'[3] The meanings of family and community are mutually consti-tutive.

These rhetorical effects, and the putative conceptual connection between family and community, are in part mystificatory—the terms' con-stant reference to each other obscures how social institutions and social processes are actually related. In public policy this really matters. As I mentioned earlier, for instance, the social policy 'community care' is actu-ally 'family care': community care sets up links between state and family which are intended to provide complementary sources of assistance.[4] This kind of discursive inexactitude is a barrier to public understanding of the interrelationships and conflicts between state organizations, kinship, eth-nic, and religious groups and social classes, and social organizations. This aspect of communitarian discourse—in which one term seems actually to operate as a code for another—generates suspicion, too, that the whole thing is really about something else: that talk of family and community actually encode talk about *gender*, about the respective roles and resources of men and women.[5]

As the passage from *Tikkun* illustrates, communitarians also emphasize presumed empirical sociological connections between family and community. Communities sustain and strengthen families, and families strengthen communities. Elsewhere it is asserted that the family is the basis

[2] Amitai Etzioni, *The Spirit of Community: Rights, Responsibilities and the Communitarian Agenda* (New York: Crown Publishers, 1991), 32.

[3] Lerner, 'Founding Editorial Statement', *Tikkun*, 1/1 (1986). In what follows in this chapter I argue that many communitarians have an insufficiently complex and critical view of intra-family relations and processes. I hasten to say that this is not a charge that can be fairly levelled at most contributors to *Tikkun*—see for instance, Anne Rouphe, 'The Jewish Family: A Feminist Perspective', *Tikkun*, 1/2 (1987). The editorial stance of the journal is based in part on psychological theories which emphasize the role of families as sources of pain and tension for individuals in their relations with others and self: Michael Lerner 'Pain at Work and Pain in Families', *Tikkun*, 6/1 (1991); Michael Lerner, 'Can the Democrats be Stopped from Blowing it Again in 1992?', *Tikkun*, 7/4 (1992).

[4] Janet Finch, *Family Obligations and Social Change* (Cambridge: Polity Press, 1989), 125 Janet Finch also points out that the old Poor Law, whatever its shortcomings, was nothing like so mystificatory as it was quite explicit about who was expected to do what for whom (pp. 117–22). See also Martin Bulmer, *The Social Basis of Community Care* (London: Unwin Hyman, 1987), 2.

[5] For instance, Bea Campbell, 'Grandaddy of the Backlash', *Guardian* (1.04.1995).

of community—'strong families are the foundation of strong commun-ities';[6] 'the stronger the community, the stronger the family—and vice versa',[7] the family is 'a basic component in the resurgence of community spirit'.[8] Families are 'embedded in wider communities which profoundly affect, for good or ill, parents' abilities to motivate their children'.[9] These putative empirical connections, despite their plausibly commonsensical appearance, are under-theorized and under-substantiated. Partly this is because political discourses of these types generally tend to be weak on sociology—this goes for communitarianism, conservatism, socialism, and liberalism. Partly it is because of problems with the conceptualizations of 'family' and 'community' that the communitarians begin with.

THE COMMUNITARIAN FAMILY

In both philosophical and political communitarianism 'family' or, just as commonly, 'the family' is often mentioned as an instance, an example, of community.[10] In the course of their discussions of what is wrong or inad-equate about individualism philosophers mention families as sites of spe-cial, particular, ethically laden relationships—family relations stand as a counter-example and alternative to the voluntary, rights-based, contracts and market exchanges that are privileged in liberal theory. The family is an exemplary cluster of unchosen relations, duties, and obligations.[11] It is also invoked as an inspiration or model for community—in the family there is a good greater than abstract justice, and there are relations that are not based on self-interest.[12] In this vein the family is more than just an instance of community: 'Family is the original human community and the basis as well as the origin of all subsequent communities. It is therefore the

[6] Mandelson and Liddle, *The Blair Revolution*, 124. See also Prime Minister Blair's speech to the Labour Party Conference, Blackpool, 29 Sept. 1998: 'I challenge us to accept that family life is the basic unit of a strong community', and the Home Office Ministerial Group on the Family, *Supporting Families*, foreword: 'Family life is the foundation on which our communities, our society and our country are built'.

[7] Tony Blair, *New Britain: My Vision for a Young Country* (London: Fourth Estate, 1996), 247.

[8] Ian Taylor, *Releasing the Community Spirit: A Framework for the Active Citizen* (Cambridge: Tory Reform Group, 1990), 12.

[9] Commission on Social Justice, *Social Justice: Strategies for National Renewal* (London: Vintage Books, 1994), 370.

[10] Alasdair MacIntyre, *After Virtue* (2nd edn.) (London: Duckworth, 1985), 221.

[11] Charles Taylor, *Philosophy and the Human Sciences* (Cambridge: Cambridge University Press, 1985), 203.

[12] Michael Sandel, *Liberalism and the Limits of Justice* (Cambridge: Cambridge University Press, 1982), 33.

norm of all communities, so that any community is a brotherhood . . . The more a society approximates to the family pattern, the more it realises itself as a community, or, as Marx called it, a truly human society.'[13] On the other hand, some communitarians resist this move, understanding the family (with its particularistic commitments and its face-to-face inter-actions) to be an imperfect model for political community, and family relations to be insufficient for civic virtue.[14] In other passages commun-itarians conceive rather of the family as the basis, the fundamental building block of community. The building blocks of a moral community 'are well known. Historically they have included families, schools and communities (which encompass places of worship and voluntary associ-ations).'[15]

So we have two understandings of family: first as an exemplar of or more strongly the original community, second as the basis or more strongly the building block of community. These two senses are straddled in the political communitarian concept of 'the communitarian family'.[16] The communitarian family is characterized as one with, ideally, two (dif-ferent sex) parents, between whom there is a cooperative and egalitarian relationship, with both marital partners deeply and actively involved in their children's upbringing, and where all members are collectively and individually active in participation in the community, where the family has many ties to social organizations. Communitarian parents understand that their moral responsibility to bring their children up well is a respon-sibility to the community.[17]

What communitarian politics means for family policy is one of the most controversial aspects of it. Critics interpret communitarianism as being primarily about neo-conservative or neo-traditional family policy;[18] and defenders of broadly communitarian ideals agree. As journalist Melanie Phillips in a rather overwrought metaphor puts it: 'The issue of the family

[13] MacMurray, *Persons in Relation*, 155.

[14] Taylor, *Philosophy and the Human Sciences*, 203.

[15] Amitai Etzioni, 'Community Watch', *Guardian* (28 June 1997); Dick Atkinson, *The Common Sense of Community* (London: Demos, 1994), 'The basic building block of com-munity for most people is the family' (p. 11).

[16] This concept can be found most clearly in the communitarianism of Amitai Etzioni and his colleagues (rather than in Tory, or Jewish, or Socialist communitarianisms).

[17] At 'The First Communitarian Teach In' at the White House in 1991 Amitai Etzioni spoke about the ideal communitarian person, and thought of former president Jimmy Carter, 'the man who has a clear spiritual core and whose wife has a persona in her own right, with her own ambitions and projects. A parent who transmits values to his children. And a member of a community who both cares about its members and reaches out to oth-ers . . .' report in *Responsive Community*, 2/1 (1991), 21.

[18] Campbell, 'Grandaddy of the Backlash', *Guardian* (1.04.1995).

is at the epicentre of the minefield.'[19] Although, as we have seen, communitarians focus on a whole range of intermediate institutions including schools, voluntary associations, and businesses, 'family' has a privileged place in the theory—as fundamental, as first.[20] Yet there is equally an insistence that communitarians recognize that 'the family' has changed— 'for good reasons as well as bad'.[21] In an evasive strategy in response to questions from a radio interviewer whether 'the family' he wishes to support includes households of same sex couples, single people with children, several single people sharing a household, and so forth, Tony Blair replied, more than once, that 'we all know what we mean by the family'. Evidently, he felt it impossible to say that such households and domestic groups were excluded from his category 'the family'; equally he could not say that they were included.[22]

Obviously politicians' ambivalence about 'the traditional family' is a canny enough response to societies and electorates that are deeply divided on issues to do with sexuality, marriage, and parenting. And probably Etzioni's project of maintaining a widely based communitarian coalition explains his on the one hand pointing to the 'fact' that 'In a wide variety of human societies (from the Zulus to the Inuit, from ancient Greece and ancient China to modernity) there has never been a society that did not have two parent families'[23] while in the same volume reporting that as he reads the social science findings it would be preferable for children to have three parents rather than two.[24]

We might, of course, reply to Blair that it is far from clear that 'we all know what we mean by the family' (as is illustrated by Etzioni's remark about children having more than two parents—whether he is serious about that or not). Family is a complex concept, and the complexity generates ambiguity. The concept has at least three elements:

---

[19] Melanie Phillips, 'Freedom and Community Reconciled', *Observer* (25 Sept. 1994).

[20] Textually, commonly it comes first, in earlier rather than later chapters of books and pamphlets. See Henry Tam, *Citizens' Agenda for Building Democratic Communities* (Cambridge: Centre for Citizenship Development, 1995), 6: 'The best place to start is where each new generation acquires its moral anchoring—at home, in the family.' The London-based centre-left think tank *Demos* published as a pamphlet just the chapter on the family from Etzioni's *Spirit of Community*: Amitai Etzioni, *Parenting Deficit* (London: Demos, 1993).

[21] Home Office, Ministerial Group on the Family, *Supporting Families* (http://www.homeoffice.gov.uk/), Nov. 1998, foreword.

[22] BBC, *World at One* (14 Oct. 1996); *Guardian* (15 Oct. 1996), 1; *Independent* (15 Oct. 1996), 9.

[23] Amitai Etzioni, *The Spirit of Community*, 60.

[24] Etzioni, *Spirit of Community*, 62.

1. A group of individuals who are genetically connected. For example, a reproductive couple, their own parents and siblings, and their biological offspring constitute a clear example. However, the question of the extent of this group will show that the concept is both fuzzy and complex. We can distinguish, for instance, between a 'descent group' (all the descendants from the mother and father of one common ancestor; each member of such a group is kin to each other), and a person's kindred (that group of people who have the relevant person in common as a relative). Here we have two contrasting ways of individuating 'a family'. Note also that genealogists conventionally include adopted children (i.e. individuals with a legal, but not a biological connection to the group) in a descent group.

2. That takes us on to another analysis of 'family': a group of individuals who are socially, economically, legally, and politically (that is related in an order of power and authority) connected. Sometimes, but not necessarily, this group will share domestic life in a household. This is not necessary—in many societies families are split between a number of households and it is quite rare for, say, grandparents, siblings and their spouses, and their children, to share a household. Typically, but not necessarily, they will be connected in a relatively dense network of social, economic, political, and legal exchanges (domestic labour, love, inheritance, authority and teaching, and so forth). This is not necessary because even where individuals are estranged the legal and biological tie (if there is one) means such a group is recognized as 'a family'.

3. Finally, a 'bare household'—that is, a group of people who share a domestic regime—may, with the addition of moral and emotional elements to their economic and social relationships, become 'a family'. Exactly what these moral and emotional elements must consist in is likely to be contested, and to vary from culture to culture. But typically, they will include items such as the unconditionality of love and care.[25]

Even if there were agreement about which cluster of relationships constituted a family, this would still not settle the questions of the extent of the family group, nor what degree of intensity or density in the members' interrelationships is necessary. The question of extension—that is, both how extensive is the network of kin and others that constitutes the family, and where lies the boundary between one family and the next—is both culturally variable and, within a culture, variable contingent on a range of factors (a variety of particular and contingent circumstances can mean that one family group can be, self-consciously, very extensive, while

[25] Some individuals who join communes have in mind the formation of a new kind of family; see for instance Angela A. Aidala and Benjamin D. Zablocki, 'The Communes of the 1970s: Who Joined and Why?', *Marriage and Family Review*, 17 (1991), 87–116, p. 89.

another from the same culture and socio-economic class can be, self-consciously, rather restricted). This also goes for the intensity of relations and density of interactions. Family groups vary tremendously both in their actual quantity and quality of interactions, and in their members' conceptions of what is proper or right.

In the United States disputes among academics and politicians about how to conceptualize 'family' have, in the 1990s, become heated.[26] In an attempt to settle the questions of its extent and of the characterizations of the relationships within a family, for social scientific and political purposes, David Popenoe argues for a normative and restricted meaning: a family is a domestic group living together in a household, functioning as a cooperative unit, particularly through the sharing of economic resources in pursuit of domestic activities; it consists of kin or people in a kin-like relationship, at least one adult and one dependent person.[27] Popenoe makes clear that this analysis or definition means that adults in intimate relationships (including we can note, interdependent adults living in the kind of domestic regime that he specifies) must be distinguished from families; as must kin who are not living together. The definition then is at variance with a good deal of ordinary usage, in which 'family' is used not only to refer to domestic groups of the sort Popenoe refers to, but also to refer to wider networks of people in households (including single person households) connected by kinship, interdependence, and obligations. In UK research among respondents from a number of ethnic groups, for instance, Geoff Dench found that some respondents (he calls these 'traditionalists') thought of family in an extended sense as stretching across households, while another group (he calls these 'alternativists') conceptualize family as confined to one household.[28]

The extent to which it is important to pay attention to how 'family' is used and thought of by persons in the populations studied is the bone of

[26] To put it mildly. Downright insulting might be more accurate: see David Popenoe, 'The Controversial Truth: Two Parent Families are Better', *New York Times* (26 Dec. 1992), 13; 'American Family Decline 1960–1990: A Review and Appraisal', *Journal of Marriage and Family*, 55 (1993), 527–555; response by Judith Stacey ibid.; David Popenoe, 'Review of J. Stacey *In the Name of the Family*', in *Responsive Community*, 7/1 (1996–7); Judith Stacey, 'Families against "the Family" ', *Radical Philosophy*, 89 (1998), 2–7. See also Teresa D. Marciano, 'Families Wider than Kin or Marriage', *Family Science Review*, 1 (1988), 115–24, and papers in *Marriage and Family Review*, 17/1, 2 (1991).

[27] Popenoe, 'American Family Decline', 529. Of course, Popenoe must mean 'at least one adult and at least one dependent person', not 'at least one adult and one dependent person'. The fact that this ambiguity detains the reader at all is that the former, more plausible, disambiguation also has some odd implications, as I go on to discuss.

[28] Geoff Dench, *The Place of Men in Changing Family Cultures* (London: Institute of Community Studies, 1996), 10–11.

contention here. One implication of Popenoe's approach is that the social scientist is responsible for concept definition. Other social scientists favour a more subjectivist approach in which the social scientist takes into account subjects' understandings and articulations. Of course, such analysis will be complex. Any such study needs to include 'ordinary participants' from different sections of the society (different social classes, different ethnic groups, different birth cohorts, migrants as opposed to people settled over several generations, different geographical regions, and so forth), and also the producers of public discourses—journalists, policymakers, political parties, political campaigners who will produce more or less clearly articulated representations of families as they are and ought to be. Such analysis delineates, of course, a much more expansive (and, to be sure, fuzzier and more complex) conception of 'family'. It will also distinguish, theoretically, between participants' experience of 'family' relations as these interact with their ideas of what those relations are and ought to be, and the symbolic (or ideological) deployment of images and ideas of 'family' for a variety of social and political purposes.[29]

The central issue in disputes about the family, though, is not the philosophy of conceptual analysis or social science methodology, but rather the politically and socially loaded questions of to what extent recent changes in family structure, family relationships including the distribution of power and authority, and the processes of parenting and growing up in a network of kinship and household relationships are a good or a bad thing—for adults, for children, for society as a whole. The central point of Popenoe's conceptualization of 'family' is that with this conception he can show that the American (he means, of course, US) family is in decline: US family groups are now (compared with the 1950s) smaller in size, constitute a smaller percentage of all households, incorporate a smaller percentage of the average person's lifecourse, have weaker control over their members' actions, are less able and willing to carry out their traditional social functions of socialization and discipline, religious practice, education, and economic production.[30] His polemical point is that this decline

---

[29] Judith Stacey makes this kind of point—she argues that the problem with Popenoe's approach is that it is positivist, empiricist, and structural-functionalist, whereas an ideological, symbolic analysis of 'family' is preferable and needed. Stacey, 'Response to Popenoe', *Journal of Marriage and the Family*, 55 (1993), 556, 'Families against "the Family" ', 6. I think that in many cases discussions of positivism, ideology, structural-functionalism, and the like generate more heat than light, and unfortunately this seems to be one of those cases.

[30] Popenoe, 'American Family Decline', 535–6.

also means the loss of extended networks, and the disintegration of the nucleus of family (and by extension all social) life.[31]

US communitarians emphasize what they interpret as the effects of the decline of proper parenting.

Gang warfare in the streets, massive drug abuse, a poorly committed work force, and a strong sense of entitlement and weak sense of responsibility are, to a large extent, the product of poor parenting. True, economic and social factors also play a role. But a lack of effective parenting is a major cause . . .[32]

They emphasize the ill-effects, on adults and children, of divorce, arguing that comparisons show that children raised in one-parent families are more likely than those raised in 'intact' families to drop out of school, to have teenage births and to be poor,[33] and also emphasize the good all-round effects of marriage on adults, children, and society at large— marriage is associated with lower risk of death, higher levels of material well being and social support, and 'appears to diminish risky behaviour'.[34]

On both sides of the Atlantic the 'broken family'—and especially that fragment of it which is headed by a lone female parent—has been represented (in both discourse and iconography) in strident terms.[35] The lone mother is depicted as a threat to society (not least via her greedy consumption of public goods in the form of welfare benefits), an emasculator of men as a class, and the begetter and parent of inadequate or otherwise problematic children.

A prominent characteristic of the political communitarian debates and polemics about family issues is the citation of social scientific data as evidence in support of communitarian policies. Critics accuse communitarians of selective, not to say biased, reading of the 'data', and point to the way communitarians and other 'neo-traditional familists' continually cite each other so as to build up impressively long-looking bibliographies of supportive interpretations.[36] A further impressive characteristic of the communitarian citations of social science, though, is their ambiguous

[31] David Popenoe, 'Fostering the New Familism: A Goal for America', *Responsive Community*, 2/4 (1992), 32.

[32] Etzioni, *Spirit of Community*, 69.

[33] Linda J. Waite, 'Social Science Finds . . . "Marriage Matters" ', *Responsive Community*, 6/3 (1996), 26–35, p. 31.

[34] Waite, 'Social Science Finds . . .', 28.

[35] Kathleen Kiernan, Hilary Land, and Jane Lewis, *Lone Motherhood in Twentieth Century Britain: From Footnote to Front Page* (Oxford: Clarendon Press, 1998), 1–2.

[36] Stacey, 'Families against "the Family" ', 3; Jyl J. Josephson and Cynthia Burack, 'The Political Ideology of the Neo-traditional Family', *Journal of Political Ideologies*, 3 (1998), 213–31, p. 216. I remain agnostic on the question whether communitarians are worse in this regard than other intellectual groups and tendencies!

presentation. I have already quoted Etzioni's assertion that '*in a wide variety* of human societies (from the Zulus to the Inuits, from ancient Greece and ancient China to modernity) *there has never been a society* that did not have two-parent families' (my emphasis), but it is worth looking at it again and emphasizing its ambiguity of scope—it veers between being a statement of restricted fact and a statement of universal fact. Linda Waite, whose article I have already cited, introduces a telling modifier when she says 'The case for marriage *is quite strong*' (my emphasis), although she fails to report thereafter the reasons for caution.[37] David Popenoe, by contrast, raises the social scientific eyebrows with confident assertions such as '*over thousands of years* the institution of the family has stripped down to its bare nucleus and now that nucleus appears to be splitting apart'[38] (my emphasis) and '*Once the only social institution in existence* . . . the family has now lost most of its social functions'[39](my emphasis), which look like nothing short of hyperbole (or nonsense).

A perusal of Anglophone social scientific research on kinship, parenting, marriage, and socialization over the last decade or so reveals a very complex and as yet inconclusive range of theoretical and statistical models of the effects of divorce on children, and the effects of different kinds of family structure, dynamics, and processes on individuals' physical and mental well-being, their careers in education, employment, and citizenship. Needless to say, a number of the problems are methodological—in particular, US research often relies on telephone interviewing as the main mode of data gathering; there are obvious limits to the validity of family members' own (usually retrospective) accounts of conflict, of levels and quality of interaction, and so on; some studies which ask interesting questions are conducted on populations of people who have sought help for various forms of ill-being, while studies on national random samples don't ask the most interesting questions. In addition, researchers report technical difficulties with modelling interaction effects, with path analysis and so on, while small-scale in-depth studies generate predictable reliability problems.

There are also theoretical problems. For instance, research on the effects of divorce on children is marred by 'a failure to distinguish between separation as a process and separation as an event'[40]—the event may occur in

---

[37] Waite, 'Social Science Finds . . .', 27.
[38] Popenoe, 'Fostering the New Familism', 32.
[39] Popenoe, 'American Family Decline', 538.
[40] Bryan Rodgers and Jan Pryor, *Divorce and Separation: The Outcomes for Children* (York: Joseph Rowntree Foundation, 1998). See also David H. Demo, 'Parent Child Relations: Assessing Recent Changes', *Journal of Marriage and the Family*, 54 (1992), 104–17, who remarks that 'a substantial amount of effort has been spent trying to isolate

the context of a whole range of processes, from destructive conflict to constructive cooperation, and it is likely (theoretically at least) that it is these processes that have consequences, not the event itself. Such theoretical reasoning is supported by the fact that, though studies often do find a higher probability of various negative outcomes for 'children of divorce' (risky behaviour like drug use, lower educational attainment and employment status, signs of distress such as depression, aggression, etc.), the differences are not large and there is a great deal of variability among children and adults who grow up in families that do not conform to the traditional or neo-traditional norms.[41]

Given these methodological and theoretical difficulties it is wise to read social science research for its theoretical and political suggestions, rather than as definite 'findings'. One theoretically and politically notable suggestion that emerges from family research literature is that individuals within a family group are not equally advantaged by the structure of that group. It is a commonplace of research and theory informed by feminism, for instance, that in the traditional two-parent family women are either disadvantaged by the lack of independence that is structurally imbricated with the status of 'housewife' or are disadvantaged by the double burden of waged work and domestic work including care. The ways women cope, their strategies for overcoming the disadvantage, range from sharing and exchanging resources with other women, to articulating a myth or family ideology that burdens and benefits are distributed within the family more evenly than they actually are, to, of course, intra-family conflict and exit.[42] One study suggests that women can alleviate the stress of family tension caused by economic difficulties with support from friends and relatives, but where men are experiencing economic instability their spouses' friendships with others worsens their experience.[43] Another suggests that girls benefit from living in a family in which rules and power structures are flexible rather than rigid, whereas fathers seem to suffer some negative

the effects of divorce and single parent family structure, but relatively little effort has been expended trying to understand the correlates and consequences of persistent marital conflict across family types and across stages of individual and family development' (p. 110).

[41] Paul R. Amato, 'Children's Adjustment to Divorce: Theories, Hypotheses and Empirical Support', *Journal of Marriage and Family*, 54 (1992), 23; Rodgers and Pryor, *Divorce and Separation*, 18–19.

[42] On exchange see Finch, *Family Obligations and Social Change*; on 'family myths', Arlie Hochschild, *The Second Shift: Working Parents and the Revolution at Home* (London: Piatkus, 1990).

[43] As the researchers put it, 'external support of wives is positively correlated with marital negativity of their husbands under conditions of unstable employment'; Elizabeth B. Robertson, Glen H. Elder, Martie L. Skinner, R. and D. Conger, 'The Costs and Benefits of Social Support in Families', *Journal of Marriage and the Family*, 53 (1991), 411.

consequences of such a family system, such as identity difficulties, and depression.[44] Boys do better with married mothers; girls do better with single mothers.[45] A great advantage of lone parenthood, according to respondents to one study, is that 'the atmosphere in the house' is satisfying. This, of course, is consistent with life in a lone-parent family being worse economically and perhaps in other ways for children.[46] Optimal conditions for one family member may not be optimal for all.

As we have seen, a central plank of the ideal model of 'the communitarian family' is that family members are outgoing—they are involved in their neighbourhoods, in their schools and other associations. The proposition that the (communitarian) family is the building block of 'community' is often stated, but as almost all attention has been paid to the controversies about varying family structures its empirical and further normative implications have been little explored. First, theoretically, the model of the communitarian family has a number of advantages. It clearly challenges the idea that families are (and should be) tightly bounded capsules.[47] Families, and individuals in their various social roles including family roles, are structured by state laws and social norms. Individuals interact in a variety of organizational and institutional settings including schools, work, locality, social services, associations, friendship networks as well as kinship and 'family'. Adults typically are members of more than one family. Discourses of various kinds, and values, shape our perceptions and experiences of 'family life' and 'families' as institutions.[48] Families,

[44] Michael P. Farrell and Grace M. Barnes, 'Family Systems and Social Support: A Test of the Effects of Cohesion and Adaptability on the Functioning of Parents and Adolescents', *Journal of Marriage and the Family*, 55 (1993), 119–32.

[45] Elizabeth G. Menaghan and Toby L. Parcel, 'Determining Children's Home Environment: The Impact of Maternal Characteristics and Current Occupational and Family Conditions', *Journal of Marriage and the Family*, 53 (1991), 426.

[46] John McKendrick, 'The Big Picture: Quality in the Lives of Lone Parents', in Reuben Ford and Jane Millar (eds.), *Private Lives and Public Responses: Lone Parenthood and Future Policy in the UK* (London: Policy Studies Institute, 1998), 83.

[47] Although note that the 'building block' metaphor is consistent with a model of the family as an entity with clear boundaries (a 'block'), which when arranged with other similar entities and bound together (with 'mortar'), makes a community. Some conservatives who believe in the 'sanctity' of intra-family relations, in the sense of the impermissibility of interference with them, might have this view. But this is quite clearly not what is intended by the political communitarians surveyed in this volume; they, by contrast, argue that 'the community' does have a clear interest in what goes on inside families (and are liable to attract conservative criticism for exactly that). See Henry Tam, *Communitarianism: A New Agenda for Politics and Citizenship* (Basingstoke: Macmillan, 1998), 70. See also Blair, *New Britain*, 'There can be no artificial line drawn around the home—families live in local communities, which are in turn part of a larger society' (p. 247).

[48] For instance Donald G. Unger and Marvin B. Sussman, 'A Community Perspective on Families', *Marriage and Family Review*, 15 (1990), 2.

then, for better or for worse are clusters of relationships with permeable boundaries, and the nature of family relationships is subject to a variety of external influences.

This model is consistent with the wide-ranging and, now long-standing, critique of 'the public versus private distinction'.[49] The concept 'community' refers to associations, locations, and institutions that mediate, or straddle so-called 'public' and 'private' areas of life, or perhaps disrupt the 'public versus private' distinction altogether. In this theoretical context the identification of 'family' with private, and 'society' or state with public, is unsettled by a number of commonplace observations. As mentioned above, state and social power enter right into families. As feminists have pointed out, 'private' advantage or disadvantage spills over into 'public' advantage or disadvantage.[50] 'Families' often occupy public spaces and a good deal of 'family life' is preoccupied with public display.[51] The communitarian model of the family is also consistent with critique of 'the burdens of privatism'. One dimension of the 'public private' distinction is the 'cult of privacy' and, especially, the cult of family privacy. Family privacy has both legitimized and concealed power and force.[52] Another line of criticism of 'privacy' as it is conceived and constructed in liberal societies is that, by downplaying individuals' roles and interactions in 'society' or, indeed, 'community', a situation is brought about in which individuals are normatively oriented only to the market for commodities, on the one hand, and the family with its intimate relations on the other.[53] Individuals

[49] See, for instance, Frances Olsen, 'The Family and the Market', *Harvard Law Review*, 96 (1983), 1497, Carole Pateman, 'Feminist Critiques of the Public/Private Dichotomy', in *The Disorder of Women* (Oxford: Polity Press, 1989); Judith Squires, 'Private Lives, Secluded Places: Privacy as Political Possibility', *Environment and Planning D: Society and Space*, 12 (1994), 387–401; Jeff Weintraub and Krishan Kumar (eds.), *Public and Private in Thought and Practice: Perspectives on a Grand Dichotomy* (Chicago: University of Chicago Press, 1997).

[50] Elizabeth Frazer and Nicola Lacey, *The Politics of Community: A Feminist Critique of the Liberal-Communitarian Debate* (Hemel Hempstead: Harvester, 1993), 72–4.

[51] Barry Wellman's network analysis, based on data gathered in Toronto, Canada, offers some intriguing hints: for example, active kin tend to get together in group contexts ('family parties', etc.) while friends meet 'more privately'. Barry Wellman, 'The Place of Kinfolk in Personal Community Networks', *Marriage and Family Review*, 15 (1990), 203.

[52] Where power and force are explicitly defended by patriarchal right, for instance, the point is that there should be no interference with or resistance to the father's disciplinary power; where patriarchy has given way to 'liberal right', the ideology of the 'private sphere', often identified with 'the family', means that vestiges of patriarchal power, and even right, can live on. For this process traced through the texts of political philosophy see Carole Pateman, *The Sexual Contract* (Oxford: Polity Press, 1988). An early feminist study of family violence, by Erin Pizzey and Alison Forbes is called *Scream Quietly or the Neighbours Will Hear* (Harmondsworth: Penguin, 1974).

[53] This line of criticism of contemporary US society and culture is especially developed in the communitarian journal *Tikkun*. Notable books are Richard Sennett, *The Fall of*

buy and privately consume all kinds of goods—even associational life has become commodified as 'entertainment' and has been more or less completely taken over by commercial enterprises. Private consumption is 'balanced' or offset only by family intimacy; and critics argue that this is not a stable system.[54] Individuals develop 'narcissistic' personalities, fixated on personal gratification,[55] and their demands for gratification by consumption spill over from the commodity market to their intimate relations—hence, frustration and dissatisfaction, conflict with intimates and problems with commitment. Further than this, this social structure fosters a positive fear of 'public life' and encounters with other people, other than in intimate relations (which as we have seen, are unrealistically idealized and fantasized) or in the safety of impersonal market exchanges (you don't have to get involved with someone from whom you are buying a commodity). According to one communitarian: people approach political groups 'with suspicion, having already internalised the societal message that it is only in families and fragile friendship networks that we can find people to trust, and that people we are likely to encounter in these groups are going to put us down or otherwise humiliate us'.[56] This becomes a self-fulfilling prophecy, too often, as the fear leads to 'holding back by some, and acting out by others', so political and 'community' meetings and projects often are rather uncomfortable experiences, from which people are only too glad to escape back to market and family. But there is pain and frustration in families, the market can't fulfil all our needs, and we are caught in a vicious circle.

The *Tikkun* editorial policy is to politicize, to make the explicit object of public discourse, the difficulties and pains of 'family life',[57] and to work towards building up confidence and the other resources for encounters in public, in civil society.[58] Other communitarians paint a less agonistic picture, arguing or hypothesizing much more straightforwardly that intra-family conflicts could be alleviated if individuals had more connections and support from outside; and that members of successful families are in a position to contribute to the 'communities' whose members can then

Public Man (London: Faber, 1986); Christopher Lasch, *The Culture of Narcissism: American Life in an Age of Diminishing Expectations* (London: Abacus Press, 1980).

[54] Nisbet made this point: 'Individuals look for community in marriage, this putting often intolerable strain on a tie already grown institutionally fragile'. Robert A. Nisbet, *The Quest for Community: A Study in the Order of Ethics and Freedom* (New York: Oxford University Press, 1953), 31.

[55] Lerner, 'Pain at Work and Pain in Families', 15.

[56] Peter Gabel, 'Community and Democracy: Creating a Parallel Universe', *Tikkun*, 10/2 (1995), 14.

[57] Lerner, 'Can the Democrats be Stopped . . .?', 20.

[58] e.g. Gabel, 'Community and Democracy', 17.

sustain each other in their personal, familial, work, local, and political lives.

Few social scientists would dispute the significance of what is usually termed in survey work 'social support'—contact and interaction with friends, neighbours, and non-intimate kin, from which can be garnered advice, discussion, and practical help. In particular, lack of social support has been associated with child abuse and neglect, and is treated as an indicator of 'extreme distress' by professionals.[59] One notable implication, for which there is a good deal of empirical support, is that labour market participation by parents has positive effects: US women employed full time are less likely to be violent to their children than women who are employed part time or unemployed.[60] Of course, the quality of 'social support' cannot be assumed a priori—well-meaning friends can give rotten advice, so 'social support' may be a harm.[61] Equally, social support is usually obtained on the basis of reciprocity, so it can be a burden.[62] For this reason, social support is a relatively fragile good, and is particularly likely to be unobtainable by those who need it most—'where needs of others can't be met, and public and private resources are few, neighbourly exchange of goods come to an end'.[63] As we have seen, too, one person's (usually, in the research literature this person is a woman) 'social support' is another person's (usually in the literature this person is a man) loss of care and attention, and reason for discontent.[64]

Another prominent 'communitarian family' theme is that there must be a degree of integration between family and school and workplace. On the one hand, there is an emphasis on schools as valuable local organizations, with the resources to cooperate with parents and other local bodies 'in the provision of neighbourhood advice and support'.[65] On the other, there is a complementary emphasis on the benefits all round of parents' involvement

---

[59] Joan I. Vondra, 'The Community Context of Child Abuse and Neglect', *Marriage and Family Review*, 15 (1990), 19–38; Shlomo A. Sarlin and Michael Shamai, 'Intervention with Families in Extreme Distress', *Marriage and Family Review*, 21 (1995), 91–122.

[60] Demo, 'Parent Child Relations', 108–9.

[61] Robertson et al., 'The Costs and Benefits of Social Support', 412.   [62] Ibid.

[63] Vondra, 'Community Context of Child Abuse', 21.

[64] I don't think the gender order in this scenario can be fixed. After all, there is a social stereotype of men's social lives (mates, the pub, the football, etc.) being heterosexual women's loss of companionship and intimacy. But my reading of social science research over the last few decades reveals that men's loss when women work for wages or socialise has been most prominently highlighted; e.g. Robertson et al. argue: 'The consistent finding that married men are happier and more satisfied with their lives than single men and married women points to the marital relationship as a primary source of emotional support for these men' (p. 413).

[65] Tam, *Communitarianism*, 76.

in schools, and in their children's education.[66] Communitarians argue that employers should not demand that employees neglect their families,[67] and parental leave has been a key communitarian policy demand.[68] These two sets of relations (communitarians also recommend close links and even integration between businesses and schools)[69] raise different normative and empirical questions.

In the case of parental leave it is quite clear that what is being sought is a redistribution of resources from employers to employees. Whether any allowances or pay during leave are borne by employers or by the state through taxation the policy means additional costs to employers who have to recruit temporary staff to cover for parents on leave and thereby incur administrative costs. Obviously, employers, especially capitalist employers, will argue that it is a normative question whether there ought to be this redistribution (and they tend to argue, on consequentialist grounds, that there should not). Others, and communitarians have been among those who have made these arguments most clearly, argue that employers will get all kinds of returns in exchange for parental leave—a loyal and committed workforce (so less industrial conflict, greater efficiency and innovation), and public goodwill (so a marketing advantage).[70] That is, they argue that these kinds of redistributions are not zero-sum. The question then is, how to persuade all employers of the communitarian case. Here, communitarians take a strategic line which emphasizes, on the one hand, the extent to which we all, already, agree that family life and parenting are important and that it is unacceptable to run an economy in a way that undermines other valuable social institutions, and on the other hand points to the existence of successful businesses that are run along democratic, consensual, and community-spirited lines.[71] That is, the argument is that employers are not being asked to do anything radical, or anything that will undermine their position; rather they are being asked to do what some of the most successful and sensible among them are doing anyway, and to uphold the values we all share.[72]

[66] Joyce L. Epstein, 'School and Family Connections: Theory, Research and Implications for Integrating Sociologies of Education and Family', *Marriage and Family Review*, 15 (1990), 116; see also Mog Ball, *School Inclusion: The School, the Family and the Community* (York: Joseph Rowntree Foundation, 1998).

[67] Tam, *Communitarianism*, 182.

[68] Al Kamen, 'A Word from the Communitarians', *Washington Post* (19 Nov. 1992); Barbara Vobejda, 'Communitarians Press Hill on Pro-Family Policies', *Washington Post* (4 Nov. 1993); Etzioni, *Spirit of Community*, 70–2.

[69] Etzioni, *Spirit of Community*, 112; Mandelson and Liddle, *The Blair Revolution*, 92–3.

[70] Tam, *Communitarianism*, 182–5.   [71] Ibid. 182–5.

[72] The editors of *Tikkun* think that constitutional legislation is needed; see their draft 'Social Responsibility Amendment to the US Constitution' which would require

The issue of close contacts between parents and schools raises some different questions. Undoubtedly, one preoccupation of protagonists in these debates is discipline of the young—schools want parents' support for their disciplinary policies, and the communitarian argument is that 'the community' needs this too.[73] What is at stake is nothing less than the proper socialization and governance of the younger generation. Second, there is emphasis on the correlation between parental involvement in children's education, and the children's attainment. Involvement includes volunteering in school, participation in school governance, and parental involvement in children's learning at home and their homework.[74] However, it must be remembered that in unequal societies parents have very different capacities to provide the 'positive home conditions that support school learning'.[75] Insofar as educational practice relies on input at home, this is bound to amplify the inequality between children of parents with the necessary resources and those without.

This point takes me to a major issue which has been touched on a number of times in the discussion so far. This is the importance of the distribution of material resources. It is fair to say, as discussed in other chapters in this volume, that the political communitarians have been concerned from the outset to emphasize the importance of non-material social goods and resources—trust, respect, civility, reciprocity, the sources of what is called social capital.[76] Contra to traditional socialists, who have always focused on the justification of and mechanisms for the redistribution of material goods—income, wealth, access to valuable goods like healthcare and education—communitarians argue that material goods are certainly not sufficient for the kinds of amelioration of human misery that progressive people look for. Sometimes, though, and critics of communitarianism have not been slow to point this out, it can seem that communitarians are implying that material goods are not necessary either. Take, for example, the argument by Joan Vondra in the article I discussed earlier. She argues, first, that there are 'communities at risk'—communities where the needs of

corporations to serve the common good: 12/4 (1997). In a review of Michael Novak's *Business as a Calling* . . . William Sullivan is sceptical about the book's implied premiss that a capitalist market system and morality will rarely conflict, or that if they do the resolution will not be a big problem, with morality generally the clear winner. William M. Sullivan, 'The Politics of Meaning as a Challenge to Neo-Capitalism', *Tikkun*, 11 (1996), 20.

[73] See for example, Carol Vincent, 'Parent Empowerment? Collective Action and Inaction in Education', *Oxford Review of Education*, 22 (1996), 465–82; Mandelson and Liddle, *The Blair Revolution*, 135–8.

[74] Epstein, 'School and Family Connections', 113–14.   [75] Ibid. 106.

[76] James Coleman, 'Social Capital in the Creation of Human Capital', *American Journal of Sociology*, 94 suppl. (1988), 95–119; Robert Putnam, 'Bowling Alone: America's Declining Social Capital', *Journal of Democracy*, 6 (1995), 65–78.

others can't be met, where public and private resources are few. In these communities, the neighbourly exchange of goods come to an end. She then goes on to say: 'What is lacking in these neighbourhoods, in other words, is a sense of community involvement, mutual caring and social cohesion'.[77] It will strike critics that this is an odd inference to draw. What is lacking, according to the author herself, is the material resources that can sustain practices of community involvement and social cohesion. The *sense* of community involvement seems to be neither here nor there, and it may well be that people continue to care, and care mutually, but simply can't back up their caring with aid. Vondra herself argues that where very poor people do maintain an orderly existence, and do not succumb to the kind of chaos that can overwhelm deprived people, it tends to be because they have strong church ties and strict family rules (she is discussing research on US populations)—the implication, that is, is that social support can compensate for the lack of material resources.

COMMUNITARIANISM, FAMILY VALUES, AND POLITICAL ANALYSIS

To recap, political communitarianism includes a theory of family, individual and community. Communitarians understand the individual as primarily a member of both family and community (or communities). The meanings of family and community are mutually constitutive. They hypothesize that family and community are mutually supporting, and, in a normative vein but because of this, that the community has a legitimate interest in the conduct of life in families.

As I have argued in earlier chapters, in my view there is both an empirical and a conceptual problem with the category 'community'. Empirically, 'the community' clearly needs disaggregating if the validity of communitarian theory is to be investigated. And communitarians are happy enough to disaggregate 'the community' into what they understand to be its constituent parts: firms and corporations, schools, neighbourhoods, villages and towns, voluntary associations, states and societies. Each of these are also communities, and they are in a 'nested' relationship: individual is nested in family, is nested in a formation of community organizations like schools, is nested in the society at large (also a community, and community of communities).[78] Conceptually, disaggregated or

---

[77] Vondra, 'Community Context of Child Abuse', 21.
[78] Amitai Etzioni, *The New Golden Rule: Community and Morality in a Democratic Society* (New York: Basic Books, 1996), 176–7.

not, it seems doubtful to me that the concept 'community' is appropriate to capture the range of social relations and conflicts that make up these organizations, institutions, and agglomerations; and theoretically, the metaphor of 'nesting' seems inadequate to capture the complex relations between institutions and agglomerations. The problem is that the connotations of the concept 'community' can effectively obscure detailed analysis of how these organizations and agglomerations work and interact with one another.

If 'the community' needs disaggregating, then so, as we have now seen, does 'the family'. For communitarians, families are made up of individuals who also have other significant memberships. What the empirical work surveyed in the previous section pressingly suggests is that these individuals also have conflicting interests and needs. It is suggested that it will be difficult to find a 'family structure' that benefits all of its members—difficult, in any case, without some major adjustments to dominant systems of gender roles and expectations. And this is a very thorny question. But, as social theory leads us to expect, the question is on a number of social agendas. The societies with which communitarians are concerned are characterized by competing constructions of 'the family', which symbolizes different values in different discourses. How kinship and family relations interact with the markets for labour and housing is a commonplace issue in public and private debate. Equally familiar is discussion of the way kinship and family relations interact with the 'emotional economy' of individuals' desires and fears. In the course of these debates many feminist critics and commentators have expressed their suspicion that communitarianism means the reinstatement of the traditional roles and relations that are believed to have contributed to a less disorderly society in the past—and that central among these are traditional gender roles. Some of the political communitarians vehemently deny that they intend that women should be reconfined to the kitchen, or that they mean 'traditional femininity and masculinity' when they speak of 'family' and 'community'.[79] Now, I see no real reason to disbelieve these people when they say this, although it would be unwise to think that all political communitarians are automatically as right minded. But the problem is that as a social theory communitarianism lacks a critical theory of power. This means that it is ill-equipped to identify, let alone analyse, the social conflict that is a systematic feature of life inside families, and inside other social groups and formations like neighbourhoods, networks, and associations (that is, life inside the so-called community). So even if political

[79] Etzioni, *Spirit of Community*, 55; Mandelson and Liddle, *The Blair Revolution*, 124–9; *Tikkun* is explicitly informed by the insights of Jewish feminism.

communitarians protest that they are not anti-feminist, the categories they work with have the consequence that feminist and other conflict will look, to them, anomalous or downright perverse, if they recognize it at all.

There is no doubt that gender is almost invariably present—if suppressed and marginalized—in discourses of community. Etzioni outlines a historical thesis: first with the industrial revolution men left the community and family, and went into waged work for long periods of each day. Second, with the post-war entry of married women into the waged labour market they too left the community and the family. These, he implies, just are the historical facts, and we must not flinch from confronting the effects they have had subseqently on the well-being of children and communities.[80] Such arguments about parents' abandonment of family inevitably raise questions about mothering as opposed to fathering, femininity as opposed to masculinity. Is the entry of women into the waged labour market bad because it means the second parent abandoning parenting, or because it means mothers abandoning parenting? Men, historians point out, have for most of the modern period at least been either absent or distant, and for significant proportions of twentieth-century European populations have been missing, killed in war. Children in every modern generation have been brought up by women, without fathers— what is the difference between that and the current results of divorce and 'unmarried motherhood'? There are many responses to these questions, and all of them involve the deployment of complicated descriptive and normative theories of gender.

Historians and sociologists concur that at the level of ideology and at the level of practice there has been an affinity between femininity and community. Community often has been women's public sphere, the site of women's political action.[81] This is because women have exploited the opportunities available to them in their own localities; and because opponents of sexual equality have heightened the barriers to their action on the wider, national, more public stage. For instance, British anti-suffragists promoted women's participation in local politics (women ratepayers had the right to vote in municipal elections half a century before any women got the vote).[82] It is widely observed that responsibility for family maintenance rests, normatively, with women. However, it is hardly the case that

---

[80] Etzioni, *Spirit of Community*, 55–7.
[81] Paula Hyman, 'Gender and Jewish History', *Tikkun*, 3 (1988).
[82] Brian Harrison, *Separate Spheres: The Opposition to Women's Suffrage in Britain* (London: Croom Helm, 1978); Anne Phillips, 'Feminism and the Attractions of the Local', in Desmond King and Gerry Stoker (eds.), *Rethinking Local Democracy* (Basingstoke: Macmillan, 1996).

everybody thinks this is right—where women take responsibility for care of their parents, for instance, there is often conflict with their brothers.[83] Beatrix Campbell reads Etzioni as arguing that the entry of married women into the labour force has deprived 'the community' of its active members. Undoubtedly, in many areas women living in run-down and disadvantaged localities are the ones who try to build community, doing battle with adult men's apathy and young men's aggression.[84] But surely, responsibility for localities, where we live, where we work, where we spend our time, should lie with everyone. The very identifications of women and the local, women and the family, pose a problem of justice and of politics.

That there is a widespread normative conviction that these are women's domain is quite consistent with many women feeling that they have had the responsibility dumped on them, and, for that matter, with women as a class being exploited. There is a question of justice here—is this gender division of labour and responsibility right and justifiable? There is a question of politics—the discontent and conflict over the distribution of these responsibilities indicates the exertion of and resistance to the power to govern.

It is a great virtue of political communitarianism that it has generated a new body of political discourse on 'the family', or rather, on marital and parental relations, on the structure and norms of households, and other social networks. This communitarian discourse comes into competition with recent feminist and related criticisms of the dominant legal, cultural, and economic constructions of 'the family' which have dwelt on the tyranny of kinship relations (especially but not only when these are organized in 'nuclear' family forms). These debates place 'family' and domestic relationships squarely in the ambit of political theory, contrary to the view, explicit in a good deal of liberal thought, that family and domestic relations are outwith politics.[85] The debate on this vexed question tends to be confusing.

[83] Wellman, 'Place of Kinfolk in Personal Community Networks', 203 on 'kinkeepers' who are usually female; Bott, *Family and Social Network,*135, 197 on gender and closeknit kin networks; Finch, *Family Obligations*, 27, 30, 40–1 on the way kin relationships are seen as women's business, although this (*a*) can cause conflict between women and men, and (*b*) is culturally variable.

[84] Beatrix Campbell, *Goliath: Britain's Dangerous Places* (London: Methuen, 1993), 44, 230; Roberta M. Feldman, Susan Stall, and Patricia A. Wright, ' "The Community Needs to be Built by Us": Women Organising in Chicago Public Housing', in Nancy A. Naples (ed.), *Community Activism and Feminist Politics: Organising across Race, Class and Gender* (New York: Routledge, 1998).

[85] See Pateman, *The Sexual Contract*; Susan Moller Okin, *Justice, Gender and the Family* (New York: Basic Books, 1989).

In some cases, the refusal to discuss family relations in the context of political philosophy and theory is made on the grounds that family relations belong to the realm of ethics and morals in general.[86] The argument goes something like this:

- There are special problems with the justification of coercion by governments, problems which do not arise in the justification of other kinds of coercion, as, for instance, the coercion of children by parents.
- Inequalities within families and households are not the direct upshot of coercion by governments; and
- Governments cannot legislate to prevent these inequalities, at least not without quite repellant 'totalitarian' implications; so
- These are not issues for political philosophy in the relevant respect.

Two responses are possible.[87] First, it might be argued that although governments typically don't legislate that, say, physical chastisement of wives is permissible, or that women should give up food in order to feed men, nevertheless the legal and administrative framework indirectly, at least, constructs a set of incentives and pressures that determines and legitimizes individuals' behaviour and transactions in households. In this sense, government and administration is implicated in these so-called private transactions. Further, the construction of incentives and of constraints is part and parcel of the same set of social and political processes. Second, it can be argued that actually *coercion as such* is the business of government, and thereby of political philosophy. So political philosophy cannot justifiably be indifferent to domestic relations.

It is also sometimes argued that intimate and domestic transactions should not be considered in the framework of thinking about justice. Many philosophers have argued that 'justice' features elements such as deliberation, detachment (justice is 'blindfolded' when she deliberates), and even-handedness. Thus, systems of 'justice' abstract away from the particulars of circumstances and actors, and, in particular, abstract away from actors' feelings about and in situations. Systems of justice such as rights, utilitarianism, and patriarchy are all (notwithstanding their great contrasts) general in their scope, abstract in their detachment from particular circumstances, and thus equipped to be detached from the emotional

---

[86] John Rawls implies something like this in *Political Liberalism* (New York: Columbia University Press, 1993); for criticism: Elizabeth Frazer and Nicola Lacey, 'Politics and the Public in Rawls' Political Liberalism', *Political Studies*, 43 (1995), 233–47.

[87] For much fuller discussion see Annette Baier, *Moral Prejudices: Essays on Ethics* (Cambridge, Mass.: Harvard University Press, 1994); Diemut Bubeck, *Care Gender and Justice* (Oxford: Clarendon Press, 1995); Okin, *Justice, Gender and the Family*.

appeal of one party against another in particular cases. Communitarians in particular are critical of the cultural dominance of rights discourse, and the social fragmentation that results when individual rights override cooperative effort, concern for others, and concern for the social whole. As we have seen, they gesture to 'the family' to show us another way of living a moral life: one where we are as concerned for the others as for ourselves, where our own happiness and welfare is dependent upon the happiness and welfare of others, and where the community, not the individual, is the source and locus of value. Within the family, it is argued, individual rights and fair decision procedures are seldom appealed to, not because injustice is rampant, but because their appeal is pre-empted by a spirit of generosity in which I am rarely inclined to claim my fair share.[88]

When set beside research data, this picture seems to overlook the good deal of reasoning about justice that does go on in kin and household relations. In intra-family exchanges between women there is often overt concern about justice—for instance, money payments pass from daughters to mothers in respect of childcare, in order that the daughter does not exploit her mother.[89] Men's reluctance to cooperate with certain aspects of domestic regimes engenders strain that can lead to family or household breakdown. Alternatively, it leads to the construction and maintenance of myths that the domestic division of labour is more egalitarian than it actually is.[90] It is evident that where negotiations about responsibility and obligation are conducted between the sexes, male protagonists tend not to notice that their sisters are not claiming their fair share—precisely because assumptions about gender intervene.[91] Thus, that the norm of family exchanges is 'sharing without reckoning', as Janet Finch puts it, is consistent with the norm's being in conflict with people's sense of justice, fairness, and grievance.

These considerations ought to worry communitarians, on the basis of two aspects of communitarian theory. First, as we have seen, for communitarians 'families' are or ought to be 'communities'. In the normative conceptions of 'community' the political communitarians have recently

[88] Sandel, *Liberalism and the Limits of Justice*, 30–1, 33–4, 169.
[89] Finch, *Family Obligations and Social Change*, 69.
[90] For recent analyses of the sexual division of domestic work see Oriel Sullivan, 'Time Coordination, the Domestic Division of Labour, and Affective Relations', *Sociology*, 30 (1996), 79–100; 'Time Waits for no Woman: An Investigation of the Gendered Experience of Domestic Time', *Sociology*, 31 (1997), 221–39; Janeen Baxter and Mark Western, 'Satisfaction with Housework', *Sociology*, 32 (1998), 101–20; on the maintenance of domestic harmony by way of a family myth about the division of labour Hochschild, *The Second Shift*.
[91] Finch, *Family Obligation and Social Change*, 181–2.

elaborated there is room for argument about the 'community's' rules, goals, etc.,[92] but the conflicts of interest alluded to here seem, to me at any rate, to go beyond this kind of reflexive and constructive project. Second, it is a key aspect of communitarian theory that the various institutions of society and state are congruent: that relations at the level of state (in its broadest sense of the people organized politically) are accordant with relations in firms, schools, families, voluntary associations, and between these. All of these organizations *are* communities; the relation of community is repeated at every level and on every scale. So the 'congruence' modelled here is more or less the geometrical congruence where there will be coincidence in the pattern of relations when these various organizations are superposed one on another.[93]

The idea that social and political institutions must be congruent is one that has wide currency in political theory, especially democratic political theory.[94] It is widely hypothesized that schools and classrooms, for instance, should be organized democratically if the children who are educated in them are to grow up to be competent and conscientious democratic citizens, and there is some empirical support for this.[95] It has been argued that 'lower class' people's experience of authoritarian decision-making and power in their families explains their submissive acceptance of a hierarchical political order and material disadvantage.[96] It is emphasized that where people participate in democratically organized voluntary associations they get a chance to learn valuable political skills and this has an effect on their political identities and engagement.[97] Susan Okin argues

[92] Robert N. Bellah, 'Community Properly Understood: A Defence of "Democratic Communitarianism" ', *Responsive Community*, 6/1 (1995), 49–54.

[93] Nancy Rosenblum, 'Democratic Character and Community: The Logic of Congruence', *Journal of Political Philosophy*, 2 (1994), 67–97 observes that congruence theories tend to emphasize either the structure of authority (family, workplace, school, state should be patterned by similar authority distributions) or affective dispositions—(that is congruence theorists argue that we should have the same kind of dispositions to care, concern etc. in family, workplace, school, and state). The political communitarians studied here are committed to both these forms of congruence. Rosenblum also picks out another strain of congruence theory, which emphasizes self-governance at different levels.

[94] For a survey see Rosenblum, 'Democratic Character and Community'.

[95] For the theory see Geraint Parry, 'Constructive and Reconstructive Political Education'; Meira Levinson, 'Liberalism, Pluralism and Political Education: Paradox or Paradigm?'; for empirical evidence Carole L. Hahn, 'Political Education in Comparative Perspective: An Empirical Study of Policy, Practices and Outcomes'; Nicholas Emler and Elizabeth Frazer, 'Politics, the Education Effect', all in *Oxford Review of Education*, 25 (1999).

[96] Harry Eckstein, 'Civic Inclusion and its Discontents', in *Regarding Politics: Essays on Political Theory, Stability and Change* (Berkeley and Los Angeles: University of California Press, 1992), 362–3.

[97] Sidney Verba, Kay Lehman Schlozman, Henry Brady, and Norman Nie, 'Race Ethnicity and Political Resources: Participation in the United States', *British Journal of*

that justice is learned, first, in the family, so the sense of justice required for liberal democratic citizenship must be instilled in the family; conversely, unjust families will prepare people badly for their tasks as citizens in a just state.[98]

Several points need to be made. First, these are clearly hypotheses that are well-formed enough to be susceptible to empirical testing, and, indeed, political scientists have begun to think about this work, although in survey research it is difficult to gather good-quality data about authority patterns, decision-making, and justice in general from within family groups. But a second point that congruence theorists overlook is that democratic citizens need to recognize and be equipped to operate in non-democratic power structures. There would be no point educating people in such a way that they were all at sea when they came up against domination. A crucial aspect of democratic politics, in other words, is the struggle for democracy. A worry that occurs to me about the congruence theory is that children who are brought up in democratic and just families, educated in democratic and just schools, work in democratic and just workplaces, socialize in democratic and just associations, will lack some crucial know-how when it comes to tackling injustice and authoritarianism. Partly, this worry is generated by the view expressed elsewhere in this book that communitarian theory lacks a necessary grasp of the tension and the conflict in individual identity and in social life. The model of community at every level, the metaphor of 'nested communities', the theory of reflexive construction of the community and the values 'we all share'—all these aspects of communitarian theory operate to eliminate (in the theory) discontent, insoluble conflicts, and the sheer perversity of social life. Nowhere is this more evident than in communitarian treatment of the question of gender, and in particular complementary gender roles in families, which is the final aspect of communitarian theory of the family I wish to discuss.

As I have mentioned, politicians such as Tony Blair and Bill Clinton are very cautious about suggesting in speeches that women are incapable of heading families alone or of raising children of both sexes perfectly satisfactorily. Nevertheless this caution is mixed with a simultaneous concern about the fact that many men are not discharging their responsibilities,

Political Science, 23 (1993), 453–97 find a difference in political engagement and sense of political efficacy between Latino citizens who attend mainly relatively authoritarian Roman Catholic churches and African American citizens who attend participatory, democratic and politically mobilizing Protestant churches. See also Robert Putnam *Making Democracy Work: Civic Traditions in Modern Italy* (Princeton: Princeton University Press, 1993).

[98] Okin, *Justice Gender and the Family*, 17–24.

financial and social, to the children they have biologically fathered.[99] This concern, in turn, generates an emphasis on the hardship attached to single parenthood, and critical comment on governments' recent attempts (in their efforts to 'restructure' welfare) to get 'welfare mothers' off benefits and into work. Journalist Melanie Phillips, who is very sympathetic to communitarian politics and often reports and comments on community projects, argues, 'The poverty and emotional and social isolation of lone parents are not caused by their worklessness but by the absence of the children's fathers. . . . Policies to shore up stable family life with two committed parents are critical to ending social exclusion'.[100]

Now of course acceptance of the view that two parents are preferable in many ways to one does not entail any particular prescription of who those two parents should be or how responsibilities and labour should be divided between them. But the concern that men are either getting away with complete neglect of their family duties, or proliferating deprived families in a series of broken partnerships, of course means that arguments about the drawbacks of parenting alone flow into a more uncompromising discourse about the need for children to be fathered by a man as well as mothered by a woman.[101]

Evidence about this need, and what children who are deprived of fathering in this sense are actually deprived of, exists mainly in the context of research about how people in families with lone parents cope compared to those in two-parent families; and research about how sex and gender interact with the distribution of resources and responsibilities within family and other networks. This kind of research turns up consistent evidence of sex differences in the maintenance of relations. We have already met the widely accepted social judgement that relationship work and kinship maintenance is women's work, and that people who take responsibility for remembering birthdays, organizing family get-togethers etc. are, as a matter of fact, most often women. These social norms show up in survey work which supports the view that women are more able than men to maintain social relations even when other social relations are going badly. This

[99] In his Labour Party Conference speech, Blackpool, Sept. 1998 Tony Blair talked about 'Responsibilities—like the belief that if you father a child, that child's got something to do with you, and the child's mother has every right to expect support'.

[100] Melanie Phillips, 'Getting Lone Parents off Benefits won't Solve any Problems', *Observer* (14 Dec. 1997).

[101] For example, David Popenoe, whose work as we have seen has been taken up by US communitarians, argues that sex differences in aggression, cognition, sensory sensitivity etc. underpin difference in male and female capabilities as regards nurturing, protection and so forth, which enjoins contrasting and complementary parental roles. David Popenoe, *Life without Father* (New York: Free Press, 1996), 209–15.

theoretically underpins the robust finding that it is more difficult for fathers than mothers to maintain relationships with non-coresident children after divorce or separation,[102] and that at times of marital conflict, men are more likely than are women to 'relate negatively' to their children as well as their marital partners.[103] So one implication that is consistent with a good deal of critical gender theory is that men's social relationships with kin are much more fragile—hence, children whose fathers are separated from their partner are likely to be without a father.

Critical gender theory has also emphasized, with support from literature, philosophy, politics, and social science, that on the whole men's experiences and points of view tend to dominate both in representations of the social world, and also practically in all kinds of social institutions and contexts. Studies of the division of domestic labour within the household find that men's perceptions, values, and attitudes are dominant in determining the division of labour and responsibility, and the quality of marital and family relations. A woman may have very clear views about a just and proper division of domestic labour, she may have egalitarian commitments and an expectation that there should be sex equality in domestic responsibilities, high self-esteem, and a belief in the value of her own work outside the household. But these will make very little difference either to the division of household labour (studies suggest that that is determined by the man's attitudes and perceptions), or to either the man's or her own experience of the quality of the partnership. What seems to determine both his and her experience of marital quality is, on the one hand, the *man's* expectations, gender role identity, attitudes, and perceptions, and on the other hand the woman's perceptions and judgements about his expectations and needs.[104]

Some of the theorists who insist that families need two different sex parents who bring different gender inputs to parenting do so with just such a theory of the centrality of patriarchal or male power in mind. For instance, in response to the observation that fathers have been absent from their families throughout the modern period—either withdrawn from the children's living space in the manner of the Victorian patriarch, or out at work as with the twentieth-century middle and working classes, or away at war or killed in battle—neo-traditionalists argue that these forms of absence

[102] Alan Booth and Paul R. Amato, 'Parental Marital Quality, Parental Divorce and Relations with Parents', *Journal of Marriage and the Family*, 53 (1994), 21–34.

[103] Jay Belsky, Lise Youngblade, Michael Rovine, and Brenda Volling, 'Patterns of Marital Change and Parent-Child Interaction', *Journal of Marriage and the Family*, 53 (1991), 487–498.

[104] Dana Vannoy and William W. Philiber, 'Wife's Employment and Quality of Marriage', *Journal of Marriage and the Family*, 54 (1992), 387–98.

are not destructive of fathers' authority (on the contrary, they can be positively enhancing of it) whereas the rejection of men by women who divorce or choose to have children alone, and men's abandonment of their children, 'kills fatherhood'.[105]

This argument about power and authority, of course, repeats and reworks arguments about the mechanisms and distribution of political power and sovereignty. Democratic and republican critics of patriarchal and monarchical theories of sovereignty argue that political power can be shared (for instance, by 'We, the people'), or even dispersed among a wide variety of state connected agencies and autonomous organizations and localities, without losing power's potency, and with the added boon of heading off the danger of tyranny. Feminist critics of domestic patriarchy, similarly, argue that domestic power can be shared between parents and other responsible adults, and also shared with children, without chaos necessarily ensuing. We may agree that parental authority must, in some sense, be 'final'—that children need very clear boundaries, for instance, and that infractions of these have to have unambiguous consequences. It may be that strategically some parents find the threat of an absent but imminent final authority indispensable ('Wait till your father gets home . . .' uttered as a warning). It may also be tempting to think that this is, strictly speaking, a cop-out, a way of ducking the ethically non-optional exercise of adult power and responsibility, a form of moral bad faith. Indeed, some lone parents who have no such handy spectre hovering on the horizon may feel a degree of moral superiority as they are endlessly responsible; while other lone parents will fervently wish that there was some credible threat they had resort to. What does, unambiguously, seem to be an ethical cop-out is to tie the attribution and exercise of this final power to gender, to masculinity. Indeed, it is impossible to think of a good reason why we should do this (if we discount the arguments which appeal to biology or to nature, and which make an unwarranted and invalid inference from sex to gender). Women and men alike must exercise parental responsibility.[106]

A less radical set of arguments for two-sex parent families elaborates the need for parents to model gender difference for the sake of children's social and moral identity. For example, Jean Bethke Elshtain argues that

---

[105] Josephson and Burack, 'The Political Ideology of the Neo-Traditional Family', 219 (citing David Blankenhorn, *Fatherless America* (New York: Basic Books, 1995)).

[106] Widows may, I suppose, appeal to the memory of their children's father, thus sustaining the potency of patriarchal power along the lines sketched by Blankenhorn. See n. 102 above. But women cannot possibly be excused moral responsibility, so why should they be excused parental responsibility?

children inescapably inhabiting a sexed body figure out the world by way of figuring out gender. Children who are learning about a complicated 'social order' will seek and must find some measure of security in these matters—they will find this security in a gender identity that maps on to their body sex.[107] But Elshtain herself is quite clear that there can be no inference from this argument to a social and gender order in which different evaluations are placed on 'maleness' or 'femaleness'.[108] Models of 'patriarchal power' are more ideological or mythical than descriptive as women as well as men exercise power and authority in societies we know about.[109] Yet Elshtain argues vigorously that, because of the 'gender health' argument outlined above, it is not desirable that 'males and females have decisions over the same activities and exercise power in identical ways over the same things'. Rather, there should be a gender division of power with 'parity and complementarity, with neither sex wholly dominant over the other, but with each dominant in particular areas of social life'.[110]

This argument raises a number of difficulties. First, it raises the same question about the exercise of parental power as came up in my discussion of the recent patriarchalists. They argue that the family must be ruled by the father. Elshtain argues that different areas of social life should be ruled by one sex or the other. This leaves open the possibility of families being ruled either by fathers or by mothers, but not by both. Which then leaves an odd moral problem for those families from which the relevantly gendered parent has disobligingly disappeared. According to this view the remaining parent has to invoke the power of the father (or the mother) in order to maintain order, rather than simply exercising adult, parental responsibility. But there is a further incoherence in Elshtain's position, which seems to imply that there is one, and only one, gender division of power per society. Thus, in one society mothers are threatening their children with paternal wrath when he puts in an appearance; in another fathers are instructing their disorderly children to wait till their mother gets back. In fact, in complicated and pluralist societies, of course, there are many local variations on the gender division of power and responsibility; and even within one socio-economic class, ethnic group or region there is variation beween families as to who controls domestic finances, disciplines children, goes out to waged work, or participates in 'public life'.

[107] Jean Bethke Elshtain, 'Symmetry and Soporifics: A Critique of Feminist Accounts of Gender Development', in *Real Politics: At the Center of Everyday Life* (Baltimore: Johns Hopkins University Press, 1997), 223; 'Against Androgyny', ibid. 239.
[108] Elshtain, 'Against Androgyny', 239.
[109] Elshtain, 'Symmetry and Soporifics', 216.   [110] Ibid. 217, 216.

The principle, which for all I know may be valid, that children have to find security in the matter of gender difference, does not settle the question 'what gender difference?' Elshtain herself wishes to move away from the lamentable status quo in which

much current male and female self-definition is defensive in relation to one another . . . human beings at least some of the time *over* define themselves as 'real men' or 'true women' defensively, given their internalised images of the opposite sex. To the extent that this is the case, we must aim to enhance our capacities to secure our male and female identities in ways that are less limiting.[111]

This introduces an ethical dimension to discourses and practices of gender and the gender socialization of children. What 'gendered' characteristics do parents and carers wish to encourage and which to discourage? It is the work of a moment to compile a very long list of both 'feminine' and 'masculine' characteristics which can be damaging to the interests of their bearers. In addition to obvious items, like certain kinds of 'flirtatiousness' in girls, for instance, we should bear in mind the gendered characteristics I discussed earlier. It would, surely, be preferable if men, as well as women, were able to sustain their social and kinship relations for themselves. Equally, there is a pressing list of virtues which any adult would wish all children to cultivate: courage, the capacity to care, diligence, self-discipline, etc.

Political communitarians tend to be caught between, on the one hand, an ideal of egalitarian and democratic flexibility in the communitarian family, in which all members sustain and care for the others, in which mothers and fathers model democracy and equality and openness to their children, in which all members play their full part in all their relevant networks—kinship, neighbourhood, school, state—and, on the other hand, a normative model of parenting which slips into a theory of gender which is unrealistically naturalistic, dualistic, and unethical. In addition, I have argued that the model of the communitarian family is unrealistically free of tension—with its open relationships, its community nested within community. Of course, communitarians can object that here I am mistaking their ideal for the real. 'We can accept', the communitarian might say 'everything you say about insoluble conflicts within family structures, but we must remind you that we are talking about how family relations ought to be'. The two points are connected: for the 'communitarian family' seems to beg a thoroughgoing critique and reconstruction of gender relations, of a kind that is clearly not on the political communitarian agenda.

---

[111] Elshtain, 'Symmetry and Soporifics', 208.

7

The Idea of a Political Community

COMMUNITY AND POLITICS

In this chapter I want to discuss the question of the normative theories
and models of 'politics' incorporated in and underlying 'communitarianism'. Once again, I will concentrate mainly on political and vernacular
communitarianism, although the work of the philosophical communitarians is also, of course, relevant. As ever, too, the relationship between
these three bodies of thought and writing is itself a problem.

Among the many critical responses to the work of the philosophical
communitarians the point was made that their prescriptions were exceedingly vague when it came to the question what political and legal institutions would need to be put in place if the communitarian society and
system of justice were to be realized. Political communitarianism, on the
other hand, is all about politics—about who, and what institutions, should
govern, how the relationships between institutions should be organized,
what strategies and tactics, including argumentative ones, communitarians should deploy in order to promote their party position and goals.

In this chapter I return to a number of issues that have arisen earlier in
the book, including the 'politics of interpretation', the 'politics of social
construction', and the ideal of community politics. One recurring theme is
the idea of 'a political community'. This term is central in political communitarianism. It is also very commonly deployed by liberal, socialist,
republican, and radical democratic thinkers. It begs a number of conceptual and theoretical questions: in what sense is a political community
'political'? in what sense is it 'a community?' If the idea of a political community is central in a political theory what implications does that have for
models of democracy, for the distribution of power and authority, and for
justice? I shall examine these issues by looking at the uneasy structure of
unity and conflict in communitarian politics.

COMMUNITARIAN POLITICS

There are a number of distinct elements to communitarian theories of politics. In this section I first discuss the value of community activism, according to communitarians, and draw attention to some problems and dilemmas arising from this theory. Second, I look at communitarian models of 'the polity', paying particular attention to the affinity communitarians express with 'republican' political thought. Third, communitarians like other political theorists tend to be committed to a distinctive set of political strategies or tactics, which are consistent with other elements of their political theory—here I discuss communitarian commitment to dialogic (as opposed to other forms of) democracy. This raises two themes that were discussed briefly in earlier chapters: the relationship between politics and interpretation, and the problems of a social constructionist politics. Fourth, and finally, I examine the idea of a 'political community'.

Community Activism

Perhaps the most obvious element of a communitarian theory of politics is the prominent and privileged place given to 'community activism'. As we have seen, the relevant political sociology and communitarian theory concentrates to a large extent on 'the local community' here—emphasizing the importance of local people's organization and action about crime, housing, leisure facilities, and other services. Action by such groups as gay people, women, and members of ethnic or religious groups, are also highlighted.[1] Of course this kind of group organization and action introduces the possibility if not the probability of conflict into local politics—the challenge for communitarian politics is to maintain local community while also acknowledging and giving due weight to memberships that transcend and possibly conflict in some respects with the locality. Communitarian theory also stresses the role of other 'communities' such as firms and schools. The point here is twofold. First, such organizations are members of their local communities, and as such have the same obligation as other members to put resources into efforts for the promotion and maintenance of genuine community relationships, and to participate in the local effort to shape the structures that govern local people. Second, schools, businesses, and other associations ought themselves to be com-

[1] Nancy Naples (ed.), *Community Activism and Feminist Politics: Organising across Race, Class and Gender* (New York: Routledge, 1998); Ann Curno et al. (eds.), *Women in Collective Action* (London: Association of Community Workers, 1982).

munities, or more like communities, so that within such organizations there is also community building to be done.[2]

Community activism, according to its promoters, has a number of political and democratic pay-offs. First, it forges 'civic bonds'. That is to say, it gives people roles and relationships outside the family and kinship structure, and separate from the markets for labour and consumption goods. So it directly constructs the infrastructure of relations of obligation and loyalty, belonging and membership, that is necessary in a democratic state where 'ordinary people' must be prepared to participate in government, where transitions from one government to another and individuals' conduct in all social settings are governed by 'the rule of law' and democratic procedures for decision-making.

Second, community politics brings 'politics' down to its proper, human, level. An obvious problem in liberal democracies has been that people feel ignorant about and alienated from the political process—to the extent that they opine that 'politics is irrelevant'. The experience of political action at the local level can show individuals the institutional links and give them an understanding of the structure of power—they may, as some of the political sociological literature shows, continue to feel alienated and disempowered, but they can no longer believe that 'politics is irrelevant'. Campaigns and negotiations about the local area, about housing or schooling are about issues that really engage people in their daily lives, and on which in the right institutional circumstances (that is, in a communitarian polity) they can have an effect. Further than this, for many people one rebarbative feature of conventional politics (writing to your councillor, attending a public meeting, watching the TV news, reading the letters pages in the paper) is that the actors don't seem real. These partial encounters with people (strangers) in roles lack any human or personal dimension. By contrast, in community politics several features are important. Encounters with members will not be confined to the particular campaigning or organizing context—rather the expectation is that you will encounter relevant others in the diurnal contexts of the neighbourhood, the shops, the school, etc.[3] Moreover, within the political context itself role multiplexity is important: having food and drink at the meeting, making business into a sociable matter, having fun.[4]

---

[2] Henry Tam, *Communitarianism: A New Agenda for Politics and Citizenship* (Basingstoke: Macmillan, 1998), 110.

[3] See papers in Curno et al. (eds.), *Women in Collective Action*; Naples, *Community Activism and Feminist Politics*; Paul Lichterman, *The Search for Political Community* (Cambridge: Cambridge University Press, 1996), 82 ff.

[4] e.g. Naples, *Community Activism and Feminist Politics*, 292.

Some communitarians are very aware on the other hand of the numerous factors that can militate against this widespread human-level encounter and action. In Chapter 6 I mentioned Peter Gabel's analysis of the way a lack of trust in our fellow citizens has a self-reinforcing effect—people's anticipation of discomfort or hostility makes defensiveness and aggressiveness a rational stance in public settings. Added to this we can note the many material barriers to participation, such as the length of waged and salaried workers' working days, and changing provision of consumption of leisure (especially for children) which takes individuals and their transport providers away from their locality. Communitarians argue that these developments damage public life.

However, it is important to note the dual significance of this normative model of multiplex and dense ties. When practised by relatively powerful people these have often been identified as a crucial mechanism of exclusion. Membership of expensive clubs brings individuals from a common socio-economic and cultural milieu together, and excludes others. Habits such as going to the pub or bar, it has been observed, exclude those who have responsibilities at home so limited time to be out. It also excludes individuals with different cultural commitments—for instance an aversion to or cultural rules against alcohol and/or places and spaces that are dedicated to the consumption of alcohol. This, and indeed any other, kind of socializing presupposes a common cultural ground which may be inconsistent with cultural differences—not to mention material differences in disposable income. Of course, the important issue is not about people's choices and abilities to join in particular cultural activities such as parties, dining in restaurants, or 'social evenings'; rather it is the way that these cultural events are effective concentrations of opportunities and resources for decision-making, so that those who are absent or effectively excluded are also excluded from decision-making. To this dilemma there are two alternative responses. One is that individuals simply have to realize and accept that the credentials and qualifications for participation in a job or a political organization include the willingness and ability to engage in the requisite cultural activities. The other is to try to eliminate the cultural paraphernalia from events and encounters—confine work to the workplace, politics to the meeting or other event, not to assume that everyone would enjoy a disco or a trip to the bowling alley, or is willing to eat in restaurants or drink in bars. With this strategy one would be retreating from the communitarian impulse that our relations should be multiplex and 'human'. (Of course, it is impossible to eliminate informal encounters and discussions of business between individuals who share cultural habits and milieux altogether.)

Finally, community activism is thought to be important simply because 'community' is thought to be the single most important resource for individuals who need to resist oppressive power and secure justice. As we saw in Chapter 5, communitarians emphasize 'community' as an instrumental value and as an absolute good. If, and only if, people can organize themselves in the kind of formation that is solid can they resist the divisive pressures that can be brought to bear on them by economically, culturally, and politically powerful actors such as governments, city authorities, corporations, etc. As we saw in Chapter 2, in 'community' individuals orient not only to each other as members of the group, but to the whole itself, and they conceive this whole as having a significance that transcends present purposes.

State Community and Individual

According to communitarian models of the polity 'the community' or 'communities' mediate the relationship between 'the state' and 'the individual'. That is to say, individuals are born into and live within a series of communities such as their family, their locality, their occupational group, their school and workplace, and so on. They also have a number of roles and statuses stemming from their individual relationship with 'the state': subject, or citizen, or immigrant etc,—but these too are actually lived out and enacted in local and immediate contexts. Communities sustain the individual in all his social roles—parent, citizen, worker. These are the 'reference groups' from which individuals draw an identity, from which they learn or negotiate norms of conduct.

Once again, it is important to note the very specific normative stance here. Rival theories idealize rather the individual's direct relationship with 'the state'. The ideal of 'cradle to grave welfare' for instance is premised on the supposition that it is a good thing for the individual not to be dependent on local and immediate communities or contexts for their welfare. After all, there is enormous inequality between communities as regards the resources they have at their command, and differences as regards the norms that govern the distribution of these resources. (Some, for instance, may not wish to educate girls; others may withhold certain goods from old people.) From this point of view, the individual's direct relationship with 'the state' can be a liberation and a guarantee of his individual rights.[5] Further, there can also be a normative commitment to the

---

[5] For example, William Beveridge, the designer of the British welfare state who was closely involved with Toynbee Hall, believed that social security must be a right, a matter of justice, which is not premised on anyone's concern in particular—that is, that

state being the primary source of identity for the individual: this is often said to be the case for French citizens, for instance. Once again, the normative thought behind such models is that 'the individual' owes his status as such to the structures of law and political power that are sustained by the state, and which local communities and lower level associations cannot and could not sustain.

Communitarians level a number of objections at this ideal picture of the individual unencumbered, as Michael Sandel puts it, by relationships and obligations, formally equal with all other citizens and subjects. It underestimates the importance of horizontal relationships and ties, and of historically continuous local communities, for the individual's social identity and for his welfare. It overlooks the danger that these 'free and equal' individuals can be enmeshed in oppressive bureaucratic structures, and because of the nature of state power can be called into a proliferation of unchosen, unwanted, and alienating relationships.[6] One way in which this dilemma between local ties and the impersonal state is resolved—theoretically—is by the ideal of the welfare state as itself a community. This indeed was a key idea underpinning the design of the British welfare state. The relation of community could be reconceptualized so as to apply at the level of the nation. Although precise analysis of what this means is lacking in the contemporary and historical accounts we can note, based on the analysis in Chapter 2, what it might mean. The welfare state can be thought of as approaching 'community' to the extent that members' relations with each other are multiple rather than simple or one-dimensional. Citizens relate to each other not only politically, in a welfare state, but also economically and culturally and, crucially, so the theory goes, their relationship is to each, to all, and to the whole thus constituted. Their relationships are dense rather than loose because each is related to each. Of course, they are not personal in the sense of face to face but this element is substituted by the mediated pooling of resources and the commitment to the well-being of all secured by redistribution to people in need. This degree of density and multiplexity based on sharing and commitment

individuals should not have to rely on 'their community' to support and sustain them. It is also notable that Beveridge thought, in Toynbee Hall fashion, of the welfare state as a reconstruction of 'community'—I discuss this further below. See Asa Briggs and Anne Macartney, *Toynbee Hall: The First Hundred Years* (London: Routledge and Kegan Paul, 1984), 61–71, 77–8; S. I. Benn, 'Individuality, Autonomy and Community', in E. Kamenka (ed.), *Community as a Social Ideal* (London: Edward Arnold, 1982), 51; Standish Meacham, *Toynbee Hall and Social Reform 1880–1914: The Search for Community* (New Haven: Yale University Press, 1987).

[6] Michael Sandel, 'The Procedural Republic and the Unencumbered Self', *Political Theory*, 12 (1984), 81–96.

generates the transcendent quality of community, the spirit of community, which is also of course expressed and promoted symbolically and culturally.

Republicanism

When communitarians have thought explicitly about political ideals and about institutional structures they have sometimes alluded to 'the republican tradition' as the most promising starting point for the development of a communitarian society and polity.[7] Alternatively, 'republicanism' is identified by some commentators as a relevant antecedent, and sometimes as a variant of, communitarianism.[8] Some recent republican thinkers have certainly thought of communitarianism as a way forward from liberal society.[9] Obviously, 'the republican tradition' is not a unified and simple object.[10] But it is possible to point to a number of features of 'republicanism' that are key in recent and current political theory.

First though there is a sense in which 'republicanism' is taken up negatively, as a kind of default position when communitarians, having criticized all the other 'isms' and 'wasms', have to find some starting point for the development of a distinctive position. Liberalism looks to the building of a society by legal and economic means; a society in which individuals are maximally free to choose their own lifecourse. As we have seen communitarians are critical both of the starting point and the consequences of this approach. Socialists look to the building of a society by way of economic cooperation, and political decision and action, in which social goods are equally distributed such that all people enjoy an acceptable level of health and welfare. Political communitarians are sceptical about the power of the state that is often assumed by socialists to be the necessary engine and mechanism for a just distribution; and are critical of the way the ideal of equality can be destructive of community integrity and

---

[7] For instance, Michael Walzer, 'The Communitarian Critique of Liberalism', *Political Theory*, 18 (1990), 16 ff.

[8] Robert Booth Fowler, *The Dance with Community: The Contemporary Debate in American Political Thought* (Lawrence, Kan.: University Press of Kansas, 1991).

[9] Paul W. Kahn, 'Community in Contemporary Constitutional Theory', *Yale Law Journal*, 99 (1989), 1.

[10] Margaret Canovan, *Hannah Arendt: A Reinterpretation of her Political Thought* (Cambridge: Cambridge University Press, 1992), 6; Adrian Oldfield, *Citizenship and Community: Civic Republicanism and the Modern World (London:* Routledge, 1990); Philip Pettit, *Republicanism: A Theory of Freedom and Government* (Oxford: Clarendon Press, 1997); J. G. A. Pocock, *The Machiavellian Moment: Florentine Political Thought and the Atlantic Republican Tradition* (Princeton: Princeton University Press, 1975); Quentin Skinner, *Liberty before Liberalism* (Cambridge: Cambridge University Press, 1998); Cass Sunstein, 'Beyond the Republican Revival', *Yale Law Journal*, 97 (1988), 1539.

autonomy. Conservatives emphasize settled relationships of authority and obligation. Although conservative communitarians are happy with this ideal of settlement, many contemporary communitarians are concerned to escape the connotations of hierarchy that have been central to many strands of conservative thought and practice.

By contrast, republicanism seeks to build, by means of public participation and decision, a society in which citizens enjoy the dignity which comes with fully participating in political decisions about the economic, social, and political structures that will govern them. This aspect of republicanism clearly has affinities with the political communitarian principles that communities should be self-governing and self-regulating, and that all individuals within a community have an obligation to participate, to uphold the community's norms and laws, to sustain it as well as themselves. 'Republicanism' has been associated with military self-sacrifice by citizens.[11] This aspect of it has been underemphasized by recent political theorists who emphasize rather the republican approach to liberty as a product of public action and cooperative relationships.[12] But it is notable that the idea of national service—or at any rate a normative expectation that people will engage in the voluntary provision of social goods— frequently recurs in communitarian discussions of policy in a communitarian society which emphasizes obligation and duty as an institutionalized correlation of rights.[13]

Republicanism is associated with the ideal of 'the government of laws not men'.[14] Again, this both is and is not what contemporary communitarians have in mind when they emphasize the overwheening importance of shared values and normative orientations. 'The rule of law' in liberal polities has turned into individual and corporate litigiousness—it has become a weapon of conflict rather than a means of harmony. Communitarians would wish to return to a legal order which is closer to the republican ideal—in which 'laws' are genuine norms of the sort that are susceptible to rational public reflection and negotiation.[15] This in turn

[11] Carole Pateman, 'The Patriarchal Welfare State', in *The Disorder of Women* (Oxford: Polity Press, 1989), 185–6.

[12] Such as Hannah Arendt, see Canovan, *Hannah Arendt*, 203, 205; also Skinner, *Liberty before Liberalism*; and the 'New Republican' group of constitutional theorists in the USA: see Sunstein, 'Beyond the Republican Revival'.

[13] Amitai Etzioni, *The Spirit of Community: Rights, Responsibilities and the Communitarian Agenda* (New York: Crown Publishers, 1993), 113–15; Tam, *Communitarianism*, 197–8; Ian Taylor, *Releasing the Community Spirit* (Cambridge: Tory Reform Group, 1990), 11–12.

[14] Oldfield, *Citizenship and Community*, 53–56, 89, and *passim*.

[15] Sandel, 'The Procedural Republic and the Unencumbered Self'; Etzioni, *New Golden Rule*, 138 ff.

would rely on personal relations and exchanges—not the personalized domination associated with 'government of (or by) men' but the horizontally structured deliberation between citizens. 'Classical republicanism'— the political theory based on the experience of the city republics of Athens and Rome, and the Italian city states—was premissed on the smallness and compactness of the unit, a city and its rural hinterland, and thus the attainability of the deliberative ideal.

In the eighteenth and nineteenth centuries republican ideals had a part to play in the construction of nation states. With the ideas underpinning the Constitution of the United States of America, and, for instance, France and later Italy, the premiss of small size was dropped. The US project was the construction of a republic, governed by laws not men, with the public participation of its citizens who thus would internalize as norms the laws of the state, but one which by virtue of its enormous territory would be more secure than the city states of Europe. Their citizens were constantly in fear of domination or conquest by power and wealth seeking men, and had constantly to be ready to spring to the military defence of the republic. This question of the size of the political and social unit is central to recent communitarian thought. Michael Sandel emphasises that the territorial extent of the United States, and the process of instituting political relationships across vast distances has led, as it turns out, to the shift from shared substantive value commitments to the institution of procedural values, and hence to the value fragmentation of the society.[16] A related theme in political communitarianism, as we have seen, is the importance of 'local communities' and relatively unified and compact entities like firms, churches, and schools.

Finally, in republican thought there is an emphasis on a conception and theory of freedom which contrasts with some strands of liberal thought and with the ideal of freedom as 'non-interference'. For republicans, as for many other political thinkers, 'freedom' is a collective achievement. Whatever the merits of thinking of it as a property of an individual (an individual is free to the extent that he is not constrained by the actions of other individuals or their products such as laws and norms) it should also be thought of as the property of collectives—societies and polities—and, as such, requires dedicated institutions and cultural effort. This in turn means that individual freedom qua non-interference cannot extend so far that individuals can absent themselves from assemblies (whatever form they take), or decline to participate in governing structures, or stay silent in the conversation that reflects upon and shapes laws and rules. For

[16] Michael Sandel, *Democracy's Discontents: America in Search of a Public Philosophy* (Cambridge, Mass.: Harvard University Press, 1996), 203–8; 'The Procedural Republic', 93.

republican freedom is fragile and easily lost.[17] This argument must be distinguished from arguments for 'positive liberty': the inference in these is that in the case of individuals liberty must be thought of as a series of capacities (for reflection, for decision and action) as well as the absence of constraint or interference; and that these capacities can only be produced and sustained in particular kinds of social environments and with the input of particular socially based goods.[18] As it happens, communitarians are likely to be sympathetic to both these lines of argument. They stress the roles of education and socialization in making people moral, civilized, and capable of conducting themselves in social and community settings.[19] They also, as we have seen, stress the political and moral importance of community autonomy—and the obligation this puts on individuals to participate in the safeguarding of that autonomy.

Political Strategies

It is important not to exaggerate the distinctiveness of communitarian political strategies. As the literature and action that is the main subject of this book makes clear many communitarians aspire to making a conventional political movement, deploying conventional tactics. A range of campaigns and pressure groups have attempted to promote communitarian ideas among citizens and have attempted to influence opinion formers and policy-makers through the usual channels of press coverage and intervention in debate, contributions to policy consultations, the dissemination of research, and so on. The communitarian journal *Tikkun* published, for instance, a draft consitutional amendment; organizations provide their supporters with model letters to representatives. However, these conventional inputs into policy-making and legislation are complemented by the specific communitarian strategy of appealing to and building up a 'spirit of community'. This can be contrasted with the alternative strategies—also of a 'horizontal' nature, that is pertaining to the relationships between citizens—of canvassing for votes, and recruiting for party or other organizational membership. The 'spirit of community' involves,

---

[17] Canovan, *Hannah Arendt*, 203; Oldfield, *Citizenship and Community*, 151.

[18] Isaiah Berlin, 'Two Concepts of Liberty', in *Four Essays on Liberty* (Oxford: Clarendon Press, 1958), also in Anthony Quinton (ed.), *Political Philosophy* (Oxford: Oxford University Press, 1967); Gerald C. MacCallum, 'Negative and Positive Freedom', *Philosophical Review* 76 (1967), 312–34, also in David Miller (ed.), *Liberty* (Oxford: Oxford University Press, 1991), 100–22.

[19] Phillip Selznick, *The Moral Commonwealth: Social Theory and the Promise of Community* (Berkeley and Los Angeles: University of California Press, 1992), 231; Tam, *Communitarianism*, 57 ff.; Etzioni, *New Golden Rule*, 161 ff.

among other things, a cognitive understanding of the benefits of mutuality, an enlightened rational understanding of self and common interest, and, more importantly, an emotional commitment to relations with others and a moral emphasis on 'what we all share'. Strategically, the latter is very important. It can be thought of as merely a matter of emphasis. Communitarians and other social theorists can emphasize that although some political discourses begin from division and difference, nevertheless the very idea of bargaining or conciliation presupposes shared practices and institutions. Conversely, an initial emphasis on what is shared—institutions for instance, and certain beliefs and values that are presupposed by those institutions, inevitably generates consciousness of difference. Indeed, in democratic politics the point of shared institutions, accepted procedures, and certain basic values is that they constitute the substructure for disagreement, conflict and competition. According to this line of thought, to speak of division is to speak of unity (by implication), and vice versa. Nevertheless, which of these is emphasized does of course have discursive effects. Furthermore, as we have seen, communitarian discourses regarding what is shared have connotations that go beyond the implication of diversity and conflict. Communitarianism takes what is shared to be the foundation for the range of relationships of community—this is the framework within which conflict proceeds. But it is also notable that appeals to 'community', the discursive invocation of 'us' and 'our' common interests, needs, nature, or values can simply be significant strategic moves in the processes of persuading, negotiating, or bargaining.

Dialogic Democracy

The emphasis on what is shared, on common ground as the precondition for political conflict, suggests an affinity between communitarianism and some models of 'dialogic democracy' (as opposed to representative democracy, or plebiscitary direct democracy). Theorists of dialogic democracy have hypothesized that dialogue under certain conditions (the absence of domination between parties, freedom from systematic distortions of meaning and from untruth) will itself increase the probability of agreements because parties who share this communicative experience will have increased understanding of each other's positions, and (more importantly) incentives to agree following from their commitment to the continued viability of the dialogue and the group.[20] (Note that a group thus described might be thought to justify the title 'community'.)

[20] David Miller, 'Deliberative Democracy and Social Choice', *Political Studies*, 40, special issue: David Held (ed.), *Prospects for Democracy* (1992), 54–67; Robert Goodin,

As is clear from this account the major question begged by models of dialogic and discursive democracy is how the institutions and norms that eliminate domination (and marginalization and exclusion), distortion, and lies are to be designed and sustained. For it is only if these conditions are met (or nearly met) that the commitment to the continued existence of the group, and the concomitant incentive to agree, is probable. Lying, distorting meaning so as to mislead or mystify, and dominating, silencing, and marginalizing certain voices are not conditions for reciprocal commitment. As we have seen in previous chapters, communitarian political and policy projects have often foundered on the impossibility of 'dialogue' let alone the ideal exchanges demanded by dialogic democracy. Relatively powerless people find that their voices are either not heard at all or, if heard, are heard as unreasonable, aggressive, shrill, uncooperative, and the like.[21] In response to and acknowledgement of this activists have recourse to disruption, symbolic demonstration, and direct action—forms of acting out and attempted coercion.

This raises an important set of issues for political theory—the question of the place of normativity or prescriptivism as opposed to reality or descriptivism; and the question of the role of rationality or reason in models of politics and in political institutions. Rawlsian liberals certainly are committed to the ideal of reason—public reason must defeat egoistic rationality, force, emotion, symbolism, and irrationality alike. Habermas's view is that in certain key human practices—communication—we are already committed to reason, to truthfulness, to cooperation, to consistency and inferential validity; thus political and other practices and institutions already have embedded in them 'particles and fragments of existing reason, however distorted these might be'.[22] Both Habermas's and Rawls's models of political decision-making, that is, treat power, emotions, and meaning as analytically and empirically distinct from reason and rationality. This is far from saying that emotion, symbolism, and irrationality are eliminated from the political process. Both Rawls and Habermas are acutely aware of their potential to distort, or undermine or thwart, the operation of reason.

'Laundering Preferences', in J. Elster and A. Hylland (eds.), *Foundations of Social Choice Theory* (Cambridge: Cambridge University Press, 1986).

[21] Chik Collins, 'The Dialogics of Community: Struggle and Identity in a Scottish Working Class Housing Scheme', paper delivered at conference 'Ideas of Community', University of the West of England, Sept. 1995; Curno et al., *Women in Collective Action*, 13–14; Ray Lees and George Smith, *Action Research in Community Development* (London: Routledge and Kegan Paul, 1975), 181.

[22] Habermas, *Between Facts and Norms*, 287.

In contrast to this analytic approach other theorists argue that emotions are themselves the objects of rationality or reasonableness conditions. Emotions and feelings can be irrational, for example if they are based on irrational beliefs; they can also be unreasonable—there is a learned component to emotion experience. The expression, display, and indeed feeling of emotions is, in human societies, subject to norms and rules.[23] For present purposes the relevant implication of this is that emotion and feeling—whether 'about' the speech and actions of others, symbols like flags and insignia, rituals, or events and circumstances quite independent of the immediate political context—is a feature of that political context, not exogenous to it. Sceptics wonder, then, whether the ideals of non-agonistic dialogue and purely reason-guided political decision meet the conditions of possibility.[24] Rationally arrived at decisions have psychological and emotional costs and pay-offs for participants (and the anticipation of these costs and pay-offs will be difficult to eliminate from the reasoning process). Many theorists have emphasized the defensible role that feeling plays in the democratic process. Consider for example the critiques of some electoral and voting systems which focus on the fact that 'strength of preference' either is not properly taken into account at all in many systems, or can be distorted. Although it is possible to analyse 'preference' entirely in terms of rational beliefs about consequences theorists seem tacitly at least to acknowledge that feeling (emotion) is salient in, say, the distinction between 'not much liking' and 'detesting' an option.[25]

Notwithstanding the view that emotions are subject to rationality and reasonableness constraints, it is clear that their presence in the forum introduces an element of discomposure, rather than the composure that is strongly connoted by models of rationality. It can also be argued that reason and rationality in any case cannot exhaust a deliberation and decision process. Rhetoric in a wide sense, including tone and timbre of voice, as well as such recognized speech strategies as eloquence, humour, hyperbole, irony, and the like are indispensable elements of deliberation. At the very least if a person is inaudible or unclear their contribution cannot be persuasive regardless of its coherence. Once again here it is important to note how the invocation of 'community' itself can be used strategically—speakers may deliberately appeal to 'community' rather than to other social

---

[23] Arlie Hochschild, 'Emotion Work, Feeling Rules and Social Structure', *American Journal of Sociology*, 85 (1979), 551–75.

[24] See Chantal Mouffe, 'Introduction: For an Agonistic Pluralism', in *The Return of the Political* (London: Verso, 1993), 2.

[25] Michael Dummett, *Principles of Electoral Reform* (Oxford: Oxford University Press, 1997), 91; also Michael Dummett, *Voting Procedures* (Oxford: Clarendon Press, 1984), 37–9; Iain McLean, *Public Choice: An Introduction* (Oxford: Basil Blackwell, 1987), 170.

aggregations because of its positive connotations, because it is an inclusive term, or because (at the same time) it is an exclusive term. Indeed, these operations need not be deliberately set in train. The term 'community' has entered public discourses as a commonplace and habitual description of relevant human groups. Here the same connotations of transcendence, unity, and the like have persuasive, or otherwise, effects.

Symbolism is equally important. Symbols and rituals such as processions, reserved places, costumes, and flags delineate the spatial and temporal boundaries of deliberative processes. Openings, decisions, and conclusions must be marked by some symbol—nods, 'ayes', the bang of a gavil, the writing of a minute, throat clearings, pauses, and turning to the next item. Symbols and rituals engage with emotion—the comfort of recognizability, the attraction of a desired identity—and therefore can undeniably have a persuasive power. In public spaces including the mass media symbols are cues to subject matter and topic, also cue substantive positions in debates, and therefore have a persuasive role.

The concern that critics can express with the Rawlsian and Habermasian programmes is that they underestimate the difficulty of separating out, in practice, reason and 'the rational' from the non-rational. Even worse, in the guise of doing this, so-called rationalist theories and practices actually carry and use a good deal of symbolic, rhetorical, and affective baggage whose true nature, though, is denied. The danger, here, is that other people's symbols, rhetoric, and emotions are named as such (and denigrated), while the so-called rationalists' own are presented as reasonable and rational.

The importance of symbolism and ritual also raises once again the significance of interpretation. The experience of a symbolic display as provocative, or aggressive, is partly a matter of the interpretation of meaning (there is also an affective component here which is itself probably linked with the understanding). The meaning of many salient symbols is contested of course—there is little consensus on what many flags (the Union Jack for instance), dress and insignia (judges' wigs, or protestant men's orange colours) really stand for and what they mean. The same goes for the experience of formal modes of speech as exclusionary or an aid to clarity, of metaphors and modes of speech as insulting or engaging, and so on. As I discussed in Chapter 3, the acceptance by an actor or onlooker of a particular interpretation of speech or gesture itself depends on the social identities and distribution of social power between the salient actors. A group who are making a claim to be heard in some forum—whether this be the pages of a newspaper or in a meeting—and whose speech is not 'hearable' or not 'acceptable' might or might not take issue with this very judgement of hearability or acceptability, depending on their resources (including organizational resources), their perception of the authority and reasonableness of those who so judge them. Indeed, applicability of the category 'reasonable' is itself the subject of interpretive dispute.

Political communitarians emphasize the importance of shared meanings as the necessary basis for agreement. But the contest of interpretation and the relative openness of meaning (especially the meanings of symbols and rituals) mean that stable and settled and clear meanings will not be shared, perhaps even in the most restricted and closed of 'communities'.

Social and Political Constructionism

Finally, the theme of social constructionism is important. The communitarian emphasis on shared values or common ground is not an emphasis on a natural or spontaneous order, but on a socially built order. Communitarians emphasize the importance of a normative order which individuals orient to as an objective reality; and of an infrastructure of institutions, practices, and routines which are socially built over time and likewise acquire a real ontological and an objective epistemological status. Communitarian politics is premissed on the belief that these social realities can be changed, reconstructed—that new institutions can be built, new practices developed, new diurnal routines can constitute a culture within which individual and collective identities will in turn be reconstructed. Building community—by promoting the density of interactions, individuals' attachment to each and to the whole—is the key communitarian strategy as well as the key communitarian good. What is notable from political communitarianism, however, is the way 'social constructionism' fades into political constructionism.

'Political construction' is exactly the mechanism that many current communitarians have in mind—the building of communities, if it occurs, will be the result of organized political effort, the effort to achieve a proper part in governance, to make a difference to public policy and to the decisions by other agents (for instance, economic enterprises and corporations) which impact on the lives and relations of people in their local and identity groups. Communitarians identify a need for relevant public policy (whether or not enforced by legislation) governing working hours, family leave, childcare support, local consultation on planning and design, the distribution of welfare provision, and so on. In this sense 'community' can only be constructed politically. Governments, it seems, might have resources for community building that individuals and organizations alone lack. But this dependence on government has clear disadvantages—

and goes against the communitarian principles that site power between the individual and the state. Recent communitarian literature emphasizes the role of social entrepreneurs, working against and in the interstices of bureaucratic and corporate power to build the new institutions and configurations of relationships that constitute community. As analysts point out, there can be 'anti-community' dynamics in the work of social entrepreneurs although the ideal of community building (as well as getting things done) tends to be prominent in their accounts.[26]

Political Community

Communitarian political theory privileges the category 'political community'. However, not only communitarians deploy this term. It is commonplace in political science and political theory. For instance, Norman Nie and his colleagues in a study of democratic citizenship in the USA discuss the empirical causes of 'a more tolerant political community' there.[27] David Miller says, for instance, 'political philosophers will simply begin an argument about how society or the political community should organise itself . . . without laying out the assumptions they are making about the kind of community in which the principles will be applied'.[28] Now, it may be that the best interpretation of passages like these is that they are used innocently, with vague intentions and indeterminate meaning. Thus, for David Miller, judging on the basis of just this quote, 'community' is nothing but a synonym for 'society' or is society organized in a particular way—politically. I am disinclined, though, to take these unanalysed uses to be wholly innocent—for political scientists, theorists and philosophers, the liberal-communitarian debates, together with critical commentary on political policies such as 'community policing' and 'community care' mean the age of innocence in this regard is past. On the other hand, perhaps in usages like this theorists are trying to hedge their bets—talking in such a way as to be indifferent between the two sides of the liberal communitarian divide.

However that may be, it is also evident that there are many conscious, non-innocent uses of the term 'political community', and usage embodies a number of important ambiguities. The first and most obvious analysis of political community is: a community in which what is shared is a political

---

[26] Charles Leadbeater, *The Rise of the Social Entrepreneur* (London: Demos, 1997); Inger Boyett and Don Finlay, 'The Social Entrepreneur', in Atkinson (ed.), *Cities of Pride*.

[27] Norman Nie, Jane Junn, and Kenneth Stehlik-Barry, *Education and Democratic Citizenship in America* (Chicago: Chicago University Press, 1996), 153.

[28] David Miller, *On Nationality* (Oxford: Oxford University Press, 1995), 185.

tie, or political institutions and their associated values. That is, a political community is just an instance of partial community—like ethnic or local or the business community. Second, though, it can seem that political community means a community in which the political tie is added to other ties—those of culture, or shared economy, shared territory. A good deal of political theory is definitely ambiguous as between these two. On the one hand, deployment of the term 'political community' seems to let the user off the embarassing hooks that come with the idea of community in its strong sense (stability, locality, dense and multiplex relations, and all the rest). On the other hand, some of those hooks, notably ideas like commitment, mutuality, shared culture and meanings—seem to be what theorists need to build up the concepts of state, society, and politics beyond the thin models deployed in empiricist political science, and in the frameworks of liberalism and Marxism.[29]

A third meaning of 'political community' is: a community which is political in the sense of 'acts politically', is a political actor. As we have seen, this idea is very clear in communitarianism, with its principles of the autonomy, integrity, and authority of communities vis-à-vis their members and in relations with each other. Communities, consisting of individuals held together by various kinds of relationship and allegiance, can make various kinds of claims—in defence of their continued existence, in defence of their members' needs and benefits, in defence of certain norms, institutions and traditions. Fourth, it can mean a community which is made politically—along the constructionist lines discussed in the previous section. Robert Nisbet's thesis is that the causes of the loss of community are themselves political—insecurity and disintegration follow upon the shifts of authority and power connected with the development of modern economies.[30] And the modern (eighteenth- and nineteenth-century) ideal of community is the 'political community'—the politically built order whether this be the Marxist utopia, the Napoleonic state, or the

---

[29] An instance I have in mind is Chantal Mouffe, 'Democratic Citizenship and the Political Community', in Mouffe (ed.), *Dimensions of Radical Democracy* (London: Verso, 1992). Mouffe argues that the democratic polity must be a community, by which she means that the bond that ties citizens to each other is an ethical bond. As my analysis in Chapter 2 makes clear, I don't believe that this is a plausible analysis of community (there can be many 'ethical bonds' that are clearly insufficient for or even antithetical to 'community' on any plausible interpretation of that term). The point is that Mouffe wishes to insist that democratic political units cannot be based on pure egoistic self-interest, mutual indifference, or simple territorial coexistence. There must be more to it than that; 'community' entails more, and it implies, albeit vaguely in context, dense relations, multiplex relations, and the orientation of each not only to the others but also to the whole.

[30] Robert Nisbet, *The Quest for Community: A Study in the Ethics of Order and Freedom* (New York: Oxford University Press, 1953). p. vii.

nation.[31] That is, Nisbet points up the paradox within the ideal of community between the centrality to the concept of unstructured personal relations and the inescapable reality of political power. It should be noted that a community which is itself the product of political agency can be constructed exogenously or endogenously. Activists and elites (including governments) can try to forge sections of the population into 'communities'. They do this by way of political mechanisms such as campaigning, mobilization, persuasion, the constitution of associations with committees, setting up channels of consultation, accountability, and so forth. On the other hand, and this perhaps is closer to current communitarian ideals, the political agency can be endogenous: individuals who have some thing in common—fate, language, territory—can construct themselves as community, forging the human relations and the boundary that that requires.

In this connection, such mechanisms as the 'social contract' can be construed as bringing into being a political community, politically. According to the social contract tradition, including its recent variants, an agreement, brought about as the upshot of some reasoning process on the part of the parties severally, transforms them from an aggregation of individuals into a duly constituted political association (or society, or polity—or community) with agreed procedures for legislation, adjudication, and administration and an agreed locus of and distribution of sovereign power. The term political community might be appropriate even given a more 'realistic' account of the founding of states and societies. However a political settlement is forged—by violent conquest, by the gradual centralization of power and the accrual of legitimacy, by the dispossession of kings in favour of the commons—a political community, in the present sense, might be said to be the upshot at the point when individuals share allegiance to a particular set of institutions and procedures.

In previous chapters I have argued that community, properly analysed, will necessarily be a fleeting moment of certain kinds of social organization. A number of other theorists recognize this. For example, Victor Turner remarks that 'the power of communitas' (qua spontaneous immediate relation of whole man to whole man) 'cannot readily be applied to the details of social existence'.[32] Although, as he goes on to discuss, many have tried. I have already discussed Farrar's observation about the short-lived but euphoric nature of the coalitions which can seem, for a while, to

---

[31] Nisbet, *Quest for Community.* 157–95.
[32] Victor W. Turner, *The Ritual Process: Structure and Anti-structure* (London: Routledge and Kegan Paul, 1969), 139.

be like communities.[33] Jeffrey Weeks, in a valuable analysis of gay politics focuses on community as something that does not exist—but that people feel should exist. As such, it is constructed in individuals' consciousness, and, as Weeks puts it, webs of narrative give meaning to the idea of sexual community for many. That is, the idea of a political community (a community which is made politically and culturally, and which is an effective claims-maker) inspires stories, actions, and orientations which tend to confirm its existence.

On the other hand, this imaginary nature of community has other political outcomes. First, comes political debunking: where something is imaginary (as where some thing is socially constructed) there will be political interests in emphasizing this. To take the case of the 'gay community' there is no shortage of arguments and analyses which focus on the extent to which gay people are socially and culturally diverse, with diverse political interests and goals, and, come to that, sexually diverse, with many understandings and practices of sexual identity and relationships between them. That is, it is argued (as it has been in the case of 'women') that the single category 'gay' falsely homogenizes a range of identities. Second, comes sociological debunking. It can be pointed out that the common characteristic whatever it is—same-sex sexual relationships, say—is a vanishingly small point of commonality, too small to sustain community. Of course, plausibly there might be many overlapping networks and chains of relationships which connect otherwise completely diverse people. But this is a very different model from 'community'.

THE NATURE OF POLITICS

The analysis so far begs the question of the concept of politics. It is worth emphasizing the elusive and contested nature of this concept. It is not easy to say what is meant when an action or an event or a relationship is described as political. And critics who attempt to reconceptualize and retheorize politics are not able to attack a monolithic body of knowledge, or fixed meanings.

[33] Max Farrar, 'Agency, Metaphor and Double Consciousness: Black Community Action in Leeds 1970–95', conference paper delivered to 'Ideas of Community', University of West of England, Sept. 1995.

Roles and Institutions

For some, politics is just what politicians or the political classes in society do.[34] This is a kind of realist approach—if politicians lie, cheat, act always so as to guard the economic interests of the class from which they are disproportionately drawn, or always act in defence of capital, keep one eye always on the constitution, or whatever, then that, in addition to fighting elections, passing laws, sitting on parliamentary committees, nominally representing constituents and party interests, is what 'politics' means. For others, politics is what goes on in a specific set of institutions—legislatures, executives, bureaucracies, electoral systems, and so on—and encompasses the relations between these and other institutions like universities, families, the judiciary, etc. Theorists who take either of these approaches will have to consider and try carefully to model the way in which normative or prescriptive models of politics (as laid out in constitutions, or in more informal discourses like theories of democracy, or social democratic ideology) interact with other causes of actions and events.

For a further group of theorists 'politics' refers to a particular mode of governance, a particular way of allocating the power to govern—that is to say through public institutions there is a visible process of deliberation and conciliation of rival interests.[35] According to this view, politics is to be contrasted with other methods of allocating power. Take, for instance, trading and bargaining in market settings, resource holders engaging in economic exchanges with others. There can be this kind of market in 'the power to govern' as there can be in any other good or bad. But the resulting allocation of the power to govern would not be a 'political' allocation, for it would be the unintended outcome of numerous trades; as in any market there would be some winners, some losers, some excluded altogether. An alternative method of allocating the power to govern might be social evolution: simply leaving the species and subgroups within it to evolve within its environment. Once again, any resulting pattern of power would be the outcome of 'spontaneous' mechanisms and processes. Both these ways of allocating power lack the deliberate and public characteristics of the political way. Alternatively, power might be allocated according to some traditional scheme, perhaps according to the prescription of sacred texts (as in, for instance, patriarchal systems); or by force and violence and the use of terror—whether this is military and quasi-military, or 'plain'

[34] Agnes Heller, 'The Concept of the "Political" Revisited' in David Held (ed.), *Political Theory Today* (Oxford: Polity Press, 1991), 331.
[35] For instance Bernard Crick, *In Defence of Politics* (1st pub. 1962), 2nd edn. (Harmondsworth: Penguin, 1992), 19.

violence (as in 'mafia' like systems of extortion). None of these ways of allocating power meets the normative conditions of politics—they lack the deliberative and public characteristics of the political way. Another way of thinking about this boundary of the political is to consider that the power to govern can be politicized—that is to say, it can be questioned, opposed, defended. Once this process of dispute reaches a certain level of articulation—once it becomes shared, public, audible—then we are crossing the threshold of politics.

Despite this, however, some theorists and others who use the term 'politics' will consider that these modes of power allocation—military force, violence, market exchange, tradition—are themselves political, albeit they are different ways of doing politics. According to this conceptualization—which also is a fair interpretation of a good deal of what participants actually say—politics is the competition for and the allocation of the power to govern, however that is done. Carl Schmitt's analysis is consistent with this view. Schmitt is concerned conceptually—and then theoretically—to delineate 'the political'. In his analysis this encompasses 'friend–foe' or allegiance–enmity relations (while 'the ethical' encompasses 'good–evil'; the legal encompasses 'right–wrong'; the aesthetic encompasses 'beautiful–ugly'). According to this approach the maintenance of friend–foe relations and structures may be done in a number of ways—the public deliberative way is not the only one.[36]

Scope

Another controversy with the concept of politics regards its scope. Some analysts have tied the concept of politics to the processes of sovereign power—the final power to decide—and thus to the state or its functional equivalent. They have expressly opposed the idea that 'political' can be a predicate of small groups and the like.[37] These may be sites of and contexts for power, and domination, but not for sovereign power, so the category political is inapplicable, except in a metaphorical extension. There are three possible responses to these conceptual strictures. One is to point out that actually, in many cases, sovereign power is in play in a very direct way. The pattern of power in a family, or between sexual partners, or in a

[36] Carl Schmitt, *The Concept of the Political*, trans. George Schwabb. 1st pub. as *Der Begriff des Politischen* (Duncker and Humblot: Munich, 1932; New Brunswick: Rutgers University Press, 1976). It is clear that Schmitt is prepared to countenance the use of force to secure 'decisions' (and social and political stability); Mouffe, 'Democratic Citizenship and the Political Community'; Paul Hirst, 'Carl Schmitt: Decisionism and Politics', *Economy and Society*, 17 (1988), 272–82.

[37] Crick, *In Defence of Politics*, 30.

school, actually is conditioned by state legislation which governs, directly or indirectly, the structure of roles in many social contexts. So, even theorists who take a purist sovereignty view of politics, looking then to a restricted scope for the concept, will find that it is actually far more extensive than they hoped. But second, it might be observed that although the concept of politics was articulated first in the context of theories of sovereign power and decision-making, it has undergone a series of shifts since then, among which is this extension in its scope. To say that this is a 'metaphorical' use is to overlook the very common process by which metaphors coalesce into meaning. Third, critics of this view might take a sceptical view of 'sovereignty', arguing that properly understood power including 'the final power to decide' is fragmented and dispersed. One might hold on to an ideal of sovereign states, and sovereign state institutions, but it will be an inaccurate model of the workings of political, let alone other sorts, of power.

The Nature of Political Agreement

A second set of problems in the conceptualization of politics is that of the nature of political agreement. Theorists in a number of traditions would agree, broadly speaking, with Arendt's distinction between public and private, political and social, cultural and domestic life. One reason for maintaining the distinction is in recognition of the plurality of social identities, and the disagreement about values, conduct, and the distribution of certain goods that these differences give rise to. Despite this diversity, the argument goes, certain agreements must be binding on all members—the criminal law, the provision of pure public goods, perhaps the provision of certain worthy goods that are necessary if the state and society are to be sustainable, a constitution, political institutions within which to carry forward legislation, administration, and the judicial function. Decisions pertaining to changes to these institutions, procedures, and principles must be agreed to by all citizens, whereas there is no need, in an orderly society, for individuals to agree about personal values (such as sexual morality) or cultural identities (religion, ethnicity, patterns of association in connection with music, leisure, art, etc.).

Some theorists, notably those who position themselves in 'the Kantian' tradition argue that this agreement must be a genuine agreement based on the understanding of reasons. Rawls, for instance, argues that anything less than this reasoned agreement—grudging acceptance, for instance, indifference, or the absence of conviction—will mean that the polity is nothing more than a modus vivendi, and that this cannot meet the needs

THE IDEA OF A POLITICAL COMMUNITY 225

for commitment and participation that generate genuine political stability.[38] Although particular characteristics and commitments, such as religious conviction, cultural identity, or kinship relations, will mean that individuals for some purposes and in some contexts will engage in reasoning and action that diverges from the kind of reasoning and action that must obtain in the public and political realm (for instance, they may practise or submit to a pattern of authoritarianism in church or in their family which would be unacceptable in a state school or in a parliament), nevertheless, in the case of public and political life, individuals will internalize norms and standards of public rationality, so that they become rationally self-governing (and therefore cooperative) individuals.[39]

There are a number of variations on this theme. For instance, Ronald Dworkin argues that underlying the bitter and venomous abortion struggles (or wars) is agreement about the intrinsic value of life.[40] Habermas's theory of ideal speech and deliberative democracy holds that the conditions of individual communicative freedom enable rational opinion and will formation on the part of individuals. It is likewise the basis of collectively rational agreement. Habermas seems to demand that citizens converge, in the long run, on the same reasons rather than agree for different reasons.[41] The hope that theorists like Rawls and Habermas have is that reason and rationality will guide political decision-making; and it is central to both their theories, diverse though they are in many other ways, that a single decision for the group or public in question will be arrived at by genuine reason. Conversely, at the level of theory of the individual, these philosophers infer that the experience of participating in and being bound by publicly reasoned decisions will also condition individual rationality.

Against these and similar views other theorists insist that the point of politics is that individuals can agree for different reasons. They may agree on procedural methods of agreement, and that in certain procedural circumstances action has been authorized, but as to the substance of the relevant decision—for instance, to make abortion legal in certain circumstances—parties may have many different reasons for agreeing. Some, for

[38] James Bohman, *Public Deliberation: Pluralism, Complexity and Democracy* (Cambridge, Mass.: MIT Press, 1996); John Rawls, *Political Liberalism* (New York: Columbia University Press, 1993), 39, 217–20; Jürgen Habermas, *Between Facts and Norms: Contributions to a Discourse Theory of Law and Democracy*, trans. William Rehg (1st pub. German 1992; Oxford: Polity Press, 1996), e.g. p. 304.
[39] Noel O'Sullivan, 'Difference and the Concept of the Political in Contemporary Political Philosophy', *Political Studies*, 45 (1997), 739.
[40] Ronald Dworkin, *Life's Dominion* (London: Harper Collins, 1993), 237–41. Dworkin does not expect agreement on abortion and euthanasia—he does not expect that laws governing these practices will command the assent of all parties.
[41] Habermas, *Between Facts and Norms*, e.g. p. 306; Bohman, *Public Deliberation*, 88.

instance, may assent now in order more effectively to dissent later; some may agree out of religious or moral conviction, others out of social pragmatism; some may be trading off an issue about which they are rather indifferent in hope of getting their way on another issue about which they feel strongly. Some may be motivated by powerful emotional reactions to issues. And so on. Neither the idea of a 'general will' nor of a unified reason are plausible. But neither are they relevant to such political process. O'Sullivan argues this fact about the absence of agreement does not rule out agreement for the time being on institutions, procedures, and offices.[42] He argues that in focusing on substantive agreement about issues (like the just constitution) as Rawlsian liberals do, an error has been made regarding the nature of politics, which is premissed on agreement about offices and institutions. It cannot be a feature of a theory of politics that agreement be attained or premissed on the values and reasons underlying individuals' choices and conclusions regarding particular issues. This means that 'politics' is a never-ending process.

Decisiveness

Some theorists, as we have seen, emphasize authoritative decision implying by this that once an authoritative decision has been made that is the end of the matter. For example, Bernard Crick argues that authoritative decisions are final, and that is the point of his strictures about the relevance of sovereign power to politics.[43] According to the theory of William Riker the significant aspect of politics is the decisiveness of political decisions; and in a situation where citizens have diverse preferences regarding the kinds of rules that should govern everyone some citizens forfeit completely the values they are committed to.[44] That is, he too emphasizes the decisiveness of political decision although he does not hope for agreement such that all are satisfied. Rawls and other US liberals emphasize the importance of agreement on what Rawls calls 'the constitutional essentials'.[45] According to Rawls the point of the social contractual underpinning to the constitution, and the relegation of certain matters, such as religion, cultural identity, kinship relations to the 'non-public sphere' as he calls it, is to once and for all get certain issues off the public agenda.[46] He is thinking of issues like racial discrimination or even racial

---

[42] O'Sullivan, 'Difference and the Concept of the Political', 744.
[43] Crick, *In Defence of Politics*, 28.
[44] William Riker, *Liberalism against Populism: A Confrontation between the Theory of Democracy and the Theory of Social Choice* (San Francisco: W. H. Freeman & Co., 1982), 205.
[45] Rawls, *Political Liberalism*, 227–30.   [46] Ibid. 151–2.

'purity', or of the basic idea that the society should extend some minimum of help to the poor, the ill, the unable. Actually, of course, although in most political systems 'constitutional' changes are harder to make than legislative and administrative changes, they are not impossible to make—there is no 'once and for all' in political life. And Riker's theory also emphasizes the way new issues break up majorities, so that the loss citizens experience in the political process is not once and for all—on new issues hitherto losers can be winners of 'scarce universal values'.[47]

Communicative Inequality and Conflict

A third set of controversies in the theory of 'politics' focuses on inequalities in communication. The ability to change the subject, to speak without interruption, to be heard, to persuade are unequally distributed and the inequality raises questions of justice. But this is not only justice regarding the distribution of these various capacities and goods. Rather, questions about the justice of the framework are also raised. The norms and standards of speech, and the styles that must be adopted if one's voice is to be heard, let alone command respect, in political institutions, must themselves be susceptible to criticism and political challenge. Again, the force of this criticism for my present purposes is the implication that politics cannot finally be settled.

In turn this point raises again the question of conflict and emotion. Everyone is likely to have some difficulty hearing 'others'. It takes a special effort to hear and understand a stranger's voice and accent, novel vocabularies, new ways of speaking. It is a moral imperative (an aspect of moral respect for persons) that we make an effort to hear and understand. But this ethical demand does not make the effort taken painless or otherwise costless. The importance of discussion and deliberation as the routes to decision are not, of course, to be downplayed. Rather it must be recognized that discussion is the site of difficult conflict. I have already mentioned the discomposing disruptive characteristics of emotions, and the view that the feeling and acting of emotions is subject to rationality and reasonableness constraints. A further point that should be made here is that notwithstanding these rationality and reasonableness constraints emotions are often contradictory and complex.

This is not to imply that conflict, agonistics, and the like are terrible and destructive or disintegrative. But it is to insist that relations within the polity, and indeed within the individual, are sites of friction, resistance,

---

[47] William Riker, *The Theory of Political Coalitions* (New Haven: Yale University Press, 1987), 229.

discontent, conflict. Membership—of any group including such loose aggregations as crowds—involves obligations; and insistence on this is a necessary corrective to certain strands of social thought which over-emphasize individual 'choice'. Of course, at some level, an individual's cooperation or otherwise is a matter of his choice. What must be made clear, however, is that although I may choose to discharge my obligations in my family, my workplace, in the shopping crowd, or wherever, this does not mean that I do not feel any burden or any pain, or any conflict, in doing so. That is, free choice does not mean freedom from friction or absence of resistance.

A good deal of political action and interaction in public consists of acting out or acting up. To begin with, the practices of demonstration and direct action invariably involve the use and display of symbols, and frequently involve elements of pantomime or carnival—with masks, costumes, humorous interactions with police, etc. But equally significant is the acting out of personal identities in public spaces—any claims-making involves the public representation of social identities, such as 'businessman', the 'arts lobby'. It may well be that the more marginal or radical the claim being made the more likely it is that pantomime and carnival will be engaged in, and the more likely that direct action tactics like stopping traffic etc. will be deployed. The spectacular and televisual nature of these events make their nature as symbolism and display very obvious. But this must not blind us to the extent that public appearance, action, and speech, by such mainstream groups as the Confederation of British Industry or Liberty also involves the public display of social identities—they equally involve 'acting out' and 'acting up'. Again, the point is that these acts and appearances inevitably engage audiences and actors like at an emotional as well as, perhaps, the critical and rational level.

Rationalists will argue that notwithstanding the descriptive accuracy of this analysis, prescriptively it must be ensured that rational judgement—not affect—guides decision. But how is emotion to be subordinated? The relationship of community might be thought to be relevant here. One thought is that cultural homogeneity between community members (that they share meanings and practices) will diminish the likelihood of antipathetic emotional reactions to speakers or displays. Note that this by no means eliminates emotion from politics—it simply substitutes positive emotion or attraction for negative emotion or repulsion. The alternative is simply to suppress emotion, just to subordinate it to reason. Depending on what theory of the subject one finds most plausible this will look more or less possible. A problem that many critics of liberalism have focused on is that the liberal commitment to 'pure reason' actually disguises the operation of emotional mechanisms such as homophily, or the (emotionally based) preference for people 'like oneself'. With developments in liberal theory such as Rawls's acknowledgement of the importance of a tradition and culture of certain values as foundational for a rationally derived, reasonable, well-ordered liberal society, this condition of homophily is explicitly accepted and indeed institutionalized. And the same implication follows from communitarian theory.

Congruence and Continuity

The foregoing arguments have raised in an elliptical way an issue that has been prominent especially in recent theories of politics—the question is the extent to which political reasoning, political morality, and political identities should be or are continuous with or congruent with non-political (for instance, personal, or cultural, or private) reasoning, morality, and identity. If there is continuity across this boundary then one's personal, political and say cultural moral reasoning will not be at odds with one another, will deploy the same principles and procedures of inference and decision. The issue, as Nancy Rosenblum points out, has been very prominent in political theory and political science where there has been a preoccupation with the outcomes of incongruence and discontinuity.[48] For instance, the theme of the discontinuity between the conduct of domestic and cultural life within certain social classes in Britain and the USA, and the values and standards of conduct in school and then in key political arenas has been much analysed.[49] The point is that individuals who do not practice rational argument and reasonable negotiation, and who do not think in general and abstract categories at home, will find participation in civil and political forums a greater strain than those for whom these modes of discourse, conduct, and reasoning are familiar and commonplace. The congruence argument holds that democratic characters are necessary for a successful democratic polity (or that communitarian characters are necessary for a communitarian polity). Varieties of congruence argument have been developed in many contexts: there are arguments that insist that the family must be the school for justice, arguments that workplace democracy must be a precondition of political

[48] Nancy L. Rosenblum, 'Democratic Character and Community: The Logic of Congruence', *Journal of Political Philosophy*, 2 (1994), 67–97.

[49] See for instance Paul Willis, *Learning to Labour: How Working Class Kids Get Working Class Jobs* (1st pub. 1977; Aldershot: Ashgate Publishing, 1993); Harry Eckstein, 'Civic Inclusion and its Discontents', in *Regarding Politics: Essays on Political Theory, Stability and Change* (Berkeley and Los Angeles: University of California Press, 1992) (the latter is discussed by Rosenblum in 'Democratic Character and Community').

democracy, the perennial arguments about the need for schools to be run in democratic and just ways, for children to learn politics and democracy in the classroom, the corridors, and the playground alike.[50]

The questions of congruence and continuity are notable and problematic in John Rawls's political liberalism. On the one hand, Rawls does require that to some extent 'democratic character' is developed in young people through the education system. Children, according to a political liberal, need to know their constitutional and civic rights, should be prepared to be fully cooperating members of society and self-supporting, should be encouraged to embrace the political virtues 'so that they want to honour the fair terms of social cooperation in their relations with the rest of society'.[51] On the other hand, a key element of Rawls's theory is that individuals can live according to some comprehensive doctrine in their domestic and cultural lives while still participating in the liberal democratic institutions of public political life, taking on the relevant public and political roles of voter and citizen. One's comprehensive doctrine has to be left behind 'at the door of the forum'. Critics doubt whether this model of individuals leaving their religious and cultural identities behind when they enter the public realm is either just or viable. Whereas for some cultural and religious identities (notably liberal, agnostic, atheist, or mainstream) there will be a good deal of congruence between an individual's reasoning and decision-making in his personal and private life, and the same processes when he participates in public institutions, this will not be true for other religions and cultures, whose members are likely to experience a degree of dissonance or incongruity between these two contexts. That is, the idea that one should leave one's particular cultural and personal identity behind at the door of the forum has very different implications depending on what that cultural identity is. Even more damaging, it turns out that some people don't really have to leave their identity behind at all—they can carry it right into the forum, and keep it on. Because the 'culture' of the forum will inevitably be biased in favour of some identities and not others.

The Distinctiveness of 'Politics'

It is important to underline the point that to say that 'politics' encompasses a series of processes that occur throughout social institutions is not

[50] Susan Moller Okin, 'Justice and Gender', *Philosophy and Public Affairs*, 16 (1987), 42–72; Carole Pateman, *Participation and Democratic Theory* (Cambridge: Cambridge University Press, 1970); Amy Gutmann, *Democratic Education* (Princeton: Princeton University Press, 1987).

[51] Rawls, *Political Liberalism*, 199.

to say that 'everything is political'. Analytically, it is possible to identify the specifically political aspects of the vast range of social phenomena and relationships without thereby committing ourselves to saying that the relevant event is, through and through, political. It is part of the task of political studies to conceptualize and study specifically political relationships and their connection with other—moral, economic, psychological, and so forth—relationships between persons. But, the other face of this argument is that 'political' entities, institutions, events, relations, and phenomena are not purely political.

On the other hand, the question whether 'political' relations etc. are, in fact, analytically, empirically, and normatively distinct from other social relations is very much a live one and very much disputed, as much as is the question of the nature of politics. A number of theorists who argue that politics is a distinct mode of activity are inspired by the thought and theory of Hannah Arendt. She argued that public action and speech by individuals engaged in talk and argument with their fellows with whom they share the world is quite distinct, both in its phenomenology and in its social effects. For example, it can be compared with labour—our interaction with and effort to overcome the physical world. Speech and communication is relevant here—the grunts, curses, and songs that accompany physical work, the efforts to coordinate our actions with others.[52] But the quality of this speech is clearly contrasted with the argumentative effort that goes into politics. Arendt is highly conscious of the fragile nature of this purely political activity—it can easily be displaced by concern with economic production and exchange, for instance, or with struggles for cultural recognition. Recently, political theorists have been inclined simply to accept that economic justice, the conditions for a viable economy, cultural recognition, and liberation from personalized structures of oppression (as in the case of the women's liberation and gay liberation movements) simply are key issues for political action and strategy, and, indeed, for political resolutions if not solutions. So Arendt's position strikes current political theorists as highly anomalous. Her argument was that attempts to solve 'social questions' by political means leads to the use of force and violence, to the abandonment of visible action in 'the worldly in between' in favour of administration and bureaucracy.[53]

Thus Arendt makes a clear distinction between 'the social' and 'the political'. There are social processes and relationships, distinct from political actions and decisions and relationships. There are political matters—

[52] Hannah Arendt, *The Human Condition* (Chicago: University of Chicago Press, 1958), 145.
[53] Hannah Arendt, *On Revolution* (Harmondsworth: Penguin, 1963), 112.

the defence of the state, the organization of governing institutions, legislation and the provision of public goods; and there are social matters including relations in households, in the labour and commodity markets, and
concerning the conduct of cultural life and religion. Arendt argues that
two important intellectual changes have occurred which mark the modern
era. First is that the scientific approach to the social world convinced many
that social life is governed by natural laws and forces, as is the physical
world. Thus, the ideal of action and deeds, the mark of political life,
fades—modern revolutions, for instance, are thought of as the outcome of
'forces' rather than deeds[54] and this encourages a view of social and political life as governed by laws that are more powerful than legislation.
Second, agitation about and efforts to change social relationships have
become the most pressing preoccupation for many. This has two outcomes. First is that attempts to deal with these politically are unsuccessful
and have perverse outcomes, and this can lead to the degeneration and loss
of admiration for political processes and relationships in general.[55]
Second, in any case, is that for those who are most involved with social
struggles, compassion becomes the prominent feature of the quest for justice; emotional and moral human feeling sits in the driving seat, so to
speak. And this kind of human feeling will be impatient with argument,
deliberation, negotiation, and conciliation. Where it is a matter of justice
and compassion, the imperative will be to use force.[56] And where force and
violence are used, authority, the mechanism of political change, is
exhausted—politics is over.[57]

Arendt's analysis of politics, evidently, is very contentious. In particular,
feminists have been hostile to her view that 'social', let alone 'domestic',
matters are not proper matters for politics.[58] After all, this move has been
made strategically by liberals, patriarchalists, conservatives, socialists, and
others to keep questions of gender justice off the political agenda. Agenda
control has come to be seen as one of the most powerful weapons in the
political armoury, so conflicts over what's on the agenda are thought of as
quintessentially political conflicts.[59] Similarly, the claims of ethnic and

---

[54] Hannah Arendt, *On Revolution* (Harmondsworth: Penguin, 1963), 253.
[55] Ibid. 60–6.   [56] Ibid. 86.   [57] Canovan, *Hannah Arendt*, 185–7.
[58] Mary G. Dietz, 'Hannah Arendt and Feminist Politics', in Mary Lyndon Shanley and
Carole Pateman (eds.), *Feminist Interpretations and Political Theory* (Oxford: Polity Press,
1991) identifies Adrienne Rich, *On Lies Secrets and Silence: Selected Prose 1966–1978* (New
York: Norton, 1979), 212 and Mary O'Brien, *The Politics of Reproduction* (London:
Routledge and Kegan Paul, 1981), 99–100 as key texts which put Arendt squarely in the canon
of sexist social theory, denigrating femininity and denying the value of women's labour.
[59] Peter Bachrach and Morton S. Baratz, 'The Two Faces of Power', *American Political
Science Review*, 56 (1962), 947–52; Steven Lukes, *Power: a Radical View* (Basingstoke:
Macmillan, 1974), 21–5.

religious minorities to be recognized as citizens and to have their particular cultural identities accepted in public life (as the cultural identities of dominant groups are taken for granted) seem to be treated by Arendt as dangerous subversion of the political process rather than a proper aspect of the competition for a just distribution of political power. Nevertheless, Arendt's insistence on politics as characterized by visibility and audibility, by communication with other human beings, by concern with a shared world, by action and speech, and, crucially, as focused on the 'worldly in between', has been a salutary reminder to many political theorists of what is lost when politics becomes 'administration' or when it is thought of as just another market in which goods and bads are exchanged.

It also should be noted that although members of social movements such as feminism have been concerned to insist on the political nature of hitherto 'private' or non-political matters, these selfsame people have also characteristically taken a view about the limits of conventionally political solutions, that is, of legislation, and of administrative decisions and distributions. It has been as obvious to those engaged in political action for gender or racial justice, for fair conditions and wages for workers, for the direction of productive effort on socially valuable goods, that legislation often has perverse outcomes, that cultural and social as much as legal and institutional changes are needed, and that governments can't legislate for culture. The point where such theorists part company from Arendt is the point at which they continue to insist that conflict over culture is a legitimate part of political life—governments can't do it, but citizens in their various social and cultural roles can and in doing so, insofar as what is at stake is the allocation of the power to govern, and modes of governance, they are acting politically. The methodological point here is that the concept of politics has to be reactive to theories of political change and how that comes about.

The Non-distinctiveness of Politics

The foregoing series of arguments have made part of a case for understanding politics to be a quite distinct aspect of social life. I now need to turn to a series of arguments that dispute this. A number of theorists vigorously dispute the idea that politics should be thought of as either analytically or normatively or empirically distinct from social life *in toto*, or from other aspects of social life (for instance, from the economy, or from culture). For example, some critics of politics emphasize the way 'the political sphere' evolved as an ostensibly separate sphere of interaction in the process of consolidation of a particular pattern of inequality, in which women, black people, domestic workers and servants, and labourers in general were excluded. This construction of separate governing institutions, and an idealization of particular modes of discourse and manners of conduct as essential to 'the political sphere' are best understood as a strategic and ideological move in the consolidation of a power structure and the exclusion of certain kinds of person and certain kinds of claim from governance.

For example, Carole Pateman in her early work insisted that if the ideals of participation and democracy have any value then they must apply equally to the economic world of work and exchange as to the conventional political realm of local councils and parliament.[60] To the extent that it is declared that democracy cannot be practised in the workplace, then democracy is not genuine. Indeed, the confinement of democracy to parliament and town governance operates in a doubly oppressive and exclusionary fashion. It denies people democratic power and justice where they most need it—in their economic lives—while offering them 'political' democracy as a sop. It effectively excludes them from political institutions, because they are denied opportunities to develop democratic and political habits and skills in the most prominent and overweening aspect of their lives. In her later work on the relationship between gender and politics Pateman takes this line of argument further. The rules of the political game, and the rules of conduct that govern participation in it, have been constructed so as to benefit those who constructed the political sphere and continue to participate in it, and so as to exclude persons whose disadvantage and subordination is necessary if some individuals are to be liberated from the pressing cares of material life so as to be able to enjoy life in the public sphere. At the same time, the claims of the disadvantaged cannot be pressed or heard in the normal political process, which is organized so as to exclude certain kinds of voices, certain kinds of claims, and certain agenda items. For instance, the identification of citizenship, in the republican and then the liberal and conservative traditions, with independence has operated to exclude both poor people and women. The identification of certain issues—to do with reproduction, sexuality, domestic and family life—as ideally 'private' similarly serves to make politics inaccessible to and irrelevant to women.[61]

More than one conclusion can be drawn from this. First, it could be argued that political institutions and procedures must be adapted so as to include the hitherto excluded. Alternatively, it can be argued that the very

[60] Pateman, *Participation and Democratic Theory.*
[61] See especially 'Justifying Political Obligation', 'Women and Consent', and 'Feminist Critiques of the Public/Private Dichotomy', in Pateman, *The Disorder of Women.*

individuation of 'the political sphere' segments life in an unacceptable way. This idea is associated with radical economic critiques which emphasize the infrastructural and causal nature of economy—production and exchange and the resulting distributions of benefits and burdens. For theorists in the Marxist tradition the separation of the political from the economic falsely presents the government's power as separate from that of the dominant economic class, whereas these two truly are closely intertwined. Further, the construction of the political sphere as separate from the economy in capitalist societies diverts efforts for social change away from the workplace (actually the source and the maintainer of unjust distributions and exploitative social relations) and into political institutions (where, as we have seen, certain people are severely disadvantaged).

Feminist theorists have turned this kind of argument in a different direction, arguing that the segmentation of social life—the maintenance of a division between political, economic, domestic, cultural etc.—can only be the product of a particular kind of gender identity, one which benefits from such segmentation. Only with the aid of domestic work performed by others can individuals cross and recross a boundary from a purely private realm of home and family, to a public world of work. Women's lives, it is argued, are much more fluid and amorphous—work, disputes about power, emotion, nurturing, exchange, all merge into one another, and allocating these aspects of diurnal existence to separate spheres is impossible and nonsensical. Further, this ambiguity of gender means that it has been difficult to address gender inequalities as properly political agenda items.

There are two lines of dissent then from the currently conventional view that 'the political' constitutes a separate sphere of life, a distinctive set of processes and procedures, taking place within a distinctive set of relationships and institutions. First, a reductionist objection can be made—it can be objected that the so-called political is epiphenomenal, or that processes and procedures that are sometimes thought of as distinctively political actually reduce to or at least rest on some other sort: economic processes and material interests, rational choice on the part of individuals, or culture, or sexual power. Second, it can be objected that this segmentation of the political is insufficiently holistic: if we are really to understand the distribution of power and resources of various kinds we have to keep the distribution of power and resources of all kinds firmly in view and examine the interactions between them. In a rather loose sense we might call this latter tendency 'deconstructive' in contrast with 'reductive'. It is deconstructive in that it looks at oppositions, separations, and the theoretical understanding of structures as balances of opposing forces, and insists rather that the relations between elements of a 'structure' so-called are actually much more amorphous, more entangled with one another, less separate and distinct than the structuralist picture suggests (or pretends).

Against these reductionist and deconstructionist attitudes to politics we can counterpose a significant celebratory strand in political theory: in which its own subject matter is seen as a sign of human advancement and realization. According to this view, in politics, human beings develop a distinct and ethically significant mode of deliberation—the self-conscious discussion of and decision about ways of ruling. Political people do not simply accept biological causes, or traditional modes of organization, or mythical justifications of their social order. Now of course this trait is not, just by itself, an unambiguous social good. The institution of politics, as has been observed, is quite consistent with a politically dominant class or group promulgating and promoting mythical justifications of the social order, or arguments in favour of traditional patterns of government, or biological or other so-called scientific explanations of why things are the way they are—in their own interests. That is, there can be politics, and the systematic exclusion of certain classes of people from the political process. Or, there can be politics and the incorporation of certain classes into a political system which is designed to subjugate them. Politics is not sufficient for justice. But this is not by itself an argument against the intrinsic preferability of a society in which the social order is raised to the level of conscious deliberation, over one in which it is simply accepted by all as unquestionable.

This refusal to accept how things are arranged, just to accept who has the power to govern our lives is, of course, central to many strains of political and social thought. One aspect, though, of the politicization of market relations, sexuality and reproduction, kinship and culture that is often underemphasized is the emotional and bodily wrench that this process can cause to many individuals. Critics complain that it spreads politics to the point where it despoils other aspects of life—private interactions, socialization and association, politically innocent popular cultural forms, and commerce. In response, the idea that politics can be 'rational', and that rational reform should be acceptable to reasonable people, overlooks the agonistic aspect of politics. This is not, of course, to say that reasonably based moral arguments are not valid; it is just to say that they won't, without power, wreak any changes in the world. And, the other side of this coin is, where there is rule there is discussion about rule, resistance to it, attempts to change it, subvert it, efforts to secure it and legitimate it, and so on. In short, there is politics.

THE COMMUNITARIAN CRITIQUE OF POLITICS

In this section I want to explore further, in the light of the foregoing analysis of the nature of 'politics', communitarian theories of politics. One question to consider is whether or to what extent communitarians share the common reductive attitude to politics. My interpretation of both political and philosophical communitarianism is that the answer to this is—to a considerable extent.

To begin with, communitarians are particularly conscious of the cultural aspects of political life. In itself this certainly does not amount to reductivism: the question of the relationship between patterns of sociability and the propensity to participate in political institutions—to vote, to stand for office, to engage in other forums where democratic decision-making about public goods goes on—is of course an important one for political science and political theory. Like many other theorists communitarians work on the hypothesis that individuals who are used to encounters and engagement with others outside their kinship circle and distinct from transactions in commodity and capital markets, will be more inclined to participate politically—to vote, to stand for office, to campaign, to participate in democratic decision-making in a variety of contexts. Further than this psychological thesis about individuals' motivations, however, is the cultural thesis that such participatory habits and forums are a matter of shared practices and values. The project of community building is on the one hand a project of building institutions, organizations, and spaces—the shared buildings and churches necessary for community events to be held, the parks and playgrounds that can form sites for public life and play that are not entirely commodified, the development of cultural events as a way of bringing people together (carnival, street parties, music, food festivals, and the like). But the very existence of this material infrastructure—the buildings, the spaces, the fund that underwrites the annual carnival—will not be doing its communitarian job if the appropriate local culture of use of these spaces is absent, if young people do not see their elders routinely using these facilities, and do not understand the values that that use articulates. The point has been made empirically by Daniel Bell in a study of residential community associations, which according to communitarian theory might be expected to foster generalized reciprocity among their members, but in the absence of the appropriate culture encourage citizens to act as private self-interested individuals.[62]

[62] Daniel A. Bell, 'Residential Community Associations: Community or Disunity?' *Responsive Community*, 4 (1995), 25–36.

This argument about the pivotal role of culture can look baffling from a policy point of view, reminiscent of the identification of the absence of 'civil society' as a key problem for putative democratic societies in transition. If the appropriate 'culture' is absent, how can we 'get one'? Culture is a complex of practices and concomitant values—from cuisine to the norms surrounding the preparation and consumption of food, music and its place in collective forms of life, conversation and the contexts in which it is conducted, patterns of sociability and the social roles involved. Not so easy to simply put one, different from the one pertaining, in place. The problem can look even more baffling in a multicultural society, where between social classes, ethnic groups, generations, and political parties there are distinct divergences regarding food, drink, music, talk, and sociability.

In the literature studied here we can find two distinct communitarian responses. One is to happily embrace cultural diversity, tying different 'cultures' to different 'communities', but for each case emphasizing the normative value of collective aspects of community and cultural life. For communitarians neither the anomic culture of existentialism, nor the individualistic cultural consumption associated with advanced commodification, meet their norms and requirements. Second, communitarians argue that the conduct of political life must be congruent with the conduct of community life. That is, the culture inhering in political institutions of the state and of the locality, must fit with the cultural life people live in their communities—their local area of residence, their schools and workplaces and churches.

On the one hand of course this requirement constitutes a critique of 'actually existing politics' in many contexts. In political settings discourse is frequently constrained in ways that are difficult to orient to (unless one is already steeped in the relevant political culture). But on the other hand, political life suffers from the shortcomings of other cultural settings. If in the course of their daily interactions individuals are suspicious of others, find interaction and conversation difficult, then it is likely that either they will behave relatively badly or be unable to enjoy political encounters.[63] Hence, the communitarian argument is that if children are brought up in communitarian families and educated in communitarian schools, in communitarian localities, then they will be both equipped and willing to engage in state political institutions if these are congruent: value the same values, involve similar patterns of interaction. Thus, political communitarians insist that community involves consensus, it involves accentuating

[63] Peter Gabel, 'The Desire for Community and the Defeat of Health Care', *Tikkun* 10/1 (1995).

what is shared (rather than what is negotiated, or contracted into), but it must also involve 'argument, even conflict, about the meaning of the shared values and goals, and certainly about how they will be actualised in everyday life'.[64] Community is consistent with democracy.

The strong communitarian implication is that any setting or organization can be more or less like a community. To the extent that it is like a community, what is shared will be privileged for practical purposes over disagreements and differences. This emphasis on what is shared, according to communitarians, is a necessary condition of stability and commitment, of a true cooperative effort. Communitarian individuals will move from family to school and workplace, engaging cooperatively albeit argumentatively with co-members. These immediate communities, together with localities, are 'nested' in the wider community of village, town or city, region or state, nation, and eventually the world. In each of these community formations members (whether they are city representatives as in national parliaments, or states as in the international community) emphasize what is shared.

We saw in the earlier examination of Rawls's and Habermas's political theory that they both argue that shared reasons should underpin political decisions. Rawls emphasizes that in public and political life citizens must converge on the reasons for decisions, these reasons being structured by the values, the institutions, and the procedures of the constitution. Values shared within restricted groups might then underpin collective decisions in particular settings in the non-public realm of cultural, community, and religious life. However, in other non-public settings other modes of decision-making—autocratic authority, or self-oriented individual rationality—may prevail. For communitarians, by contrast, shared values must underpin decisions in any context. To this extent at least, the strong distinction between public and non-public (or more conventionally between public and private) is attenuated in communitarianism. The distinction between public and private has conventionally been analysed in terms of differences in standards of conduct—whereas in public life particular standards of conduct and patterns of interaction can be prescribed (otherwise public institutions will scarcely be viable) a person in their private life should be less constrained by norms or regulation of their conduct. Conventionally whereas life in public comes within the sights of state law, some aspects at least of life in private escape this scrutiny. On all of these points communitarians diverge from hitherto mainstream, liberal and conservative, understandings and analyses. Communitarians

[64] Robert N. Bellah, 'Community Properly Understood: A Defence of Democratic Communitarianism', *Responsive Community*, 6/1 (1995), 49–54.

emphasize normative regulation rather than legal, in many areas of life, but are far less tempted to think that there should be aspects of life, let alone considerable areas of life, that escape norms. The ideal of the communitarian family entails the entry of norms governing relations between parents and children, between marital and sexual partners, right into the heart of private life. If individuals are to attain the skills and desires necessary to enable them to be good citizens and effective community members, then their lives within their families, their personal lives, must model these modes of conduct and patterns of interaction.

A number of theoretical problems are suggested at this point. First, there is the question whether this degree of congruence throughout areas of life best equips individuals politically. As I discussed in the previous section, there are degrees of incongruity that seem to disable individuals, either preventing them from participation in political forums or setting the costs of participation very high. But communitarians seem to postulate a high degree of congruity which presents its own problems. The worry is whether individuals who are raised in communitarian (or let us say, democratic communitarian) families, and attend democratic communitarian schools in democratic communitarian neighbourhoods, and so on, will be properly equipped to tackle authoritarianism or anomie when they encounter them. Such individuals, let us concede, will have democratic and communitarian instincts and expectations, but the lack of serious conflict in their lives may well mean that they lack important political skills.

Another worry is that these pervasive democratic and communitarian norms (the practical emphasis on what is shared, the presumption of the value of stability, the integrity of local cultures) may mean that certain voices are literally unhearable, certain positions absolutely invisible. This as we have seen is a criticism that can equally be levelled at Rawls and Habermas as at the philosophical and political communitarians: both emphasize what is shared—shared languages, shared discourse, shared reasons, shared values. However, we have seen the ethical and the political importance of both voice and hearing. It is important for justice that voices should not go unheard just because they are strange, or new, or present difficulties to hearers. It is important that participants in a political forum cultivate their abilities to hear so that they do not inadvertently marginalize or dominate those with 'different' voices. Attention to these values and skills of voice and hearing makes hearing the different, the excluded, the radical a political imperative.[65] What this means is that, for

[65] It is imperative that the politics of the different not be settled beyond and at the margins of democratic politics—Seyla Benhabib, 'Democracy and Difference: Reflections on the Metapolitics of Lyotard and Derrida', *Journal of Political Philosophy*, 2, (1994), 17, 23.

public and for political purposes, the voices and positions and demands of the 'unreasonable', of those who do not share 'our' values, must be central to the political process.

POLITY AND COMMUNITY

Should the polity be, or be thought of as, a community? The answer to this relies, of course, on conceptual analysis. As we have seen many theorists use the terms 'community' and 'political community' very loosely. So, liberal and democratic theorists often refer to 'political community' seeming to mean only a society which is politically constituted, or which is governed by political institutions. Another interpretation of such usages is that a group or plurality of people is being referred to—a group which shares some thing or set of things. This usage can be relatively thin: the implication could be only that the group of people have a common subjection to some set of governing institutions and structures. Or (and as we saw in Chapter 2 this comes closer to some accepted meanings of 'community') it might be implied that the group of people share more than one thing, that they are related by sharing not only institutions, territory, state or national symbols, a legal system, etc., but also values, political culture, national and political identity, a sense of allegiance, and so on. This is closer to my interpretation of the meaning of 'community' because as we saw there is the strong conceptual implication in usage and analyses of community that individuals are related to each other in multiple and complex ways. This multiplexity and complexity enhances the 'entity' status of the whole and accentuates the sense in which to be related to each is to be related to the whole.

Other theorists attempt to be even more specific about the specialness of the relation of community. For instance, Chantal Mouffe argues that democratic polities must be communities—communities in the sense that the relation between citizens is 'an ethico-political bond'.[66] As analysis however this must be too vague—the relations between persons in all kinds of collectives and aggregates is 'ethical': within kinship groups, within social institutions like schools, even within relatively anonymous aggregations like crowds ethical principles and constraints govern and even constitute people's relations with one another. Equally, to specify that a bond is political as well as ethical does not differentiate between a democratic polity and any other kind—presumably the bond between

---

[66] Mouffe, 'Democratic Citizenship and the Political Community', 285.

co-subjects of a tyrant is both ethical and political. Nor does it distinguish between a polity and other kinds of aggregations and collectives. As we have seen, there will be a political element to relations between members of all kinds of groups, wherever there are questions of governance and power.

It may be helpful to look at the question whether it makes sense to think of a polity as a community through the framework of the conceptual analysis of community conducted in Chapter 2. Co-members of a polity share a number of goods: symbols, institutions, procedures. Many political theorists believe that a successful democracy also requires that members share at least some values and practices, and standards of reason. In a political society the dominant relation between persons is political—persons are connected as fellow citizens or subjects, and as co-participants in the political process as voters, candidates, party members, and so on. These roles involve particular obligations and constraints on action. But it is important to note that these political relations are complex. Co-nationals and fellow citizens are usually also related to each other culturally, although this cannot simply be taken to mean that they share a culture.

The extent to which these political relations involve the kind of 'transcendent' quality that is implied by the concept 'community' is arguable. A number of critics and theorists insist that political relations and state unity can only be achieved by the use of symbols, and rituals as symbols, which relate each to each and to the whole at an imaginary level. Notably, Benedict Anderson argues that large, multicultural religiously pluralist modern states like Indonesia are only viable if citizens, aided by symbols such as flags and anthems, and by representations such as maps and portraits of leaders, each imagine themselves as connected to their fellow citizens and to the state.[67] David Miller argues that state institutions must deploy myths and associated symbols of 'nationhood' in such a way that all citizens orient to these in such a way as to understand themselves as related to their fellow citizens and to the whole.[68] In these theories of politics we find an emphasis, that is, on the need (if the polity is to work) for members to be related in a way that transcends material relations. Partly this is because material relations (apart from inhabiting the same geo-political territory) between co-citizens do not obviously exist so must be imagined. Partly, it is because the ideal of the 'human to human' or 'soul to soul' relation might itself be thought to be important for the viability of the state. (The extent to which the second as opposed to the first of these

[67] Benedict Anderson, *Imagined Communities*, 2nd edn. (London: Verso, 1991), 170–8.
[68] David Miller, *On Nationality* (Oxford: Clarendon Press, 1995), 17, 33–40.

considerations is emphasized will, of course, reflect the extent to which the theorist in question is tending to communitarianism.)

Another important element of the concept 'community' is that of 'boundedness'. Undoubtedly, polities have boundaries that, compared to other social aggregations, are relatively definite and relatively difficult to cross. In most states there are a range of legal and civil statuses that contribute to citizenship: liability to military service in time of war, liability to pay taxes, the right to bear a passport, rights of residence, the right to work, the rights to state-funded education and healthcare. Typically, these different rights and obligations encompass different populations—residents and even visitors to a country may have to pay tax although they have no right to vote and are passport holders from another state for instance. But together they draw a relatively definite boundary around 'the citizens' which will coincide with a territorial boundary. To this extent, polity and community can seem to coincide.

A difficulty arises though when we consider the nature of the political boundary—not the boundary of the state that is constructed and enforced politically (and usually militarily) but the boundary encompassing those who participate in the political process of the state. Here things cannot be so clear cut. The status of citizenship cannot settle the question of whose voice must be attended to in the political process—for citizenship is precisely a good whose distribution might be an issue and the generator of political dispute. Those who lack formal legal and political rights might be those persons whose voices urgently should be attended to. Obvious examples will include migrant workers, asylum seekers, and children. Equally significant are people who while holding formal rights lack the resources to get a fair hearing in the political process. Familiar examples include ethnic minorities, women as a group, people with physical and mental disabilities, homeless people, jobless people. All of these groups and many more have formed (and will in the future form) political movements whose aim is to dismantle barriers to their participation. Some of these barriers are legal, some are cultural. Many groups and individuals aim to join in the process as it is already in train; others conclude that the process itself will have to be changed if their participation is to be enabled.

Many political theorists wish to design a political settlement: a constitution that establishes rights to basic goods; or standards of reason that will guide future legislation and administration; or a social and political order that will support orderly agreement in matters of government while allowing diversity in religion and culture; or a set of political institutions that guards certain individual rights while enabling parties, social groups, and political movements to participate in governance. For many this settlement depends on agreement about procedures, convergence on values, shared culture; and as we have seen in many cases this agreement and sharing is theoretically resolved as community, with its implications of all and the whole, and of transcendent relations.

My argument in this and the foregoing chapters has suggested three final points. First, conflict based on interest divergence disrupts the ideal of community. Recent communitarians insist that the ideal of community is consistent with disagreement, with diversity in certain respects, with arguments about values, principles, and preferences and with change. But my reading of political and cultural studies of conflicts over development and neighbourhood regeneration, and over the participation of incoming groups (women, ethnic minorities, young people, tenants) suggests that it is difficult to maintain that community is a salient factor in the resolution of these disputes. Communitarians argue that if only the value of community were to take its proper place in human relations these divergences of interest and the conflicts they generate would be overcome or avoided. But that demand amounts to a demand that shared goods and complex relationships take on the transcendent qualities that can overcome divergences and conflicts, which is close to becoming circular.

Second, in any case, conflict and divergence is invariably accompanied by tension, aggression, and emotion. This is also true for politics in general. Politics is the competition for the power to govern. For governors the competition for and the securing of that power cannot be a friction-free, unfelt, or costless process. Resistance is invariably engendered in the governed (no matter how benign the rule). Some recent communitarians would want to acknowledge all this—and, further perhaps agree that because primary human relationships are antagonistic in various ways, this antagonism and the internal conflicts it engenders are likely to be acted out in the context of all kinds of human relations and social settings. But, they would argue, community settings—shared goods, complex relationships, human-to-human encounter, boundedness—are the best settings for holding individuals who feel and suffer these conflicts, and the best framework for minimizing the adverse social consequences of these antagonisms. In response, we can note the contrasting arguments that emphasize the freeing effects of simple relationships and loose networks. To argue this is by no means to go to the opposite extreme of the anomic society and the lonely individual, the lack of sustaining institutions and networks that the communitarians associate with liberal individualism and negative freedom and rights.

Finally, contemporary democratic politics cannot be consistent with the boundary nature and maintenance associated with the concept community. This is not to say that there is no boundary to the polity: rather the conflicts over what topics, what ways of speaking, whose voices, what rituals, what meanings, what claims, testify to the boundary as well as testifying to its unstable and contested nature. The boundary of the polity is as likely as a community boundary to be symbolic. But whereas the members of a community must be in a position legitimately to keep certain kinds of would-be entrant out (or the community itself with its shared values and peculiar pattern of relationships would be dissolved) this cannot so obviously be the case for a political society. Certainly political systems can and do delegitimize certain kinds of claims and certain kinds of action. But communities appeal to and constantly seek to build 'the spirit of community'. This political societies, with their contested boundaries and their conflicts, cannot do.

Appendix I

Analysing Political Communitarianism

I constructed the corpus of 'political communitarianism' on the basis of observed differences between books like those authored by Amitai Etzioni and Henry Tam and the recognized body of philosophical books and articles that constituted the 'communitarian' contributions to the 'liberal v. communitarian debates'. The Etzioni and Tam books are much more directly political (in the sense of intended to be read as direct interventions in policy debates, and directed at an audience of policy-makers and voters rather than theorists and philosophers) than philosophical. They seem to fit into a distinctive corpus of literature including books and pamphlets by established politicians (e.g. Ian Taylor, Frank Field), some output of pressure groups and policy studies organizations (e.g. the Citizenship Foundation), speeches by politicians such as Tony Blair, Al Gore, Hillary Clinton and Bill Clinton, and above all the press coverage of these ideas by broadsheet journalists in the UK and USA. A complete list of this corpus of 'political communitarianism' is given in Appendix II; some of these items (not print journalism) also appear in the main bibliography.

I conducted a reasonably systematic search of the press for coverage of communitarianism and communitarian issues. For the *Guardian* and *The Times* (including the *Sunday Times* and the *Financial Times*) I searched the printed indexes for 1988–98. The *Guardian* contains numerous entries under the heads 'community', 'communitarianism', 'community action', 'community development', and the like; *The Times* far fewer. I also searched the *Washington Post* for the same period, via their Internet Index and copying service. I physically searched the *Observer*. I selected items that report or comment on either communitarianism as a political position, or community activism and community organization where the political implications of this are articulated or otherwise prominent. I am conscious that had I included more US papers, from different regions, my analysis of 'political communitarianism' might vary somewhat—for instance, the *Los Angeles Times* would probably have yielded coverage of commuity activism on the part of members of different ethnic groups.

I also read complete runs of two notable US 'communitarian' periodicals: *Tikkun* and *The Responsive Community*.

I decided to analyse the bulk of this corpus of 'political communitarianism' using the software package for text analysis 'QSR NUD.IST'. (I excluded from this analytic exercise the books authored and edited by Amitai Etzioni, so as not to bias the corpus too much towards his particular version and project of communitarianism, and on the grounds that he is, in any case, either the author of or the subject of a fair amount of press coverage).

I assembled copies, transcripts, or notes from all the documents. These were coded manually—I read them for passages that featured discussion of 'community', 'communitarianism' and the like including passages featuring discussion of contrasts with or negations of community. So this exercise yielded two basic codes: Community and Anti-community.

The relevant passages were then transcribed and imported into NUD.IST. The resulting word-processed documents were then coded manually, yielding the following initial coding scheme:

Communitarianism	Varieties	US
		Tory
		British Socialist
		Jewish
		Spiritual
		Beyond Left and Right
Community	Examples of	family
		neighbourhood
		voluntary associations
		workplace
	Kinds of	ethnic
		spiritual
		religious
		territorial
		interest
		adversity
		democratic
Communitarian	Hypotheses	Strong families make strong communities
		Strong communities can deal with crime
		A good society depends on good community
	Principles	Communities have rights
		Communities have voice
		Politics of meaning
		Communities need power
		Community at every level
		Community groups as social capital
		Individual rooted in community
		Generations are linked
	Values	civic spirit
		solidarity
		equality

Values	democracy
	voluntary service
	social capital
	common good
	participation
	political power
Roles	entrepreneurs
	community leaders
	active citizen
Names	Douglas Hurd
	Bill Clinton
	Hillary Clinton
	Al Gore
	Amitai Etzioni
	Tony Blair
	Gordon Brown
The community	Global
	national
	local
Family	Family as starting point
	Families must participate in community

This initial coding scheme formed the basis for further coding and recoding conducted within Nud.ist. In this exercise the application of codes to text is reviewed, and the relationships between codes explored and analysed. This resulted eventually in an expanded coding scheme:

Varieties of communitarianism	US
	Tory
	British Socialist
	Jewish
	spiritual
	moral
Examples of community	family
	neighbourhood
	voluntary associations
	workplace
	state
	human race
Kinds of community	ethnic
	spiritual
	religious
	territorial
	interest

	adversity
	democratic
	moral
Communitarian hypotheses	Strong families make strong communities
	Communities can deal with crime
	A good society depends on good communities
Communitarian principles	communities have rights
	communities have rights to defend themselves
	communities have voice
	people need meaning in their lives
	communities need power and authority
	community should exist at every level
	community groups are social capital
	individual and community:
	individual rooted in community
	individual and community both valuable
	individuals should participate in community
	less rights and more responsibilities
	generations linked
	community, not state government
	community, not state, not market
	community, beyond left and right
Communitarian values	civic spirit
	solidarity
	equality
	democracy
	voluntary service
	social capital
	common good
	participation
	political power
	cleanliness
	responsibility
	self-discipline
	mutuality
Community roles	entrepreneurs
	community leaders
	active citizens
Names	Douglas Hurd
	Hillary Clinton
	Bill Clinton

Names	Al Gore
	Amitai Etzioni
	Tony Blair
	Gordon Brown
	Dick Atkinson
	Charles Lerner
The Community	global
	national
	local
Family	Family as the starting point
	Families must participate in wider community
	2 parents necessary
Discourse	reportage
	interview
	opinion
	policy document
Anti-community	poverty
	lack of care
	crime
	dirt
	privatization
	selfishness
	government betrayal
	capital
	solitude
Communitarian politics	consensus
	local activism
	community development
	human scale

A number of searches were then conducted which greatly aided the analysis for and composition of sections on, for example, 'the family' and 'communitarian politics'. The program's coding and search facility enabled detailed analysis of the meaning of community for different writers and actors. A number of analytic hypotheses were also explored, by conducting cross-referencing searches exploring the relationships between, for instance, varieties of communitarianism and theories of community and community breakdown.

Appendix II

Bibliography: Political Communitarianism

1. *Books, pamphlets and reports*

Atkinson, Dick, *The Common Sense of Community* (London: Demos, 1994).
—— *Cities of Pride: Rebuilding Community, Refocussing Government* (London: Cassell, 1995).
Blair, Tony, *New Britain: My Vision for a Young Country* (London: Fourth Estate, 1996).
Commission on Social Justice/Institute for Public Policy Research, *Social Justice: Strategies for National Renewal* (London: Vintage Books, 1994).
Etzioni, Amitai, *The Spirit of Community: Rights, Responsibilities and the Communitarian Agenda* (New York: Crown Publishers, 1991).
—— *The New Golden Rule: Community and Morality in a Democratic Society* (New York: Basic Books, 1996).
Field, Frank, *Making Welfare Work: Reconstructing Welfare for the Millenium* (London: Institute of Community Studies, 1995).
Harris, Robin, *The Conservative Community: The Roots of Thatcherism—and its Future* (London: Centre for Policy Studies, 1989).
Leadbeater, Charles, *The Rise of the Social Entrepreneur* (London: Demos, 1997).
Mandelson, Peter, and Liddle, Roger, *The Blair Revolution: Can New Labour Deliver?* (London: Faber, 1996).
Tam, Henry, *Citizen's Agenda for Building Democratic Communities* (Cambridge: Centre for Citizenship Development, 1995).
—— *Communitarianism: A New Agenda for Politics and Citizenship* (Basingstoke: Macmillan, 1998).
Taylor, Ian, *Releasing the Community Spirit: A Framework for the Active Citizen* (Cambridge: Tory Reform Group, 1990).

2. *Periodicals*

Tikkun: a Bi-monthly Jewish Critique of Politics, Culture and Society (Oakland, Calif.: Institute for Labour and Mental Health), Vol 1, 1986–
The Responsive Community (Washington DC) Vol 1 1990–

3. *British Government Documents*

Cabinet Office, Social Exclusion Unit, *Bringing Britain Together: A National Strategy for Neighbourhood Renewal*, Cm. 4045, Sept. 1998.

Department of Education and Employment, *Excellence in Schools*, Cm. 3681, July 1997.

Department of Education and Employment, *New Start: A Journal for Everyone Helping Young People to Stay in Learning*, issue 3, 'Focus on Mentoring', July 1998.

Department of the Environment, Transport and the Regions, *Guidance on Local Transport Plans* (http:/www.local-transport.detr.gov.uk/Hp9811/08.htm).

Home Office, Research and Statistics Directorate, Offenders and Corrections Unit, Paul Ekblom 'Community Safety and the Reduction and Prevention of Crime: a conceptual framework for training and the development of a professional discipline', August 1998.

Home Office, *Guidance on Statutory Crime and Disorder Partnerships,* Crime and Disorder Act 1998.

Home Office, Ministerial Group on the Family, *Supporting Families*, Nov. 1998.

Labour Party, Speech by Rt. Hon Tony Blair MP, Prime Minister and Leader of the Labour Party, Labour Party Conference 1998, Blackpool, UK, 29 Sept. 1998.

4. *Print Journalism*

Barone, Michael, 'After Reagan, How about a Great Communitarian?', *Washington Post* 29.11.87, p. L01.

Baxter, Sarah, 'I am the Way and I am the Truth', *Sunday Times* 19.03.95, p. 7.

Blair, Tony 'The Right Way to Find a Left Alternative', *Observer* 09.05.93, p. 20.

Brown, Gordon, 'Beware the Mask of Tory Social Concern', *Observer* 01.12.90, p. 20.

Campbell, Bea, 'Grandaddy of the Backlash' *Guardian* 01.04.95, p. 31.

Davis, Marcia, 'Open Arms', *Washington Post* 20.02.96, p. B01.

Etzioni, Amitai, 'Sizing Up America', *Washington Post* 05.10.97, p. X07.

—— 'Community Watch', *Guardian* 28.06.97, pt. 1.

Glazer, Sarah, 'Teaching Kids Values, but Whose?', *Washington Post* 10.09.96, p. Z14.

Hattersley, Roy, 'Let's Proclaim our Beliefs', *Observer* 29.09.91, p. 23.

Hetherington, Peter, 'Well-Heeled Take on Kerb Crawlers', *Guardian* 02.06.97, p. 11.

Holman, Bob, 'Helping Self-Help', *Guardian* 11.06.97, Soc. p. 9.

Holtham, Gerald, 'It's not all over yet', *Observer* 24.09.95, p. 4.

Kamen, Al, 'A Word from the Communitarians', *Washington Post* 19.11.92, p. A21.

Kelly, Gerard, 'Off the Self Sociology', *Times Higher Education Supplement* 24.03.95, p. 21.

Kettle, Martin, 'Blair Puts Faith in Community Spirit', *Guardian* 13.03.95, pt. 1 p. 2.

Popenoe, David, 'The Controversial Truth: Two Parent Families are Better', *New York Times* 26.02.92, p. 13.

Phillips, Melanie, 'Dumping Granny on the Doorstep', *Guardian* 20.7.90, p. 23.

—— 'Riddle behind Howard's Volunteers', *Observer* 20.03.94, p. 27.

—— 'Power to the People in the War on Crime', *Observer* 24.04.94, p. 27.

—— 'When a Community Stands up for Itself', *Observer* 17.07.94, p. 25.

—— 'The Race to Wake Sleeping Duty', *Observer* 02.04.95, p. 25.

—— 'Freedom and Community Reconsidered', *Observer* 25.09.94, p. 27.

—— 'Getting Lone Parents off Benefits . . .', *Observer* 14.12.97, Review p. 2.

Power, William F., 'Can a Nation of Individuals give Community a Sporting Chance?', *Washington Post* 03.02.95, p. D01.

Rogaly, Joe, 'Blair's Community Spirit', *Financial Times* 18.03.94, Weekend p. 1.

Sherrill, Martha, 'Hillary Clinton's Inner Politics', *Washington Post* 06.05.93, p. D01.

Simmons, Michael, 'No Need to Duck Out', *Guardian* 11.06.97, Soc. p. 9.

Smith, Sam, 'Bringing Politics Back Home', *Washington Post* 01.11.94, p. A23.

Steele, Jonathan, 'Clinton Policies Caught in Communitarian Crossfire', *Guardian* 12.04.95.

Taylor, Paul, 'An Agenda Focussed Less on Rights and More on Responsibilities', *Washington Post* 19.11.91, p. A19.

Trueheart, Charles, 'The Case for the Group Ethic', *Washington Post* 5.2.91, p. C07.

Vobejda, Barbara, 'Communitarians Press Hill on Pro-Family Policies', *Washington Post* 04.11.93, p. A06.

Wainwright, Martin, 'People Power is Bringing Hope', *Guardian* 06.12.95, p. 4.

Walker, Martin, 'Community Spirit', *Guardian* 13.03.95, pt. 2 p. 10.

Young, Michael and Gerard, Lemos, 'Roots of Revival', *Guardian* 19.03.97, Soc. p. 2.

'Labour Vision of a Future Britain', *Observer* 23.10.94, p. 27.

'Communitarian Conceits', *The Economist* 18.03.95, p. 20.

'Communitarianism: Down with Rights', *The Economist* 18.03.95, p. 31.

'First Lady Tries to Turn over a New Leaf', *The Times* 12.01.96, p. 11.

'Communities and Crime', *Guardian* 02.06.97, p. 10.

Bibliography

Note: this bibliography contains selected items from the corpus of 'political communitarianism', but no press items have been included—a full list of press items is included in Appendix II.

ABERCROMBIE, NICHOLAS, HILL, STEPHEN, and TURNER, BRYAN, S., *Sovereign Individuals of Capitalism* (London: Allen and Unwin, 1986).

AIDALA, ANGELA, and ZABLOCKI, BENJAMIN, D., 'The Communes of the 1970s: Who Joined and Why?', *Marriage and Family Review*, 17 (1991), 87–116.

ALMOND, GABRIEL, and VERBA, SIDNEY (eds.), *The Civic Culture Revisited* (Newbury Park, Calif.: Sage Publications, 1989).

AMATO, PAUL, R., 'Children's Adjustment to Divorce: Theories, Hypotheses and Empirical Support', *Journal of Marriage and the Family*, 54 (1992), 104–17.

ANDERSON, BENEDICT, *Imagined Communities,* 2nd edn. (London: Verso, 1991).

ARBLASTER, ANTHONY, *The Rise and Decline of Western Liberalism* (Oxford: Basil Blackwell, 1984).

ARENDT, HANNAH, *The Human Condition* (Chicago: University of Chicago Press, 1958).

—— *On Revolution* (Harmondsworth: Penguin, 1963).

—— *On Violence* (London: Allen Lane, 1970).

ATKINSON, DICK, *The Common Sense of Community* (London: Demos, 1994).

—— (ed.), *Cities of Pride: Rebuilding Community, Refocussing Government* (London: Cassell, 1995).

AUSTIN, J. L., *How to Do Things with Words* (Oxford: Clarendon Press, 1962).

AVINERI, SHLOMO, and DE-SHALIT, AVNER (eds.), *Communitarianism and Individualism* (Oxford: Oxford University Press, 1992).

BACHRACH, PETER, and BARATZ, MORTON S., 'The Two Faces of Power', *American Political Science Review*, 56 (1962), 947–52.

BAGGULEY, PAUL, et al., *Restructuring: Place Class and Gender* (London: Sage 1990).

BAIER, ANNETTE, *Moral Prejudices: Essays on Ethics* (Cambridge, Mass.: Harvard University Press, 1994).

BAILEY, NICK, LEES, RAY, and MAYO, MARJORIE, *Resourcing Communities* (London: Polytechnic of Central London, 1980).

BALL, MOG, *School Inclusion: The School, the Family and the Community* (York: Joseph Rowntree Foundation, 1998).

BALL, TERENCE, FARR, JAMES, and HANSON, RUSSELL L., 'Editors' Introduction', to *Political Innovation and Conceptual Change* (Cambridge: Cambridge University Press, 1989).

BALLASTER, ROS, BEETHAM, MARGARET, FRAZER, ELIZABETH, and HEBRON, SANDRA, *Women's Worlds: Ideology, Femininity and the Woman's Magazine* (Basingstoke: Macmillan, 1991).

'Barclay Report', *Social Workers, their Role and Tasks* (London: Bedford Square Press, 1982).

BARNES, J. A., 'Class and Committees in a Norwegian Island Parish', *Human Relations*, 7 (1954), 39–58.

BAXTER, JANEEN, and WESTERN, MARK, 'Satisfaction with Housework: Examining the Paradox', *Sociology*, 32 (1998), 101–20.

BELL, COLIN, and NEWBY, HOWARD, *Community Studies: An Introduction to the Sociology of the Local Community* (London: George Allen and Unwin, 1971).

BELL, DANIEL, A., 'Residential Community Associations: Community or Disunity?' *Responsive Community*, 4 (1995), 25–36.

BELLAH, ROBERT N., 'Community Properly Understood: A Defence of Democratic Communitarianism', *Responsive Community*, 6/1 (1995–6), 49–54.

—— et al., *Habits of the Heart: Individualism and Commitment in American Life* (Berkeley and Los Angeles: University of California Press, 1985).

BELLAMY, RICHARD, *Liberalism and Modern Society* (Oxford: Polity Press, 1992).

BELSKY, JAY, YOUNGBLADE, LISA, ROVINE, MICHAEL, and VOLLING, BRENDA, 'Patterns of Marital Change and Parent–Child Interaction', *Journal of Marriage and the Family*, 53 (1991), 487–98.

BENHABIB, SEYLA, 'Liberal Dialogue versus a Critical Theory of Discursive Legitimation', in N. Rosenblum (ed.), *Liberalism and the Moral Life* (Cambridge, Mass.: Harvard University Press, 1989).

—— 'Autonomy, Modernity and Community: Communitarianism and Critical Social Theory in Dialogue', in *Situating the Self* (Cambridge: Polity Press, 1992).

—— 'Democracy and Difference: Reflections on the Metapolitics of Lyotard and Derrida', *Journal of Political Philosophy*, 2 (1994), 1.

BENINGTON, JOHN, 'The Flaw in the Pluralist Heaven: Changing Strategies in the Coventry CDP', in Ray Lees and George Smith (eds.), *Action Research in Community Development* (London: Routledge and Kegan Paul, 1975).

BENN, S. I., 'Individuality, Autonomy and Community', in Eugene Kamenka (ed.), *Community as a Social Ideal* (London: Edward Arnold, 1982).

BEN-SASSON, H. H., 'The Northern European Jewish Community and its Ideals', in H. H. Ben-Sasson and E. Ettinger (eds.), *Jewish Society through the Ages* (London: Vallentine Mitchell, 1968).

BENTON, TED, *Philosophical Foundations of the Three Sociologies* (London: Routledge and Kegan Paul, 1977).

—— *The Rise and Fall of Structuralist Marxism* (Basingstoke: Macmillan, 1984).

BERGER, PETER, and LUCKMANN, THOMAS, *The Social Construction of Reality* (Harmondsworth: Penguin, 1967).

BERLIN, ISAIAH, 'Two Concepts of Liberty', in *Four Essays on Liberty* (Oxford: Clarendon Press, 1958), also in Anthony Quinton (ed.), *Political Philosophy* (Oxford: Oxford University Press, 1967).

BHASKAR, ROY, *Reclaiming Reality* (London: Verso, 1989).

BLACK, ANTHONY, 'Communal Democracy and its History', *Political Studies*, 45 (1997), 5.

BLAIR, TONY, *New Britain: My Vision for a Young Country* (London: Fourth Estate, 1996).

BLAKEMORE, DIANE, *Understanding Utterances* (Oxford: Blackwell, 1992).

BLUNKETT, DAVID, and JACKSON, KEITH, *Democracy in Crisis: The Town Halls Respond* (London: Hogarth Press, 1987).

BOHMAN, JAMES, *New Philosophy of Social Science: Problems of Indeterminacy* (Oxford: Polity Press, 1991).

—— *Public Deliberation: Pluralism Complexity and Democracy* (Cambridge, Mass.: MIT Press, 1996).

BOOTH, ALAN, and AMATO, PAUL R., 'Parental Marital Quality, Parental Divorce and Relations with Parents', *Journal of Marriage and the Family*, 53 (1994), 21–34.

BOTT, ELIZABETH, *Family and Social Network* (1st pub. 1957), 2nd edn. (London: Tavistock, 1971).

BOURDIEU, PIERRE, *The Logic of Practice* (1st pub. French 1980), trans. Richard Nice (Oxford: Polity Press, 1990).

BOYETT, INGER, and FINLAY, DON, 'The Social Entrepreneur', in Dick Atkinson (ed.), *Cities of Pride: Rebuilding Community, Refocussing Government* (London: Cassell, 1995).

BOYTE, HARRY C., and EVANS, SARA M., 'The Sources of Democratic Change', *Tikkun*, 1/1 (1986).

BRENT, JEREMY, 'Community without Unity', paper delivered to conference 'Ideas of Community', University of the West of England, Sept. 1995.

BRIGGS, ASA, and MACARTNEY, ANNE, *Toynbee Hall: The First Hundred Years* (London: Routledge and Kegan Paul, 1984).

British Youth Council, *The Voices of Young People* (London: British Youth Council, 1986).

BRYANT, BARBARA, and BRYANT, RICHARD, *Change and Conflict: A Study of Community Work in Glasgow* (Aberdeen: Aberdeen University Press, 1982).

BRYANT, RICHARD, 'The New Slums—Community Action Response', in Paul Henderson et al. (eds.), *Successes and Struggles on Council Estates: Tenant Action and Community Work* (London: Association of Community Workers in the UK, 1982).

BUBECK, DIEMUT, *Care Gender and Justice* (Oxford: Clarendon Press, 1995).

BUBER, MARTIN, *Pointing the Way*, ed. and trans. Maurice S. Friedman (Freeport, NY: Books for Libraries Press, 1957).

—— *A Believing Humanism: My Testament 1902–1965*, trans. and introd. Maurice Friedman (New York: Simon and Schuster, 1967).

—— *I and Thou* (1st pub. 1923), trans. and Prologue by Walter Kaufman (New York: Charles Scribners' Sons, 1970).

BULMER, MARTIN, *Neighbours: The Work of Phillip Abrams* (Cambridge: Cambridge University Press, 1986).

—— *The Social Basis of Community Care* (London: Unwin Hyman, 1987).

BUNGE, MARIO, 'New Sociology of Science, Part 1', *Philosophy of the Social Sciences*, 21 (1991), 524–60.

BUNNAG, JANE, 'The Way of the Monk and the Way of the World', in H. Bechert and R. Gombrich (eds.), *The World of Buddhism* (London: Thames and Hudson, 1991).

BUTCHER, HUGH, COLLIS, PATRICIA, GLEN, ANDREW, and SILLS, PATRICK, *Community Groups in Action: Case Studies and Analysis* (London: Routledge and Kegan Paul, 1980).

BUTLER, JUDITH, 'Variations on Sex and Gender', in Seyla Benhabib and Drucilla Cornell (eds.), *Feminism as Critique* (Oxford: Polity Press, 1987).

—— *Gender Trouble: Feminism and the Subversion of Identity* (New York: Routledge, 1990).

—— *Bodies that Matter* (New York: Routledge, 1993).

BYNNER, JOHN, and STRIBLEY, KEITH M., *Social Research: Principles and Procedures* (Harlow: Longman, 1978).

Cabinet Office, Social Exclusion Unit, *Bringing Britain Together: A National Strategy for Neighbourhood Renewal*, Cm. 4045 (London: Stationery Office, Sept. 1998).

CAMERON, DEBORAH, *Feminism and Linguistic Theory* (Basingstoke: Macmillan, 1985).

—— (ed.), *The Feminist Critique of Language* (London: Routledge, 1990).

CAMPBELL, BEATRIX, *Goliath: Britain's Dangerous Places* (London: Methuen, 1993).

CANOVAN, MARGARET, *Hannah Arendt: A Reinterpretation of her Political Thought* (Cambridge: Cambridge University Press, 1992).

CARLING, ALAN, 'Analytical and Essential Marxism', *Political Studies*, 45 (1997), 768.

CLARK, DAVID B., 'The Concept of Community', *Sociological Review*, 21 (1973), 397–416.

CLARK, H., 'Taking up Space: Redefining Political Legitimacy in New York City', *Environment and Planning A*, 26 (1994), 937–55.

COCKBURN, CYNTHIA, *The Local State: Management of Cities and People* (London: Pluto Press, 1977).

COHEN, A. P., *The Symbolic Construction of Community* (London: Routledge, 1985).

COHEN, ERIK, 'Persistence and Change in the Israeli Kibbutz', in E. Kamenka (ed.), *Community as a Social Ideal* (London: Edward Arnold, 1982).

COHEN, G. A., 'Back to Socialist Basics', *New Left Review*, 207 (1994), 3–16.

COLEMAN, JAMES, 'Social Capital in the Creation of Human Capital', *American Journal of Sociology*, 94 suppl. (1988), 95.

—— *The Foundations of Social Theory* (Cambridge, Mass.: Harvard University Press, 1990).

COLEMAN, WIL, and SHARROCK, WES, 'Unconstructive', in I. Velody and R. Williams (eds.), *The Politics of Constructionism* (London: Sage, 1998).

COLLINS, CHIK, 'The Dialogics of Community: Struggle and Identity in a Scottish Working Class Housing Scheme', paper delivered to conference 'Ideas of Community', University of the West of England, Sept. 1995.

Commission on Social Justice/Institute for Public Policy Research, Report of the, *Social Justice: Strategies for National Renewal* (London: Vintage Books, 1994).

CONNELL, JAMES P., and KUBISCH, ANNE C., 'Evaluating Comprehensive Community Initiatives', unpub. 1996.

CONNOLLY, WILLIAM E., *The Terms of Political Discourse*, 2nd edn. (Oxford: Basil Blackwell, 1983).

COOKE, IAN, and TUNNAH, EDDIE, 'Urban Communities and Economic Regeneration: A Liverpool Case Study', paper delivered to conference 'Ideas of Community', University of the West of England, Sept. 1995.

COOKE, PHILLIP (ed.), *Localities: The Changing Face of Urban Britain* (London: Unwin Hyman 1989).

COOTE, ANNA, and CAMPBELL, BEATRIX, *Sweet Freedom: The Struggle for Women's Liberation*, 2nd edn. (Oxford: Basil Blackwell, 1987).

CORNELL, DRUCILLA, 'Beyond Tragedy and Complacency', *Northwestern University Law Review*, 81 (1987), 693.

—— 'Feminism, Negativity, Subjectivity', in Seyla Benhabib and Drucilla Cornell (eds.), *Feminism as Critique* (Oxford: Polity Press, 1990).

CRAWFORD, ADAM, 'Appeals to Community and Crime Prevention', *Crime, Law and Social Change*, 22 (1995), 97–126.

—— *The Local Governance of Crime: Appeals to Community and Partnerships* (Oxford: Clarendon Press, 1997).

—— *Crime Prevention and Community Safety: Politics, Policies and Practices* (London: Longman, 1998).

CREEL, AUSTIN B., and NARAYAN, VASUDHA (eds.), *Monastic Life in the Christian and Hindu Traditions: A Comparative Study* (Lewiston, NY: Edward Mellen Press, 1990).

CRICK, BERNARD, *In Defence of Politics* (1st pub. 1962), 2nd edn. (Harmondsworth: Penguin, 1992).

CROW, GRAHAM, and ALLAN, GRAHAM, *Community Life: An Introduction to Local Social Relations* (Hemel Hempstead: Harvester Wheatsheaf, 1994).

CURNO, ANN, LAMMING, ANNE, LEACH, LESLEY, STILES, JENNY, WARD, VERONICA, and ZIFF, TRISHA (eds.), *Women in Collective Action* (London: Association of Community Workers, 1982).

DAHLGREN, PETER, and SPARKS, COLIN (eds.), *Communication and Citizenship: Journalism and the Public Sphere in the New Media Age* (London: Routledge, 1991).

DAVIDSON, DONALD, 'On the Very Idea of a Conceptual Scheme', *Inquiries into Truth and Interpretation* (Oxford: Oxford University Press, 1984).

DAY, GRAHAM, and MURDOCH, JONATHAN, 'Locality and Community: Coming to Terms with Place', *Sociological Review*, 41 (1993), 82–111.

DEAKIN, NICHOLAS, and WRIGHT, ANTHONY (eds.), *Consuming Public Services* (London: Routledge, 1990).

DEMO, DAVID H., 'Parent Child Relations: Assessing Recent Changes', *Journal of Marriage and the Family*, 54 (1992), 104–17.

DENCH, GEOFF, *The Place of Men in Changing Family Cultures* (London: Institute of Community Studies, 1996).

DENNETT, DANIEL, 'Darwin's Dangerous Idea', *The Sciences* (May 1995), 34–40.

DENNIS, NORMAN, *Public Participation and Planners' Blight* (London: Faber and Faber, 1972).

Department of Education and Employment, *Excellence in Schools*, Cm. 3681 (London: The Stationery Office, July 1997).

—— *New Start: The Journal for Everyone helping young people to stay in learning*, issue 3, 'Focus on Mentoring' (July 1998).

Department of the Environment, Transport and the Regions, *Guidance on Local Transport Plans* (http://www.local-transport.detr.gov.uk/ltp9811/08.htm).

DERRIDA, JACQUES, 'Différance', in *Margins of Philosophy* (1st pub. French 1972), trans. Alan Bass (Hemel Hempstead: Harvester Wheatsheaf, 1982).

DE-SHALIT, AVNER, 'David Miller's Theory of Market Socialism and the Recent Reforms in Kibbutzim', *Political Studies*, 40 (1992).

DICKENS, PETER, *One Nation? Social Change and the Politics of Locality* (London: Pluto Press, 1988).

DIETZ, MARY, 'Citizenship with a Feminist Face: The Problem with Maternal Thinking', *Political Theory*, 13 (1985), 19.

—— 'Feminism and Theories of Citizenship', in Chantal Mouffe (ed.), *Dimensions of Radical Democracy* (London: Verso, 1992).

—— 'Hannah Arendt and Feminist Politics', in Mary Lyndon Shanley and Carole Pateman (eds.), *Feminist Interpretation and Political Theory* (Oxford: Polity Press, 1991).

DOWNES, STEPHEN M., 'Socialising Naturalised Philosophy of Science,' *Philosophy of Science*, 60 (1993), 452–68.

DUMMETT, MICHAEL, *Voting Procedures* (Oxford: Clarendon Press, 1984).

—— *Principles of Electoral Reform* (Oxford: Oxford University Press, 1997).

DURKHEIM, EMILE, *The Division of Labour in Society* (1st pub. French 1893), trans. George Simpson (New York: Free Press, 1933).

DWORKIN, RONALD, *Taking Rights Seriously*, 2nd edn. (London: Duckworth, 1978).

—— *Laws Empire* (London: Fontana, 1986).

—— 'Liberal Community', *California Law Review*, 77 (1989), 479–504.

—— *Life's Dominion: An Argument about Abortion, Euthanasia and Individual Freedom* (London: Harper Collins, 1993).

ECKSTEIN, HARRY, 'Civic Inclusion and its Discontents', in *Regarding Politics: Essays on Political Theory, Stability and Change* (Berkeley and Los Angeles: University of California Press, 1992).

EKBLOM, PAUL, 'Community Safety and the Reduction and Prevention of Crime: A Conceptual Framework for Training and the Development of a Professional Discipline' (London: Home Office Research and Statistics Directorate; http:l/www.open.gov.uk, August 1998).

EKMAN, PAUL, 'Facial Expressions and Emotion', *American Psychologist*, 48 (1993), 384–92.

ELSHTAIN, JEAN BETHKE, 'Against Androgyny', in *Real Politics: At the Centre of Everyday Life* (Baltimore: Johns Hopkins University Press, 1997).

—— 'Symmetry and Soporifics: A Critique of Feminist Accounts of Gender Development', in *Real Politics: At the Centre of Everyday Life* (Baltimore: Johns Hopkins University Press, 1997).

—— 'The Mothers of the Disappeared: Passion and Protest in Maternal Action', in *Real Politics: At the Centre of Everyday Life* (Baltimore: Johns Hopkins University Press, 1997).

ELSTER, JON, 'The Market and the Forum: Three Varieties of Political Theory', in Jon Elster and Aanund Hylland (eds.), *The Foundations of Social Choice* (Cambridge: Cambridge University Press, 1986).

—— *The Cement of Society: A Study of Social Order* (Cambridge: Cambridge University Press, 1989).

—— *Nuts and Bolts for the Social Sciences* (Cambridge: Cambridge University Press, 1989).

—— 'The Possibility of Rational Politics', in David Held (ed.), *Political Theory Today* (Oxford: Polity Press, 1991).

EMLER, NICHOLAS, and FRAZER, ELIZABETH, 'Politics: The Education Effect', in Elizabeth Frazer (ed.), *Political Education*, special issue of *Oxford Review of Education*, 25 (1999).

EPSTEIN, JOYCE L., 'School and Family Connections: Theory, Research and Implications for Integrating Sociologies of Education and the Family', *Marriage and Family Review*, 15 (1990), 99–126.

ETZIONI, AMITAI, *The Spirit of Community: Rights, Responsibilities and the Communitarian Agenda* (New York: Crown Publishers, Inc., 1993).

—— *The Parenting Deficit* (London: Demos, 1993).

—— (ed.), *New Communitarian Thinking: Persons, Virtues, Institutions and Communities* (Charlotesyville: University Press of Virginia, 1995).

—— *The New Golden Rule: Community and Morality in a Democratic Society* (New York: Basic Books, 1996).

FARRAR, MAX, 'Agency, Metaphor and Double Consciousness', paper presented to conference 'Ideas of Community', University of West of England, Sept. 1995.

FARRELL, MICHAEL P., and BARNES, GRACE M., 'Family Systems and Social Support: A Test of the Effects of Cohesion and Adaptability on the Functioning of Parents and Adolescents', *Journal of Marriage and the Family*, 55 (1993), 119–32.

FELDMAN, ROBERTA M., STALL, SUSAN, and WRIGHT, PATRICIA A., 'The Community Needs to be Built by Us: Women Organizing in Chicago Public

Housing', in Nancy Naples (ed.), *Community Activism and Feminist Politics: Organising Across Gender, Race and Class* (New York: Routledge, 1998).

FIELD, FRANK, *Making Welfare Work: Reconstructing Welfare for the Millenium* (London: Institute of Community Studies, 1995).

FINCH, JANET, *Family Obligations and Social Change* (Cambridge: Polity Press, 1989).

FISH, STANLEY, *Is There a Text in this Class?* (Cambridge: Mass.: Harvard University Press, 1980).

FISHMAN, ARYEI, *Judaism and Modernisation on the Religious Kibbutz* (Cambridge: Cambridge University Press, 1992).

FORD, REUBEN, and MILLAR, JANE, *Private Lives and Public Responses: Lone Parenthood and Future Policy in the UK* (London: Policy Studies Institute, 1998).

FOUCAULT, MICHEL, *The Archaeology of Knowledge*, trans. A. M. Sheridan Smith (London: Tavistock, 1972).

—— *Madness and Civilisation* (London: Tavistock, 1967).

—— *The Birth of the Clinic* (London: Tavistock, 1973).

—— *Power/Knowledge: Selected Interviews and Writings*, ed. and trans. Colin Gordon (Brighton: Harvester, 1980).

—— 'Questions of Method', in G. Burchell, C. Gordon, and P. Miller (eds.), *The Foucault Effect: Studies in Governmentality* (Hemel Hempstead: Harvester Wheatsheaf, 1991).

FOWLER, ROBERT BOOTH, *The Dance with Community: The Contemporary Debate in American Political Thought* (Lawrence, Kan.: University Press of Kansas, 1991).

—— 'Community: Reflections on Definition', in Amitai Etzioni (ed.), *New Communitarian Thinking: Persons, Virtues, Institutions and Communities* (Charlottesville: University Press of Virginia, 1995).

FRANZWAY, SUZANNE, COURT, DIANNE, and CONNELL, R.W., *Staking a Claim: Feminism, Bureaucracy and the State* (Cambridge: Polity Press, 1989).

FRASER, JOHN, 'Community, the Private and the Individual', *Sociological Review*, 35 (1987), 795.

FRAZER, ELIZABETH, 'Construction and Social Construction', *Imprints*, 1 (1997), 71.

—— and LACEY, NICOLA, *The Politics of Community: A Feminist Critique of the Liberal-Communitarian Debate* (Hemel Hempstead: Harvester, 1993).

—— —— 'Politics and the Public in Rawls' Political Liberalism', *Political Studies*, 43 (1995), 233–47.

FREEDEN, MICHAEL, *Ideologies and Political Theory* (Oxford: Clarendon Press, 1996).

FRIEDMAN, MARILYN, 'Feminism and Modern Friendship: Dislocating the Community', *Ethics*, 99 (1989), 257–90.

FUDGE, COLIN, 'Decentralisation: Socialism Goes Local', in Martin Boddy and Colin Fudge (eds.), *Local Socialism? Labour Councils and the New Left Alternatives* (Basingstoke: Macmillan, 1984).

GABEL, PETER, 'The Desire for Community and the Defeat of Healthcare' *Tikkun*, 10/1 (1995), 36.

—— 'Community and Democracy: Creating a Parallel Universe', *Tikkun*, 10 (1995), 14.

GADAMER, H.G., *Truth and Method*, 2nd edn. rev. trans. J. Weinsheimer and D. G. Marshall (London: Sheed and Ward, 1975).

GAMBETTA, DIEGO, 'Can we Trust Trust?', in Diego Gambetta (ed.), *Trust: Making and Breaking Cooperative Relations* (Cambridge: Cambridge University Press, 1988).

—— *Were They Pushed or Did They Jump?* (Cambridge: Cambridge University Press, 1987).

GARDBAUM, STEPHAN A., 'Law, Politics and the Claims of Community', *Michigan Law Review*, 90 (1992), 685.

GATENS, MOIRA, ' "The Oppressed State of My Sex": Wollstonecraft on Reason, Feeling and Equality', in Mary L. Shanley and Carole Pateman (eds.), *Feminist Interpretations and Political Theory* (Oxford: Polity Press, 1991).

GEERTZ, CLIFFORD, 'Thick Description: Toward an Interpretive Theory of Culture', in *The Interpretation of Culture* (1st pub. 1973) (London: Fontana, 1993).

GIDDENS, ANTHONY, *Central Problems in Social Theory: Action, Structure and Contradiction in Social Analysis* (Basingstoke: Macmillan, 1979).

GLENDON, MARY ANN, *Rights Talk: The Impoverishment of Political Discourse* (New York: Free Press, 1991).

GOLDMAN, LAWRENCE, *Trinity in Camberwell: A History of the Trinity College Mission in Camberwell, 1885–1985* (Cambridge: Trinity College, 1985).

GOODIN, ROBERT, 'Laundering Preferences', in J. Elster and A. Hylland (eds.), *Foundations of Social Choice Theory* (Cambridge: Cambridge University Press, 1986).

—— 'Review Article: Communities of Enlightenment', *British Journal of Political Science*, 28 (1998), 531–58.

GRANOVETTER, MARK, 'The Strength of Weak Ties', *American Journal of Sociology*, 78 (1973), 1360–80.

—— 'The Strength of Weak Ties: A Network Theory Revisited', in Peter Marsden and Nan Lin (eds.), *Social Structure and Network Analysis* (Beverly Hills, Calif.: Sage Publications, 1992).

—— 'Economic Institutions as Social Constructions: A Framework for Analysis', *Acta Sociologica*, 35 (1992), 3–11.

GRAYSON, DAVID, 'Business and the Community', in Dick Atkinson (ed.), *Cities of Pride: Rebuilding Community, Refocussing Government* (London: Cassell, 1995).

GRIFFIN, GABRIELE (ed.), *Feminist Activism in the 1990s* (London: Taylor and Francis, 1995).

GROSSER, GEORGE, *New Directions in Community Organisation* (New York: Praeger, 1976).

GUTMANN, AMY, *Democratic Education* (Princeton: Princeton University Press, 1987).

HABERMAS, JÜRGEN, *On the Logic of the Social Sciences* (1st pub. German 1967), trans. T. McCarthy (Oxford: Polity Press, 1988).

—— *Knowledge and Human Interests* (1st pub. German 1978), trans. Jeremy J. Shapiro (Oxford: Polity Press, 1987).

—— *Between Facts and Norms: Contributions to a Discourse Theory of Law and Democracy* (1st pub. German 1992), trans. William Rehg, (Oxford: Polity Press, 1996).

HACKING, IAN, *Rewriting the Soul: Multiple Personality and the Sciences of Memory* (Princeton: Princeton University Press, 1995).

—— 'On Being More Literal about Construction', in I. Velody and R. Williams (eds.), *The Politics of Constructionism* (London: Sage, 1998).

HAHN, CAROLE L., 'Political Education in Comparative Perspective: An Empirical Study of Policy, Practices and Outcomes', in *Oxford Review of Education*, special issue, *Political Education*, 25 (1999).

HAMPSHIRE, STUART, 'Social Objects', *Proceedings of the Aristotelian Society*, 76 (1975–6), 1–27.

HARDING, SANDRA (ed.), *Feminism and Methodology* (Bloomington: Indiana University Press, 1987).

—— *The Science Question in Feminism* (Milton Keynes: Open University Press, 1986).

HARLOE, MICHAEL, PICKVANCE, C. G., and URRY, JOHN (eds.), *Place Policy and Politics: Do Localities Matter?* (London: Unwin Hyman, 1990).

HARRIS, ROBIN, *The Conservative Community: The Roots of Thatcherism—and its Future* (London: Centre for Policy Studies, 1989).

HARRISON, BRIAN, *Separate Spheres: The Opposition to Women's Suffrage in Britain* (London: Croom Helm, 1978).

HARTSOCK, NANCY, 'The Feminist Standpoint: Developing the Ground for a Specifically Feminist Historical Materialism', in Sandra Harding and Merrill Hintikka (eds.), *Discovering Reality: Feminist Perspectives on Epistemology, Metaphysics and the Philosophy of Science* (Dordrecht: Reidel, 1983), and in S. Harding (ed.), *Feminism and Methodology* (Bloomington: Indiana University Press, 1987).

HECHTER, MICHAEL, 'The Role of Values in Rational Choice Theory', *Rationality and Society*, 6 (1994), 318–33.

HEGEL, G. W. F., *The Philosophy of Right*, trans. T. M. Knox (Oxford: Clarendon Press, 1952).

HELD, VIRGINIA, 'Mothering versus Contract', in Jane Mansbridge (ed.), *Beyond Self Interest* (Chicago: Chicago University Press, 1990).

HELLER, AGNES, 'The Concept of the "Political" Revisited', in David Held (ed.), *Political Theory Today* (Oxford: Polity Press, 1991).

HENDERSON, PAUL et al. (eds.), *Successes and Struggles on Council Estates: Tenant Action and Community Work* (London: Association of Community Workers in the UK, 1982).

HENRY, PATRICK G., and SWEARING, DONALD K., *For the Sake of the World: The Spirit of Buddhist and Christian Monasticism* (Minneapolis: Fortress Press, 1989).

HIRST, PAUL, 'Carl Schmitt, Decisionism and Politics', *Economy and Society*, 17 (1988), 272–82.

HOBBES, THOMAS, *Leviathan*, introd. by Kenneth Minogue (London: Dent, 1973).

—— *Leviathan*, introd. J. C. A. Gaskin (Oxford: Oxford University Press, 1996).

HOCHSCHILD, ARLIE, 'Emotion Work, Feeling Rules and Social Structure', *American Journal of Sociology*, 85 (1979), 551–75.

—— *The Second Shift: Working Parents and the Revolution at Home* (London: Piatkus, 1990).

HOLLIS, MARTIN, *The Cunning of Reason* (Cambridge: Cambridge University Press, 1987).

Home Office, *Guidance on Statutory Crime and Disorder Partnerships* (Crime and Disorder Act 1998) (http//www.homeoffice.gov.uk/).

Home Office/Ministerial Group on the Family, *Supporting Families* (http:/www.homeoffice.gov.uk/) Nov. 1998.

HONIG, BONNIE, *Political Theory and the Displacement of Politic* (Ithaca, NY: Cornell University Press, 1993).

HONT, ISTVAN, and IGNATIEFF, MICHAEL (eds.), *Wealth and Virtue: The Shaping of Political Economy in the Scottish Enlightenment* (Cambridge: Cambridge University Press, 1983).

HYMAN, PAULA, 'Gender and Jewish History', *Tikkun*, 3 (1988).

JAGGAR, ALISON M., *Feminist Politics and Human Nature* (Brighton: Harvester, 1983).

JONES, PETER D'A., *The Christian Socialist Revival 1877–1914: Religion, Class and Social Consciousness in Late Victorian England* (Princeton: Princeton University Press, 1986).

JOSEPHSON, JYL J., and BURACK, CYNTHIA, 'The Political Ideology of the NeoTraditional Family', *Journal of Political Ideologies*, 3 (1998), 213–31.

KAHN, PAUL W., 'Community in Contemporary Constitutional Theory', *Yale Law Journal*, 99 (1989), 1.

KAMENKA, EUGENE (ed.), *Community as a Social Ideal* (London: Edward Arnold, 1982).

KATZ, JACOB, 'The Jewish National Movement', in H. H. Ben-Sasson and E. Ettinger (eds.), *Jewish Society through the Ages* (London: Vallentine Mitchell, 1968).

KEANE, JOHN (ed.), *Civil Society and the State: New European Perspectives* (London: Verso, 1988).

—— *Democracy and Civil Society* (London: Verso, 1988).

KELLER, EVELYN R., *Reflections on Gender and Science* (New Haven: Yale University Press, 1985).

KEMMIS, DANIEL, 'A Question of Locus: Sovereignty and Community', *Responsive Community*, 1/3 (1991).

KIERNAN, KATHLEEN, LAND, HILARY, and LEWIS, JANE, *Lone Motherhood in Twentieth Century Britain: From Footnote to Front Page* (Oxford: Clarendon Press, 1998).

KING, DESMOND, 'Government beyond Whitehall: Local Government and Urban Politics', in P. Dunleavy et al (eds.), *Developments in British Politics*, 4 (1993).

—— and STOKER, GERRY (eds.), *Rethinking Local Democracy* (Basingstoke: Macmillan, 1996).

KITZINGER, CELIA, *The Social Construction of Lesbianism* (London: Sage, 1987).

KLEIDMAN, ROBERT, 'Volunteer Activism', *Social Problems*, 41 (1994), 257–76.

KUHN, THOMAS, *The Structure of the Scientific Revolutions*, 2nd edn. (1st pub. 1962) (Chicago: Chicago University Press, 1970).

—— *The Essential Tension: Selected Studies in Scientific Tradition and Change* (Chicago: University of Chicago Press, 1977).

KUMAR, KRISHAN, *Utopia and Anti-Utopia in Modern Times* (Oxford: Basil Blackwell, 1987).

LACEY, NICOLA, *State Publishment: Political Principles and Community Values* (London: Routledge, 1988).

LANGE, LYDIA, 'Rousseau and Modern Feminism', in M. L. Shanley and C. Pateman (eds.), *Feminist Interpretations and Political Theory* (Oxford: Polity Press, 1991).

LASCH, CHRISTOPHER, *The Culture of Narcissism: American Life in an Age of Diminishing Expectations* (London: Abacus Press, 1980).

LEADBEATER, CHARLES, *The Rise of the Social Entrepreneur* (London: Demos, 1997).

LEECH, KENNETH, *The Social God* (London: Sheldon Press, 1981).

LEES, RAY, and MAYO, MARJORIE, *Community Action for Change* (London: Routledge and Kegan Paul, 1984).

—— and SMITH, GEORGE, *Action Research in Community Development* (London: Routledge and Kegan Paul, 1975).

LEONARD, PETER (ed.), *The Sociology of Community Action*, Sociological Review Monograph no. 21 (Keele: University of Keele, 1975).

LERNER, MICHAEL, 'Founding Editorial Statement', *Tikkun*, 1 (1986).

—— 'Surviving a Bush Presidency', *Tikkun*, 4 (1989), 17.

—— 'Pain at Work and Pain in Families', *Tikkun*, 6 (1991).

—— 'Can the Democrats be Stopped from Blowing it Again in 1992?', *Tikkun*, 7/4 (1992).

LEVINSON, MEIRA, 'Liberalism, Pluralism and Political Education: Paradox or Paradigm', *Oxford Review of Education* special issue *Political Education*, 25 (1999).

LICHTERMAN, PAUL, *The Search for Political Community* (Cambridge: Cambridge University Press, 1996).

LICHTHEIM, GEORGE, *A Short History of Socialism* (London: Fontana, 1975).

LLOYD, GENEVIEVE, *The Man of Reason: 'Male' and 'Female' in Western Philosophy* (London: Methuen, 1984).

LONEY, MARTIN, *Community against Government: The British Community Development Proiect 1968–78—A Study of Government Incompetence* (London: Heinemann, 1983).

LORENZ, EDWARD H., 'Flexible Production Systems and the Social Construction of Trust', *Politics and Society*, 21 (1993), 307–24.

LUKES, STEVEN, 'Methodological Individualism Reconsidered', *British Journal of Sociology*, 19 (1968), 119–29.

—— *Power: A Radical View* (Basingstoke: Macmillan, 1974).

MACCALLUM, GERALD C., 'Negative and Positive Freedom', *Philosophical Review*, 76 (1967), 312 also in David Miller (ed.), *Liberty* (Oxford: Oxford University Press, 1991).

MACINTYRE, ALASDAIR, *After Virtue: A Study in Moral Theory*, 2nd edn. (London: Duckworth, 1985).

—— *Whose Justice? Which Rationality?* (London: Duckworth, 1988).

—— *Three Rival Versions of Moral Enquiry* (London: Duckworth, 1990).

MCKENDRICK, JOHN, 'The Big Picture: Quality and Quantity in the Lives of Lone Parents', in Reuben Ford and Jane Millar (eds.), *Private Lives and Public Responses: Lone Parenthood and Future Policy in the UK* (London: Policy Studies Institute, 1998).

MACKINTOSH, MAUREEN, and WAINWRIGHT, Hilary (eds.), *A Taste of Power* (London: Verso, 1987).

MCLEAN, IAIN, *Public Choice: An Introduction* (Oxford: Basil Blackwell, 1987).

MACMURRAY, JOHN, *Persons in Relation* (London: Faber and Faber, 1961).

MANDELBAUM, MAURICE, 'Societal Facts', *British Journal of Sociology*, 6 (1955) repr. in Alan Ryan (ed.), *Philosophy of Social Explanation* (Oxford: Oxford University Press, 1973).

MANDELSON, PETER, and LIDDLE, ROGER, *The Blair Revolution: Can New Labour Deliver?* (London: Faber and Faber, 1996).

MARCIANO, TERESA D., 'Families Wider than Kin or Marriage', *Family Science Review*, 1 (1998), 115–24.

MARX, KARL, *Capital* (1st pub. 1867), vols. i, ii, iii (London: Lawrence and Wishart, 1954–59).

—— and ENGELS, FRIEDRICH, 'The German Ideology', in David McLellan (ed.), *Karl Marx Selected Writings* (Oxford: Oxford University Press, 1977).

MAYHEW, LEON H., *The New Public* (Cambridge: Cambridge University Press, 1997).

MEACHAM, STANDISH, *Toynbee Hall and Social Reform 1880–1914: The Search for Community* (New Haven: Yale University Press, 1987).

MEAD, GEORGE HERBERT, *On Social Psychology*, (ed.), Anselm Strauss (Chicago: University of Chicago Press, 1956).

MEADOWCROFT, JAMES (ed.), *The Liberal Tradition: Contemporary Reappraisals* (Cheltenham: Edward Elgar, 1996).

MELUCCI, ALBERTO, 'Social Movements and the Democratisation of Everyday Life', in John Keane (ed.), *Civil Society and the State* (London: Verso, 1988).

MENAGHAN, ELIZABETH G., and PARCEL, TOBY L., 'Determining Children's Home Environments: The Impact of Maternal Characteristics and Current Occupational and Family Conditions', *Journal of Marriage and the Family*, 53 (1991), 426.

MILLER, DAVID, 'In What Sense Must Socialism be Communitarian?', *Social Philosophy and Policy*, 6/51 (1989), 57.

—— 'Deliberative Democracy and Social Choice', *Political Studies*, 40 (1992), 92.

—— *On Nationality* (Oxford: Oxford University Press, 1995).

MOORE, G. E., *Principia Ethica* (Cambridge: Cambridge University Press, 1903).

—— 'Reply to my Critics', in P. A Schlipp (ed.), *The Philosophy of G. E. Moore* (Evanston, Ill.: Northwestern University Press, 1942).

MOORE, HENRIETTA L., *A Passion for Difference* (Oxford: Polity Press, 1994).

MOSSE, GEORGE L., 'Nationalism, Fascism and the Radical Right', in E. Kamenka (ed.), *Community as a Social Ideal* (London: Edward Arnold, 1982).

MOUFFE, CHANTAL, 'Democratic Citizenship and the Political Community', in C. Mouffe (ed.), *Dimensions of Radical Democracy* (London: Verso 1992), also in *The Return of the Political* (London: Verso, 1993).

—— *The Return of the Political* (London: Verso, 1993).

MOYNIHAN, DANIEL R., *Maximum Feasible Misunderstanding: Community Action in the War on Poverty* (New York: Free Press, 1970).

MULHALL, STEPHEN, and SWIFT, ADAM, *Liberals and Communitarians*, 2nd edn. (Oxford: Blackwell, 1996).

MULHAUSLER, PETER, and HARRE, ROM, *Pronouns and People: The Linguistic Construction of Social and Personal Identity* (Oxford: Basil Blackwell, 1990).

NAPLES, NANCY A. (ed.), *Community Activism and Feminist Politics: Organising across Race, Class and Gender* (New York: Routledge, 1998).

NEAR, HENRY, *The Kibbutz Movement: A History*, vols. i and ii (Oxford: Oxford University Press, 1992).

NIE, NORMAN, JUNN, JANE, and STEHLIK-BARRY, KENNETH, *Education and Democratic Citizenship in America* (Chicago: Chicago University Press, 1996).

NISBET, ROBERT A., *The Quest for Community: A Study in the Ethics of Order and Freedom* (New York: Oxford University Press, 1953).

NOZICK, ROBERT, *Anarchy, State, and Utopia* (Oxford: Basil Blackwell, 1974).

—— *The Examined Life* (New York: Simon and Schuster, 1989).

O'BRIEN, MARY, *The Politics of Reproduction* (London: Routledge and Kegan Paul, 1981).

OFFE, CLAUS, 'New Social Movements: Challenging the Boundaries of Institutional Politics', *Social Research*, 52 (1985).

OKIN, SUSAN MOLLER, 'Justice and Gender', *Philosophy and Public Affairs*, 16 (1987), 42–72.

—— *Justice Gender and the Family* (New York: Basic Books, 1989).

OLDFIELD, ADRIAN, *Citizenship and Community: Civic Republicanism and the Modern World* (London: Routledge, 1990).

OLSEN, FRANCES, 'The Family and the Market', *Harvard Law Review*, 96 (1983), 1497.

O'SULLIVAN, NOEL, 'Difference and the Concept of the Political in Contemporary Political Philosophy', *Political Studies*, 45 (1997), 739.

PALEY, JOHN, THOMAS, JIM, and NORMAN, JERRY, *Rethinking Youth Social Work* (Leicester: National Youth Bureau, 1986).

PARRY, GERAINT, 'Constructive and Reconstructive Political Education', *Oxford Review of Education*, 25 (1999).

—— MOYSER, GEORGE, and DAY, NEIL, *Political Participation and Democracy in Britain* (Cambridge: Cambridge University Press, 1992).

PATEMAN, CAROLE, *Participation and Democratic Theory* (Cambridge: Cambridge University Press, 1970).

—— *The Sexual Contract* (Oxford: Polity Press, 1988).

—— *The Disorder of Women* (Oxford: Polity Press, 1989).

—— ' "God Hath Ordained to Man a Helper": Hobbes, Patriarchy and Conjugal Right', in Mary Lyndon Shanley and Carole Pateman (eds.), *Feminist Interpretations and Political Theory* (Oxford: Polity Press, 1991).

PEACOCKE, CHRISTOPHER, *A Study of Concepts* (Cambridge, Mass.: MIT Press, 1992).

PEET, RICHARD, and THRIFT, NIGEL, *New Models in Geography: The Political Economy Perspective*, vols. i and ii (London: Unwin Hyman, 1989).

PETTIT, PHILIP, *Republicanism: A Theory of Freedom and Government* (Oxford: Clarendon Press, 1997).

PHILLIPS, ANNE, *Local Democracy: The Terms of the Debate* (London: Commission on Local Democracy, 1994).

—— 'Feminism and the Attractions of the Local', in Desmond King and Gerry Stoker (eds.), *Rethinking Local Democracy* (Basingstoke: Macmillan, 1996).

—— *Democracy and Difference* (Oxford: Polity Press, 1993).

PIZZEY, ERIN, and FORBES, ALISON, *Scream Quietly or the Neighbours will Hear* (Harmondsworth: Penguin, 1974).

PLANT, RAYMOND, 'Community: Concept, Conception and Ideology', *Politics and Society*, 8, (1978), 79–107.

PLATO, *The Republic*, trans. and introd. Desmond Lee, 2nd edn. (Harmondsworth: Penguin, 1974).

PLUMWOOD, VAL, *Feminism and the Mastery of Nature* (London: Routledge, 1993).

POCOCK, J. G. A., *The Machiavellian Moment: Florentine Political Thought and the Atlantic Republican Tradition* (Princeton: Princeton University Press, 1975).

POPENOE, DAVID, 'Fostering the New Familism: A Goal for America', *Responsive Community* 2/4 (1992), 32.

—— 'American Family Decline 1960–1990: A Review and Appraisal', *Journal of Marriage and the Family*, 55 (1993), 527–55.

—— 'Review: Judith Stacey *In the Name of the Family*', *Responsive Community*, 7/1 (1996–7).

POPENOE, DAVID, *Life without Father* (New York: Free Press, 1996).

POWER, ANNE, and TUNSTALL, REBECCA, *Swimming against the Tide* (York: Joseph Rowntree Foundation, 1995).

PUDDIFOOT, JOHN E., 'Some Initial Considerations in the Measurement of Community Identity', *Journal of Community Psychology*, 24 (1996), 327–36.

PUTNAM, HILARY, 'The Meaning of Meaning', in *Mind Language and Reality*, Philosophical Papers, 2 (Cambridge: Cambridge University Press, 1975).

PUTNAM, ROBERT, *Making Democracy Work: Civic Traditions in Modern Italy* (Princeton: Princeton University Press, 1993).

—— 'Bowling Alone: America's Declining Social Capital', *Journal of Democracy*, 6 (1995), 65–78.

QUINE, WILLARD VAN ORMAN, *Word and Object* (Cambridge, Mass.: MIT Press, 1960).

RALLINGS, COLIN, TEMPLE, MICHAEL, and THRASHER, MICHAEL, *Community Identity and Participation in Local Democracy* (London: Commission for Local Democracy, 1994).

RAWLS, JOHN, *A Theory of Justice* (Oxford: Oxford University Press, 1971).

—— 'Kantian Constructivism in Moral Theory', *Journal of Philosophy*, 77 (1980).

—— *Political Liberalism* (New York: Columbia University Press, 1993).

RAZ, JOSEPH, 'Morality as Interpretation: on Walzer's *Interpretation and Social Criticism*', *Ethics*, 101 (1991), 403.

RICH, ADRIENNE, *On Lies Secrets and Silence: Selected Prose 1966–1978* (New York: Norton, 1979).

RICHARDS, I. A., *Practical Criticism* (London: Routledge and Kegan Paul, 1929).

RIKER, WILLIAM, *Liberalism against Populism: A Confrontation between the Theory of Democracy and the Theory of Social Choice* (San Francisco: W. H. Freeman and Co., 1982).

—— *The Theory of Political Conditions*, (New Haven: Yale University Press, 1987).

ROBERTSON, ELIZABETH B., ELDER, GLEN H., SKINNER, MARTIE L., and CONGER, D., 'The Costs and Benefits of Social Support in Families', *Journal of Marriage and the Family*, 55 (1991), 403–16.

ROBINS, KEVIN, 'Prisoners of the City: Whatever Could a Postmodern City Be?', in Erica Carter, et al. (eds.), *Space and Place: Theories of Identity and Location* (London: Lawrence and Wishart, 1993).

ROBSON, BRIAN, *Those Inner Cities: Reconciling the Economic and Social Aims of Urban Policy* (Oxford: Clarendon Press, 1988).

RODGERS, BRYAN, and JAN, PRYOR, *Divorce and Separation: The Outcomes for Children* (York: Joseph Rowntree Foundation, 1998).

ROSENBERG, ALEXANDER, *Philosophy of Social Science* (Oxford: Clarendon Press, 1988).

ROSENBLUM, NANCY, (ed.) *Liberalism and the Moral Life* (Cambridge, Mass.: Harvard University Press, 1989).

—— 'Democratic Character and Community: The Logic of Congruence', *Journal of Political Philosophy*, 2, (1994), 67–97.

ROUPHE, ANNE, 'The Jewish Family: A Feminist Perspective', *Tikkun*, 1/2 (1987).

ROUSSEAU, JEAN JACQUES, *The Social Contract and Discourses* (1st pub. 1750–62), trans. and introd. G. D. H. Cole (London: Dent, 1973).

ROYCE, JOSIAH, *The Problem of Christianity*, ii (New York: Macmillan, 1913).

SALECL, RENATA, *The Spoils of Freedom: Psychoanalysis and Feminism after the Fall of Socialism* (London: Routledge, 1994).

SANCTION, ANDREW, 'British Socialist Theories of the Division of Power by Area', *Political Studies*, 24 (1976), 158–70.

SANDEL, MICHAEL, *Liberalism and the Limits of Justice* (Cambridge: Cambridge University Press, 1982).

—— *Liberalism and its Critics* (Oxford: Basil Blackwell, 1984).

—— 'The Procedural Republic and the Unencumbered Self', *Political Theory*, 12 (1984), 81–96.

—— *Democracy's Discontents: America in Search of a Public Philosophy* (Cambridge, Mass.: Harvard University Press. 1996).

SARLIN, SHLOMO A., and SHAMAI, MICHAEL, 'Intervention with Families in Extreme Distress', *Marriage and Family Review*, 21 (1995), 91–122.

SAUSSURE, FERDINAND DE, *Course in General Linguistics* (1st pub. French 1916) trans. R. Harris (London: Duckworth, 1983).

SCANNELL, PADDY, *Radio, Television and Modern Life: A Phenomenological Approach* (Oxford: Basil Blackwell, 1996).

SCHMITT, CARL, *The Concept of the Political* (1st pub. 1932), trans. George Schwabb (New Brunswick: Rutgers University Press, 1976).

SCHNEIDER, JOSEPH W., 'Defining the Definitional Perspective on Social Problems', *Social Problems*, 32 (1985), 232–4.

SCOTT, JOHN, *Social Network Analysis: A Handbook* (London: Sage, 1991).

SCRUTON, ROGER, (ed.), *Conservative Texts: An Anthology* (Basingstoke: MacMillan, 1991).

SEARLE, JOHN, *The Construction of Social Reality* (Harmondsworth: Penguin, 1995).

'Seebohm Report', *Report of the Committee on Local Authority and Allied Services*, Cmnd. 3713 (London: HMSO, 1968).

SELZNICK, PHILLIP, 'The Idea of a Communitarian Morality', *California Law Review*, 77 (1987), 445.

—— *The Moral Commonwealth: Social Theory and the Promise of Community* (Berkeley and Los Angeles: University of California Press, 1992).

SENNET, RICHARD, *The Fall of Public Man* (London: Faber, 1986).

SINGH, DEVENDRA, 'Adaptive Significance of Female Physical Attractiveness: Role of Waist to Hip Ratio', *Journal of Personality and Social Psychology*, 65 (1993), 293–307.

SISMONDO, SERGIO, 'Some Social Constructions', *Social Studies of Science*, 23 (1993), 515–53.

SKELCHER, CHRIS, MCCABE, ANGUS, and LOWNDES, VIVIEN, *Community Networks in Urban Regeneration* (Bristol: Policy Press, 1976).

SKINNER, QUENTIN, 'Some Problems in the Analysis of Political Thought and Action', *Political Theory*, 2 (1974), 277–303.

—— 'From Hume's Intentions to Deconstruction and Back', *Journal of Political Philosophy*, 2 (1996), 142–54.

—— *Reason and Rhetoric in the Philosophy of Hobbes* (Cambridge: Cambridge University Press, 1996).

—— *Liberty before Liberalism* (Cambridge: Cambridge University Press, 1998).

SMITH, DOROTHY, 'A Sociology for Women', in Sandra Harding (ed.), *Feminism and Methodology* (Milton Keynes: Open University Press, 1987).

SMITH, TERESA, 'Decentralisation and Community', *British Journal of Social Work*, 19 (1989), 137–49.

SPECHT, HARRY, *Community Development in the UK: An Assessment and Recommendation for Change* (London: Association of Community Workers, 1975).

SPIVAK, GAYATRI C., *In Other Worlds: Essays in Cultural Politics* (New York: Routledge, 1988).

SQUIRES, JUDITH, 'Private Lives, Secluded Places: Privacy as Political Possibility', *Environment and Planning D: Society and Space*, 12, (1994), 387–401.

STACEY, JUDITH, 'Response to David Popenoe "American Family Decline"', *Journal of Marriage and the Family*, 55 (1993), 556.

—— 'Families against the Family', *Radical Philosophy*, 89 (1998), 2–7.

STACEY, MARGARET, *Tradition and Change: A Study of Banbury* (Oxford: Oxford University Press, 1960).

—— 'The Myth of Community Studies', *British Journal of Sociology*, 20 (1969), 134–47.

—— *Power, Persistence and Change: A Second Study of Banbury* (London: Routledge and Kegan Paul, 1975).

STEWART, JOHN, 'A Future for Local Authorities as Community Government', in John Stewart and Gerry Stoker (eds.), *The Future of Local Government* (Basingstoke: Macmillan, 1989).

STOKER, GERRY, *The Politics of Local Government,* 2nd edn. (Basingstoke: Macmillan, 1991).

—— 'Introduction: Normative Theories of Local Government and Democracy', in Desmond King and Gerry Stoker (eds.), *Rethinking Local Democracy* (Basingstoke: Macmillan, 1996).

—— and YOUNG, STEPHEN (eds.), *Cities in the 1990s* (London: Longman, 1993).

SULLIVAN, ORIEL, 'Time Coordination, the Domestic Division of Labour and Affective Relations: Time Use and the Enjoyment of Activities within Couples', *Sociology*, 30 (1996), 79–100.

—— 'Time Waits for No Woman: An Investigation of the Gendered Experience of Domestic Time', *Sociology*, 31 (1997), 221–39.

SULLIVAN, WILLIAM, 'The Politics of Meaning as a Challenge to Neo-Capitalism', *Tikkun*, 11 (1996).

SUNSTEIN, CASS, 'Beyond the Republican Revival', *Yale Law Journal*, 97 (1988), 1539.

TAM, HENRY, *Citizen's Agenda for Building Democratic Communities* (Cambridge: Centre for Citizenship Development, 1995).

—— *Communitarianism: A New Agenda for Politics and Citizenship* (Basingstoke: Macmillan, 1998).

TAYLOR, CHARLES, *Philosophy and the Human Sciences* (Cambridge: Cambridge University Press, 1985).

—— *Human Agency and Language* (Cambridge: Cambridge University Press, 1985).

—— *Sources of the Self: The Making of the Modern Identity* (Cambridge: Cambridge University Press, 1989).

—— 'Cross Purposes: The Liberal Communitarian Debate', in Nancy Rosenblum (ed.), *Liberalism and the Moral Life* (Cambridge, Mass.: Harvard University Press, 1989).

TAYLOR, IAN, *Releasing the Community Spirit: A Framework for the Active Citizen* (Cambridge: Tory Reform Group, 1990).

TAYLOR, MARILYN, *Unleashing the Potential: Bringing Residents to the Centre of Regeneration* (York: Joseph Rowntree Foundation, 1995).

THAKE, STEPHEN, *Staying the Course: The Role and Structure of Community Regeneration Organisations* (York: Joseph Rowntree Foundation, 1995).

THOMPSON, JOHN B., *Studies in the Theory of Ideology* (Oxford: Polity Press, 1984).

TONNIES, FERDINAND DE, *Community and Society* (Lansing, Mich.: Michigan State University Press, 1957).

TOQUEVILLE, ALEXIS DE, *Democracy in America* (1st pub. 1835–40), trans. Henry Reeve, rev. Francis Bowen, ed. Phillips Bradley (New York: Vintage Books, 1945).

TURNER, VICTOR, *The Ritual Process: Structure and Anti-structure* (London: Routledge and Kegan Paul, 1969).

TUSHNET, MARK, 'The Possibilities of Interpretive Liberalism', *Alberta Law Review*, 29 (1991), 276–92.

UNGER, DONALD G., and SUSSMAN, MARVIN B., 'A Community Perspective on Families', *Marriage and Family Review*, 15 (1990), 2.

VANNOY, DANA, and PHILIBER, WILLIAM W., 'Wife's Employment and Quality of Marriage', *Journal of Marriage and the Family*, 54 (1992), 387–98.

VELODY, IRVING, and WILLIAMS, ROBIN (eds.), *The Politics of Constructionism* (London: Sage, 1998).

VERBA, SIDNEY, SCHLOZMAN, KAY LEHMAN, BRADY, HENRY, and NIE, NORMAN, 'Race, Ethnicity and Political Resources: Participation in the United States', *British Journal of Political Science*, 23 (1993), 453–97.

VINCENT, CAROL, 'Parent Empowerment? Collective Action and Inaction in Education' *Oxford Review of Education*, 22 (1996), 465–82.

VONDRA, JOAN I., 'The Community Context of Child Abuse and Neglect', *Marriage and Family Review*, 15 (1990), 19–38.

WAGNER, PETER, *A Sociology of Modernity: Liberty and Discipline* (London: Routledge, 1994).

WAITE, LINDA J., 'Social Science Finds . . . Marriage Matters', *Responsive Community*, 6/3 (1996), 31.

WALDRON, JEREMY, 'Particular Values and Critical Morality', *California Law Review*, 77 (1989), 561.

WALZER, MICHAEL, *Spheres of Justice: A Defence of Pluralism and Equality* (Oxford: Basil Blackwell, 1983).

—— *Interpretation and Social Criticism* (Cambridge, Mass.: Harvard University Press, 1987).

—— 'The Communitarian Critique of Liberalism', *Political Theory*, 18 (1990), 6–23.

—— *Thick and Thin: Moral Argument at Home and Abroad* (Notre Dame, Ind.: University of Notre Dame Press, 1994).

WARNKE, GEORGIA, *Justice and Interpretation* (Oxford: Polity Press, 1992).

WEBER, MAX, *Economy and Society* (1st pub. German 1921; New York: Bedminster Press, 1968).

WEEKS, JEFFREY, 'The Idea of a Sexual Community', paper delivered to conference 'Ideas of Community', University of West of England, Sept. 1995.

WEINTRAUB, JEFF, and KUMAR, KRISHAN (eds.), *Public and Private in Thought and Practice: Perspectives on a Grand Dichotomy* (Chicago: University of Chicago Press, 1997).

WELLMAN, BARRY, 'Studying Personal Communities', in Peter V. Marsden and Nan Lin (eds.), *Social Structure and Network Analysis* (Beverly Hills, Calif.: Sage, 1982).

—— 'The Place of Kinfolk in Personal Community Networks', *Marriage and Family Review*, 15, (1990). 195–228.

WIENER, JONATHAN M., 'Quentin Skinner's Hobbes', *Political Theory*, 2 (1974), 251.

WILLIAMS, BERNARD, *Making Sense of Humanity* (Cambridge: Cambridge University Press, 1995).

WILLIAMS, RAYMOND, *Keywords* (rev. edn. 1983) (London: Fontana Press, 1976).

WILLIS, PAUL, *Learning to Labour: How Working Class Kids Get Working Class Jobs* (1st pub. 1977) (Aldershot: Ashgate Publishing, 1993).

WILKINSON, SUE, and KITZINGER, CELIA, 'The Social Construction of Heterosexuality', *Journal of Gender Studies*, 3, (1994), 307–16.

WILSON, E. O., *Sociobiology: The New Synthesis* (Cambridge, Mass.: Belknap Press, 1975).

WITTGENSTEIN, LUDWIG, *Philosophical Investigations*, trans. G. E. M. Anscombe (Oxford: Basil Blackwell, 1958).

WOOLEVER, CYNTHIA, 'A Contextual Approach to Neighbourhood Attachment', *Urban Studies*, 29 (1992), 99–116.

WUTHNOW, ROBERT, *Sharing the Journey: Support Groups and America's New Quest for Community* (New York: Free Press, 1994).

YOUNG, KEN, GOSSCHALK, BRIAN, HATTER, WARREN, *In Search of Community Identity* (York: Joseph Rowntree Foundation, 1996).

YOUNG, MICHAEL, and WILLMOTT, PETER, *Family and Kinship in East London* (London: Routledge and Kegan Paul, 1957).

Index

Abrams, Phillip 149
anti-individualism 21–3
Arendt, Hannah 224, 231–3
association, *see* social relations
Austin, J. L. 59 n.
authoritarianism 38
authority 105, 200

Barnes, J. A. 69
Benington, John 157
Berger, Peter 133
Blair, Tony 12, 25, 35, 36, 37, 39, 41, 177, 197
Blakemore, Diane 59 n., 60 n., 91 n., 97n.
Bott, Elizabeth 69
boundaries 7, 67, 69, 70–1, 82–3, 166, 243–5
Boyte, Harry 139
Brown, Gordon 12, 39, 102
Bryant, B and Bryant, R 161–2
Buber, Martin 24–5, 65, 139
Buddhism 24
bureaucracy, bureaucrats 5, 22, 72, 138, 140, 141, 143, 156, 157, 161, 168, 170, 208
Butler, Judith 59 n., 94 n.

Campbell, Beatrix 193
capitalism 34, 188
cause 89, 123, 124, 125, 134
   see also social mechanisms
Christian thought and practice 24, 25, 26–8, 31, 39
civility 170, 189
Clinton, Bill 13, 197
Clinton, Hillary Rodham 39
coalitions 46, 109, 164, 165, 167
Cockburn, Cynthia 158
Cohen, A. P. 70–1, 81
Commission on Social Justice 30
commune 75
communion 25, 75, 83
communitarianism 1, 8, 13
   antecedents and sources of 23–32
   communitarian hypotheses 37–8, 190
   communitarian principles 35–6, 145–6

communitarian values 21, 22, 23, 34, 37, 38–9
dialogic communitarianism 3, 8
philosophical communitarianism 8, 11, 13–15, 19, 20–3, 61–5, 86–8, 143–5, 203
political communitarianism 4–6, 8, 10–15, 32–42, 87, 143, 145, 203
vernacular communitarianism 4–5, 11, 87, 142, 150, 163–4
see also liberal *v* communitarian debates
community:
   community activism 4–5, 7, 10, 41, 141, 204–5, 207
   community building 140, 152, 162, 205
   as a category 76
   concept of 4, 5, 7–8, 9, 10, 42, 44–5, 46, 61–85, 141, 190–1
   community development 141, 153, 157, 160
   community entrepreneurs 140
   as an entity 45, 61, 66, 77–8
   as an idea 4–5, 10
   occupational communities 142
   'partial communities' 73, 106, 141–2
   'political community' 62, 203
   in public policy 4, 7, 10, 174
   as a relation 31, 45, 61, 66, 78, 141
   as a value 31, 76, 152
   community *v* society 67–8
   community studies 45–6
   theory of 42–4
   community workers, community work 156, 157, 158–60, 161, 168
Community Action Programme 144, 154
Community Development Programme 153, 155–7
concepts 49–52
conceptual analysis 47–60, 61–3, 65–6, 74–6, 94–5
conflict 1, 164, 167
   over meaning and interpretation 101–3, 104–5, 108–10
   political conflict 109, 156–7, 158, 233, 236, 240, 244
   theory 157–8, 162
Confucianism 24

Stacey, Judith 180n
Stacey, Margaret 67 n., 69, 149, 150
state
   state and individual 10, 43, 207–8
   state power 2, 157, 158–9, 209, 223–4
   welfare state 208–9
Stewart, John 147
Stoker, Gerry 148
structure:
   structure/structurelessness 70, 79, 220
   structural analysis 71
   structuralism 158–9, 162
subject:
   community as 78
   interpretive subject 95
   social construction of 127–9
symbolic, symbols 70–1, 81, 83, 216, 242

Tam, Henry 38
Taylor, Charles 46 n., 52 n., 57 n., 62–3,
   79, 87, 95–6, 103, 105–6, 144, 145
theory:
   theory and concept 48–9, 52–4, 57, 66
   see also political theory
Tikkun 33, 34, 37, 38, 174, 186
Toynbee Hall, see settlement

transcendence 25, 40, 42, 83, 84, 85, 165,
   242
trust 19, 22, 136, 186, 189, 206
Turner, Victor 70, 220

Urban Programme 153

values, see communitarian values
violence 185, 232
voice 214, 215, 227, 243

Wagner, Peter 135
Walzer, Michael 19, 57 n., 62, 86, 87–8,
   103, 105, 129–30, 144–5, 167
'War on Poverty' 144, 153, 154–5
Weeks, Jeffrey 81, 221
Wellman, Barry 149, 150, 185 n.
Williams, Bernard 112 n.
Wittgenstein, Ludwig 51–2, 55, 57, 58, 71,
   94, 100, 107
Wollstonecraft, Mary 121

Young, Michael 35, 149

Zionism 25, 29